# The Battle for Zimbabwe

## THE FINAL COUNTDOWN

### GEOFF HILL

ZEBRA

Published by Zebra Press
an imprint of Struik Publishers
(a division of New Holland Publishing (South Africa) (Pty) Ltd)
PO Box 1144, Cape Town, 8000
New Holland Publishing is a member of Johnnic Communications Ltd

First published 2003

1 3 5 7 9 10 8 6 4 2

PUBLISHING MANAGER:  Marlene Fryer
MANAGING EDITOR:  Robert Plummer
EDITOR:  Marléne Burger
PROOFREADER:  Ronel Richter-Herbert
COVER AND TEXT DESIGNER:  Natascha Adendorff
TYPESETTER:  Monique van den Berg

Set in 10 pt on 13.5 pt Plantin Light

Reproduction by Hirt & Carter (Cape) (Pty) Ltd
Printed and bound by Paarl Print, Oosterland Street, Paarl, South Africa

ISBN  1 86872 652 5

**www.zebrapress.co.za**

Log on to our photographic website www.imagesofafrica.co.za for an African experience

# The Battle for
# Zimbabwe

*The most fearful curse has to be, 'May you fall in love with Africa.'
It beats the old Chinese one hands down, though it also
guarantees that you will live in interesting times.*

*Having an affair with Africa, like any great love, will take you through
conflicting emotions of hate and desire, joy and despair. And, if you stay
long enough, it will drive you insane and, in your madness, you will finally
realise that, come what may, this is where you were meant to be.*

*This book is dedicated to my parents who gave me that curse and to
my wife who encouraged me to keep writing – another act of lunacy.*

# Contents

*Photographs between pages 148 and 149*

# List of maps
# and illustrations

# Preface

When my publishers, Steve Connolly and Marlene Fryer, first came up with the idea for this book, they were clear about what was needed.

Much of the recent work on Zimbabwe, they said, had been researched and written outside the country, and cobbled together from press reports. This book had to be based on personal interviews, hundreds of them if necessary, with people in both the ruling ZANU-PF party and the opposition, and with ordinary Zimbabweans inside the country and those in exile.

The writing was fairly swift, but the interviews took more than two years, and my only regret is that I can't name the brave souls who risked so much to tell me their stories. They came from all races and all sides of politics, from the media, industry, agriculture, the War Veterans' Association and the Central Intelligence Organisation, Zimbabwe's feared secret police.

Many had fallen victim to the violence that has consumed Zimbabwe for so long, while others had tortured and even murdered people themselves. Either way, I hope that sharing their stories was a healing process, though I have no doubt that each of them has a long journey ahead in their quest to find some meaning in all that they have been through.

The tragedy of Zimbabwe is not that things went bad, but that the danger signals were there for years, and little was said or done by the international community to halt the slide.

The Organisation of African Unity has never been strong in defending human rights, but the rest of the world has been equally neglectful when it comes to speaking out for people in developing countries, and Zimbabwe is simply one more sad example.

Thankfully, we live in changing times, and freedom and democracy are part of the new order, and those who tread on the rights of others do so at their peril. Zimbabwe has *not* changed that much in recent years, and that is why it now stands out as a pariah in a world that has found new values since the end of the Cold War.

The fact that it has taken more than twenty years to set up trials for those accused of the Cambodian massacres under Pol Pot, and almost as long to prosecute the torturers who held up various dictatorships in South America, is evidence that little effort was made at the time to stop the crimes taking place. By contrast, people accused of more recent actions in Yugoslavia, Rwanda, Sierra Leone and East Timor have already been charged and brought to trial. And there is little doubt that the abuse of human rights in Zimbabwe is linked to an effort by a small minority to stay in power no matter what, because stepping down might render them liable to prosecution.

But that is only a small part of the truth. History is not a simple matter of cause and effect, but a long process of events that, collectively, deliver a set of circumstances in which a nation finds itself. In this book I have tried to lay out, as best I can, the history of the country and the people who have a stake in it. Some of the tragedy is recent, but other parts go back many years, and it is important to understand how things developed if we have any hope of creating a better future for all Zimbabweans.

In telling this story, some names and places have been changed to protect the innocent, and, in a very few cases, I have blended several events into one to create a better flow, but I have been careful not to tamper with the facts.

Special thanks go to Robert Plummer, Ronel Richter-Herbert, Marléne Burger and the team at Zebra Press, and to Dr Len Weinstein and his staff, Di and Rachel, who did so much to help the torture victims I interviewed. Also thanks to ET, NM and TC.

There are a few other people who played a special role in making this book possible. You know who you are: my deepest gratitude for your effort, kindness and friendship.

Finally, my thoughts go out to the thousands of people, on all sides, who have fought for the land between the Limpopo and the Zambezi, and to the memory of those who lost their lives doing so. May the survivors find the peace and freedom that has so long eluded the country.

I hope I have delivered what my publishers had in mind, and that the book will help readers everywhere to better understand this extraordinary country. Most of all, the task brought home to me the words of British writer Thomas Hardy (1840–1928): 'While much is too strange to be believed, nothing is too strange to have happened.'

GEOFF HILL

# Abbreviations

AI:            Amnesty International
ANC:           African National Congress
ANZ:           Associated Newspapers of Zimbabwe
AU:            African Union
BSAC:          British South Africa Company
BSAP:          British South African Police
CAZ:           Conservative Alliance of Zimbabwe
CBD:           central business district
CBZ:           Commercial Bank of Zimbabwe
CFU:           Commercial Farmers' Union
CHOGM:         Commonwealth Heads of Government Meeting
CIO:           Central Intelligence Organisation
COSATU:        Congress of South African Trade Unions
DA:            Democratic Alliance
DRC:           Democratic Republic of Congo
ESAP:          Economic Structural Adjustment Programme
EU:            European Union
Frelimo:       Mozambique Liberation Front
GMB:           Grain Marketing Board
GW:            Global Witness
IFP:           Inkatha Freedom Party
IMF:           International Monetary Fund
KANU:          Kenya African National Union
MDC:           Movement for Democratic Change
MMPZ:          Media Monitoring Project of Zimbabwe
NDP:           National Democratic Party
NEPAD:         New Partnership for African Development
NGO:           non-governmental organisation
NOCZIM:        National Oil Company of Zimbabwe
OAU:           Organisation of African Unity
PAC:           Pan Africanist Congress

PTC:        Post and Telecommunications Corporation
RBZ:        Reserve Bank of Zimbabwe
Renamo:     Mozambique National Resistance
SABC:       South African Broadcasting Corporation
SADC:       Southern African Development Community
UANC:       United African National Council
UDI:        Unilateral Declaration of Independence
UMNIC:      United Nations Interim Administration Mission in Kosovo
VOP:        Voice of the People (radio station)
WVA:        War Veterans' Association
ZANLA:      Zimbabwe African National Liberation Army
ZANU-PF:    Zimbabwe African National Union-Patriotic Front
ZAPU:       Zimbabwe African People's Union
ZBC:        Zimbabwe Broadcasting Corporation
ZCC:        Zimbabwe Council of Churches
ZCTU:       Zimbabwe Congress of Trade Unions
ZDF:        Zimbabwe Defence Force
ZDI:        Zimbabwe Defence Industries
ZESN:       Zimbabwe Election Support Network
ZIPRA:      Zimbabwe People's Revolutionary Army
ZLP:        Zimbabwe Liberators' Platform
ZNA:        Zimbabwe National Army
ZUJ:        Zimbabwe Union of Journalists
ZUM:        Zimbabwe Unity Movement

# 1

# Across the river

Paradise, my South African taxi driver, pulled off the road onto a dirt strip and parked between a pick-up truck and a minibus. It was late afternoon, and this was one of those areas in Johannesburg where I wouldn't have parked a wheelbarrow, let alone my own car.

Many stories about crime in South Africa are exaggerated, but, even so, every day 55 people are murdered, 817 homes are broken into and 280 vehicles are stolen (including 39 hijackings),[1] and the area of bushland where Zimbabwean exiles hold their meetings, on the fringe of the country's richest city, was not a healthy place to be late on a Sunday.

Paradise pulled a lever and the back of his seat reclined until it was nearly horizontal. 'I'll stay here,' he said. 'I don't understand what those guys say anyway, and if there's trouble, you just come back and we can get out quickly.'

I picked up my camera and tape recorder and walked to a clearing beyond the trees. I was facing into the sun, already low in the sky, and against the light the hundred or so people sitting on the ground were etched in silhouette. I got the feeling that some of them had been there for a while.

In accordance with tribal custom, men were grouped together on one side and women on the other. Most were in their twenties and thirties, but a few older people sat at the back and children stayed with their mothers. Mine was the only white face there, but no one seemed to notice.

I was making my way to the front of the men's group when someone grabbed me by the ankle.

'Where have you been?'

'Hey, Clever, *ndiepe yako* [where are you at in life]?' I asked in Shona, the language spoken by the majority of Zimbabweans.

The young man stood up, extended his fist and we 'shook hands' the way blacks do in Johannesburg, touching each other's clenched fist and then bringing the hand up to the heart.

'Where have you been?' he asked again, and his eyes told me that he was off his medication. 'My pills are finished and I need to see you.'

Clever hailed from near Gokwe, a small town in the centre of Zimbabwe, but

1

he had worked in Bulawayo and in his spare time was a security officer with the Movement for Democratic Change (MDC), the first serious opposition the ruling ZANU-PF party had faced in twenty years. Not yet twenty-five, he'd been kidnapped twice, and both times his friends had raided the militia camps where he was being held and rescued him. He, in turn, had conducted four raids on the camps to save other abductees.

Finally, he had been picked up by the Central Intelligence Organisation (CIO), Zimbabwe's dreaded secret police, and tortured so severely that he had lost the hearing in one ear and would never have children. Once again, he had escaped – but this time he fled the country and joined more than two million Zimbabwean exiles already living in South Africa. I had come to know a number of them, though it wasn't often that I attended their meetings.

I had first met Clever while photographing an anti-Mugabe demonstration in Johannesburg, and later interviewed him for an article, which was published in a British weekend newspaper. But when he told me the full extent of his injuries I took him to my doctor, who did what he could to repair the damage. That was three months before, and since then Clever had been under the care of a state psychiatrist who prescribed anti-depressants, which I paid for. Small thanks for the information he and his friends had given me.

'Bring your prescription tomorrow,' I said. 'Meet me at the usual place and we'll get your pills from the chemist.'

Some of the other people I had met at previous demonstrations came over and I found myself surrounded as they told me their news. I had interviewed hundreds of exiles, and when people have shared their suffering with you, you somehow become a witness to their progress.

There was Violet, not yet twenty but with an eight-month-old daughter strapped to her back. She had been pregnant when her husband was shot by soldiers near Harare, and when the child was born three months later, she chose the name Chipo, meaning 'the gift'.

The last time I had seen her, while photographing a protest march in Pretoria, Violet was living on her own in one of the townships near Johannesburg, and struggling to survive.

'I now have a job,' she told me in perfect English. 'It's only part time, stacking shelves in a supermarket, but it's a start, and my sister has come from Zimbabwe to look after Chipo.'

Violet reached behind her and pulled forward a woman even younger than herself, who was obviously shy about meeting strangers. She cast her eyes downwards, as though she expected me to scold her.

'This is Matilda,' said Violet, but her sister said nothing, and at the first chance she moved to the back of the crowd. Standing next to Violet was Dennis,

who had finished his O-levels in the eastern border town of Mutare just two years before, but now made a living selling refuse bags at the roadside. His older brother Robson, equally well educated, had found part-time work as a gardener. Both had been forced into militia camps at home, but they had suffered no more than a few beatings before they escaped.

'When you interviewed us last time, you said you were going to London,' Robson reminded me. 'Did you bring us anything?'

I pulled a wallet of pictures out of my camera bag, and in no time a crowd had gathered, passing between them the photographs I had taken at a demonstration outside the Zimbabwe high commission in The Strand. There was much excitement as people recognised friends who had fled to the United Kingdom.

Since 1999, Zimbabwe has been in a state of undeclared civil war. On the one side is President Robert Mugabe and his ruling Zimbabwe African National Union-Patriotic Front (ZANU-PF), which controls the army, police, youth militia and CIO. On the other side is the MDC, which, despite having fifty-four members of parliament or 45 per cent of the elected seats, is more like an underground movement than a political party, often meeting in secret to avoid being targeted by government agents.

For most of the people at the gathering in Johannesburg, Mugabe, born in 1923, was probably older than their grandparents, and few would have been out of nappies when he came to power in 1980. Now, he seemed set to stay there for life, and some writers in the press had suggested he feared going the way of Slobodan Milosevic, the former president of Yugoslavia, who had gone on trial in The Hague for crimes against humanity. Certainly there would be enough evidence to convict Mugabe if he ever stands down or is defeated at the polls.

Torture and murder have long been the instruments of war between the ruling ZANU-PF and the opposition MDC, and neither side plays clean, but independent organisations such as Amnesty International have concluded that most of the abuse has been carried out by Mugabe's party. Yet, for all the power at his disposal, he has been unable to break the support the MDC enjoys among the population.

'Excuse me. *Pamusoroyi!*' I said in Shona, as I pushed my way out of the circle of people who were still looking at the photographs.

'*Tujhele,*' I repeated in Ndebele, the language of most people at the meeting, and I moved to the edge of the clearing where beefy young men had been posted in case of trouble.

I recognised one of them. Although I couldn't remember his name, he always wore a black stetson, and was easy to pick out.

'*Makadi* [how are you]?' he asked in Shona, as he smiled and raised his hat.

'I'm fine,' I said. 'Are you expecting any problems?'

3

'I think those two guys standing at the back are spies,' he said, nodding in their direction. 'Their clothes are too smart.'

Officials from the South African home affairs department – responsible for dealing with illegal immigrants – often infiltrate large gatherings of Zimbabweans, and their presence, along with that of CIO agents, keeps many people away.

'Are you worried?' I asked.

He shook his head. 'They know we outnumber them here but we must stick together.'

The speaker had arrived, and although this was not so much an official meeting of the Johannesburg branch of the MDC as a regular gathering of the exile support group, he was a senior member of the opposition on a visit from Zimbabwe. As he reached the front of the crowd, someone handed him a megaphone and he put it to his mouth.

'*Chinja!*' he shouted, but his thin voice was lost in the open air.

He switched on the megaphone.

'*Chinja!*' he boomed, and his audience raised their right hands and gave the open-palm salute of the MDC.

'*Maitiro!*' they roared.

'*Chinja!*' he repeated, and again they responded, completing the two-word phrase that means 'let's change the way we do things'.

The two men my friend suspected of being government agents joined in, perhaps worried that if they didn't, they *would* be taken for spies.

'Yes! Change!'

The speaker switched to English. He was about thirty years old, clean-shaven and dressed in a T-shirt and jeans.

'We are going to change Zimbabwe,' he promised.

'We will chase these cruel and corrupt gangsters from power. We will bring back prosperity. We will reclaim the billions from the president's bank accounts in Malaysia. But we need your help. Let us make it safe for you to go home!'

A roar of approval met the mention of what was probably the uppermost priority on the minds of his audience … the chance to go home.

Opinion varies as to how many of these political and economic refugees can claim legal status in South Africa. Some estimates put the figure as low as 10 or 20 per cent. According to the same analysts, in the absence of dramatic change, as many as 3 000 Zimbabweans could be crossing the border into South Africa every day by the middle of 2004. Catching and repatriating them would require a staff of thousands, and President Thabo Mbeki's government has more pressing budgetary concerns.

It is common knowledge that Mugabe sends CIO agents to South Africa to keep tabs on his exiles, but theirs is not an easy job. International agreements between governments allow only a reciprocal number of 'declared' intelligence staff to operate from embassies, and if, for example, the British intelligence service, MI6, has four people based at their high commission in Pretoria, South Africa can station four 'spooks' in London, and the same rules apply to neighbouring states.

'The South Africans are very sticky about this,' an American diplomat told me. 'They allow only the agreed number into the country and get very upset if undeclared agents try to work on their patch.'

Realistically, Mugabe would need several thousand agents in Johannesburg alone, but Zimbabweans have also settled in cities such as Durban, Cape Town, Bloemfontein and Port Elizabeth, to say nothing of every town and hamlet in between.

Revolving teams of CIO enter South Africa on holiday visas, stay for a month and go back. They have their own accommodation in Hillbrow, once the Bohemian heart of inner-city Johannesburg, but now a slum, populated almost exclusively by exiles from the rest of Africa. Mugabe's spies park their Land Rover Defenders in the street and drink in the pub at the Dorchester Hotel or at the Jungle Inn across the road, and the South Africans take no action against them, provided they comply with the conditions of their tourist visas. But if they try to harass anyone, including their own nationals, they are out.

As for turning up at meetings, that is more risky. Many of the exiles fled their country after being tortured by the CIO. In Johannesburg, however, the victims feel safe, and are not afraid to take revenge. In 2003, at least one CIO agent was allegedly murdered in Johannesburg, killed by the very people he had interrogated near Bulawayo less than twelve months earlier.

In Zimbabwe, the police have to be informed before any public meeting can take place, though ZANU-PF holds rallies at will. If any other party tries its luck, the police, army and militia will move in and hand the organisers over to the CIO for questioning. Troops use tear gas, sticks, boots, rifle-butts and even live ammunition to reinforce Mugabe's message that ZANU-PF intends to stay in power, no matter what.

But at meetings in South Africa, Mugabe's agents can do no more than listen, catch a name in conversation, recognise a known dissident or take notes as the speaker rouses the crowd.

'We know that Mugabe is good at stealing elections, but we are still pushing for a proper one, under international supervision. And when that happens, you must convince your loved ones in Zimbabwe that, unless they vote against Mugabe, they will not be reunited with you. And thousands, millions more of their sons and daughters will end up here or in Botswana or England. Outside our beloved country.'

For most of the people at the meeting, going home to see family or attend a funeral – let alone to vote – would mean jumping the border, travelling via Mozambique or Botswana, or paying 'traffic men' who, for a fee, could smuggle just about anyone through passport control.

As soon as an illegal immigrant presents his or her passport to a South African official, the game is up. No entry stamp or, at best, a holiday visa issued at the high commission in Harare a year or two before ... allowing the traveller to spend three months in the country.

Since Mugabe has banned Zimbabweans living abroad from voting, most exiles have no say in their country's future, but at meetings such as this, they cheer and applaud as though tomorrow might bring a new beginning, a dream they share with their host nation. Another million refugees from the north will play havoc with South Africa's already high unemployment figures, and Mugabe's antics have tarnished the image of the subcontinent as a place to do business.

For Mbeki, there is no easy way to deal with the problem on his doorstep. His chosen path has been the much-criticised policy of 'quiet diplomacy', avoiding confrontation with Harare and rarely criticising the regime in public. But he has little option, short of risking a split in his ruling African National Congress (ANC). Hardliners on the left of the party see Mugabe as a messiah, and some have gone so far as to suggest that his policies of virtual one-party rule and nationalisation of the economy are just what South Africa itself needs to bridge the divide between the small number of haves and the millions who go without.

Then there are the MDC links with the Zimbabwe Congress of Trade Unions, Tsvangirai's original power base and still a force within the opposition. The Congress of South African Trade Unions (COSATU) has been vocal in its support for the MDC, while simultaneously criticising Mbeki's government for not doing enough to help the working class in South Africa. Some of the more paranoid elements in the ANC believed that COSATU was on the brink of forming its own political party, and with 1.8 million members the movement certainly has the structure, resources and manpower to take on all comers, but has thus far limited itself to industrial issues. However, the theory was that, if the MDC became the ruling party in Zimbabwe, it might encourage South African workers to follow suit and form a party of their own.

More than two-thirds of all Zimbabwe's imports and exports move through South Africa, and closing the border – or even threatening to do so – would bring Mugabe to his knees in less than a week. But Mbeki chooses not to throw his weight around, and has even suggested that it would be wrong for the world to interfere in the internal affairs of an independent African state. During his years in exile fighting against South Africa's former apartheid government, he adopted a different stance, and openly pleaded for sanctions and international pressure.

By contrast, the developed world has run out of patience amid claims that the presidential election that returned Mugabe to power for another seven years in 2002 was marred by violence, vote-rigging and intimidation. The European Union (EU), the US, Canada, Australia and New Zealand all imposed a package of so-called 'smart sanctions' against Zimbabwe, citing not just the flawed election but what they alleged was an ongoing campaign of state-sponsored violence, torture and murder directed at the MDC. Foreign aid was frozen, trade with government agencies was restricted, an arms embargo was enforced and travel bans were imposed on senior members of ZANU-PF, whose personal assets and bank accounts in the participating countries are open to seizure.

But it was never supposed to come to this. Admittedly, post-colonial Africa has generated more than its share of atrocities, like the massacre of hundreds of thousands of people in Burundi and Rwanda, despotic warlords in Somalia and child slavery in Sudan. Perhaps because of the horrors that have beset the continent, when the former Rhodesia was renamed Zimbabwe in 1980 and the eight-year civil war came to an end, the new state carried the hopes and prayers of the world as a model of peaceful coexistence.

Mugabe, who came to power in British-sponsored elections, talked reconciliation and invited his former opponents, the white commanders of the Rhodesian security forces, to stay on and create a new army, air force and police service made up of their members, who were mostly black, and soldiers from the two guerrilla armies.

During the war, Beijing had sided with Mugabe's Shona tribe, which made up 70 per cent of the population, and armed his Zimbabwe National Liberation Army (ZANLA) with guns, mines and rockets while he commanded them from exile in neighbouring Mozambique.

Joshua Nkomo, leader of the minority Matabele tribe (an offshoot of South Africa's Zulu nation), which accounted for only 20 per cent of Zimbabwe's population was been backed by Moscow, used Zambia as the springboard for a guerrilla campaign waged by his Zimbabwe African People's Union (ZAPU).

Together, the movements led by Mugabe and Nkomo formed what became known as the Patriotic Front, and their mutual enemy was the white, African-born prime minister of Rhodesia, Ian Smith, whose Rhodesian Front government had held out against black majority rule since 1965.

Rhodesia's minority white population had trickled in from 1890, when Cecil John Rhodes convinced the Matabele chief, Lobengula, to sign a deal giving Rhodes prospecting rights across the entire country. The Matabele had conquered the Shona, and so were able to sign away the northern lands in addition to their own. Rhodes used the agreement to add one more colony to the burgeoning British Empire, and it was named Rhodesia in his honour.

As with Australia and Canada, Rhodesia saw a huge influx of white immigrants after the Second World War, and by the 1960s only a handful of settlers could trace their lineage back to the Pioneer Column that had originally occupied the territory. Even so, they developed a Rhodesian identity and defined themselves as white Africans.

Between 1956 and 1968, Britain gave independence to all her former colonies in Africa, but denied it to Smith unless he instituted democratic reforms that would see more blacks elected to parliament and, ultimately, a black majority government. At the time, Rhodesia's population numbered 3.5 million blacks and 250 000 whites.

Smith refused, and on 11 November 1965 issued a unilateral declaration of independence (UDI), severing all ties with London but reserving the right of allegiance to Queen Elizabeth as the country's head of state. Ian Smith is one of only two leaders in history to have taken their own independence from Britain, the other being George Washington who, on 4 July 1776, proclaimed the thirteen original colonies of America free from the rule of King George III.

In Rhodesia, the civil war that followed UDI wore down protagonists on all sides. By 1979, 36 000 combatants and civilians were dead, the same number had been injured and 1.5 million people had been displaced, and no armed force was even close to victory.

The Rhodesian government had scrapped most racial discrimination by 1976, and in March 1979 everyone was given the vote. But Mugabe and Nkomo refused to come home from exile or take part in the election, and both vowed to continue the armed struggle. Bishop Abel Muzorewa was elected prime minister and the name of the country was changed to Zimbabwe Rhodesia, but the West refused to recognise the new state.

The conflict might have dragged on for another decade but for a peace deal brokered at the end of 1979 by Britain's newly elected Conservative Party government, led by Margaret Thatcher. In elections that were as free as could be expected after a war, Mugabe won fifty-seven of the eighty seats reserved for blacks, while Nkomo took twenty and Muzorewa claimed the last three. Ian Smith's Rhodesian Front won all twenty of the seats reserved for whites.

When Zimbabwe attained legal independence on 18 April 1980, it was Africa's second largest manufacturing base, and the Zimbabwe dollar was almost on par with the British pound and 30 per cent stronger than the South African rand.

In those days, thousands would turn out for ZANU-PF meetings, just to catch a glimpse of the hero who had achieved justice and equality for the majority. Robert Mugabe was not only popular at home, but had a huge following in Africa and beyond. Here was a man who would show the world that Africa could produce at least one success story, a free country that would disprove white-ruled South Africa's argument that Third World democracy could lead only to corruption, tyranny and economic disaster.

Furthermore, he would show that Ian Smith had been nothing more than a paranoid old man who should have embraced democracy years before and saved his country from so much needless suffering and loss of life.

Mugabe was fêted in Europe, America and Australia. He made several speeches at the United Nations headquarters in New York, and was beloved among leaders throughout the developing world, spearheading the Commonwealth's battle against apartheid in South Africa and serving as chairman of both the Organisation of African Unity and the Non-Aligned Movement.

He took an already excellent school system and expanded it to make primary education both free and compulsory, extended health care and encouraged small business. His government was friendly to large corporations and especially to the established white agricultural sector, whose cash crops were not only the major source of foreign currency, but fed the nation with maize, wheat, potatoes and livestock. Food exports went to Malawi, Zambia, Botswana and Mozambique, and Zimbabwe was South Africa's largest trading partner in Africa.

White politicians who had run the Rhodesian Front changed their party's name to the Conservative Alliance of Zimbabwe (CAZ), but in black politics there was little opposition to Mugabe, except in Matabeleland, where Joshua Nkomo's ZAPU had the sole mandate.

Five years later, the press had been nationalised and Mugabe had imported North Korean instructors to train a special army unit, the Fifth Brigade, now known to have murdered somewhere between 10 000 and 30 000 of Nkomo's followers in an effort to liquidate the opposition. Elections became a formality, and anyone who envisaged standing against ZANU's candidates could expect a visit from the CIO.

In December 1987, Nkomo, his people beaten into submission, agreed to merge his party with Mugabe's to create ZANU-PF, and Zimbabwe became a de facto one-party state.

Over the next fifteen years the economy faltered, and Mugabe used state funds to finance ruinous military expeditions, first into Mozambique in the late 1980s when his troops helped the ruling Frelimo party in its fight against pro-Western Renamo guerrillas, and later in the Congo to shore up the government of Laurent Kabila, who had overthrown the US-backed dictator, Mobutu Sese Seko.

In 1997, money that did not appear in the national budget was paid to veterans of the bush war in order to quash an internal revolt. Mugabe simply ordered the Reserve Bank to print more currency. The value of the Zimbabwe dollar plummeted, inflation moved into double (and later triple) digits, and the first signs of grass-roots opposition to ZANU-PF began to emerge throughout the country.

Six years later, Mugabe stood accused of rigging elections and destroying the economy through agrarian reforms that saw all but 300 of Zimbabwe's 4 000 white commercial farmers driven off their land in a matter of months. The flow of foreign currency dwindled to a trickle, and eight million people were left in a state of famine.

I lived through the war of the 1970s and have followed Zimbabwe's progress ever since, and it strikes me how similar ZANU-PF's latter-day message is to that of the white minority government before pressure from South Africa and America forced Ian Smith to accept the concept of majority rule in 1976. Up to then, he had vigorously opposed the idea, arguing that black rule had been a disaster everywhere in Africa, and that democratic institutions inherited from the colonial powers that withdrew in the 1950s and 1960s had swiftly been abandoned. One by one, the new nations had become either one-party states or military dictatorships. The press was nationalised, political opposition outlawed and rulers treated their countries as private domains.

And Smith's claims were supported by fact. From January 1956 – when Sudan became the first colonial territory to gain independence – until white-ruled Rhodesia capitulated in 1979, not a single African state saw regime change through the ballot box. During the same period, however, there were fifty successful coups (and more than eighty attempts), eighteen heads of state were assassinated and six were forced to resign.

Smith had also accused black nationalists such as Mugabe of being funded by foreign governments. Their opposition to his policies was not, he claimed, a legitimate expression of the people's will, but a plot by outside forces, notably the communists, to take over the country.

From the late 1990s, similar claims were made at ZANU-PF meetings: the opposition MDC was a puppet of the West, funded by Britain, Europe and America, and, if they were elected to government, Zimbabwe would become the slave of some foreign master.

Within the ranks of ZANU-PF, all Zimbabwe's ills were blamed on the World Bank, Europe, the British, the whites and the economic programmes imposed by the International Monetary Fund (IMF). At the heady levels of the CIO's top brass and some of the more radical cabinet ministers, the party faithful would cite dark forces who could not be named, but were part of an international conspiracy to destroy the country.

The opposition agreed as far as the IMF was concerned, but in their version the letters stood for: *It's Mugabe's Fault!*

But MDC officials tended to avoid going too far back when attacking Mugabe's track record, because many of them had originally been members of ZANU-PF and had done nothing to curb the party's heavy-handed rule, which started less than two years after Mugabe came to power.

Even South African human rights activists such as Archbishop Desmond Tutu and Helen Suzman, who fought hard to bring freedom to their own country, failed to criticise Mugabe in the 1980s when he was torturing and killing his political opponents, and when he might still have listened to an outside voice.

Suzman subsequently admitted this that had been a mistake, even suggesting that liberal politicians in South Africa had let Zimbabwe down.

'We were so involved with our own problems here,' she told me at her home in Johannesburg. 'As a result, we ignored what was going on elsewhere. In those days, it wasn't fashionable to criticise black governments, but I daresay we could have done more.'

However, in her opinion, failure to censure Mugabe at an early stage did not lessen the ANC government's responsibility to intervene in the crisis that ensued.

'They are weak,' she said. 'Mbeki and all of them. Too weak to deal with a thug like Mugabe, and that's why he could get away with it, because he knew that the one country that could do something to stop him wouldn't raise a finger.'

The free schooling Mugabe introduced with such success has produced Africa's best-educated workforce, which is why Zimbabweans find work abroad so easily. According to Suzman, this helps to explain, at least in part, why tyranny was not answered with mass uprisings.

'Jumping the border is a lot easier than rioting in Harare and getting shot or tear-gassed.'

Despite South Africa's falling job market, the Zimbabweans, more often than not, have found steady employment, creating the inevitable backlash as happened with the Asians in Australia or Turkish migrant workers in Germany.

From 1994 to 2002, more than 500 000 South Africans lost their jobs,[2] and in the squatter camps and informal settlements around Johannesburg, residents adopted a harsh policy towards foreigners who tried to set up home, chasing them away and sometimes even burning their shacks. As had happened with the Jews in Europe before World War II, a culture of popular wisdom sprang up, and if you spent time in the townships, it wasn't long before you heard the stories: most of the criminals in South Africa hailed from elsewhere and were responsible for everything from break-ins and carjackings to rape and murder. However, no one I spoke to could ever produce statistics to back up such claims.

But what made Zimbabweans so employable? I put the question to some of the restaurant owners at Sandton Square, a posh piazza north of Johannesburg, where the rich go to eat.

'It's simple,' one of them told me after I agreed not to use his name for fear that officials would raid his establishment looking for illegal immigrants. 'Our staff is 80 per cent Zimbabwean and they know how to work. What's more, a Zim waiter will add 10 or 15 per cent to the bill.'

I asked him to elaborate.

'Bring your notebook and come sit here and watch,' the owner said as he guided me to a table and ordered each of us a glass of wine. Across the way, a middle-aged couple studied the menu while waiting for someone to take their order. A waiter approached.

I don't recall the whole conversation, but it went something like this.

'Good evening sir, good evening madam,' said the waiter, as he placed a carafe of water and two glasses on the table. 'How are things at home?'

'Uhh, uh, fine. Good evening,' mumbled the man.

'Let me get you the wine list,' the waiter offered, returning with it a moment later.

'We have a very good price this week on some of our Merlots. And while you're deciding, can I bring you some rolls, or garlic bread perhaps?'

The restaurant owner touched me on the elbow. 'See what I mean? Because of our history, or maybe it's education, I don't know, but most black South Africans don't have the confidence to engage whites in conversation. They won't even do it with wealthy black patrons.

'They wait for the guest to ask for the wine list and then stand in silence until the table is ready to order. The Zimbabweans sell the menu and boost the client's order. The waiter actually directs them to a range of choices, but he never gets pushy.'

I still wasn't sure how this linked back to education, so I approached one of my former teachers, Dr Manfred Schroenn, who retired as inspector of English education in KwaZulu-Natal before becoming an education consultant based in Pietermaritzburg. Manfred had a gift for teaching literature, and I owe much of my love of language to his talent for bringing text and characters to life.

'In Rhodesia under white rule, there was a good black school system and people like Mugabe and his cabinet are products of that,' he told me. 'The problem was that when students finished their education, there were no jobs, because all the best positions were reserved for whites.'

South Africa, he said, was different. 'Here there was a clear policy of denying blacks a quality education, and sadly, despite some brave attempts in Kenya and Tanzania, education and literacy were not big winners in the rest of Africa in the 1960s and 1970s either.

'What makes young black people from places like Zimbabwe so different is that they grew up in households where their parents – and possibly even their grandparents – were literate and had a wider understanding of education. Youngsters who are able to discuss their homework with their elders gain a lot more from the school experience. We are starting to see that in South Africa, but it will take time to erase the damage done to the school system under apartheid,' said Manfred.

'The good news is that, since the advent of democracy in 1994, black South Africans are starting to feel empowered, and I believe this is reflected in the public attitude, which can only be a positive thing.'

I told him what I had seen at the restaurant.

'Education gives you confidence,' he said. 'Workers from Zimbabwe are no more or less intelligent than people in South Africa, but they may be less reticent about striking up a conversation with their clients or even challenging the boss on issues they disagree with.'

But Manfred felt that factors other than education could be involved in the willingness of South Africans to employ Zimbabweans.

'The same kind of assertiveness is developing among South Africans, though it's never fair to generalise, and there could be many other reasons why restaurateurs choose to employ people from Zimbabwe.'

The quality of Zimbabwe's education system is borne out by a UNESCO study that shows the country had a 70 per cent literacy rate at the time of independence, compared with 47 per cent in Kenya and Tanzania. South Africa scored an impressive 76 per cent in urban areas, but in former homelands such as Venda, on the border of Zimbabwe, less than half the population could read and write.

Back at the meeting, people were still paying attention to every word from the speaker, even after thirty minutes. Most had sat down again, and some of the men joined their wives and children. Young jocks stood guard while others patrolled the area.

A commotion broke out somewhere near the back, but hardly any heads turned and the speaker didn't miss a beat. The security guards had converged on a man who was taking photographs with a small flash camera. They searched him and found a business card in his pocket that upset them, though I never discovered what it was.

'That's not me. It's a card I picked up when I went there yesterday,' he shouted, but his cries were drowned by the megaphone as the men moved him off behind the trees.

The chanting began again. 'Change! Now! *Chinja maitiro!*'

In another thirty minutes the meeting was over, but like a crowd of worshippers at a village church or synagogue after the service, no one wanted to leave. There was so much to talk about, news of people back home, details of who had got married or had a child or died. One man was telling his friends that his cousin in the UK had sent him an aeroplane ticket and he'd be leaving within a week. A woman had got her visa for Australia, where she would join her brother.

I found myself in conversation again with some of the people I had interviewed at previous meetings or protests.

'The building in Hillbrow where we used to stay is being pulled down next week,' said Robson. 'But there are still some refugees living in the basement and they have nowhere to go.'

In the rundown suburbs, penniless immigrants from Africa's more destitute countries sleep on the streets in summer, and in winter creep into any sheltered space to escape the cold in a city where early morning temperatures can plunge to –4°C (28°F).

A distant cousin of Robson and Dennis was one of the people who would be homeless after the building came down, and he would be moving in with them for a while, despite the fact that their flat was already overcrowded.

Matilda had come back and was a little less shy, and she took Chipo while Violet caught up with friends.

It was late and I had a deadline to meet, so I turned to head back to the trees where Paradise was waiting.

'One picture please!'

It was the man in the cowboy hat, and although it was growing dark I pulled out my camera and moved close to him so that the built-in flash could do its work. But before he could set his pose the other people I'd been talking to crowded around him, and it turned into a free-for-all with everyone determined to be in the shot.

When I finally worked the shutter, there must have been forty people, all young, all smiling and waving as though they didn't have a care in the world.

But the camera *does* lie, and at a rough guess, half of them would not have had a proper meal that day and probably had no place of their own to sleep that night.

Nonetheless, the following weekend, at meetings such as this one, people would again come together to share their dream of seeing real change in a country where madness has taken hold, resulting in the death of thousands and the displacement of millions, all in little more than twenty years.

# 2

# A bird's-eye view

To understand Zimbabwe, you need to know something about the country's history and the psyche of its people. The issues are complex, and many factors contributed to the crisis that began escalating in 2000.

The first inhabitants were the Bushmen or San people, who lived there for perhaps 100 000 years before they were wiped out by other black tribes moving south from the equator. There was probably a viable San population as recently as the mid-1800s, and evidence of their passing can be seen in countless rock paintings that adorn the walls of caves and overhangs in just about every hill and mountain across the country.

More than a thousand years ago, the land was settled from the north by the Shona, whose origins lie in the Great Lakes region east of Congo. But the Matabele and the white colonists came from South Africa, and this will also be our starting point for a virtual tour of Zimbabwe.

It's a short flight from Johannesburg to Harare. On a good day, with favourable winds, you'll get there in one hour twenty minutes, whereas Cape Town is a two-hour haul from Johannesburg.

In the late 1990s, when I used to fly the route once or twice a month, the aircraft operated by South African Airways and the private carrier, Comair, were always full. Air Zimbabwe (Air Zim for short) had better in-flight service than its two competitors, but the national carrier was so unreliable that it struggled to average a 50 per cent load factor. The ageing President Mugabe and his young wife, Grace, used Air Zim as their private fleet, commandeering aircraft and either occupying all of business class or simply taking over the whole aircraft.

There were many stories – mostly urban myths – about Robert Mugabe arriving at Harare International Airport ten minutes before departure of a scheduled flight to London and tossing off the other passengers, but in reality this only happened a few times a year.

His usual entourage would include members of his immediate and extended family, ministers, senior public servants, and writers and photographers from the state media. When he took over the business-class cabin on a London flight

(Air Zim has no first class), other passengers might find themselves on a detour to Libya, Nigeria or Egypt, or wherever else the president wanted to go, and the flight would arrive at Heathrow hours later than expected.

I once asked his photographer why the president couldn't give a day or two's notice of his travel plans, and was told: 'That would compromise security and make it easy for people who want to assassinate him.'

Flying north from Johannesburg, the border between the two countries is clearly visible from the air. The river that Rudyard Kipling called 'the great, grey, greasy Limpopo' is one of the continent's major waterways, flowing west to east for more than 1 500 kilometres, and forming, in turn, South Africa's border with Botswana, then with Zimbabwe, before crossing into Mozambique and pouring its silty waters into the Indian Ocean north of the capital, Maputo.

In the dry season it is barely a trickle, but when the rains are good the Limpopo comes down in full spate, uprooted trees and the carcasses of livestock and wild animals tossing and churning in a frothy mess of torrents and whirlpools as it rushes east, the force of the water pushing the flotsam far out to sea, until whatever is not eaten by sharks eventually washes back onto the beach. Two and a half trillion litres of water rush down to the river mouth each year, enough to fill Sydney Harbour five times over.

In 1927, Sir Ralph Freeman, the man who would later build the Sydney Harbour Bridge, was commissioned by the Rhodesian government to span the Limpopo. He designed a road and rail bridge 478 metres long, on which work began in May 1928. Floods almost scuppered the project but the bridge was completed in just twelve months, the total cost of £130 000 being met by a charitable trust bequeathed by Sir Alfred Beit (1853–1906), a business associate of Cecil John Rhodes. The vast fortune with which he endowed Rhodesia on his death is still used today for the annual Beit scholarships.

From 33 000 feet, you can't see Beit Bridge or the lines of cars and pedestrians waiting to cross in both directions, but the wide brown line of the river is clearly visible.

Almost from the moment of take-off at Johannesburg, an agricultural patchwork unfolds far beneath the aircraft as it makes its way across South Africa's Limpopo province. Squares of freshly ploughed earth are bordered by fields of maize, lucerne or big yellow blocks of sunflowers. Those areas that are not cultivated are marked off for cattle or game.

Some of it is commercial land, mostly in white hands, and large tracts are farmed by black villagers who generate food and cash crops in the fields around their huts. But nothing lies empty until you reach the Limpopo. The moment the aircraft flies over the river, the signs of cultivation disappear and passengers stare down at an olive-green wilderness. Streams and rocky outcrops make a

statement here and there, and sometimes you see a village or a farm, hemmed in by bush on all sides and visible for only an instant.

This is primarily game and cattle country, with some citrus and mango orchards, but with only 13 million people and – because of AIDS and emigration – an on-the-ground population of probably no more than 8 or 9 million, Zimbabwe has never faced the same pressures as South Africa, with its population of 45 million.

At 390 000 square kilometres, Zimbabwe is one-and-a-half times the size of Britain, but fits into South Africa three times. Almost a quarter of South Africa is semi-desert, but while Zimbabwe has some areas of arid bushveld, there is nothing as dry as the Kalahari. Annual average rainfall is 828 millimetres, nearly double South Africa's 464 millimetres, though both countries suffer periodic drought.

Once across the Limpopo, there are no towns for 200 kilometres until you fly over Masvingo. With a population of only 71 000, it is the country's fifth largest city, but the Masvingo province is the biggest in Zimbabwe and home to the Karanga, one of the four key groups that make up the Shona tribe. Around Masvingo, patches of farmland are visible, but the bush soon closes over the coloured squares. It's only when you get to within kilometres of Harare that the intensive farming so evident in South Africa can be seen.

The Zimbabwe economy is, of course, a lot smaller than that of its neighbour. Indeed, the entire gross domestic product (GDP) is only one-tenth of Gauteng's, the province that surrounds Johannesburg and Pretoria. Still, Zimbabwe is a bit like South Africa in microcosm, with the same crops – maize, wheat, fruit, barley, tobacco, coffee, tea and sorghum – and minerals such as gold, silver, chrome, tin, copper and small quantities of precious and semi-precious stones.

The one crop in which Zimbabwe led the field in both quantity and quality was tobacco, but that was before commercial farming collapsed as a result of Mugabe's land reform programme. In everything else, the numbers were always much smaller on the northern side of the Limpopo, even before the advent of political unrest and economic chaos.

From the air, on a clear day, great expanses of country are visible, and if you fly with a pair of binoculars, it is possible to make out some of the features.

While the Limpopo forms Zimbabwe's southern border, the northern boundary is marked by the Zambezi, which rises in Zambia and flows briefly into Angola, before winding back into Zambia and down to the border, where it spills over a ledge to create the world's largest curtain of falling water.

At a width of 1 600 metres, the Victoria Falls are one of Africa's most popular tourist attractions. In 1851, when explorer and missionary David Livingstone became the first white person to see them, he named the falls after his queen, and wrote in his diary: 'Scenes so lovely must be gazed upon by angels in their flight.'

In the visitors' book at one of the hotels near the falls, a more recent traveller described them as 'a cross between a plumber's nightmare and a tourist's wet dream'.

From there the Zambezi – which at 2 600 kilometres is the tenth longest river in the world – spills into Lake Kariba, where it spreads out to a surface area of 5 000 square kilometres. When it was built in 1960, Kariba was the largest man-made lake in the world, 230 kilometres long and 30 kilometres wide in places. On a clear day, the flat, shining surface can be seen from an aircraft over Harare.

From Kariba the Zambezi flows into Mozambique, where another dam holds back its waters at Cabora Bassa, and then, like the Limpopo, it spills into the Indian Ocean.

South of Victoria Falls lie the great game lands of Hwange and Matetsi. In the

1960s the government set up hunting blocks where, for a trophy price that could run into thousands of US dollars, the very rich were able to bag an elephant or a lion. Nowadays, though, most tourists prefer to shoot with a camera.

Hunting and tourism used to be Zimbabwe's third biggest source of foreign currency after mining and agriculture. However, from 2001 to 2003, tourist receipts fell by 80 per cent, and the number of visitors dwindled from two million a year to the point where lodges closed their doors and the famous Meikles Hotel in Harare, Zimbabwe's answer to Singapore's Raffles, put half its rooms in mothballs.

By 2003, there were still three or four flights a day from Johannesburg to Victoria Falls, but many of the tourists went straight from the airport across the bridge to Livingstone in neighbouring Zambia, where a South African resort group had built a new complex.

Lake Kariba was also a mecca of recreation in its day, but by 2003 the hotels stood empty, except on long weekends when people from Harare – or at least those who could find petrol for the trip – headed north to what they called 'Zimbabwe's Riviera'.

The collapse of tourism meant that for locals, hotels were cheap, and they could pay in Zimbabwe dollars, which was a boon at a time when foreign currency was expensive and in short supply.

Three mountain ranges lie along Zimbabwe's eastern border with Mozambique. Furthest north is Nyanga, a well-developed area with several hotels and casinos. Just a three-hour drive from Harare, it is popular as a weekend retreat, especially in mid-summer.

The town of Mutare lies on the border, and twenty kilometres south is the Bvumba range, with its English-style inns and country homes. The southernmost peaks are those of Chimanimani, heart of the country's coffee plantations.

The highest point in Zimbabwe is Mount Inyangani [the Place of Shouting], close to Nyanga, but at 2 620 metres it is much lower than Africa's most famous mountains, such as the Uhuru Peak of Kilimanjaro at 5 895 metres, or Mount Kenya, with its snow on the equator, at 5 199 metres. Even the Drakensberg range in South Africa reaches an impressive 3 450 metres, but in Zimbabwe's eastern highlands the lower altitude means that you can walk without puffing, though the nights are still cool enough for cuddling.

The entire region is a wonderland of waterfalls, caves and thick native forests interspersed with plantations of imported pines, firs and Australian eucalyptus or gum trees, which grow taller here than on their home continent.

South of Chimanimani lies the lowveld, with citrus and sugar plantations. Here the country's second largest national park, Gona re Zhou [Place of the Elephant], almost touches the South African border, and is part of the Peace

Parks Project to create the world's biggest game reserve, along with South Africa's Kruger National Park and a large chunk of Mozambican wilderness.

Much of Zimbabwe lies above 900 metres, creating a temperate climate, though the low country along the Zambezi and near Gona re Zhou in the south-east is hot. In summer, the mercury often tops 40°C.

From the air, Harare looks white, the predominant colour of the buildings. Dams and rivers encircle the city, the grass is green, and where the suburbs end, farmland takes over. It's clear that, more than a century ago, the city fathers did well when they planned what used to be known as Salisbury.

Like most Third World cities, Harare has grown bigger than ever intended, and from overhead you can see the dormitory towns of Chitungwiza in the south – home to a million people – and Tafara [Place of Happiness] in the east.

There are no real squatter camps such as those around Nairobi, Dar es Salaam, Johannesburg or even Cape Town. Chitungwiza and a dozen other high-density suburbs are well laid out and their streets have electric lights. From a distance the neat, boxy homes all look alike, but on closer inspection they are clearly distinguished by individual style and taste.

Tarred roads link these suburbs to the city, but except for work, residents have little need to venture that far, as each township has its own shopping centres, a community hall that can be hired for a nominal fee, hospitals or clinics, schools, a police station and a beerhall, which forms the centre of social life for the men and offers a base from which an army of prostitutes ply their trade.

In 2001, Harare got a new airport at a cost of more than Z$4 billion (then US$72 million). Tenders were invited but ignored, and the most expensive bid, made by Mugabe's nephew Leo, was accepted. Aircraft still touch down on the world's longest commercial runway, built in the days before jet travel to accommodate propeller-driven Viscounts and Dakotas, which struggled to take off in the summer heat. At 4 700 metres, the runway is 20 per cent longer than the one at Johannesburg, and is also longer than New York's JFK, London's Heathrow and Charles de Gaulle in Paris.

African leaders are big on pictures and have their portraits hung in all government buildings. Some, like the late Kamuzu Banda of Malawi or former Kenyan president Daniel arap Moi, insisted that their likeness should decorate the walls of shops, banks and all other public places. But Mugabe went one better, with huge gilt-framed portraits of himself on each of the four walls in the airport arrivals hall and two on the wall facing passengers as they line up to have their passports stamped.

The old terminal, built in the 1960s, served the nation in the days when more than a dozen long-haul carriers flew to Harare – Alitalia, British Airways, Aeroflot, Balkans, Air India, Swissair, Austrian, KLM, Lufthansa, Qantas and

SAA – but forty years later, only BA and SAA frequented the big new airport with its long empty corridors waiting to welcome passengers who never came.

Part of the attrition was beyond Harare's control. Aeroflot, Alitalia and Air India moved first to Johannesburg, then withdrew from southern Africa altogether. But for the big airlines such as KLM, Lufthansa and Qantas, the destination became too unstable and passenger numbers simply evaporated. Those carriers had, in any case, serviced Harare via Johannesburg, and their strategy around the world was to dump less viable destinations in favour of a regional hub, be that Bangkok, Lagos, Rio or, in this case, Johannesburg.

Malawi, Botswana and Mozambique fell victim to the same policy, but they had never enjoyed as much international air traffic as Harare. The real lunacy was to build an expensive new airport while all this was happening, and this in a country where, at the time, nearly half the population was living below the poverty line.

Until 2000, Harare was perhaps the most liveable inland city in Africa. The streets were clean, the skyline modern, municipal workers quickly attended to potholed roads during the rainy season, and the network of tarred roads far exceeded anything found to the north. Swaziland, South Africa, Lesotho, Botswana and Namibia all have excellent highways, but Zambia and Malawi are a nightmare for drivers, while in Kenya and Tanzania the roads have more holes than a cheese grater and some stretches are all but impassable.

Harare's streets are wide and traffic jams are few, and many of South Africa's major chain stores, including Edgars and Woolworths, have long had branches in the capital, while franchise restaurants such as News Café and Ocean Basket offer the same fare as they do down south, albeit at hugely inflated prices that reflect the parallel exchange rate rather than the ludicrous rates published by the Reserve Bank of Zimbabwe.

In July 2003, according to the government, one rand was worth Z$105, and the pound traded at 1 300:1, while the greenback was set at 824. But no currency was available at these rates, so people had to resort to black-market traders who charged 300 for the rand, 3 700 for the pound and 2 400 for the US dollar. The banks displayed the official rates, and on inquiry clients would be told that no currency was available. But if you were a regular customer (and one who could be trusted not to talk about the deal), the teller would sell you as much foreign currency as you wanted at black-market rates. The state passed a law making this illegal, but government departments were among the worst offenders.

A visitor might well recognise some of the banks with names such as Barclays and Standard, which opened here a century ago, but the late 1990s saw an explosion of good, local banks, such as Century and Kingdom. ZANU-PF's own bank, CBZ, was the only one granted facilities in the new airport terminal, and payments for all government services – even school fees – have to be made through CBZ: corruption with a clean face.

Street children are as much of a problem in Harare as anywhere else in Africa, approaching motorists at every intersection. Many are from Mozambique and few are orphans. Having learned that people would sooner give cash to an urchin than to an adult beggar, their parents spend the day sitting in the shade while the children, aged from five to fifteen, accost drivers and shuttle back and forth to deliver the day's takings.

Adult street people work the municipal parking bays along all the main streets, waving oncoming cars to vacant spots and offering to look after the vehicle in your absence. Decline, and you risk a nasty coin scratch on your car's bodywork.

If you go along with this protection racket, a fee of a few hundred Zim dollars is in order; it sounds a lot, but in real terms it translates to a few British pence on the parallel market.

The only difference between Harare's exclusively male 'car guards' and those who provide a similar service in Johannesburg is the attitude. Harare's hustlers not only offer a broad, toothy grin as they wave you to your spot, they have a line in patter that would match the best American sales pitch.

A typical exchange with one of these parking attendants might go something like this:

'Good morning, sir. How are you today?'

'I'm fine. What's your name?' (This is important if you want him to feel a sense of attachment to your car.)

'I'm Kingston, sir. For extra, I can wash your car and clean the windscreen and I don't break the aerial when I wash.'

'No, I won't be gone for long enough. Just watch it and make sure no *tsotsis* [thieves] come near it.'

At this point, Kingston may puff out his chest and flex an arm to show an impressive bicep. 'I'm very strong. I will beat them until they run away!'

And when you return, your car is there, untouched, and Kingston (or whoever) still has his smile.

On just about any street in Harare, two things stand out. First, it's how neatly dressed the pedestrians are – the men in smart shirts, often with ties and jackets, and the women clearly having taken care to look their best. Some of the women wear trousers, but most opt for dresses or skirts, and the notion of getting dressed up to go to town is alive and well. Even the street men tuck in their hand-me-down shirts, and it is rare to see anyone barefoot.

The other big feature is the trees, thousands of them across the city, on every spare patch of soil – on pavements, traffic islands, church grounds and vacant plots, in parks and in schoolyards. Some, like the flame trees, are indigenous, but many exotic species have been planted, including countless South American jacarandas, which, in September, burst into purple blossom with the approach of spring.

Long after the city council was bankrupted, public funds pilfered or frittered away, it continued to employ an army of litter collectors who patrolled the streets with their bins on wheels, spiking papers and cigarette butts, making Harare cleaner than many cities in developed countries.

Another tradition that has been maintained is the planting of showy annuals in parks and other public places, their flowers creating an atmosphere of cheer and goodwill, which is reflected in the ready smiles of the street men, newspaper vendors and hawkers – who sell sweets and cigarettes from makeshift corner stands – refuse collectors, gardeners, and even the police and traffic officers.

In fact, anyone walking around the CBD would be hard pressed to imagine how much hunger, horror and pain these people have endured, and that makes their tragedy so much greater. Awful things happen to the nicest people, and Harare is a city of very nice people. In contrast, when I visit well-fed cities such as London, the pedestrians look permanently pissed-off.

For most of Harare's recent past, there was never any sign of a police or military presence on the streets, except when trouble was about. Like the British bobbies, Zimbabwe's patrolmen never carried firearms. Even at the height of the civil war in the 1970s they were not armed, and perhaps as a result of this criminals rarely were, either. But things change, and Harare could not escape the sight of policemen carrying Chinese-made automatic rifles or reports of people being carjacked at gunpoint.

Even so, the city remains one of the safest in Africa, with crime levels way below those of Nairobi or Lusaka, and not even in the same league as Lagos and Johannesburg.

But a new menace came from Mugabe's efforts to politicise the youth. In 2000, militia training camps were set up across the country, and thousands of young people joined the National Service Campaign in exchange for a regular meal. But many more were shanghaied, literally kidnapped, and forced to undergo training.

Their green drill trousers led people to dub them the 'Green Bombers', and their duties included patrolling the streets and managing bus queues, sometimes demanding ZANU-PF membership cards before allowing people into a shop. They acted with impunity, beating up anyone who disputed their authority. The Hitler Youth would be a good analogy.

After America sent its armed forces into Afghanistan, people began calling these young thugs the Taliban, but thanks to the irrepressible humour that sustains the Zimbabwean spirit come what may, it wasn't long before they were being referred to as the 'Talibob', a play on the president's first name.

Around Harare, roadblocks are a way of life. The police only pull cars off the road if they want to conduct a physical search, but every vehicle has to stop for the driver to be questioned while traffic builds up behind. Most are then waved on with a smile, but anyone who makes a fuss will almost certainly be directed to the side of the road and searched, and depending on the mood of the police, things could turn nasty.

You get the feeling that no one's in a rush anyway. Harare lacks the sense of urgency that marks the pace in Johannesburg and, to a lesser extent, Cape Town. Here, life moves slowly and no one cares, or maybe after forty years of living under conditions of a police state they no longer notice.

Roadblocks are more plentiful towards the end of the month, when police wages have been spent and they demand money from black drivers in exchange for letting them pass. Whites are almost never asked for a bribe.

Suburban homes used to be open to the streets when I grew up here in the 1960s and 1970s, and the most you would see was a hedge or a chicken-wire fence. Even during the war, no one bothered about urban security. But within two years of Mugabe coming to power, law and order had broken down to such a degree that the police could not protect the people, and high concrete walls began to go up everywhere.

The collapse of normal policing was linked to a shortage of transport. There were plenty of vehicles, but the newly appointed inspectors and superintendents, many of them former guerrillas with little training, took a fancy to the police cars and Land Rovers, appropriating them for personal use and leaving the rest of the force do their work on foot.

If you called the local station to say you were being robbed or murdered, the usual response was to ask you to drive to the station and collect the duty officer.

By the mid-1990s, theft and home break-ins had become a serious problem, and the typical garden wall had been topped with razor wire or an electric fence.

It didn't take long before private companies filled the gap left by the police. A client's home was fitted with alarms, which were linked to a command centre. At the first sign of trouble, a reaction squad was sent to the rescue, but none of the staff carried guns. In South Africa it would be suicide for their counterparts to react to a crime without a truckload of weapons.

Zimbabwe's only other city of any size is Bulawayo, 400 kilometres south-west of Harare. An American tourist once remarked that the people of Bulawayo had taken the Spanish concept of *manyana* and wound it down to half speed.

Whatever the case, Bulawayo is a delight for drivers. Cecil John Rhodes decreed that the streets of the town should be wide enough for a wagon driver to turn a full span of twelve oxen, and traffic jams are virtually unheard of.

The area is home to the Matabele people, whose language is so different from

Shona that members of the two tribes must either learn the other's language or converse with one another in English. Most Matabele have a fair grasp of Shona, but the reverse is not true. The government has deliberately staffed the region's public service with Shonas, who generally refuse to learn Ndebele and insist on conducting business in their own tongue.

Bulawayo has an identity all its own, but from the mid-1980s the city lost much of its skilled workforce as people started emigrating to South Africa. The only constant was the face of Mugabe on the walls of public buildings, though when Bulawayo became a stronghold of the MDC after the 2000 general election, a lot of the portraits were taken down by workers who had voted for the opposition.

One of the best places in town is the Bulawayo Club, a huge, high-ceilinged building opposite the post office. The walls are panelled with dark wood, game heads look down on patrons, and ceiling fans keep the air cool on summer days when the temperature can easily reach 30°C.

The club was founded in 1895, and has such an air of colonial charm about it that one might expect to pass David Livingstone or Karen Blixen on the wide spiral staircase that leads from the lobby to the first-floor dining room. Until 1977, membership was open only to whites, but today it is common to find a majority of black members taking coffee on the balcony, or drinking beer or pink gins in the main bar, which looks like something out of a novel by Somerset Maugham.

I used to lecture in both Harare and Bulawayo, and perhaps more than anything, this brought home to me the difference between the Shona and the Matabele. If someone in a class in Harare thought I had made a mistake in the lecture, he or she might see me afterwards and ask if I could explain the concept again. In Bulawayo, people will raise their hands and stop you in mid-stride.

The Matabele are no less courteous than the Shona, just more assertive.

I don't know much about anthropology, but I suspect that the difference has something to do with the history of the two tribes. It is important to know where Zimbabwe has come from if you want to understand where the country may be headed in the future.

# 3

# Strangers at the gate

By the year 2000, more than half of Zimbabwe's population was too young to remember the civil war of the 1970s, or had not even been born until it was over. The country's often tumultuous past had been consigned to the history books, and the earliest human settlement of the land between the Zambezi and the Limpopo was something the Shona preferred not to talk about.

For untold millennia, the Bushmen or San people occupied most of southern Africa, including Zimbabwe, living in a lush, well-watered but isolated Eden, where game was plentiful and the trees were heavy with fruit.

A nomadic people, they neither raised cattle nor grew crops, and when the great herds of antelope caught the smell of distant rain in their nostrils and migrated north or south, the San followed. When the herds stopped to graze, San families would shelter in caves, painting the rockface with plant dyes, recording great hunts and sometimes orgies, but mostly sketching the animals they saw around them. Their art is among the oldest on earth, and there are thousands of sites across Zambia, Zimbabwe, Botswana and South Africa where it can be seen.

In the second century AD, other tribes began moving down the length of Africa from present-day Burundi and the Democratic Republic of Congo. Many of these original migrants died out, but by the year 1000 some had settled in the valleys south of the Zambezi, where they planted fields and built their shelters. The Shona people had arrived in the country they would make their own.

By the twelfth century the Shona were building with stone, creating the temple and walled enclosures at Great Zimbabwe, from which the country takes its name. The ruins of that edifice are the largest free-standing stone structure in Africa after the pyramids. In places, the walls are five metres thick and up to ten metres high, yet there is no cement or fixing agent between the more than one million granite blocks preserved on an 800-hectare piece of land.

An enterprising people, the Shona had colonised most of present-day Zimbabwe by 1400, and 400 years later the San were all but extinct.

Sub-tribes such as the Karanga and the Rozvi made contact fairly early with Arab traders, who ventured into the hinterland after sailing south in their dhows, returning to their homes with gold taken from the ground by the Rozvi, using slow and simple methods. The people of Great Zimbabwe also fashioned the precious metal into ornaments for themselves, but even as tales of the riches to be found in Mwana Mutapa's kingdom reached the shores of foreign lands, the inhabitants were dying out, their natural resources depleted and their numbers eroded by internecine war.

During Great Zimbabwe's golden age, other branches of the same central African people had also migrated south. The Korekore settled north-east of present-day Harare near the town of Mount Darwin, and extended their domain to the Zambezi, where a pre-Shona group, the Tongas, dwelt on either side of the river. The Tonga lifestyle centred on fishing, and it was they who named the waters Zambezi, which means 'great river'.

Four main branches of the Shona would survive: the Karanga, Korekore, Zezuru and Manyika. They share a common language, chiShona, and include a number of smaller but significant clans such as the Ndau, who populate much of Mozambique and are found as far north as Malawi.

The Shona held sway over Zimbabwe until 1840, when the Zulu chief Mzilikazi swept into the country from the south, slaughtering all before him.

There's a legend, which is almost certainly not true, but worth repeating anyway. As the San were driven from their prehistoric home, they placed a curse on the land between the Zambezi and Limpopo, swearing that while others might live there, no one would ever truly control it, for it still belonged to the Bushmen and there would never be peace on stolen land.

If it was the San curse that visited revenge on the Shona, it was a mighty and terrible hex.

In 1822, Mzilikazi was a trusted general in the army of Shaka, warrior king of the Zulu nation, in what is now the South African province of KwaZulu-Natal. Shaka's regiments roved the country, subjugating or wiping out other tribes and plundering their settlements with impunity.

Mzilikazi's last raid on the Zulu king's behalf took him to an area near present-day Johannesburg, where his warriors attacked the local tribes. In accordance with Shaka's rules of conquest, they killed the men and slaughtered the children, and when the battle was done, rounded up the women and cattle as booty for the monarch.

But Mzilikazi set aside some of the plumpest cows for his own herd and sent only part of the spoils to Shaka, who dispatched a messenger with orders that the general should report in person with the rest. Mzilikazi knew that to obey meant certain death, as Shaka would have to make an example of him, so he clipped the feathers from the messenger's headdress (an unpardonable insult in Zulu custom) and sent him back to the king.

In a rage, Shaka ordered his best warriors to teach Mzilikazi a lesson, and the general and his army were routed at a hill called enTumbane. The general and 300 of his men escaped and ran hundreds of kilometres to the north-west, until they reached a valley near the present-day town of Bethal, 150 kilometres south-east of Johannesburg, where Mzilikazi felt they would be safe from Shaka's wrath.

He named his new kraal Phumuleni [the Resting Place], and immediately embarked on a campaign of oppression against the native Sotho people, taking their women as wives for his soldiers, killing the men and rounding up their cattle to build up his own herd. The marauders called themselves Zulus, but the BaSotho referred to anyone who had run away from authority as amaTebele, and the name stuck. Others, however, said the name related to the big shields carried by the warriors.

The newcomers prospered, and by 1825, captives who were not used as slaves had been pressed into military service, making the Matabele a mixed tribe, though Mzilikazi and his original warriors held the top ranks.

With prosperity came the fear that Shaka would raid the kraal, so the Matabele moved north to where Pretoria now stands, and it was here that spies reported in 1828 that the Zulu king's half-brother, Dingaan, had slain him and seized the throne.

Two of the first white men to visit Mzilikazi's kraal were Robert Schoon and William McLuckie, traders who had trekked up from the Cape. The king received them well, but the visitors were outraged by the harsh conditions under which the Sotho and other conquered tribes were living. Their huts had been burned and their cattle confiscated, they had no oxen to pull their ploughs, and for 150 kilometres in all directions from Mzilikazi's seat, the people were destitute.

Over the next eight years, many white travellers paid homage to the chief, including David Livingstone's father-in-law Robert Moffat, who struck up a lifelong friendship with Mzilikazi, while French and American missionaries were given permission to settle in the area.

The Cape had been under British occupation since 1795, and in 1834 descendants of the original Dutch settlers who had arrived in 1652 loaded their ox-drawn wagons and rode into the unknown interior to get as far away as possible from the yoke of English rule.

Some of these pioneers or *voortrekkers* – literally, those who went first – settled less than 100 kilometres south of the Matabele heartland. While other newcomers had sought the self-proclaimed Matabele king's permission to pass through his territory, the Voortrekkers dismissed him as a minor thug and refused to recognise his authority. On 24 August 1836, a Matabele unit on patrol killed four members of a hunting party led by Stephanus Erasmus. Another group of Voortrekkers living nearby was also attacked, twelve of them killed and four taken prisoner – a boy who was rescued, a man who was later put to death and two girls who were kept by the Matabele and grew up in the tribe.

Mzilikazi decided it was time to punish those who had invaded his realm, and sent his armies against a group of settlers living in fifty wagons along the Vaal River to the south. The Matabele attacked, and while the Voortrekkers tried to hold the enemy at bay, the warriors rounded up horses, 5 000 cattle and 50 000 sheep, and took them back to the king.

In the battles that followed the use of rifles gave the Voortrekkers an unfair advantage, and some scholars have argued that they pushed Mzilikazi out of South Africa and into Zimbabwe. But the whites were few in number and hardly posed a threat to the Matabele. The Zulus, however, were a different matter.

Dingaan had heard exaggerated stories of Mzilikazi's raid against the Voortrekkers. The 5 000 cattle grew in the telling until they were a herd that stretched to the horizon, while the sheep were so numerous that a man could not walk past the flock in one day. Dingaan sent an army to seize these riches, and they launched a surprise attack on the renegade king in October 1837. Mzilikazi's personal regiment, the *izimPhangele* [plunderers], died in the first wave, and the Matabele defence collapsed as warriors fled, leaving the raiders to make off with virtually all their sheep and cattle.

A month later, the kraal was attacked again, this time by the Voortrekkers, who took the remaining livestock. His kingdom in ruins, Mzilikazi gathered the remnants of his tribe and fled across the Limpopo River, where the army split in two. One group made their way to what became Bulawayo, and the other, under Mzilikazi, pushed north through Botswana, then east into what is now the Hwange National Park, south of Victoria Falls.

A local Shona chief named Hwange challenged them, but while the Matabele were no match for Dingaan's massive army, they slaughtered the Shona with ease and took the chief prisoner. Hwange was rumoured to have two hearts, and Mzilikazi ordered the soldiers to cut him open, but there is no record of what they found. The defeat of Hwange's people was perhaps the first destruction of a Shona village by the Matabele in what would later become wholesale slaughter.

The other group of Matabele had received no word from their king, and assumed that he and his followers had perished. With spring at hand they wanted to perform the traditional ceremony of *ncwala* [first fruits ceremony], but a ruler had to bless the event, so they appointed Mzilikazi's eldest son, Nkulumana, as heir to the throne.

When this news reached the king, who was still enjoying the game lands of Hwange, he was furious and mustered his army to march south. When word of their advance reached Nkulumana, he sent a messenger to meet his father and beg forgiveness, explaining that they had truly thought him dead.

Mzilikazi was prepared to accept the apology, until he asked what great ceremonies of weeping had been held to mark his passing. On learning that none had taken place, he was enraged, but when he reached the unauthorised royal kraal he acknowledged that his people had chosen a beautiful place for the Matabele to make their home, and declared that this would be his new seat of power. His first act was to order the deaths of not only Nkulumana, but also all his brothers and their advisers. The youngest prince, Lobengula, who was just a boy, was smuggled to safety by his mother and hidden in the mountains until his father's rage subsided.

Legend has it that Lobengula was looked after by one of the two Voortrekker girls who had lived with the tribe since being captured in 1836, and that this explained why he was always at ease in the company of whites.

The year was 1840 and the Shona had long since abandoned Great Zimbabwe. The Karanga living in the Motobo Hills south-east of the kraal were soon chased back to Masvingo by the Matabele, who kept their women. Another clan fled north, but half of them turned back when a woman called Nyamazane suggested that peace could be made with the conquerors if she married Mzilikazi. She did, and her people were accepted into the tribe.

The king regarded all the land between the Limpopo and the Zambezi as his domain and all the people living in it as his subjects. Over the next half-century the Shona were hunted relentlessly, and all other tribes had to pay the Matabele a tax just to stay alive.

The Karanga, Zezuru, Manyika and Korekore, along with the Rozvi people who had built Great Zimbabwe, had grown soft and fat over the centuries. The Shangaan had raided the Manyika in the south-east, and there had been some minor skirmishes but no real battles, so the Shona were unprepared for war. The Matabele viewed the northern tribes with contempt, calling them tripe eaters, but took care to cultivate those who posed a threat to their new-found prosperity, such as the Shangaan in the south-east and the Voortrekkers, with whom Mzilikazi signed a non-aggression pact before setting up an embassy across the Limpopo.

White hunters, traders and missionaries visited the king, and as long as they showed proper respect their safe passage was assured. But many returned to South Africa with tales of how the other tribes had been persecuted and were now starving in subjugation. The Shona population dwindled to perhaps as low as 100 000, and the survivors took to living on high ground from where they could at least see the approach of the Matabele. Even now, many hilltops in Zimbabwe feature low stone walls, built to protect Shona cattle overnight.

Robert Moffat was a regular guest at the royal kraal and was allowed to establish a mission station just beyond its limits. The king enjoyed eating the roast fat from slaughtered cattle, and was renowned for the amount of beer he could drink at one sitting. Moffat treated him for gout, but his poor diet repeatedly inflamed the condition. By the time the missionary retired to England in 1860, Mzilikazi, aged seventy, was barely mobile. But his mind was as sharp as ever. A steady stream of hunters and prospectors made their way to his seat, and he would keep them waiting, sometimes for days, to underline his power. He maintained a lifelong distrust of all Zulus, lest they be spies from his former home, and any groups led by Zulu guides were turned back at the Limpopo.

When Mzilikazi died in 1868, Lobengula fled into the Matobo Hills and hid until he saw how people viewed the succession. There were influential generals who would have liked to be king, but no one wanted to start a war within the tribe. Lobengula became the obvious choice to unite a nation in mourning. No sooner had he been installed as king than he put to death those generals and other leaders who had fostered visions of power. When the executions were over, Lobengula renamed his capital guBulawayo, the place of great killing.

Among the earliest visitors to Mzilikazi's kraal had been Henry Hartley and a young German adventurer, Karl Maunch. Hartley and the old king had formed a good relationship from the start, and Lobengula had accompanied the hunter on some of his expeditions.

In 1865, Hartley discovered the ancient gold mines of the Rozvi, and was told by local inhabitants how their ancestors had worked the mines before the Matabele came. Hartley kept his find to himself, but on his next visit he teamed up with Maunch and they took rocks from the site back to South Africa, where the samples caused great interest. There was gold in the quartz, though the seams were thin, but Maunch was unable to curb his excitement.

'The extent and beauty of the goldfields are such that I stood, as it were, transfixed, and for a few minutes was unable to use the hammer,' he wrote in one account.

In 1867 a German-American called Adam Renders, who lived with a black wife near the Limpopo, became the first white person to see the ruins of Great Zimbabwe, but he made no fuss about the discovery. In 1871, however, Karl Maunch heard the story and implored Renders to take him to the site. His first glimpse was from the crest of a nearby hill at night, under a full moon. The vision must have been splendid, and the German's imagination ran wild.

'I do not think I am far wrong if I suppose that the ruin is a copy of Solomon's Temple,' he wrote.

Maunch grabbed all the glory of the find and sent dispatches to newspapers in London, Europe and South Africa, claiming he had solved the riddle of the ancients. He cut a piece of wood from a lintel above one entrance to the great stone enclosure, and, from the perfume, identified it as Lebanese cedar. In fact, it was African sandalwood.

By 1870, people claiming to be hunters, but really looking for gold, poured across the Limpopo, many of them ignoring the Matabele altogether. Lobengula lacked his father's aggression, and let them pass. However, he continued to raid and tax the Shona, who had been reduced to a hidden people, creeping down from the hills to water their cattle and running for cover at the sight of strangers. While Robert Moffat and his famous son-in-law, David Livingstone, had exposed the horrors of slavery and been instrumental in having it abolished throughout the civilised world, no one bothered about the continued practice in Africa, showing a singular disregard for black-on-black violence that would also become evident a century later, when African colonies became independent.

Lobengula had entrenched his position as ruler and made peace with the Shangaan – the only other belligerent tribe in the region – by taking several of their royal maidens as his wives. When his sister, Mcengence, objected to such contamination of the royal bloodline, the king had her killed, and thereafter it seemed that he would rule in peace for the rest of his life.

Some prospectors had ventured as far north as present-day Harare, while others had set up in the mountains to the east, and ivory hunters were taking trophies by the ton. But although Maunch entertained ideas of annexing the area for Germany, none of the newcomers had made any attempt, as yet, to make Matabeleland their own. That was about to change, and the ensuing invasion would alter life between the Limpopo and the Zambezi forever.

On 22 October 1844, Louisa Peacock, daughter of a wealthy landowner and banker in far-off Lincolnshire, married Francis William Rhodes, a widowed vicar nine years her senior. The first two children born of their union died shortly after birth, but nine others followed,[1] six of them arriving after Francis was given his own parish in 1849 at Bishops Stortford in Hertfordshire, north of London.

Their fourth son, Cecil John, uttered his first cry at 7.30 pm on Tuesday, 5 July 1853, and when he drew his last breath at the age of forty-nine in 1902, he was one of the richest men in the world. He had conquered both the Matabele and the Shona, founded a country that bore his name, played a pivotal role in starting the Anglo-Boer War, and established a fund that helped to educate, among others, astronomer Edwin Hubble, lateral thinker Edward de Bono, Australian prime minister Bob Hawke and US president Bill Clinton.

Though millions of words have been written about Rhodes, much of his life remains the stuff of myth and legend. Far from being a poor and sickly youth who arrived in South Africa penniless and made his fortune from the diamond fields at Kimberley, Rhodes came from a comfortably well-off family. His great-grandfather was an eighteenth-century property mogul, and his grandfather made a fortune in the building industry.

His mother's family was not only wealthy but also well connected, and Louisa's father was a member of the British parliament for many years. Of all her children, Cecil was Louisa's favourite. At school, he displayed 'signs of superior intelligence', and one teacher remembered him as 'a very bright little boy'. He wanted to become a lawyer, but two years after his eldest brother Herbert moved to South Africa to try his hand at growing cotton, Rhodes joined him, having been given a clean bill of health by the family doctor, John Morris, before leaving home.

He arrived in Durban on 1 September 1870 with £2 000 (the equivalent of £100 000 in 2003)[2] in his pocket, a gift from his mother's sister, Sophie. Three years earlier, the discovery of diamonds near Kimberley had drawn a legion of foreign dreamers, crooks, con men, prospectors, whores and speculators to South Africa, where both the Cape Colony and Natal were under British rule, while the Voortrekkers had set up independent Boer republics in the Transvaal and Orange Free State.

So intoxicating was the prospect of fortune that Cecil's brother, Herbert, had rushed to the new diamond fields to see for himself whether the stories he had heard were true. He returned with accounts of diamonds just waiting to be plucked from the gravel of the Vaal River, but Cecil reminded him that their dream was to grow cotton, and cotton it would be.

From Durban, the siblings travelled to a farm in the Umkomaas Valley near Pietermaritzburg, and while Cecil supervised the clearing of the land – building a good rapport with the black labourers – Herbert began spending more and more time in Kimberley. Cecil's earliest investment in South Africa was in the country's first railway line, a short piece of track that ran around Durban harbour.

Since 1868, the bottom had dropped out of the international cotton market, and the next time Herbert and his friend, Captain Rolleston, returned from the diamond diggings with a good haul of stones, the brothers agreed that it was time to move.

'To hear Rolleston talk and see his diamonds makes one's mouth water,' Cecil wrote to his mother.

Many people had struck it lucky, he wrote, and of late there had been 'three whoppers, one worth £8 000, another £10 000 and another £8 000. The man who found the £10 000 diamond had offered his claim the evening before for 15/- and nobody would buy it.'[3]

The contrast between the farm and the diamond fields could not have been greater. When the Rhodes brothers arrived in 1872, more than 50 000 people were working the diggings. The 'town' was a collection of tents with a few wood-and-iron pubs and a dozen shops, where everything sold at grossly inflated prices. Prospectors had already dug a hole fifteen metres deep, and on the floor of the crater some 30 000 men worked in shifts, hauling out the soil in buckets and sifting the sand to find the gems. Each claim measured just seven by nine metres, and the whole site was little bigger than a football field.

After sundown the miners drank, gambled and spent money on prostitutes, and there were nightly brawls between the tents and gunfights at the saloons.

By law, no miner could own more than one claim, and the greatest challenge for every man was how to reach his claim without trampling on other workers. A network of ropes and high wires had been strung over the hole, and men moved around on these like acrobats performing in a giant circus.

Cecil threw himself into the work, digging for long hours and sorting stones while he discussed claims with fellow miners and advised them how to invest their money. Within a few weeks, Herbert decided to take a trip back to England, returning with the second eldest Rhodes son, Frank, after which all three brothers worked their claim.

While other diggers gambled, drank away their profits or squandered them in the vice dens, Cecil bought more railway shares. In Herbert's absence, the value of the claim and Cecil's investments had grown to £5 000. With a friend called Charles Rudd he set up a plant that could freeze water, and made money by selling ice to the hotels where patrons could enjoy a cold drink in the heat of the day. At supper with various confidants he theorised on how, if the law were changed, it would be easy for a few men to buy up the claims of hundreds of heartbroken miners who had yet to find a stone of any value.

Soon after Frank's arrival, Cecil suffered a mild heart attack, which his doctor said was caused by too much work. It was later discovered that he had an enlarged heart, and this is what eventually killed him, the organ filling so much of his chest that he could no longer breathe.

Leaving Frank and Rudd at the diggings, Cecil and Herbert borrowed a wagon and set off to explore the countryside north of Kimberley for a few weeks, so that Cecil could recuperate. They travelled as far as what would become the Botswana border, passing through miles of uninhabited veld teeming with wild animals. They met small Afrikaner farming communities and were entertained by friendly tribes in the area. Cecil wrote in his diary that the country was unlikely to stay unspoiled for long.

On returning to Kimberley, he drew up a will, leaving all the money he had to Britain's secretary of state for colonies, with instructions that it be used to expand Queen Victoria's empire in Africa.

When his mother died in 1883, Cecil returned to England and became an Oxford undergraduate, dividing his time over the next few years between England and South Africa as he studied for a degree and built his investments. In 1874, the law on ownership of single claims was amended, and Cecil spent all the money he could lay his hands on buying out other miners. One of his natural gifts was the power of persuasion, and he would talk with reluctant sellers late into the night, convincing them that there was no future in Kimberley and then offering to buy their mining rights for the price of a coach ride back to Cape Town.

Before long, Cecil and his main business rival, Barney Barnato, owned more than half the claims in Kimberley between them. The farm on which the first diamond had been found had belonged to an Afrikaner, Nicolaas de Beer, and when people inquired about the mining operation, they often asked how things were going 'over at De Beers'. Rhodes adopted the name for his company, and by the twenty-first century, De Beers would control more than 90 per cent of the world's diamond trade.

Having consolidated his share of the industry, Cecil turned his attention to Johannesburg, where Australian prospector George Harrison had found a rich seam of gold in 1886. A year later Rhodes formed the Gold Fields group of companies, which, like De Beers, had it written into the articles of association that they could finance settlement expeditions north of the Limpopo.

At the age of thirty-five, Rhodes had amassed a vast fortune. He had heard Karl Maunch's stories of Great Zimbabwe and Henry Hartley's tales of ancient gold mines, and now he was wealthy enough to stop waiting for the secretary for colonies to move on Africa. Instead, he would open up the continent himself, and realise his dream of a British railroad from Cape Town to Cairo.

Whereas armies had failed to overwhelm the Matabele, prospectors were driving their king to distraction. Men came seeking permission to search for gold, diamonds, silver and emeralds, while missionaries begged to set up schools where they might convert the people to a new set of beliefs. Ambassadors from Portugal and Germany had promised Lobengula protection in exchange for the right to mine gold, but some of his generals believed that having crushed the mighty Zulu army at Isandhlwana in 1879, the British would move north to make war on the Matabele.

After Robert Mugabe came to power in 1980, there was a concerted effort to diminish the role of the Matabele in both Zimbabwe's past and present. The massacres from 1982 to 1987, known as Gukurahundi, saw between 10 000 and 30 000 Matabele slain by Mugabe's private army, the notorious Fifth Brigade. There was also visibly less development and government spending in the south than in Mashonaland. Matabele history was largely edited out of school textbooks, and Lobengula denigrated as a fool.

Eyewitness accounts, however, portray him as a wily old ruler who made every effort to save his people.

A Shona friend of mine told me that Lobengula gave Cecil John Rhodes the right to annex his country in exchange for some bags of sugar. Wanting to share the spoils with his subjects, the king poured the sugar into a river so that the waters would always run sweet. I put this piece of folklore to other well-educated Shona people, and the story holds currency, but the recorded facts surrounding the Rudd Concession are very different.

From 1885 there was a permanent white presence in Matabele and Mashona territory. Miners had begun working gold deposits at Penhalonga near the present town of Mutare on the Mozambique border, missionaries had won the right to establish schools, and hunters such as Frederick Courtenay Selous were hauling wagonloads of ivory to South Africa.

The Portuguese and French were both keen to exploit the country's considerable natural resources, but no one wanted to take on the Matabele, especially given how hard it had been for the British to conquer the Zulu. The neighbouring Tswana were a different matter. Hunters and prospectors from the Transvaal had crossed into what is now Botswana with a view to creating a new Boer republic, and Germany had shown some interest in annexing the area bordering its colony of South West Africa. In a pre-emptive move, Britain placed the entire territory under its protection on 27 January 1885, and named the new colony Bechuanaland.

Lobengula's warriors raided the Tswana almost as often as they harassed the Shona, though pickings in the Kalahari Desert were less bountiful. The Tswana chief, Kgama, told the British government at the Cape that if they intended to protect him, they could start by holding back the Matabele, and in June 1885 Major Samuel Edwards and two lieutenants were sent to Bulawayo to explain the new situation. They were granted an audience with the king, who seemed impressed and wanted to know more about Kgama's treaty with the British, especially as it related to protection against other foreign powers.

He gave the trio free reign to traverse his country, and they compiled the first official report on the people living north of the Limpopo. They put the Matabele population at 175 000, organised around the Zulu system in which all males were enrolled in military regiments at an early age and lived in villages reserved exclusively for each unit. Marriage was forbidden unless the regiment performed heroically in battle, after which the king might grant them wedding honours and all the men would be married on the same day to brides who had been reserved for them.

This enforced chastity might have sprung from Shaka's alleged homosexuality, but in any event, in both his kingdom and in Mzilikazi's, sex before marriage was punishable by death for both men and women, and there is evidence that the desire to take a wife inspired the warriors to fight more fiercely.

However, Major Edwards found that under Lobengula's reign, little more than lip service was paid to the discipline that had previously been enforced so rigidly. Pregnancy was rife among unmarried women, and the right to marry was granted to virtually any regiment that had carried out a successful raid against the Shona.

Of special note, in view of later history, are the Edwards party's observations on the Shona. The future of the country, they wrote, lay with this 'industrious people, hounded out of their country by Mzilikazi's dogs of war'. Edwards noted that considerable trade had formerly been done with the Portuguese on the Zambezi, and that the Shona now reared 'numerous cattle of a small but hardy breed', their agriculture being 'far in advance of the other natives'.

The problem with Shona advancement, he concluded, was that they lived 'in fear and dread of the Matabele'. Selous had made similar comments in his writings, and the idea took hold in both Britain and South Africa that Mashonaland was a more desirable territory than that around Bulawayo, but that in order to acquire it, a deal would have to be made with Lobengula.

When the Edwards report became known in Pretoria, it immediately raised the spectre of the Boer republic being sandwiched between British colonies in the Cape and Natal to the south, and Matabeleland to the north.

The Transvaal government was on good terms with Lobengula and warned him not to trust the British. In June 1887, they drew up a treaty and sent it to Bulawayo with Piet Grobler, a fluent Zulu linguist who farmed near the Limpopo and enjoyed a sound relationship with both the Tswana and the Matabele.

But Grobler found that Major Edwards had again visited Bulawayo in the interim, accompanied by a British government representative, John Fry, and they had persuaded the king to make no deals. They had gone so far as to warn him that Britain intended seizing the Transvaal gold mines near Johannesburg – which they eventually did, thereby causing the Anglo-Boer War in 1899 – and that when this happened, the Boers would use any treaty in place to flee into Matabeleland and set up their own republic.

Lobengula told Grobler that after Fry and Edwards had left, there had been a succession of envoys, all bearing letters from prospecting houses in the Cape, begging the king to grant them mining concessions in Mashonaland. One group had given him a barrel organ, while another contingent brought a cup of solid silver.

He had given all these visitors permission to hunt, but warned that if any of them picked up so much as a single rock sample, they would not leave his land alive.

The king was deeply worried about this rash of interest in his domain, so on 30 July 1887, he put his X to the Transvaal treaty, endorsing seven principles of peace with his neighbours and allowing President Paul Kruger to set up a consulate in Bulawayo. The treaty also covered the extradition of criminals and, most worrying to the British, established a military alliance.

When news reached the colonial government in Cape Town, there were fears that Kruger might be poised to annex Matabeleland. A former missionary, John Moffat, who had been made assistant commissioner for Bechuanaland, was sent to speak to Lobengula without delay.

Moffat had grown up in Africa and was the brother of David Livingstone's wife, Mary, and son of the famous Botswana missionary, Robert Moffat, who had befriended Mzilikazi many years before. He and his family were always welcome at Bulawayo, but this was no time to talk to the king. It was the annual *ncwala*, and Moffat stayed in Bulawayo until the end of January before he was granted a proper audience.

Lobengula denied signing any treaty with Grobler and readily put his mark to a new one with the British, in which he pledged peace between his people and those of Queen Victoria, and undertook to negotiate with no other foreign power without first consulting the British high commissioner in Cape Town.

For their part, in what became known as the Moffat Treaty, the British recognised all Shona land as being part of the Matabele kingdom. When the treaty was ratified in London, the Portuguese objected, but the deed was done.

On 28 April 1888, President Kruger appointed Grobler as his consul in Bulawayo, and around the same time Moffat, whose ability to influence Lobengula had become legendary, was recruited by Cecil John Rhodes.

Rhodes had been elected a member of the Cape parliament in 1881, and when Bechuanaland became a protectorate, he lobbied strongly for the southern regions of the territory to be incorporated with the Cape. The British government declined, and instead declared the area a crown colony. Rhodes resigned his seat in protest and went to London, where he convinced the colonial office to change its mind. The territory became part of what is now South Africa, though from 1977 to 1992 it enjoyed nominal independence as Pretoria's puppet republic of Bophuthatswana.

The signing of the Moffat Treaty filled Rhodes with excitement at the prospect of setting up a private company to annex the fabled land of Ophir. If the stories about King Solomon's mines were only half true, the northern claims would rival or even outshine the Transvaal gold deposits.

The race was on, and Moffat told Rhodes that unless they acted swiftly, any one of a dozen new concession seekers might sway Lobengula to sign away his country. The Portuguese had already granted a charter to a private company engaged by Lisbon to mine the goldfields of the Manyika, and their traders and marshals had penetrated as far as Mount Darwin, 140 kilometres north-east of present-day Harare.

The turning point came with the death of the Transvaal consul, Piet Grobler.

Since the establishment of British Bechuanaland, relations between the Tswana and the Matabele had grown ever more tense. Lobengula had sated his army's bloodlust by sending them into the Tonga territories in present-day Zambia, but Kgama's impudence in signing the treaty still upset the generals.

On 8 July 1888, Grobler rode south with two companions, George Cameral and William Lotriet, to meet his wife Elsie, waiting across the Limpopo to be escorted to their new home near the royal kraal. Along the way, the three men were confronted by some of Kgama's soldiers, who accused them of trespassing on Tswana land. To keep the peace, Grobler penned an admission of guilt, promising 200 cattle as a fine, but as he signed the document, Kgama's men attacked, and although they were driven off by gunfire, Grobler was injured in the leg. He managed to reach the river, where his wife nursed him until he died sixteen days later.

The party's Matabele escorts rushed back to the king with news of what had happened, and Lobengula accused the British of having put Kgama up to it. The truth never did emerge, but whether Kgama was acting in concert with the British high commissioner, with Cecil John Rhodes, or on his own, Grobler's death gave Rhodes the opportunity he had been waiting for.

With the consent of the British governor at the Cape, Rhodes sent Moffat to Bulawayo where he and his companion, a clergyman named Helm, assured Lobengula that a full commission of inquiry would be set up and the results delivered to him. They also impressed on the king that the only way to secure a lasting peace was to trust the British, and, like Kgama, place his fate in their hands.

Moffat agreed to stay on and advise the king, but his real mission was to ensure that no other concession seekers could gain a foothold until a negotiating team sent by Rhodes had arrived and made a deal with the Matabele.

Meanwhile, the British government sent a telegram to Paul Kruger that read: 'Her Majesty's Government regards the territory north of the South Africa republic and the Bechuanaland Protectorate, south of the Zambezi, east of the 20th degree longitude and west of the Portuguese province of Sofala, as exclusively within the British sphere of influence.'

It was the end of Matabele independence.

The inquiry was conducted and the incident was blamed on Grobler, the report even suggesting he had been shot accidentally by one of his own men. The final report, preserved in the British archives, is one of the best examples of the lies and duplicity used by the British government to advance its interests.

Lobengula was now alone. The Transvaal Boers had been warned off Matabeleland by the British, relations with the Tswana tribes had hit an all-time low, and concession seekers from all over Europe were pushing him for a deal. He needed someone on his side, and Rhodes seized the moment.

He sent his friend, Charles Rudd, with whom he had set up the ice-making plant in Kimberley fifteen years earlier, to negotiate the concession. The Rudd party arrived on 20 September 1888, carrying £10 000's worth of gold coins and an envelope bearing the royal crest, which contained a letter of introduction from Sir Hercules Robinson, high commissioner at the Cape and a close friend of Rhodes.

Lobengula received them in habitual manner – seated on the base of a covered wagon, while his visitors sat on the ground. The talks continued for several weeks, and it became clear that the king had no interest in money (Rhodes was reportedly shocked by this), but wanted rifles for his army. He also expressed curiosity about how big England was and whether the white queen really was as powerful as he had heard. If so, perhaps she was the one to best protect his interests.

Rudd shamelessly exploited Lobengula's belief (no doubt created by the official envelope) that they spoke with the authority of the British government.

The concession, he was told, had to be a monopoly, because two or more bulls in one enclosure would always fight, and the concessionaires would need to raise a military force of their own to keep out trespassers and defend the territory. In exchange, the king would receive a pension, 1 000 Martini-Henri rifles, 100 000 rounds of ammunition and a gunboat on the Zambezi. Far from destroying the fighting power of the Matabele, Rudd promised, the deal would strengthen it.

On 29 October 1888, Lobengula made his mark on the paper. Things moved quickly after that. Rudd hastened back to Kimberley to hand the charter to Rhodes, who travelled to London at the earliest opportunity to raise capital for a company that would control all the land between the Limpopo and Zambezi.

Lobengula had the foresight to send two of his headmen to England as well, to determine what kind of country he was dealing with, and they even met privately with Queen Victoria. But Rhodes had already made the queen's brother-in-law a director of the charter company, and any officials who opposed his plans were afforded the same privilege, so the king's emissaries learned nothing Rhodes did not want them to.

The foreign office was told that if the British did not move at once – and since Rhodes was willing to pay for the venture it would cost them nothing – the French, Germans and Portuguese would take the country.

The idea of giving rifles to the Matabele was opposed by various people, notably a prominent clergyman in Kimberley, Bishop Knight-Bruce, who had travelled extensively in Mashonaland and written a number of newspaper reports about the wretched state of the Shona. At a public meeting on 8 December 1888, Knight-Bruce warned: 'Everyone must know that [the rifles] would be used to assist in the murder of hapless innocents', and described the idea as a piece of 'devilry and brutality'.

The speech was widely reported in South Africa and abroad, prompting the British colonial secretary, Lord Knutsford, to cable Rhodes for an explanation.

Rhodes arranged for his friend the high commissioner to reply to Knutsford. His letter of 26 December contained perhaps one of the most callous statements made by any British official in the late nineteenth century.

'The actual loss of life and bloodshed is diminished in native wars by the substitution of the rifle for the stabbing *assegai* [spear],' wrote Sir Hercules.

Rhodes returned to the Cape from England having secured a considerable sum of money, a glittering board of directors and the sure knowledge that no one would interfere with the plans for his new venture, to be known as the British South Africa Company (BSAC). He recruited a twenty-three-year-old fortune hunter, Frank Johnson, to lead the invasion. It was clear that once Lobengula realised he had been duped, the Matabele would try to drive out any settlers, and military advisers estimated that it would take 2 500 men and a million pounds to win the war that would inevitably erupt.

Johnson, however, undertook to deliver the territory within nine months with just 250 men and at a cost of £87 500. When Selous, the seasoned hunter who had explored more of Mashonaland than perhaps any other Englishman, agreed with Johnson, Rhodes set them the task of putting together a corps of pioneers. Recruitment notices published in Kimberley offered each volunteer 3 000 acres of farmland and fifteen mining claims of his choice. On the advice of Rhodes, Johnson chose most of his men from wealthy families, the logic being that if the Pioneer Column was surrounded and cut off by the Matabele, rich and influential fathers would have a better chance of convincing the British government to mount a rescue.

On 11 July 1890, the Pioneer Column crossed into Matabele territory. It consisted of 180 colonists, 62 wagons and 200 volunteers, and a special police unit set up by the BSAC. A support party followed with a further 110 men, 16 wagons, 250 cattle (to be used as food) and 130 spare horses.

The group was commanded by Johnson, with Selous acting as guide, and included Rhodes's personal physician, Leander Starr Jameson, who would become the first governor of the occupied territory. Had Lobengula sent his army to halt the Column's advance at the Bechuanaland border, it is possible that he might have changed history. But he did nothing except take his wrath out on one of his headmen, Lotshe, who had spoken in favour of the concession during the talks with Rudd. The king concluded that Lotshe had been bribed, and he and 300 members of his extended family were clubbed to death, along with their cattle, goats, dogs and chickens.

The route chosen by Selous bypassed Bulawayo and took the Column to the centre of the country. Not far from Great Zimbabwe, the pioneers founded the first town, which they named Fort Victoria (now Masvingo). Meeting no resistance from either the Matabele or the Shona, they proceeded to the northern plateau that Selous had selected as the site of the capital. On 12 September 1890, they raised the British flag at a place they named Fort Salisbury, after the British prime minister of the day. In the heart of modern Harare, a flagpole still stands on the spot next to Africa Unity Square in Second Avenue.

The next day, a small party set off for the home of Chief Mutasa, east of Salisbury and close to the Portuguese border. There was still a fear that Lisbon might extend the area it claimed as Mozambique and encroach on Mashonaland. The chief received the visitors with great hospitality, listened to their offers of protection from both the Portuguese and the Matabele, heard their plans to mine the region and build roads and railways, then put his mark to a treaty.

After one last muster parade in Salisbury, the pioneers took off in all directions, each determined to peg the best claims around old mining ruins, and the lushest farmland. In his book *Pioneers of Mashonaland*, one of these early settlers, Adrian Darter, wrote: 'Extravagant reports of alluvial gold and rich reefs were the order of the day. Old workings were eagerly sought for and, in that way, many a Mashona rice field was pegged off. Rushes, stark, staring mad rushes possessed the pioneers and prospectors.'

Rhodes tried to negotiate with the Portuguese to buy one of their ports and a strip of land that would give his new territory access to the sea. His first choice was Maputo (formerly Delagoa Bay or Lourenço Marques), but because of the geography such a purchase would have cut Mozambique off from the Transvaal, and the Portuguese refused to entertain the idea.

In many ways the failure to secure a port determined the country's destiny, because Rhodesia, and later Zimbabwe, would forever be at the mercy of neighbouring states with direct access to the sea.

Within weeks, the BSAC had established a presence all over Mashonaland and began building surprisingly good relations with the local inhabitants. However, the expedition's initial success did not last long. Salisbury experienced unusually heavy rains that year, which made movement around the town difficult and travel across virgin veld virtually impossible. Next came malaria, and those who managed to survive found nowhere near enough gold to support their expectation of untold riches. Mail and supplies were bogged down, and contracts that required prospectors to hand over 50 per cent of all gold to the BSAC would bankrupt even those who had made reasonable strikes. There was no alluvial gold to be panned from the rivers or picked up as nuggets, and deeper veins would take costly equipment and years of work to extract. Many of the men thus fell back on the next-best promise of wealth – farming – and marked out their land with no regard for Shona occupation.

The disillusioned drifted back to South Africa, selling their claims for next to nothing to those who elected to stay. Henry Borrow ended up with 52 000 hectares, which in time would become the Harare suburb of Borrowdale.

In terms of the Rudd Concession, only mining rights had been granted, not permission to occupy the country, and in Bulawayo the fury of the Matabele generals mounted each time spies reported new settlements. The rifles and ammunition had been delivered, and with so many pioneers weakened by malaria, any attack was bound to succeed. But Lobengula held his army in check, promising to renegotiate the kingdom's future with more honest brokers.

Rhodes had bargained on the Matabele attacking the Pioneer Column and Johnson's assurance that he had enough men and guns to destroy Bulawayo at the first sign of aggression, thus giving the British undisputed control of the country. But when Lobengula let the Column pass unhindered, the BSAC was forced to breach the terms of the charter in order to meet its commitments to the volunteers.

The king thus had every right to declare the concession null and void, and the next time German entrepreneur Eduard Lippert visited the royal kraal from the Transvaal at the beginning of 1891, Lobengula surprised him by agreeing to grant Lippert all surface mining rights for the next 100 years, as well as the right to lay out farms and towns in all territory under BSAC control.

Rhodes did the only thing he could and bought out Lippert for £30 000 cash and 15 000 shares in the BSAC. A few months later, Rhodes visited Salisbury for the first time. Having no wish to confront Lobengula, he travelled via Beira in Mozambique, and was met by Frank Johnson at Penhalonga, just north of Mutare, with the news that the pioneers had decided to call the country Rhodesia, in honour of their benefactor. By September 1892, the white population numbered 857 men – 184 of them accompanied by their wives – 80 single women and 146 children.

With the Matabele already alienated, the settlers had also aroused Shona anger by occupying huge tracts of their traditional land. At the beginning of 1893, Lobengula sent a delegation to inform the governor, Dr Jameson, that he intended to reclaim Mashonaland by sending an army to exact the annual tax of cattle and crops. Jameson raised a force of 250 unpaid volunteers and nearly 500 Shona soldiers, and offered each white man a 2 400-hectare farm and twenty gold claims in Matabeleland. Half of Lobengula's cattle herd would also be divided among the volunteers, the rest being seized by the BSAC. The Shona, who were willing to risk their lives against the Matabele, would get little reward beyond liberation from the constant raids.

The battle was swift, and realising that his warriors were no match for the settlers with their Maxim guns, Lobengula set fire to Bulawayo and fled north. The exact location of his grave remains a mystery, and many Matabele believe he died in exile in western Zambia round 1923.

Zimbabwean writer Peter Godwin, whose childhood memoirs, *Mukiwa*, became an international bestseller in the mid-1990s, showed little pity for the Matabele king.

'Before one dissolves into a sobbing heap at Lobengula's terrible fate at Rhodes's hands,' he wrote in a political essay, 'we should remember that Lobengula was a bloodthirsty tyrant himself, whose people had arrived as colonists themselves, only a generation before, wiping out most of the Mashona who lived there, and treating the rest as slaves.'

But it could as easily be argued that Lobengula was a product of his history, dating back to his father's origins in Shaka's army. Mzilikazi had been forced out of the Transvaal by the Boers and the Zulus, and had to find safe harbour for his people. His approach to the Shona was no more brutal than that of Shaka, who dealt with rival tribes and enemies mercilessly, marching entire regiments off a high cliff above the Indian Ocean to plunge to their deaths on the rocks below, and killing an estimated two million people in a decade of conquest.

As for Rhodes, however perfidious the act that amounts to one the greatest confidence tricks in history, the truth is that if the Pioneer Column had not laid claim to Rhodesia, someone else would have, and the eventual outcome would have been much the same.

When the defeated Matabele fled, some 125 000 cattle were rounded up and shared as agreed, and Jameson laid out a new town, keeping the original name of Bulawayo. By April 1894, 6 804 gold claims had been pegged by white settlers and 859 farms laid out. Two months later, the number of claims had jumped to 11 000.

Selous, who had led the original Column to Salisbury, warned Rhodes and Jameson that, given the rate at which the country was being carved up by white settlers, there would soon be nothing left for either the Shona or the Matabele, and that war would be inevitable. His concerns were dismissed, but the Matabele had regrouped in the Matobo Hills and the Shona were becoming increasingly restive over the loss of their land, which had deprived them of the ability to sustain themselves and graze their cattle.

Preoccupied with gold fever and the quest for farms, the BSAC had effectively stopped gathering intelligence, and its officers were oblivious to the growing resentment in both the north and south of the country. On 24 March 1896, reports flooded into Bulawayo that men, women and children at outlying camps, stores and farms had been murdered. The timing could not have been worse. Jameson had been taken prisoner in the Transvaal after leading a badly planned raid on Pretoria, designed to seize the Boer republic for Britain, and there were only seventy-seven company horses – and even fewer rifles – left in Bulawayo.

Whites who had survived the attacks sought sanctuary in the town, where three patrol squads were assembled and a small group of defenders assigned to protect the settlement. From Salisbury, 312 white volunteers and 250 Shona troops were dispatched to help put down the rebellion. With BSAC control of Matabeleland virtually restored almost three months later, the Shona attacked miners and settlers around Salisbury on 16 June.

For a people who had spent decades running away from their enemies, the Shona put up a valiant struggle, especially in the Mazowe Valley, thirty kilometres east of the capital. Unlike the Matabele, they had no rifles and fought mainly with spears, making the outcome a foregone conclusion.

After the uprisings, Rhodes travelled to Bulawayo and negotiated a lasting peace with the Matabele. The Shona were shown no such respect, and their spirit medium, an old woman called Ambuya Nehanda, who had been partly responsible for driving them to battle, was arrested and hanged without trial.

With the 'native question' settled, railways were extended from Mafeking and Beira to form a network across Rhodesia. Roads, shops, schools and mission stations were built, and coal was found in the domain of the Shona chief, Hwange, the original victim of Mzilikazi's invasion.

Rhodes died in 1902 and was buried at a place of his choosing, called World's View, in the Matobo Hills near Bulawayo. During the Anglo-Boer War, Rhodesia sided with Britain, and imperial troops from Canada and Australia entered the country from Beira to attack Paul Kruger's republic from the north.

By 1896, Rhodesia's white population stood at 5 000, but in less than three decades it had increased sevenfold to 35 000 in 1923. Despite the feverish pegging of farms by the early settlers, there was little agricultural activity to speak of, and of the 12 000 whites in the country in 1904, only 545 were involved in farming. Indeed, it was the Shona with their crops of maize and rice who sold food to the settlers, and since the Matabele had stopped raiding their lands, it looked as though the prophecies of Major Edwards and Frederick Selous would prove accurate and that Shona industry would lie at the heart of the future economy. In 1908 the government decided to actively promote white agriculture, and a land bank was created to finance new farms.

The demand for Shona land grew, but the 1896 rebellion had cost many black lives and the BSAC's expansion went unchallenged. More land was lost when white Rhodesians returning after the First World War were given farms as their reward. On the other hand, black troops who had served with equal distinction were simply demobilised and sent home.

In 1910, the British colonies of Natal and the Cape united with the former Boer republics to form the Union of South Africa. Rhodesia was invited to become the fifth province, but declined. On 7 November 1923, a second attempt to make Rhodesia part of South Africa was roundly rejected by the white electorate, with 5 989 voting in favour of the proposal, and 8 744 opting for the country to become the empire's first self-governing colony, with essentially the same status as Canada or Australia.

The land between the waters of the Zambezi and Limpopo had come of age.

# 4

# The making of Mugabe

When the results of the 1923 referendum were announced, Bona Mugabe was six months pregnant, and the summer heat only added to her discomfort at Kutama Mission in the Zvimba district, seventy-five kilometres north of Salisbury.

She and her husband Gabriel already had two children, Miteri (known as Michael) and Raphael. Gabriel worked as a carpenter, while Bona helped out at the Jesuit mission founded ten years earlier by a French priest, Jean-Baptiste Loubiére.

Father Loubiére had not been in the first wave of missionaries who followed the Pioneer Column when the Shona and Matabele wars ended. He was ministering to souls in Mozambique at the time, but when he fell in love with a Portuguese girl, his order sent him to a remote corner of Rhodesia to do penance by establishing a new mission from scratch.

From May to September the Zvimba district was dry and dusty, but when the summer rains came the sand turned to mud and mosquitoes bred in the puddles. By December, a third of the population would be ill with malaria.

Loubiére's first convert was the local chief. In what they called a migration of beliefs, the villagers not only followed suit but also built a church, and called the mission Kutama, which means to migrate. Had they known how strict the new order would be, they might have thought twice before embracing the Jesuit teachings. Father Loubiére banned all Shona customs and traditions, and he and his assistant, a black priest named Joseph Dambaza, began a crusade to convert as many souls as possible to their rigid interpretation of the Bible.

Prayers and confession were mandatory and mass was a daily ritual, with a warning that anyone who failed to follow the narrow path of righteousness would burn in the fires of hell for all eternity. Spirit mediums, which had played such an important role in the Shona rebellion and would again come to prominence in the guerrilla war of the 1970s, were either hounded out of the parish or made to recant their beliefs.

Bona thrived on the unmitigated diet of Christianity, but Gabriel found it hard to swallow. Their third son, Robert Gabriel, was born at the mission on 22 February 1924. Bona dearly wanted a daughter, but her next pregnancy produced yet another boy, named Donald, and it was not until October 1934 that she gave birth to a girl, Sabina.

The Great Depression had hit Rhodesia hard. Gabriel was struggling to find work, and before Sabina's birth he left to take up a contract in Bulawayo, and never returned. Adding to Bona's problems was the death of her eldest son, Michael, after eating poisoned maize in circumstances that have never been resolved.

Robert and his brothers began their education at the mission, which had been taken over after Loubiére died in 1930 by an Irish priest, Father O'Hea. He had nothing but contempt for the colonial government in Salisbury, and fully respected the need of his flock to blend Christianity with their traditional beliefs. He relaxed the discipline and brought his church in line with the more progressive missions in the country.

O'Hea came from a wealthy family, and used his own money to extend primary education at the mission and to build a school where he could train the most promising students to be teachers. But the real need was for a hospital, and in 1933 O'Hea turned to the government for help, inviting the prime minister, Godfrey Huggins, to visit Kutama and see the work being done there. The governor, Cecil Rodwell, who was nothing more than a figurehead, made the journey as well, and in the presence of Robert, aged nine, he asked the priest why he was so passionate about the idea of healing the sick.

'After all,' he said, 'there are so many natives in the country already.'

Mugabe neither forgot nor ever forgave the comment.

Once the hospital was built, Father O'Hea spent more and more time tending patients and less of his day saving souls. Mass and even confession sometimes fell by the wayside, men started drinking, fights broke out in the village and the strict discipline imposed by Father Loubiére disintegrated.

Before he even reached his teens, Robert Gabriel Mugabe decided that he would never drink alcohol, and remained a strict teetotaller throughout his life.

Before his death in 1970, Father O'Hea recalled Robert as having 'an exceptional mind with an exceptional heart', and his contemporaries remember him as quiet, studious, intelligent and not much of a team player.

In their excellent biography *Mugabe*,[1] David Smith and Colin Simpson quote one of his childhood friends, David Garwe, who also went on to become a teacher.

'We all knew him as a very clever lad. He was by far the youngest boy in his class, and though he was three years younger than me, he was only one class below.

'I suppose the fact that he was younger and smaller may have kept him a little apart from everyone. I don't remember him taking part in sport or school plays. He always seemed to enjoy his own company.'

Robert sailed through school, and when he expressed a desire to train as a teacher, O'Hea agreed. In 1944 he graduated with his diploma, and left Kutama the next year to fill a range of teaching posts across the country.

The Second World War had come and gone with little impact around Zvimba, except that some of the white farmers from the district had gone away to fight. Rhodesia served gallantly, and was also used as a base for training pilots from all over the empire. A flying school was set up at Gwelo (now Gweru) in the centre of the country, and its graduates included the later jockey and author Dick Francis, as well as the future Rhodesian prime minister, Ian Smith.

More than 14 000 black Rhodesian volunteers also went to war, mostly as private soldiers and non-commissioned officers in the Rhodesia African Rifles, serving in Egypt, Libya and Burma. It would be more than thirty years before blacks could be promoted to the rank of officer in the Rhodesian armed forces, and when the war ended in 1945, returning black soldiers were simply demobilised, while their white counterparts were rewarded for their service to the crown with farms and pensions.

At that time, Mugabe was teaching at Dadaya Mission, where a colleague, Ndabaningi Sithole, introduced him to black nationalism. Sithole came from the minority Ndau tribe at Chipinge in the south-east, an area largely spared from raids in the days of Lobengula, and where the Shona rebellion had passed unnoticed.

In 1985, I interviewed Sithole in Washington DC after he had been forced into exile by Mugabe. He told me he believed his former colleague had been odd from the start.

'He was so impossibly self-absorbed,' Sithole recalled. 'You never knew what he was thinking, except that it probably had to do with himself. There was little in the way of team spirit about the man, though I wouldn't call him arrogant, rather aloof. Sometimes he would discuss things with other teachers and, on other occasions, you would ask him something and he would just look at you and not reply, as though your question was not important enough for him to consider.

'When he wanted something, he could charm anyone and get his own way. But when you needed a favour, Robert was probably the last person you would ask. It was rather a one-way street with him, and I got the impression that he put himself first in everything.

'Even so, you forgave him because of the bright mind that made you believe here was a man who had the potential to do something really great. Sadly, in later years, that intellect was used for evil instead of good, and I wondered if it hadn't even driven him mad. Or perhaps he was always near the edge to begin with.'

Sithole, who died in 1998, said he had dreamed of a country where all the people, Shona, Matabele, white and even minor tribes like his own, could share both the power and the wealth. But, first and foremost, he felt the need to do away with discrimination.

'It was not just a separateness,' he told me, 'it was the humiliation of not being able to use a toilet at a garage or in a department store because these were reserved for whites only. It was nothing as severe as South Africa, but it was still intolerable to be treated in my own country as something that was foreign and dirty.'

After the colonisation of Rhodesia, discrimination was not so much a conscious policy as one that evolved. Two cultures had been thrown together and were expected to coexist despite their obvious differences. One group could read and write and had a knowledge of the world, the other was living in the Iron Age and, at the time of conquest, had not yet invented the wheel. Any thoughts of an instant union between the two would have been naive at best. But by the time Mugabe and Sithole were teaching at Dadaya, hundreds of thousands of blacks had been through school and were ready to enter the mainstream as equals in the business and social world. Instead, they were blocked at every turn.

Unlike South Africa after the National Party came to power in 1948, Rhodesia never formalised job reservation for whites, but, in practice, whites held all the positions that mattered in both commerce and the thriving industry that sprang to life from 1923 onwards, as well as on the railways. The best a well-educated black could hope for was a job making tea or sweeping the floor. Teaching was the exception, but blacks could only educate pupils at black schools. Shona and Ndebele were not taught at white schools, and a white person who spoke the languages was regarded as something of an oddity.

While segregation certainly existed de facto, Rhodesia never barred blacks from taking part in elections on racial grounds. However, legislation governing land ownership effectively limited the ballot to white citizens. Under British dominion, the country was a meritocracy, with a qualified franchise based on educational qualifications and ownership of property. As far back as the 1923 referendum, sixty blacks out of a population of 900 000 were included on the voters' roll. Of the 35 000 whites living in Rhodesia at the time, 20 000 qualified as voters. A small number who failed to meet the requirements were excluded from the ballot.

In 1926, a Land Commission set aside 21.1 million acres of communal land for dispensation by tribal chiefs to their subjects, in keeping with tradition. Another 49 million acres were open to purchase by anyone, and 7.5 million acres were reserved for purchase by blacks only, the fear being that whites would otherwise buy up all available land. No land was specifically designated for whites, but they had already been given the best farms as rewards for service in the pioneer corps, during the Matabele and Mashona rebellions or the First World War, and owned all the urban residential plots in private hands.

Discrimination notwithstanding, race relations were historically far less confrontational than in South Africa or, for that matter, the southern states of America. However, Ron Reid Daly, a Rhodesian soldier who served in Malaya during the early 1960s and later founded the Selous Scouts, the first truly multiracial unit in the Rhodesian Army, believes more could – and should – have been done to foster a fully integrated society.

'If whites had been taught the Shona and Ndebele languages in schools from the 1940s and 1950s, and been instilled with the richness of native culture, there would have been a whole different understanding between the races,' he told me. 'I would go so far as to say that the eventual civil war and all that bitterness of the 1970s might even have been avoided.'

In 1949, aged twenty-five, Robert Mugabe won a scholarship to Fort Hare University in South Africa. Rhodesia did not have its own tertiary institution until 1956, but with the nationalist ideas Mugabe had espoused through his friendship with Sithole, he could not have found a more fertile breeding ground for his embryonic ideology. Student politics at Fort Hare, in the Eastern Cape, were dominated by ardent activists such as Nelson Mandela and Oliver Tambo of the African National Congress (ANC), Robert Sobukwe (who would go on to lead the Pan Africanist Congress (PAC)) and Zulu leader Mangosuthu Buthelezi.

Mugabe read a Bachelor of Arts degree and passed without difficulty. By his own account, it was during his time at Fort Hare that he became increasingly hostile towards whites, but on a personal level he was more interested in improving his academic qualifications than getting involved in politics.

He ordered copies of books by Marx and Engels from London, and in Salisbury attended meetings of the Capricorn Society, set up by Colonel David Stirling, founder of the British Special Air Service (SAS), who had settled in Rhodesia after the Second World War. Stirling was shocked by the extent of the racial divide he found in Rhodesia, and established the society in a bid to encourage social and political dialogue between black and white.

Around the same time, Mugabe renewed his childhood friendship with James Chikerema, an early nationalist and son of Father Loubiére's assistant, Joseph Dambaza. James was somewhat older and had gone to study in South Africa before Mugabe, only to be deported back to Rhodesia because of his radical Marxist beliefs. While James's goal was to rid Rhodesia of both the whites and their religion, Mugabe found it possible to reconcile Marxism with his Roman Catholic upbringing and beliefs.

In 1957 the Gold Coast – renamed Ghana and led by the charismatic Kwame Nkrumah – became the first British colony to gain independence. Armed with no less than three academic degrees, Mugabe went to teach at St Mary's College in the seaside town of Takoradi, west of Ghana's capital, Accra. There he not only experienced at first-hand a conquered black people assuming power, filling posts as cabinet ministers, senior government officials and company directors, but met a fellow teacher, Sally Heyfron, and her twin sister Esther.

Robert became a regular guest at the Heyfron home, and when he burned himself in an accident, Sally visited him in hospital. At the end of 1960 she accompanied him back to Rhodesia, where they were married in 1961.

Africa was changing fast, and Rhodesia was no exception. In the post-war boom, tens of thousands of new, mostly British, immigrants had arrived in the country. In 1946, the white population was a mere 82 000. By 1960, it had swelled to 223 000. Several attempts by successive governments in Salisbury to gain full dominion status had been rejected, but Rhodesia ran its own elections, passed its own laws through a de facto sovereign parliament, and the governor, as representative of the queen, could act only on the advice of the prime minister.

A 1953 referendum had voted in favour of union with the protectorates of Northern Rhodesia (now Zambia) and Nyasaland (now Malawi) to create the Central African Federation, and the commercial wisdom of this decision had long been evident, with a migrant labour system serving industry in Southern Rhodesia, copper mining in Northern Rhodesia, and tea and coffee production in Nyasaland. Winston Churchill's government had strongly endorsed the federation, formed after a conference at London's Lancaster House. Rhodesia had intended sending an all-white delegation, but when Churchill insisted on black representatives being included, Joshua Nkomo was plucked from his position as leader of the rail trade union and flown to London. Often described as a Matabele, Nkomo was actually a member of the minor Kalanga tribe, whose home was west of Bulawayo. Addressing the conference, he supported the principle of federation, but said it would be difficult to sell the idea to Rhodesia's black majority unless active steps were taken to include them in business and society as equal partners.

With Nigeria (1960) and Tanganyika (1961) having followed Ghana to independence, however, the federation was doomed, and nationalist leaders in all three territories demanded an end to colonial rule. In Nyasaland, the moving force was Hastings Banda, a medical doctor, who had lived in England for so long that he had all but forgotten how to speak his native Chichewa, while Kenneth Kaunda led the way in Northern Rhodesia.

Since 1957, James Chikerema had been mobilising support for his ideals, forming the City Youth League with George Nyandoro and Edison Sithole, and demanding a reduction in bus fares. By the time British prime minister Harold MacMillan delivered his famous 'winds of change' speech to the South

African parliament in 1960, black Rhodesians had taken up the chant of 'One Man, One Vote!'

MacMillan used the 'winds' phrase – coined by one of his predecessors, Stanley Baldwin, in relation to Asia twenty-five years earlier – to bring home to South Africa's prime minister and arch-segregationist Hendrik Verwoerd that the political tide had turned, but he also had his own agenda. He had seen the potential value of the European Union that was being mooted, and believed that this was where Britain's future sphere of influence would lie. Colonies were frowned upon by the Americans, who might use their continued existence to hold Britain back from playing a meaningful role in the new world order.

'The winds of change are blowing down Africa,' MacMillan warned. 'The most striking of all impressions I have formed since I left London a month ago is the strength of African national consciousness.'

In January 1960, Chikerema and his colleagues formed the National Democratic Party (NDP), and a number of blacks were killed during riots in Salisbury and Bulawayo. On 20 July, Mugabe returned home from Ghana to see his mother, and encountered a crowd of 7 000 protestors who had gathered in Salisbury to present their grievances to the prime minister, Sir Edgar Whitehead.

Whitehead sent a message through the police that he would address the meeting, but he had no intention of doing so. When two representatives made their way to his office, he refused to see them, and issued an order banning political gatherings in the black townships.

Mugabe was inspired by the sight of the crowd and met some of their leaders, including Leopold Takawira and Edgar Tekere, who both implored him to return to Rhodesia permanently and help them with the struggle. As the day wore on, speeches were made and Mugabe was asked to say a few words about what he had seen in Ghana. He took the podium and spoke about the great new order that Nkrumah was building, the vision of an Africa free from domination, where black people were masters of their own destiny.

'The nationalist movement will succeed only if it is based on a blending of all classes of men,' he said, as the crowd roared its approval.

Robert Mugabe had entered politics.

The following day, police with batons tried in vain to break up the crowd. They returned with dogs, and as people dispersed the ringleaders were arrested. Riots erupted in the townships, and by the end of the day more than 100 blacks had been detained and many more injured. A week later, a similar riot occurred in Bulawayo and eleven blacks were shot.

In the townships, NDP thugs intimidated those who were reluctant to get involved in politics, and the government introduced the notorious Law and Order Maintenance Act (1960), which gave the authorities wide-ranging emergency powers, including detention without trial. Sir Robert Tredgold, the federal chief justice, resigned, denouncing the legislation as the gateway to a police state.

In a bid to resolve the situation, Commonwealth secretary Duncan Sandys convened a conference in Salisbury, attended by representatives of both the government and the NDP. With Ndabaningi Sithole and Joshua Nkomo acting as the chief negotiators, agreement was reached on a new constitution that would include a bill of rights, wider black franchise and special clauses protecting non-white Rhodesians, which could only be abolished after the holding of separate referendums for the white, black, coloured and Indian communities.

Ian Smith, Whitehead's finance minister, resigned in protest against the proposals. Nkomo and Sithole accepted them, but subsequently rejected the constitution after NDP supporters accused them of not gaining enough concessions for the black majority. Mugabe, by now the NDP's publicity secretary, described the proposed constitution as a sell-out.

However, it was adopted by parliament and endorsed by a referendum of white voters and the minority of blacks who were qualified to cast their ballots.

Robert and Sally Mugabe had decided to settle in Salisbury, but because the Rhodesian government had passed a Land Tenure Act prohibiting blacks from buying property in any of the 'white' suburbs, they had to live in the satellite town of Highfield, just off the road to Bulawayo. Their home became a meeting place for nationalists, and before long was placed under surveillance by the authorities. Robert was an easy target for attention, because whereas other blacks would doff their caps to the police, he was more inclined to speak his mind. In April 1961, his name featured in newspaper reports after he told a policeman who was trying to search him at the airport, 'We are taking over this country and we will not put up with this nonsense.'

In December, he told a crowd of 20 000 at an NDP meeting in Highfield: 'If European industries are used to buy guns which are aimed against us, we must withdraw our labour and our custom and destroy those industries.'

A week later the NDP was banned, its vehicles and other assets seized and the leaders, including Mugabe, barred from addressing public meetings for four months. Within less than a fortnight, the NDP had regrouped as a new party, the Zimbabwe African People's Union (ZAPU).

In June 1962, Nkomo went to New York and succeeded in having the UN General Assembly pass a resolution calling for an all-party conference to draw up a new constitution for Rhodesia. On his return in July, ZAPU stepped up its programme of industrial strikes. Intimidation was rife, and anyone in the townships who showed less than full support risked a beating from gangs of youths moving from house to house at night, demanding to see ZAPU membership cards.

The government retaliated by making it a crime to try to force anyone to join a political party against their will. The new law carried a maximum jail term of ten years.

By September 1962, ZAPU had also been banned and the leaders detained. Nkomo was in Lusaka when the crackdown came, and instead of returning to Salisbury, he went to Dar es Salaam. When he did eventually go home, he was duly arrested and held along with the entire ZAPU executive. While in detention, he made it clear to his colleagues that he had lost faith in the internal struggle and that, on being released, they should go into exile and fight the government from beyond Rhodesia's borders.

With the extended franchise, the bill of rights and a rapidly growing black middle class that would make thousands more people eligible to vote each year, the scene was already set for blacks to outnumber whites in almost every constituency within twenty years, resulting in significant power-sharing within eight or ten years and majority rule by 1981. But the nationalists were impatient. While other African states were being handed the tools of government on a plate, discrimination remained in force in Rhodesia. Public parks, buses, cinemas, hotels and many other facilities had been opened to all races, but integration was far from a way of life. Black parents could not send their children to schools of their choice, only to those set aside for their use. Health care was free and among the best in Africa, but black and white were treated at separate facilities.

And then there was the elusive promise of personal advancement. As Africa's colonies had become independent, their leaders had quickly entrenched and enriched themselves, doing away with frugal white administrations in favour of luxury cars, mansions and frequent trips abroad. While the Rhodesian government practised fiscal discipline, the country was rich enough to offer good pickings for anyone drawn to the better things in life.

The 1962 election was a watershed. Ian Smith and another hardliner, Winston Field, had formed a new party, the Rhodesian Front, and were seeking a mandate to keep power in white hands indefinitely. Sir Edgar Whitehead's government made it clear that, if re-elected, laws would be changed to allow blacks to participate equally in most aspects of society. Both parties were in favour of full independence from Britain.

In his book *Triumph or Tragedy, Rhodesia to Zimbabwe*,[2] Mike Hudson argued that the 1962 election was a crucial milestone in the country's history.

'This, rather than UDI or indeed any other event, perhaps even including the 1980 election, was the decisive point in deciding whether Rhodesia was to evolve in peace or turn to civil war with all the consequences of that tragic happening,' he wrote.

The nationalists, led by Joshua Nkomo, chose to boycott the election, and a high level of intimidation kept blacks away from the polls, with only 12 200 of the 65 500 who qualified casting their votes. While 65 000 was but a fraction of the four million blacks living in Rhodesia, it was a sizeable proportion of the total count, since there were fewer than 130 000 white voters, and a high black turnout was crucial for Whitehead's party. There were a number of marginal constituencies, and Whitehead claimed afterwards that he could have taken the election with just 500 more black votes. But in the event, his United Federal Party won just twenty-nine seats to the Rhodesian Front's thirty-five.

Winston Field was the new prime minister, and his government moved quickly to introduce tough new legislation limiting freedom of speech and creating a mandatory death penalty for acts of sabotage.

The ZAPU leaders were released, and Mugabe travelled to Northern Rhodesia, from where he enraged Field with a public address in which he said: 'This fascist settler cowboy government is preparing to unilaterally declare Rhodesia independent from Britain, for the settlers to subject millions of Africans to slavery.'

When he returned to Salisbury three months later, he was detained. Both Sally and Nkomo had already been arrested after addressing political rallies, and Nkomo tried again to convince his executive that the only way to pursue the struggle was from exile. He told them President Julius Nyerere of Tanzania had offered them sanctuary while they built up an army, and the committee voted in favour of the proposal. Mugabe opposed it, but accepted the outcome.

Robert, Sally and several top party officials flew to Dar es Salaam, where Nyerere told them bluntly that he had never given such advice to Nkomo and that they were not welcome to set up a ZAPU office in his country. Nkomo had also promised that donor funds would be available in Tanzania to help the organisation, but the Mugabes didn't even have enough to pay for their accommodation. Sally, who had lost a child at birth the year before, was pregnant again and awaiting the outcome of her appeal against a prison sentence, and Mugabe was not only furious, but felt betrayed. It was clear that Nkomo had to go, and six members of the executive flew to Ethiopia to lobby support from the Organisation of African Unity (OAU) for a proposed government in exile. But the leaders in Addis Ababa held the same view as Nyerere: the struggle could be waged only from inside Rhodesia.

Nkomo was scheduled to travel to Yugoslavia, but sensing that he was about to face a revolt he returned home, where a young lawyer who had joined ZAPU, Edison Zvobgo, showed him the minutes of discussions held in Dar es Salaam at which it was decided that Nkomo should step down as leader.

In June 1963, Nkomo suspended Mugabe, Sithole, Takawira and Moton Malianga from the executive. They received the news in Dar es Salaam, and responded by voting to replace Nkomo with Sithole. Shortly afterwards, Sithole's supporters named the breakaway party the Zimbabwe African National Union (ZANU), appointing him leader and Herbert Chitepo the party chairman. Nkomo remained at the helm of ZAPU, but a rift had been created that would never be healed.

In London, the Commonwealth and Colonial Office had agreed to grant independence to both Northern Rhodesia and Nyasaland, and a conference was arranged at Victoria Falls to formally disband the Central African Federation. Winston Field refused to attend unless the British gave a prior commitment that Rhodesia, too, would be given independence. London would agree to this only on condition that the 1961 constitution was amended to extend majority power.

In his memoirs, the British foreign secretary at the time, Lord Home, pondered the stalemate. 'Ought the British Government to have faced the Governments of Northern Rhodesia and Nyasaland with the independence of all three parts or none? It would have been possible and perhaps in terms of real politics, we could have done so with a reasonably clear conscience, but, hitherto, when handing over power to another Government, we had always done so to a majority.'

In hindsight, this was perhaps the greatest mistake Britain made in its handling of the Rhodesia problem. The crown had never wielded any real authority in Salisbury. First it was the BSAC, then the Rhodesian government, yet, for as long as Rhodesia remained a colony – even if only in name – the United Nations, and especially the developing world, would hold the British government responsible for anything and everything that went wrong.

Granting independence to a white-dominated government would be difficult, but camouflaging it in the break-up of a federation would have been an entirely different matter, and one that would have saved successive administrations in Whitehall a great deal of trouble.

Field held a trump card because, without Rhodesia's cooperation, dismantling the federation would have been messy, if not impossible, and had he been a stronger negotiator, he could probably have got his independence.

The federation was dissolved on 31 December 1963. Ian Smith, who was at the conference, claimed consistently that the British had agreed, in private, to grant Rhodesia independence no later than the other two territories. According to Smith, Field had enough faith in British honour not to demand a written agreement, but British delegates always denied that any such deal had been done.

In August 1963, Sally Mugabe gave birth to a son in Dar es Salaam, and in keeping with the Shona tradition of naming children after events in play when they are born, Robert called him Nhamodzenyika, or 'the Suffering Country'. In later years he said his son had been 'a sign of hope at the centre of a storm'.

He revelled in the new role of father and doted on the child, dividing his time between raising funds to cover the exile group's living expenses in Dar es Salaam, meeting ambassadors and others with influence, and supporting Sally in the months after the birth.

It soon became clear that both Nyerere and the OAU had been correct when they advised the nationalists to pursue their struggle from inside Rhodesia. Despite being harassed by the authorities, Nkomo was visible to the people and quickly became the sole black political voice in the country, while Sithole's group was all but forgotten.

In December 1963, the Mugabes made a decision that would chart their fate far beyond the moment. Both were facing prison terms emanating from their earlier arrests and the added charge of jumping bail, but Robert was determined to return to Rhodesia. He was equally adamant that Sally should take Nhamodzenyika to the safety of the Heyfron family in Ghana.

Robert would never see his son again. He was arrested on arrival in Salisbury, and held without bail. Party chairman Herbert Chitepo defended him in a trial that ran from January to March 1964, during which Robert took full advantage of the chance to speak his mind. The government, he warned, would declare itself independent of Britain and plunge the country into years of conflict. He had not fled to escape the law, he said, but in an effort to serve the black majority.

'It was necessary in the interests of the nation that I took speedy action and left. We all had to sacrifice our personal interests,' Mugabe told the judge and media from the dock.

He was sentenced to indefinite detention under the Law and Order Maintenance Act, and would spend the next eleven years behind bars.

In April 1964, a month after the trial ended, Ian Smith replaced Winston Field as prime minister, and the breaking of ties with Britain became a certainty. Smith travelled to London, and British prime minister Harold Wilson, whose Labour Party was in power, reciprocated by visiting Salisbury, but no acceptable compromise could be reached. Smith had asked the various government department heads to report on the likely consequences of unilateral independence, and they had all warned that it would be a disaster. Wilson and the Secretary for Commonwealth Affairs, Arthur Bottomly, had in turn drawn up six principles for independence:

- Retention of all clauses in the 1961 constitution that would pave the way for majority rule.
- Guarantees that the constitution would not be amended to the disadvantage of the majority.
- A greater say in politics for the black population, with immediate effect.

- Phasing out of racial discrimination.
- A test to ensure that independence on these terms was acceptable to the majority.
- No oppression of the majority by the minority, or vice versa.

Smith argued, with some justification, that it was the British government that had written and endorsed the 1961 constitution at the conference in Salisbury where they signed the final draft along with Nkomo and Sithole. Now, just three years later, they were making new demands.

Unable to make any headway in Whitehall, Smith called a referendum, and the existing electorate voted overwhelmingly in favour of independence. He also arranged an *indaba* [meeting] of all tribal chiefs, who pledged the support of their subjects for the idea as well. In reality, both the authority and the salaries of the chiefs were determined by the government of the day, and they would have been unlikely to say anything else. From 1980 their loyalties lay with Mugabe's regime, and they would doubtless stand just as firmly behind any alternative ruler.

In May 1965, the Rhodesian Front won all fifty 'white' seats in a general election, and in October, Wilson travelled to Salisbury to meet with Smith and various black leaders, most of whom had to be taken out of detention to see him. In a move that surprised many observers, Wilson promised that whatever happened, Britain would never use force to resolve the Rhodesian situation. In fact, he had already canvassed this option with his army, navy and air chiefs, and been told that the entire high command would resign if ordered to act against Rhodesia. The Second World War had ended only twenty years before, and many senior officers had served alongside Rhodesian soldiers in battle, and would not be willing to take up arms against their former comrades. More than anything, Wilson's reassurance was for home consumption.

Britain's economy was in a parlous state, renewed tensions were brewing in Northern Ireland, and it is doubtful whether a military campaign could have been successfully mounted against Rhodesia. South Africa and the Portuguese territories of Mozambique and Angola would not have allowed access, and invading from the north would have created impossibly long lines for both logistics and communication. When the federation was dissolved, all military equipment from Zambia and Malawi had gone to Salisbury, and the Rhodesians had a well-equipped army that knew the terrain.

But more than anything, it was domestic politics that tied Wilson's hands. Facing an election with a majority of only one parliamentary seat, he dared not go to the polls while fighting a long and bloody battle against people of British descent.

Wilson offered a final carrot: a royal commission on the issue of independence, with no preconditions and headed by Australian prime minister Sir Robert

Menzies, who was known to be sympathetic to Smith. London and Salisbury would abide by the commission's recommendations.

The two men agreed, and Wilson returned to face vehement protest from his party's left wing, which saw the deal as a sell-out of black rights. He buckled under the pressure, announcing that he could no longer guarantee acceptance of the proposed commission's verdict, and reserved the right to reject it. For Smith, it was the final straw in what he saw as years of British duplicity.

On 11 November 1965, the cabinet agreed to a unilateral declaration of independence (UDI), and the prime minister announced the decision on Rhodesian radio and television.

'They left us with no option, nothing at all,' Smith told me during an interview in 2001 at his home in Harare. 'What were we supposed to do? Every time we agreed to something, from the 1961 constitution to the break-up of federation to the royal commission, they put new obstacles in our way. We had no other choice.'

Wilson moved quickly to isolate Smith's government, declaring British sanctions against Rhodesia and then convincing the United Nations to do the same. In order to impose the boycott, the UN had to agree that Rhodesia was a threat to world peace.

This ridiculous move showed not only how little logic prevailed in the General Assembly, but also how much Smith had miscalculated the results of his action. No one cared about the rash of military coups in the rest of Africa, Chinese genocide in Tibet, America's growing war in Vietnam or the conflict in Northern Ireland, but a small landlocked country in Africa was a different thing – because it had a government whose colour differed from those it ruled.

A Commonwealth Heads of Government Meeting (CHOGM) in Lagos from 10 to 12 January 1966 applied similar double standards. The host country of Nigeria had grown increasingly despotic under the rule of prime minister Sir Abubakar Balewa, while in neighbouring Ghana, Kwame Nkrumah had declared a one-party state and jailed the opposition. Both Kaunda in Zambia and Banda in Malawi had consolidated power in their own hands and nationalised the press, but neither Wilson nor the other CHOGM delegates made reference to these attacks on freedom. Balewa made it plain that if the British government backed down over Rhodesia, he would nationalise their extensive interests in Nigeria's oil industry. Wilson found himself with little room to manoeuvre.

Three days after CHOGM, in the early hours of 15 January, Balewa was overthrown by a group of young majors who dragged him from his home, shot him dead and dumped his body in a ditch. Neither Wilson nor the Commonwealth secretariat saw fit to comment, and Britain continued to supply arms to the Nigerian government.

At UDI, the Rhodesian economy was small. Items as basic as potato crisps, washing powder, cornflakes and toothpaste were imported from either South Africa or Britain, and the export economy was confined to tobacco and, to a lesser extent, mining.

Within five years, all that had changed. A massive programme of industrialisation had turned the country into the largest manufacturing base outside South Africa, and in respect of most items, Rhodesia became self-sufficient. Employment boomed, drawing more than 30 000 new white immigrants in addition to hundreds of thousands of blacks who abandoned the poverty and economic chaos of Zambia to seek work in Salisbury.

Still incarcerated, Mugabe found prison life a difficult adjustment to make. The government, fearful that conspiratorial cliques might form among the jailed nationalists, moved them at regular intervals. Mugabe began his term in Salisbury, after which he was taken to Gwelo in the centre of the country, and then to Que Que, closer to Bulawayo, before being returned to Salisbury in 1966. Exercise time was limited, a dozen men shared one large cell with only enough beds for half that number, and a bucket in the corner was the toilet. Under Mugabe's rule, the same cells held up to fifty inmates and the beds had all been removed, leaving prisoners to sleep on the floor.

With Nkomo and Sithole behind bars as well, ZAPU and ZANU were in open conflict in the townships, with party thugs carrying out nightly raids, burning the homes of opponents and killing members of the rival party.

As the number of political detainees grew, the government decided they should be isolated from the common criminals, lest they turn the jails into ideological battlegrounds.

At Que Que there were no cells, just a large fenced enclosure in which the prisoners could build their own huts and create a community. Mugabe found himself living in a hut next to Leopold Takawira, whom he had first met at the demonstration of 7 000 in Salisbury in 1960. The prison warders allowed the men to conduct their political activity within the village, and Mugabe was soon making speeches to his fellow inmates and encouraging them to maintain their morale for the fight ahead.

'These months,' he told them, 'no matter how long it takes, must not be wasted.'

Aid organisations provided the prisoners with books, and the better educated, like Mugabe, taught the others. Before long, he was elected 'headmaster'.

His personal regimen was strict, rising early, doing a range of exercises and meditation before breakfast, then teaching several classes before pursuing his own studies well into the night. In later life, even at the age of seventy-nine, his bodyguards found it hard to keep up with his daily routine.

Sympathetic black prison warders smuggled letters to his friends and their replies back into the camp. Herbert Chitepo, the most senior party official not in jail, was encouraged to set up a war machine in exile and send guerrillas back into Rhodesia. There was only one country from which this could be done. Mozambique was under Portuguese rule while Botswana was (and remained) neutral, so it had to be Zambia.

The first group of fighters, known as the Zimbabwe African National Liberation Army (ZANLA), returned from Zambia in April 1966 and murdered a farmer seventy kilometres outside Salisbury. On their way back, the Rhodesian army cornered and killed them all at Sinoia, north of the capital.

Mugabe, now back in Salisbury, was working on his fourth degree by correspondence with London University, and continued his relentless campaign to boost the morale of the other prisoners. Soon after the Sinoia incident he was visited by his sister Sabina, who told him that Nhamodzenyika had died of malaria in Ghana. Sally's twin sister Esther, who had become a doctor, had nursed the boy at hospital in Accra, but to no avail.

A prisoner who was in the same jail as Mugabe later described his response to the news of his only child's death.

'He just cried and cried. He lost interest in everything. His life, it seemed, amounted to nothing any more. He was a man lost inside himself. His grief was total.'

Mugabe pleaded with the prison authorities to release him on bail, even to have Rhodesian soldiers or police accompany him to Ghana so that he could bury his child and comfort his wife, but they refused. In reality, the government could not possibly have granted his request. Ghana had become a dictatorship, and there would have been nothing to prevent any escort being detained and Mugabe set free.

Four years later, Leopold Takawira died in detention due to lack of treatment for late-onset diabetes. Despite a sudden loss of weight, the prison doctor had not detected the condition.

While Mugabe never said so, these two events may have helped to foment his racist attitude towards whites.

Ian Smith and Harold Wilson met twice after UDI, both times aboard British warships anchored in the Mediterranean. The first attempt at reconciliation was frosty, but at the second Wilson virtually offered Smith independence in exchange for a return to legality. Smith took the proposals back to his cabinet, which rejected them on the grounds that past experience had shown the British could not be trusted to deliver.

Although jailed, Sithole was still nominally in charge of ZANU, but his behaviour had become erratic and the other detainees went out of their way to avoid him. He became obsessed with the idea of assassinating Smith, and through whispers to the guards, arranged for some of his lieutenants to assemble outside the prison.

He wrote his instructions, stuffed them inside oranges and threw the fruit over the wall to his waiting men. Also waiting outside were several members of the police Special Branch, who collected the oranges and found the notes.

In 1969, the Rhodesian press hummed with the story of Sithole's treason trial and his plans to kill the prime minister. He was found guilty and, facing the death penalty, he asked to make a statement to the court.

'My Lord, I wish to publicly dissociate myself in word, thought and deed from any subversive activities, from any terrorist activities and from any form of violence,' he said.

When news of the statement reached his fellow inmates, they branded him a coward, and took a poll on leadership of their ZANU committee. Mugabe won. Sithole was sentenced to six years in maximum security, away from other prisoners, but was allowed to return to the general political cells in March 1973. His former comrades shunned him, and until his release eighteen months later, he increasingly lost touch with the struggle.

Some analysts believe that Ian Smith's biggest mistake was detaining Sithole in the first place, arguing that if he had not been held, he would have gone into exile and worked with Chitepo and others to rebuild the party, and Mugabe would never have gained control of ZANU.

However, having met all the leaders who were still alive in 1980 – Nkomo, Muzorewa, Sithole, Chikerema and Mugabe, and interviewed many of them – my personal view is that Sithole was the only one who might have ended up being a worse tyrant than Mugabe. He came across as deeply insecure and suspicious of everyone and anyone around him, and seemed to find great difficulty creating bonds of genuine trust with people – all traits of the great dictators.

Following UDI, most diplomatic missions remained open in Salisbury, but when Rhodesia became a republic in 1970 and replaced the British monarch with a non-executive president as head of state, all the legations closed, except for those of Greece, Portugal and South Africa. The British and UN sanctions had become something of a joke. Imports continued to arrive via Mozambique and South Africa, and Rhodesia was still exporting tobacco and minerals and selling beef and maize to a number of African countries, notably Gabon, Malawi and even Zambia.

In 1973, after a series of guerrilla attacks – and in characteristic hot-headed manner – Smith closed the border with Zambia. As with UDI, this was easy enough to do, but almost impossible to reverse without one side being seen to back down.

Sally Mugabe moved to London, where she lobbied on behalf of her husband.

But change, when it came, would originate not in England, South Africa or Rhodesia itself, but in Lisbon.

The Portuguese had stubbornly held onto their African territories and were fighting guerrilla wars in Guinea-Bissau, Angola and Mozambique. Every young Portuguese man was forced to do national service in the colonies, and the casualty rates were out of control. On 25 April 1974, the military high command in Lisbon mounted a coup against President Marcello Caetano's dictatorship, and announced that all colonies would be granted immediate independence.

ZANU guerrillas were already piggybacking on Frelimo in Mozambique, and in December 1972, Rex Nhongo led the first major attack on a farm in the Mount Darwin area north-east of Salisbury. In theory, Sithole was still ZANU's president, despite the vote by the jailed executive, but it was Herbert Chitepo who directed the war from exile in Lusaka.

With the Portuguese gone from Mozambique, ZANU would be poised to inflict real damage, but Lisbon's capitulation had brought war to South Africa's very door. Up to that time, John Vorster's government in Pretoria had worried little about its own security. The Rhodesians had mopped up incursions by ZANU, and while Frelimo had enjoyed some success against the Portuguese, there had been no discernible danger of Mozambique falling to the communist-backed guerrillas. The coup in Portugal changed the equation, and Vorster decided it was time to make peace with the rest of Africa.

He initiated talks with Kaunda in Zambia, and they agreed to push the men under their influence to attend a conference at Victoria Falls. Vorster would send a South African Railways carriage to park halfway across the bridge and serve as a 'neutral' venue. Kaunda would send the exiles in Lusaka to the conference, and South Africa, Rhodesia's main supplier of fuel and armaments, would have no problem persuading Smith to do as he was told.

It was the start of a series of shuttles that verged on farce, but also illustrated the integrity of Kaunda and Nyerere. To prepare the ZANU delegation, members of the executive needed to meet outside Rhodesia, and Kaunda asked Smith to send the party leader to Lusaka. The jailed ZANU executive elected to send Mugabe, but no sooner had he flown to Lusaka in a private jet than Kaunda and Nyerere made it plain that they still recognised Sithole as the boss, and sent Mugabe back to Rhodesia, and to jail. He returned to Lusaka at a later stage to take part in the discussions, and Sally came from London to see him for the first time in more than ten years. She fainted at the airport, and Mugabe visited her at the private clinic patronised by Kaunda. Two days later, Mugabe was on his way back to jail again. Kaunda and Nyerere could easily have used the talks to free Mugabe, but they had promised Smith that he would return, and they saw to it that he did.

In December 1974, Smith, acting on Vorster's orders, declared a ceasefire against the guerrilla groups and released all jailed nationalists, including Mugabe, Nkomo, Sithole and Bishop Abel Muzorewa, who had organised a civil disobedience campaign in 1972.

According to Mac Maharaj, a veteran South African anti-apartheid activist who served in Nelson Mandela's cabinet, a study of ZANU in exile is necessary in order to understand the political crisis that beset Zimbabwe in the late 1990s.

'They had immense difficulties holding themselves together during the struggle, and they really never changed. It was an organisation with deep divisions, even in those days,' he told me at the end of 2002.

One of the first high-profile victims of these difficulties was Herbert Chitepo. A brief look at the circumstances surrounding his murder sheds some light on why Mugabe had to rule his own party with the proverbial iron fist.

After the split between ZANU and ZAPU, both parties reverted to the tribal origins of their leaders. Nkomo's support base became largely Matabele, while the Shona gravitated towards ZANU.

It was not until the Movement for Democratic Change (MDC) was formed in 1999 that members of both tribes embraced one party, and even then the question of ethnic identity continued to simmer below the surface.

However, ZANU also had to contend with internal divisions between the four Shona clans. Mugabe's Zezuru, because of their geographical dominance around Salisbury, had become the best educated and most intellectual. The Korekore from the north-east were still largely rural folk, but had provided support and recruits for the guerrilla army. The Manyika, including Chitepo, came from the eastern highlands and tended to support politicians from their own area.

But it was the Karanga from the south-central region, men such as Chitepo's military commander, Josiah Tongogara, who held the trump card, because of their numbers.

With the release from prison of so many nationalists into what was essentially a power vacuum created by years of bannings and imprisonment, the race was on to see who would lead the struggle.

In 1973, while Mugabe was still in jail, fractures had emerged at a ZANU congress in Lusaka, with Karangas taking over key portfolios including finance, defence, information and the guerrilla war. Chitepo, while still chairman, was left with foreign affairs and politics.

By the time Mugabe and Sithole were released at the end of 1974, ZANU was at breaking point. Trainee guerrillas complained about inhuman treatment, beatings and torture in their camps, and at a largely Manyika base at Chifombo in eastern Zambia the men revolted and jailed their commanders, electing one of their number, a young lawyer called Thomas Nhari, as leader. They supported

Chitepo and blamed Tongogara and other Karangas for their ill treatment and lack of direction in the war.

With a group of fighters from the camp, Nhari went to Lusaka and kidnapped Tongogara's wife and several party chiefs, including Kumbirai Kangai, who was destined to become an important member of Mugabe's cabinet after 1980. They were on their way to seize Tongogara at his home when the Zambian police stopped and arrested them.

Tongogara took a group of soldiers and went to Chifombo, where he regained control of the camp in a battle that cost more than forty lives.

As the head of ZANU in Zambia, Chitepo had to try the rebels, and those found guilty were shot. But the battle between the Karanga and the Manyika continued, and over the next few months more than 100 people were kidnapped, tortured and murdered.

The Manyikas believed that Chitepo had sold them out by executing people from his own tribe, while the Karanga were convinced that Nhari had acted on his behalf. Chitepo told Kaunda that he feared for his life, and believed Tongogara was trying to kill him. On 18 March 1975, he died when his car detonated a landmine planted in the driveway of his Lusaka home.

Tongogara fled to Mozambique, while Kaunda had most of the ZANU high command arrested and launched an investigation. Tongogara was apprehended and jailed for eighteen months.

ZANU's official stance was that the Rhodesians had killed Chitepo, but that has since been disproved, though the full details of the matter have never been revealed. Tongogara denied involvement, and some of Mugabe's critics would later suggest that he might even have had a hand in clearing the way for new leadership, but no evidence has come to light to support this notion.

In Salisbury, Sithole was in trouble again, having been arrested for trying to relaunch the local branch of ZANU, which was still a banned organisation. With Chitepo dead and Tongogara behind bars, there was only one man the party could turn to.

Robert Mugabe took over the military and political leadership, but had to find a base from which he could direct the struggle. Rhodesia was impossible, and in Zambia Kaunda was still fuming over the murder of Chitepo. The only safe haven was Mozambique. After the coup in Lisbon, the military junta had moved quickly to dismantle colonial rule, handing over power immediately in Guinea-Bissau and scheduling Angolan independence for 11 November 1975 – by which time Angola would be engulfed in civil war. No elections were held in either colony.

In Mozambique, Frelimo was headed by a charismatic male nurse, Samora Machel, who was installed in the capital, Maputo (then Lourenço Marques), and gradually assumed control of the government over a twelve-month period, again without any elections. Independence was set for June 1975, and in April, Mugabe and Edgar Tekere, whom he had first met at the mass rally in 1960, crossed the border and went to Maputo.

Machel made it clear to Mugabe that he would not tolerate incidents such as Chitepo's assassination, but assigned him a house on the coast north of the capital, and had him watched around the clock. Finally, Machel granted him permission to travel, and he went to Tanzania to gain the support of Nyerere, sending word back to Rhodesia that anyone who was unhappy with the situation at home should join him in Mozambique. Thousands answered the call and were housed in refugee camps. Tongogara was released from jail and became Mugabe's supreme commander, turning the refugees into soldiers.

Meanwhile, Nkomo, Sithole and Muzorewa took part in the train summit at Victoria Falls, which produced no solutions to anyone's problems. Weary of détente, Nkomo went into exile in Zambia, and invited his Matabele supporters to join him there with a view to waging war. He set up training camps outside Lusaka, and named his military wing the Zimbabwe People's Revolutionary Army (ZIPRA).

By 1976, two fronts had opened up, with ZIPRA infiltrating Rhodesia from Zambia, and Mugabe – now based in Maputo and supported by both Nyerere and Machel – dispatching his ZANLA guerrillas from the east. The Rhodesian army began to feel the strain, and periods of military service were extended.

Initially, American secretary of state Henry Kissinger was not unduly concerned about a regional conflict, but he became worried soon enough when China began arming Mugabe and the Russians started shipping thousands of tons of weapons to Nkomo. Rhodesia was rapidly becoming a war in which the US had no role, and if Rhodesia fell, key American investments in South Africa could be jeopardised. And there was the Cape sea route to consider.

Kissinger embarked on a series of covert meetings with John Vorster in Europe. With the Portuguese withdrawal from South Africa's flanks, Rhodesia stuck out like a sore thumb above the northern border, and Vorster made it clear that he would rather deal with a moderate black government in Salisbury than have a war on his doorstep.

In September 1976, Kissinger visited Pretoria, determined to break the Rhodesian resolve. If he could get Smith to announce publicly that he would accept majority rule within two years, it would be difficult for Salisbury to renege on the idea. Vorster told Smith that he had two choices: black rule or the closure of Beit Bridge.

On 23 September, the Rhodesian leader made a radio and television broadcast announcing that elections would be held on the basis of universal franchise. The

British government would sponsor a conference in Geneva, at which all parties concerned would thrash out a final deal.

The white population was shocked. The independence of Mozambique had brought a torrent of Portuguese immigrants, pushing the white population up to 330 000, but now large-scale emigration began, as Rhodesians fearing imminent black rule moved to South Africa, Australia, Canada and Britain.

The Geneva conference went ahead as planned, and was attended by the Rhodesian government and all the key black players, including Mugabe and Nkomo, but no agreement could be reached.

Smith then negotiated a power-sharing deal with Muzorewa, Sithole and a tribal leader, Chief Chirau, who had no real support. All discrimination would end and free elections based on universal franchise would be held under the supervision of international observers. Nkomo was also invited to the table, but it was too late. He had his army set up in Zambia, and although he came close to agreeing when Smith flew in to see him in 1977, Nyerere talked him out of it.

'That was Nkomo's biggest mistake,' one of his supporters told me on condition of anonymity while serving in Mugabe's government. 'If Josh had come in then, his ZIPRA troops along with the Rhodesian army would have liquidated ZANU in no time, and we would have been saved from Mugabe.'

In June 1979, after elections rated free and fair by observers, Muzorewa became prime minister of Zimbabwe Rhodesia, a clumsy name designed to appease white fears. In the same year, Margaret Thatcher came to power in Britain, and despite an election manifesto that promised to recognise the Muzorewa government, she gave in to pressure from her foreign secretary, Lord Carrington, and the Australian prime minister, Malcolm Fraser – an avid supporter of Mugabe – and opted for an all-party conference in London.

In an effort to disrupt supply lines to ZAPU and ZANU, the Rhodesian army and air force had inflicted huge damage on the railways and roads in both Zambia and Mozambique. And they had acquired a secret weapon in the form of a new rebel movement.

Within two years of coming to power, Samora Machel had all but destroyed his country's economy. He closed the border with Rhodesia, losing millions of dollars in port revenues, and scared away the South African tourist trade, which had been the single biggest foreign exchange earner. Every scrap of land was nationalised, along with all private companies, after which he declared war on the country's black middle class, rounding up anyone with enough schooling to form an opinion and sending them to re-education camps scattered across rural Mozambique. According to a US Senate report, more than 200 000 people were jailed and some 30 000 died in detention.[3] When a revolt broke out in one of the camps in central Mozambique, the inmates killed the guards, stole their rifles and sought refuge in Rhodesia. Soon, there was a two-way flow of refugees, with Rhodesian blacks moving east to Mugabe's training camps and Mozambicans running in the opposite direction to escape Machel's regime.

As with ZANU's internal struggle, Frelimo's problems were tribal-based. Machel came from the Shangaan nation, which sprawls across southern Mozambique and the Mpumalanga province of South Africa, whereas his opponents were from Sithole's Ndau tribe, which had been split when the colonial border between Rhodesia and Mozambique was arbitrarily drawn, with no regard for ethnic ties.

The Rhodesians seized the moment and formed the exiles into the Mozambique Resistance Movement (Renamo), which continued to wage war until 1994. In 1986, while returning to Maputo from Lusaka, Machel died when his aircraft flew into a mountain on the South African side of the Mozambican border. There were suggestions that South Africa had deliberately caused the fatal crash so that the less radical Joaquim Chissano could become president, but in the absence of concrete proof, Machel's death was labelled an accident.

Chissano did succeed him, and after two decades of civil war eventually agreed to a multiparty democracy, with Renamo becoming the official opposition. The party leader, Afonso Dhlakama, was one of the first escapees from Machel's re-education camps.

In 1979, with the Rhodesian armed forces on his threshold, Renamo mounting raids at will and ZANU eating him out of house and home, Machel put pressure on Mugabe to attend Thatcher's peace conference, making it clear that if he did not agree to take part in a new, British supervised election, he would not be allowed to continue using Mozambique as the springboard for his armed struggle. Kaunda issued a similar ultimatum to Nkomo, and at the end of 1979 an agreement was reached and signed by the two guerrilla leaders and Muzorewa.

A British governor, Lord Soames, was appointed in Salisbury, and Commonwealth observers monitored the elections in February 1980. But the vote was for peace rather than for any one party. The black population had been shot at and tortured by both the guerrillas and the army, and were ready to support any leader who could stop the war.

The problem was that both Mugabe and Sithole still called their parties by the same name, so Mugabe changed his to ZANU-PF, the latter initials standing for 'Patriotic Front', a term he and Nkomo had used when negotiating with the British.

Muzorewa won three seats, Mugabe fifty-seven, and though Nkomo swept all of Matabeleland, this gave him only twenty seats. On a special roll reserved for whites, Smith's Rhodesian Front won all twenty seats.

Nkomo was genuinely shocked at the Shona rejection of his party, since he had always seen himself as a national leader rather than a tribal chief.

In some quarters, Bishop Muzorewa's failure to secure more than three seats was an even bigger shock. Despite the fact that intelligence agents on the ground had been warning Salisbury for weeks that Mugabe's guerrillas had applied enough intimidation, especially in the rural areas, to win the election, Muzorewa himself, the whites, and the British and South African governments had all relied on reports from Rhodesian intelligence, which suggested that he would emerge a clear victor.

Under the peace accord, all guerrillas were supposed to be confined to camps inside Rhodesia during the run-up to the elections, but Mugabe had violated the agreement and sent young *mujhibas* [collaborators] into the camps instead, dispatching his trained soldiers to conduct a terror campaign against villagers, telling them that if ZANU did not win, there would be an even more horrific war than the one they had already faced.

The British had agreed that any party guilty of intimidation would be barred from the poll, but after fifteen years of haggling over Rhodesia, they were keen to rid themselves of the problem, and looked the other way.

Mugabe had a working majority of six in a 100-seat parliament, and on 18 April, Britain granted formal independence to Rhodesia. At midnight the Union Jack – a flag that had not flown over the country since 1923 – was lowered, and the new Zimbabwe flag raised. Prince Charles travelled from Britain to hand over a power his country had never commanded, and with Sally in the audience, Robert Gabriel Mugabe took the oath of office and became prime minister at the age of fifty-six.

During his first few months in office, he preached reconciliation, telling the whites that while they might have hated him in the past, 'you cannot escape the love I feel for you'. He even visited Smith and thanked him for handing over such a strong economy.

But the spirit of cooperation was not to last.

# 5

# Into madness

Mugabe's victory was hailed around the world. Throughout the Commonwealth, within the so-called Non-Aligned Movement (which had become something of a joke following the admission of Cuba and Soviet-occupied Afghanistan) and even the United Nations, Zimbabwe's new leader was fêted and solicited for advice on how to solve problems not only in Africa, but all over the Third World.

Many of his first cabinet members were better educated than their white predecessors who had run the country until the middle of 1979. Dr Bernard Chidzero, married to a French Canadian, had degrees in psychology and political science, and had obtained his doctorate in Montreal. He held several posts at the UN before returning to Zimbabwe to help run the economy. Edison Zvobgo was a lawyer who had practised at the bar in Salisbury before taking a master's degree and a doctorate in diplomacy in the United States. Nathan Shamuyarira had a BSc from Princeton, and, after taking his doctorate, lectured in politics at the University of Dar es Salaam.

Mugabe himself had six academic degrees to his credit.

Josiah Tongogara had not made it home, having died in a car accident in Maputo. Many Zimbabweans old enough to remember Tongo, as he was affectionately known, believe that Mugabe had him killed because he had become too popular, but no evidence was ever presented to support this suspicion.

While the final vestiges of discrimination had been abolished by the time ZANU-PF came to power, affirmative action had not been implemented. But Mugabe moved swiftly to correct this situation. Tongogara's deputy, Rex Nhongo, and Joshua Nkomo's military chief, Lookout Masuku, were each given the rank of major general under command of Lieutenant General Peter Walls, whom Mugabe asked to stay on and oversee the integration of ZANLA, ZIPRA and the Rhodesian Army.

Many white Rhodesian soldiers, as well as some black members of the Selous Scouts and other units, moved seamlessly into the ranks of the South African Defence Force in the run-up to independence, fearing reprisals or unwilling to serve with and under their former enemies. In fact, they had nothing to fear. As Ron Reid-Daly told me: 'You have to salute Mugabe for one thing. There were no witch-hunts. No one in the armed forces, black or white, was hounded by the new government, and the integration was a total success.'

Mugabe also made an early point of reassuring the agricultural and business sectors, making it clear that while he was a socialist at heart, he would support free enterprise, and recognised that economic transformation would be a gradual process.

With the war over, farmers could work their lands without fear of attack, and commerce and industry no longer had to contend with constant and lengthy disruptions while employees performed military service. But in the first ten years of independence, economic growth was slowed by a brain drain as the white population fell from 300 000 to just more than 100 000. In due course, however, this wave of emigration was offset by the return of black Zimbabweans, products of the country's superb education system who – finding their career paths blocked – had taken jobs in Britain or America. Their white countrymen were amazed by the competence and abilities the exiles brought home.

'When I see the transformation of this country and the thousands of well-educated black people slipping so effortlessly into the economy, I really wonder why we didn't introduce a real democracy many years ago,' one writer confessed in a letter to the *Herald*.

'As whites, we were conned for years by the Rhodesian Front into believing that hell and damnation would follow if we embraced real change. And what a waste of life there was because of this.'

She signed herself 'A proud white Zimbabwean'.

But there were early warning signs that Mugabe was not comfortable with too much democracy, and his ministers began attacking the press whenever newspapers ran stories that did not praise the new government.

Nathan Shamuyarira, Minister of Information, quickly turned the Zimbabwe Broadcasting Corporation (ZBC) into a ZANU-PF mouthpiece, appointing Gray Tichatonga, a former party propaganda boss, to manage radio and television news. All members of government had to be referred to as 'comrade' rather than 'mister' or 'doctor'. Broadcasters who balked at the new policies were free to leave. On a visit to Australia in October 1980, Tichatonga told the *Sydney Morning Herald*, 'The only way we can maintain political control is through fear.'[1]

Though neither came even close to military victory during the war, Mugabe and Nkomo had both believed their respective armies would eventually take the country by force. ZANU-PF and ZAPU had thus been primed to rule with absolute authority and without the messy business of elections, parliament, democracy and, least of all, a free press to criticise their decisions.

With only twenty seats, Nkomo was in no position to do anything except form a political opposition, take up arms again – an option that Kaunda would not countenance being exercised from Zambia – or accept Mugabe's offer to form a government of national unity. He chose the latter, and became Minister for Home Affairs.

Mugabe had often spoken in Mozambique about the desirability of a one-party state, but there was no way to consolidate his power while the press watched his every move. There were two daily newspapers, the *Herald* in Salisbury and the *Chronicle* in Bulawayo, one national weekend newspaper, the *Sunday Mail*, and the parochial *Sunday News* in Bulawayo. There was also a weekly publication in Manicaland, originally known as the *Umtali Post*, which changed its name to the *Manica Post* when Umtali became Mutare in 1981.

The parent company of all five publications, Zimbabwe Newspapers, thus had a monopoly, and the Argus Group in South Africa, which published *The Star* in Johannesburg and dailies in all other major centres, owned 46 per cent of the company's shares. However, a board of directors in Salisbury made all the decisions regarding ZimPapers, as it was generally known. These included the appointment of editors, but until 1978 there had been no senior black editorial or advertising executives at any of the newspapers.

Immediately after the election, Shamuyarira told ZimPapers chairman and managing director George Capon that he wanted to see a new and more cooperative approach by the press, reflecting the changes that had taken place in the country. Capon replied that the company had always supported the government of the day, but that editorial policy and decisions on news coverage were the responsibility of individual editors, who were not subject to interference by management.

In the middle of 1980, Shamuyarira went to South Africa and made it clear to the Argus Group directors that unless they sold their share of ZimPapers to his government, the company would be nationalised. The group capitulated, and the Nigerian government gave Mugabe the money to take over the investment.

I was working at the *Manica Post* when Capon came to Umtali to brief staff on the change. In the common room, he bought us drinks and lied that the Argus Group had sought other buyers, but that only the government had been able to come up with the cash. He even suggested that any transformation would be minimal and that we should 'all go about our business with the least possible disruption'.

Having accepted Shamuyarira's offer to stay on and oversee the change, he then went out of his way to turn the newspaper group into a ZANU-PF lapdog.

Within weeks all the editors – with the exception of sixty-year-old Jean Maitland-Stewart at the *Manica Post* – had been fired and replaced with people acceptable to the party. Jean remained a fiery critic of the government, especially at local level, where a new town council was helping itself to ratepayers' money.

A Mass Media Trust was set up to run the company, ostensibly to keep the government at arm's length from the editors, but this never worked in practice.

Shamuyarira called a news conference, and dressed up the purchase as an effort to free the press rather than bring it to heel.

'By removing South African influences,' he said, 'we have leapt forward on the long march to true liberation and independence.'

Ironically, despite the best efforts of the apartheid regime to muzzle its critics, South Africa still had the freest press on the continent, and its English-language newspapers were a constant thorn in the government's flesh.

Asked how the international community might respond to the takeover of Zimbabwe's press, Shamuyarira said he anticipated a favourable reaction. 'There is nothing unusual in what we have done,' he said, 'and the world should see this as a natural development in the consolidation of our independence. Some may misinterpret our intentions, but they would be wrong.'

Before vacating their chairs, the departing editors all warned of the dangers inherent in state-owned media. The *Sunday Mail* observed that the Mass Media Trust could never be independent if the government appointed its directors.

The *Sunday News* was even more concerned, pointing out that it would be easy to say 'let's see how it works', but warning that all African governments had made it a policy to gag the press, and that Zimbabwe would be no exception. 'Sooner or later, these newspapers will be vehicles reflecting government and nationalist policy.'

The *Chronicle*'s prediction would prove most accurate. 'The prospect, alas, is bleak,' wrote the editor, 'and not only for newspapers, but for other freedoms, and democracy itself.'

Any doubt over the government's intention was dispelled when the new chairman of the Mass Media Trust addressed the press a few days later. Robert Mandebvu had been ZANU-PF's representative in Libya during the war, and had his own views about how reporters should do their job.

'We will not interfere with the right of the press to report the truth,' he said, 'but journalists will also have to remember that they are citizens of the country and should be wary of issues that may discredit or embarrass the government. The press will now be controlled by the people.'[1]

Shamuyarira agreed, saying that like any other freedom, the right to publish was 'relative and not absolute'.

Nkomo was shocked, and described the takeover as a complete tragedy. Although he was a member of the cabinet, it was clear that he had not been aware of the ultimatum to the Argus Group.

Most black opinion, however, was on the side of the government, and welcomed the effort to control the newspapers. Even the president of the Zimbabwe Union of Journalists, Philemon Nandu, said there was little likelihood that the government would interfere, and another writer, Gilbert Mawarire, said it was nonsense to suggest that Mugabe would try to silence the press.

Jay Jay Sibanda, a former teacher and leader of a support group for the two million Zimbabweans in exile in South Africa by 2003, told me about the feelings that prevailed at the time.

'We loved ZANU-PF and we worshipped Mugabe. After believing for so long that we would never really rule the country, here was the man who had made it all happen, and in our eyes, he could do no wrong. If he said that his party should control the press, we were ready to believe him. We were naive, and we paid for it dearly.'

The new editors lost no time positioning their publications behind the government, and freezing out comments by opposition parties and even dissenting voices inside ZANU-PF.

By the end of 1980, the 32 000 guerrillas who had moved to assembly points inside the country ahead of the elections, were still there. Trained men, many armed, were sitting around with nothing to do. It was a recipe for turmoil.

Gun battles broke out in the black townships around Salisbury as fighters slipped away from the boredom of the camps and went to town for women and beer. But in Matabeleland, something more sinister was happening. Nkomo's men were disappearing from their bases and going back to the bush, not into Zambia as before, but inside Zimbabwe.

As Minister for Home Affairs, Nkomo was responsible for the police, whose job it was to hunt down the deserters who were labelled 'dissidents'.

Soon, the renegades were not just moving around, but robbing stores and murdering white farmers.

There is still much debate about how much Nkomo knew. I have spoken to senior men in ZAPU who insist that, while ZIPRA did have armed members at large, the murders were carried out by former ZANLA guerrillas sent to Matabeleland to discredit Nkomo.

In February 1981, Nkomo was demoted to Minister without Portfolio, and at the first Independence Day celebrations on 18 April that year Mugabe spoke of the need to unite the country. There was little doubt about what he meant: the battle was on to consolidate all power in the hands of ZANU-PF.

On the same day, Salisbury's name was changed to Harare, Umtali became Mutare, and street names across the country were renamed after dead war heroes such as Chitepo and Tongogara, some of whom had been murdered by their own comrades.

In August, *Manica Post* assistant editor Stan Higgins and I went to Inyanga, seventy kilometres from Mutare, to compile our monthly feature on the resort town. Asian-looking soldiers had been seen drinking at hotels in Mutare, and from the lawns of the Montclair Hotel at Inyanga we looked down into a valley and saw rows of army tents. Without a word to the nation, Mugabe had brought 106 North Koreans into Zimbabwe to train a special brigade that would answer not to parliament, but directly to the prime minister.

The story ran that week, and Jean wrote an editorial condemning the North Korean presence as a form of neo-colonialism. She was arrested the next day and taken to Mugabe's house, where he told her she had no right to criticise his decisions. George Capon then fired her.

A young journalist who had worked as a government press secretary took her place. Geoff Nyarota understood that editors had to be subservient to ZANU-PF, but in later years he would turn against the party and become its greatest critic.

Guerrillas from both ZANLA and ZIPRA were being absorbed into the new national army, but thousands of Nkomo's men had begun deserting, and dissident activity had made Matabeleland ungovernable. In November 1980, Mugabe's treasurer, Enos Nkala, had addressed a mass rally in Bulawayo and threatened that ZANU would eventually destroy ZAPU. The result was a two-day battle during which ZIPRA and ZANLA fought each other in the streets of the Bulawayo suburb of Entumbane.

By the beginning of 1981, fewer than 20 000 guerrillas had been integrated into the armed forces, and hundreds of ZIPRA fighters were demobilised and given housing in Entumbane. In February, there was another fight in the Midlands province, in which 300 people were killed.

The government asked Enoch Dumbutshena, the former chief justice of Zimbabwe, to hold an inquiry into the matter, but the findings were never released. On 17 February 1982, Nkomo was fired from the government, and Mugabe announced that huge arms caches had been found in Matabeleland on farms owned by ZAPU.

The press pilloried Nkomo, who found it hard to get his side of the story into the papers. He insisted, right up to his death in 1998, that the government had planted the guns, grenades, rocket launchers and tons of ammunition.

Nkomo's commanders, Dumiso Dabengwa and Lookout Masuku, were arrested for treason, but the government was unable to secure their conviction. However, Mugabe had declared a state of emergency that allowed him to detain people indefinitely, and Dabengwa and Masuku remained behind bars. Masuku died in prison – his supporters believed he was poisoned – and Dabengwa was released after four years.

At the end of 1982, Mugabe's new unit, the Fifth Brigade, was deployed to

Matabeleland. What followed contributed greatly to ZANU-PF's determination, two decades later, to cling to power.

The soldiers set up extermination camps along the lines of those used by Pol Pot in Cambodia and Idi Amin in Uganda, and began to systematically eliminate the opposition. As they moved around the province, the Fifth Brigade marched to a song in which they pledged to defend not Zimbabwe, but Mugabe, with their lives. Thousands of men, women and children were rounded up, tortured and killed. Families were herded into their huts and the grass roofs set on fire. Anyone trying to escape through the flames was shot.

Gordon Mpofu was a child at the time, but was thirty-five years old and living in Johannesburg when he told me what had happened to his family.

'They came to our village and accused my father of helping the dissidents. He denied it, and so they assembled us all in the area between our huts and made us sit on the ground.

'Then they took my mother and tied rope around her ankles and hoisted her, upside down, into a tree, so that her head was maybe a metre off the ground. As we watched and cried, one of the soldiers gouged out her eyes with a knife, while others made a fire underneath her and baked her head until she was dead. I can still hear her screaming for help.

'My father was tied to the next tree, from where he was forced to watch.

'When my mother was dead, they beat my father with their rifle butts until he vomited and finally passed out. By the time they left our village, he was dead.'

Equally barbaric incidents were repeated all across Matabeleland, but the press neither reported them nor as much as questioned why a third of the country had been sealed off.

Estimates vary on how many people died in what became known as Gukurahundi, which means 'the wind that blows away the chaff before the rains', but the numbers range from 10 000 to 30 000. The truth probably lies somewhere in between.

In March 1983 Nkomo fled, dressed as a woman and travelling on foot, first to Botswana and then into exile in Britain. On arrival he held a news conference and accused Mugabe of slaughtering his people. 'Things are worse now than they ever were under Ian Smith,' he said. 'This is the worst government in the history of the country.'

Nkomo may have been right, but according to those Shona willing to even talk about the terror campaign, Gukurahundi generally met with approval in Mashonaland.

'First of all, in those days, we would never criticise anything Mugabe did,' Jordan Mashonganyika told me after going into exile in London. 'And, secondly, there was an unspoken feeling that this was revenge for the bad days our grandparents used to talk about before white rule, when the Matabele used to come and slaughter us and steal our cattle.'

Ambassadors and high commissioners in Harare knew full well what was going on, but said nothing. They reported the massacres to their governments at home, but the official silence was deafening.

When the Australian Broadcasting Corporation ran a documentary on the genocide, Prime Minister Malcolm Fraser – an outspoken advocate of human rights during the Smith regime – declined to comment. Indira Gandhi had been a constant voice of support for the guerrillas, but her government in India was mute.

Perence Shiri, who later became commander of the Zimbabwe Air Force, led Gukurahundi. After the massacres he was invited to Britain to attend a course in military procedure. The ministers in charge of the campaign, Sydney Sekeramayi and Emerson Mnangagwa – who would become both speaker of parliament and Mugabe's heir apparent – were criticised by no one, and to all intents the atrocities never took place.

To understand how Zimbabwe could descend into such madness without rebuke, one has only to remember Africa's appalling record on human rights, and how other leaders got away with even worse than Gukurahundi. I would go so far as to say that Mugabe, as one of the old men of Africa, matured politically at a time when violence was the norm rather than the exception, and he might genuinely have seen the Matabeleland campaign as a legitimate way of consolidating power.

Perhaps the greatest horror of apartheid is that, if a black tribe that made up only 15 per cent of South Africa's population had perpetrated it, the policy would have raised the ire of no one in the international community. Radical as that statement may be, one has only to look at ethnic cleansing in Indonesia or the murder of millions of people in Burundi and Rwanda, the dreaded Idi Amin and Milton Obote – who was almost as ruthless as Amin – or General Mengistu Haile Mariam, who starved thousands to death in Ethiopia, and at the lack of world condemnation for Third World dictatorships in general.

Before becoming the Swedish ambassador to Zimbabwe, Kristina Svensson was an active member of the anti-apartheid movement. I once asked her why her country had remained silent throughout the 1970s and 1980s on human rights in the rest of Africa.

'It was a period of post-colonial consolidation,' she told me. 'The period of one-party rule was necessary, and Sweden supported it.'

But if one accepts that argument, the notion of a universal declaration of human rights becomes meaningless, because the rights of some would become subjective and less important than those of others.

In 1989 South African journalist Donald Woods toured Australia to raise awareness for International Refugee Week. I was working for the *Australian* newspaper in Sydney and attended one of his briefings. Best remembered as the editor of the Eastern Cape newspaper the *Daily Dispatch*, and for being a friend of the black activist Steve Biko, who died in police custody in 1976 (their story was told in Richard Attenborough's film *Cry Freedom*), Woods had impressive credentials when it came to human rights, and his plea for change in South Africa touched my heart.

He spoke passionately about his country, where Nelson Mandela was still imprisoned, and about the campaign he had spearheaded in London to get British banks to withdraw their investments from South Africa. He had been active in Europe as well, pushing a range of multinationals to disinvest.

But his visit to Australia was in aid of Refugee Week, and compared with East Timor, Tibet, Afghanistan, Uganda and a score of other countries, the number of political refugees who had been forced to flee South Africa was tiny. At question time, I asked Woods whether the world would care more about the East Timorese or the Tibetans or Afghans if they were a different colour from the people who were persecuting them.

There was silence in the room before Woods, to his credit, took the challenge and replied: 'I quite agree with you. The world is full of terrible regimes, and we must fight abuse wherever we find it.'

His answer drew a round of applause, and when it died down, he added: 'But we need to focus our energies on the main problem, which is South Africa.'

The point of this story is not to diminish the stature of Woods, but to illustrate the mindset that allowed people such as Obote, Mengistu, Amin and Mugabe to misrule their countries with impunity. It's hard to counter Mugabe's complaint of unfair criticism against him and his government when decades of equal and greater abuse elsewhere failed to evoke international censure.

If independence in Africa had not been such a shambles, the history of southern Africa might have been very different. As it was, the backlash against political opponents in virtually every former colony served only to harden resolve in Salisbury and Pretoria – and, for that matter, in Lisbon until 1974 – against black majority rule.

As the colonial powers withdrew, the economies of the newly independent African states collapsed one after another, not because foreign interests conspired against the new rulers or because they lacked the opportunity to succeed, but due to corruption, waste, inefficiency and outright theft by those in power. Human rights were the greatest casualty in every instance, but for more than forty years, African tyranny was little more than a footnote on international agendas.

In many ways, the independence of Ghana in 1957 was to have been the litmus test for democracy in Africa, but the government of Kwame Nkrumah was one of the earliest examples of post-colonial political decline. When Ghana was declared a republic in 1960, Nkrumah's position changed from prime minister to president, but his conduct was that of an absolute monarch. He awarded contracts worth millions of dollars without reference to cabinet, let alone parliament. He set up a special company, the National Development Corporation, to receive 'gratuities' from foreign business people seeking the nod for a government deal, but the money was actually used to fund the ruling party or Nkrumah's personal expenses.

Not a word of criticism was raised in Europe, Britain or America, even when his policies began to impoverish the nation. In 1961, Nkrumah launched a range of state enterprises to develop fishing, farming and a steelworks. A total of fifty state corporations were created, providing jobs for those who supported him, but leaving Ghana with little real development and a huge foreign debt.

In 1962, there was an attempt on Nkrumah's life. He ordered the arrest of his foreign minister, Ako Adjei, and several other members of the cabinet, but they were acquitted due to lack of evidence. Nkrumah sacked the judges, appointed new ones and ordered a retrial, at which the men were found guilty.

The press was muzzled, with Nkrumah providing 'guidance' to editors on how best to report events. Special courts presided over by judges appointed by Nkrumah were set up to try those accused of political offences, and when verdicts displeased him, he passed a law allowing him to set aside the courts' decisions.

In 1964, books deemed 'counter-revolutionary' or critical of his philosophies were banned and all copies were removed from libraries. Later that year, Nkrumah declared Ghana a one-party state, making it a crime to oppose the ruling party.

In just nine years, Ghana had become a dictatorship, the freedom Nkrumah had espoused in his fight against colonialism, forgotten. Profiteers from the USA, Britain, Cuba, Israel, Russia – anyone willing to flatter the government and pay a bribe – had made money by exploiting Nkrumah's demented vision, while nothing was done by the United Nations, the Commonwealth, Britain, America, China or the Soviet bloc to halt the destruction of Ghana's economy and democracy.

The only countries that raised the alarm were in Africa. Tanzania's Julius Nyerere fell out with Nkrumah over the latter's hard line on the rapid unification of the continent – one of his passions – and neighbouring West African states objected to Ghana offering refuge to dissidents fleeing dictatorships in their own countries.

And there were many dictators to run away from.

Togo, Ghana's neighbour, gained independence from France in 1960. In 1963 the head of the army, General Eyadema, overthrew the government and made himself the sole source of power. Political activity was banned, the press was controlled and no criticism or even discussion of Eyadema's rule was tolerated. He managed to overcome divisions between north and south and largely rid the country of corruption, but at the cost of all the recognised human freedoms.

Niger, to the north, had also been granted independence by France in 1960, and in no time at all the president, Hamani Dori, banned all opposition and proclaimed himself the sole legitimate ruler. He and his ministers spent their time embezzling foreign aid and amassing personal fortunes, and the president's wife became one of the richest women in Africa. Madame Dori and her personal guards were killed in a coup in 1974 when Colonel Seyne Kountché seized power, and while his Supreme Military Council allowed no political activity, Kountché virtually wiped out corruption and resuscitated the country's farming sector. Within five years, Niger was at least able to feed itself.

With the exception of Gambia, all West African states had become dictatorships within a few years of winning independence, and countries in southern and East Africa fared little better.

Jomo Kenyatta, who led Kenya to independence from Britain in 1963, and who is often hailed as one of Africa's great statesmen, passed a law making it a capital offence to discuss what might happen to the country when he died. His KANU party funded itself from state coffers, while the opposition had to raise money from the public, with Kenyatta using the police to spy on them and thwart their efforts. He banned private broadcasting and turned the government-owned Voice of Kenya radio and television service into a KANU mouthpiece.

In Tanzania, Nyerere nationalised the majority of privately owned property and declared a one-party state. Elections were held every five years, but only his ruling Ujaama Party was allowed to field candidates.

Uganda came under the tyranny of Milton Obote, whose rule was so harsh that when General Idi Amin mounted a coup in 1971, crowds rushed into the streets to welcome the change. However, Amin took Uganda on his own journey into madness, and by the time he was overthrown by Nyerere's army in 1979, an estimated 300 000 people had died at the hands of the state.

Both Malawi and Zambia became dictatorships within five years of independence, while the former Belgian Congo was plunged into rebellion and war just one day after independence on 30 June 1960. By 1965, the American-sponsored Mobutu Sese Seko had become supreme dictator.

All across Africa, the earning power of working people collapsed while heads of state lined their own pockets, the media was gagged, dissenters were tortured and jailed, and, with the exception of Amnesty International and a few civic groups, virtually no voice was heard in the West clamouring for human rights in

Africa – except when it came to Rhodesia and South Africa. Throughout the Cold War, the unwritten rules of engagement meant that any tyrant denounced by the West was assured of support by the communist bloc, and vice versa.

When Mugabe came to power in 1980, the Soviets had plenty of their own men in Africa, including Machel in Mozambique, Neto – and later Dos Santos – in Angola, and Mengistu in Ethiopia. The French maintained an even tighter hold on the leaders of their former colonies, none of which was a democracy, while Britain and America supported a host of one-party states in East, West and southern Africa.

In Mugabe's defence, one would have to acknowledge that by the standards applied in Africa from the mid-1950s – when the first colonies became independent – until the fall of the Berlin Wall in 1989, he was not an exceptionally bad leader. But when the Cold War ended and human rights became a primary factor in international relations, Mugabe found it difficult to adjust, and from 1990 onwards his increasingly repressive regime was an aberration on a continent where most governments had succumbed, however grudgingly, to calls for greater political freedom.

In 1984, the Catholic Commission for Justice and Peace, which had been harshly critical of abuses by Smith's forces throughout the war in the 1970s, compiled a report based on interviews with victims of Gukurahundi and handed it to Mugabe, but did not release it for public consumption until 1998, when Zimbabwe's government was accused of murder.

Most of the victims were shot in public executions, often after being forced to dig their own graves in front of family members and fellow villagers. The largest number of dead in a single incident involved sixty-two young men and women shot on the banks of the Cewale River at Lupane on 5 March 1983. Seven survived with gunshot wounds, the other fifty-five died. More than once, the Fifth Brigade killed large groups of people at Lupane and Tsholotsho by burning them alive in their huts.

Simultaneous with the Fifth Brigade's deployment in Matabeleland, the government introduced a strict curfew, preventing anyone from entering or leaving the region, banning all forms of transport and restricting movement from dusk till dawn. Stores were closed in order to control food supplies, anyone travelling by bicycle or donkey cart was shot on sight, and no journalists were allowed anywhere near the area, making it all but impossible to report on the horrors being perpetrated against Nkomo's supporters. Only when some individuals managed to escape the containment did stories of the atrocities begin to surface.

The earliest accounts could not be independently verified, but offered evidence that the Fifth Brigade was trained or ordered to specifically target civilians. Dozens, sometimes hundreds, of people would be rounded up and marched at gunpoint to a school or beerhall, where they would be forced to sing Shona songs praising ZANU-PF and were beaten with sticks. These gatherings usually ended with public executions of former ZIPRA fighters, ZAPU officials or anyone else chosen at random, including women. Some incidents involved as many as two hundred soldiers and seldom fewer than forty.

When I spoke to Margaret Thatcher's foreign secretary, Lord Peter Carrington, chief negotiator of the peace accord that put Mugabe in power, he conceded that more could – and should – have been done in the early days to save the people of Africa from their leaders.

'Our record in Africa after independence has not been good,' he told me in a telephone interview. 'Of course it was difficult, but we could have done more. And we should have.'

Carrington resigned when he failed to foresee Argentina's invasion of the Falkland Islands in 1981, and was thus no longer in office when Mugabe started slaughtering his own people. But his successors took a decision not to comment or intervene, a policy that could only have been sanctioned by Mrs Thatcher.

In 2002, journalists Fergal Keane and Mark Dowd made a documentary for the BBC's *Panorama*, in which they asked how much Whitehall knew about Gukurahundi. Sir Martin Ewans, high commissioner in Harare at the time, admitted on camera that his instructions from London were to 'steer clear of it' when speaking to Mugabe.

'I think Matabeleland was a side issue,' he said. 'The real issues were much bigger. We were extremely interested that Zimbabwe should be a success story, and we were doing our best to help Mugabe and his people bring that about.'

His deputy, Roger Martin, actually witnessed some of the beatings, but agreed with his boss. 'The big picture involved keeping the show on the road for most of the country, recognising that this series of atrocities was happening in limited areas of Matabeleland, but not severing relations and watching the whole thing go down the tubes faster,' he said in the programme, screened on Sunday, 10 March 2002.

But Sir Robin Renwick, a retired diplomat who served as British ambassador in both Pretoria and Washington, disagrees.

'When this sort of thing happens in Bosnia or Kosovo,' he said, 'the world gets its act together and acts, and Milosevic ends up facing a war crimes tribunal in The Hague. Now if we really want to do something about these situations in Africa, we can't fail to try to do something similar.'

Could pressure from Britain have forced Mugabe to act differently at the time? Probably not. But if the Thatcher government had taken the matter to the United Nations, Zimbabwe might have been required to explain what was happening in the country, and thousands of lives could have been saved. As it was, when asked by the media what was happening in Matabeleland, Mugabe denied that anything untoward was taking place, blaming negative reports on 'reactionary foreign journalists'.

For all practical purposes, Zimbabwe was a one-party state by 1986. For the most part, command of the armed forces was in the hands of former ZANLA guerrillas, whose loyalty to Mugabe was unquestioned. Nkomo had returned from exile but was powerless, and for the time being, any resolve among the Matabele to oppose the government had been crushed.

While Mugabe was the prime minister, the Reverend Canaan Banana held the office of president. Little more than a figurehead, Banana was a Matabele and had long been active in politics, but had never been drawn into the squabbles that divided the nationalists. His neutrality made him the perfect choice as nominal president, a man to whom politicians from either camp could speak in confidence. It was from his office that the eventual *rapprochement* between Nkomo and Mugabe emanated.

During an interview in 2002, he told me how it happened:

When people talk about the unity accord, they talk as though the accord arrived one day in a three-piece suit and said 'I am here.' It was nothing of the sort. This was a protracted, hazardous journey. Initially, when the split between ZANU and ZAPU happened in the 1960s, the OAU made efforts to bring the parties together, but this did not occur until the Geneva Conference of 1976, when they came together to create a negotiating platform.

But this was just an organisational approach. Nkomo had established himself as an undisputed nationalist leader over a period of many years throughout the country, and you can imagine how difficult it must have been for him to accept Mugabe as leader.

Initially, when the so-called dissident issue came up, there was a very deep attitude of mistrust between Nkomo and Mugabe. To talk about cooperation or unity at all was not possible, so one had to address first and foremost the question of attitudes and relationships to try to remove the feelings of mistrust.

The very first meeting was in 1986, during Gukurahundi, and Simon Muzenda, Maurice Nyagumbo and Emerson Mnangagwa attended it on the ZANU side, and Joseph Msika, John Nkomo and Naison Ndhlovu on the ZAPU side. We tried to agree about the basis of discussions, and they went away to report and set up a number of committees.

When these committees met, they were even further apart, so I said, let's try this thing again at the highest level, and I invited Mugabe and Joshua Nkomo to State House. Initially I spoke to each of them separately. Mugabe was bent on wanting to resolve the civil war by military force alone, and my argument was that you needed a political solution. Nkomo expressed total distrust of Mugabe.

So, I could see that communication was non-existent, and I first had to deal with the issue of trust. During the subsequent meetings, there were lots of bitter exchanges and shouting matches, but sometimes it is important to open the wound in order to dress it.

I even said to them, 'Get it out. Put it on the table and discuss it.' But I also said, 'Zimbabwe is greater than these two parties and than the two of you, so we have to find a way out of this problem.'

Initially, there were three things blocking the way. First was the question of leadership and who would head the new party. Next was the name. Would we call it ZANU or ZAPU or a mix of the two or something completely new? And finally, of course, the principles upon which that unity would be predicated.

Nkomo had always seen himself as a nationalist leader drawing support from across the country, and in the old days, if you looked at the ZAPU leadership, there were more Shonas than Ndebele, so the idea that Nkomo was an Ndebele leader was not true, and he did not need to prove that.

Mugabe suggested that Nkomo should remain with a constituency, but he declined because he said he was a national leader, and I respect him for that. So he had at the back of his mind that it would be difficult for him to play second fiddle.

One of the greatest problems was the name, and I believe that ZANU was unfair, but ZAPU had to come in under the name of ZANU-PF. I asked Mugabe why he could not compromise on this, but he said: 'We are in power, and if we lose our name we become irrelevant.' So I said to Joshua, 'What is important is not the name but the content and to what extent ZAPU is going to play a prominent role in the unified government.'

There are those who look back now and say that it was not really unity. Nkomo's party was simply swallowed by ZANU-PF. But Nkomo really did enter the deal in good faith. I can remember his words at the signing ceremony: 'Unity is not an event but a process, and there are no winners and no losers.' But he felt let down in the end. I was close to him up to his death and he felt let down that the other side had not moved. He also felt let down by the people of Zimbabwe, who did not return his candidates in the elections.

On 22 December 1987, Nkomo signed the peace accord merging ZAPU with ZANU, and was given the meaningless post of vice-president. At the same time the constitution was changed, abolishing Banana's position and making Mugabe executive president with wider powers than any leader had enjoyed since the first parliament was opened in 1923.

Mugabe could decree legislation and have it passed retroactively by parliament, he appointed judges and was personally exempt from any legal action. One of his first moves was to issue a blanket amnesty for all soldiers of the Fifth Brigade, rendering them immune from prosecution.

The era of dictatorship had arrived, and the only voice of opposition was that of Ndabaningi Sithole, whose Ndau people in Chipinge had returned him to parliament as their representative.

In 1990, Mugabe enlarged parliament from 100 to 150 seats, with only 120 seats elected. Mugabe appointed the other 30, so that in future elections ZANU-PF would have to win only 46 seats to gain a majority, while other parties would need 76.

Edgar Tekere, the man who had walked into Mozambique with Mugabe in 1976, quit the government and began speaking out against the president's new powers. This was not what he had fought for, said Tekere.

He formed the Zimbabwe Unity Movement (ZUM), and stood as an alternative candidate in the presidential election. The state-controlled media shut him out of all debate, while the police harassed members of the public trying to attend his meetings.

Mugabe had already taken Smith's spy force, the Central Intelligence Organisation, and merged it with the police Special Branch, but now he made the CIO a department of the presidency, so that only he and his closest allies knew what they were doing and what information they were gathering on his opponents ... and his colleagues.

ZANU-PF's power was total, and Mugabe lifted the state of emergency. In July 1990 he hosted CHOGM, and the Commonwealth leaders drew up the Harare Declaration, laying out the minimum standards of human rights and freedoms that all member countries were required to apply. Mugabe's government was in breach of almost every one of the principles, but, in fairness, so were most member countries in Africa.

This was perhaps the last Commonwealth meeting that carried any weight. The 'old boys' club' of former colonies had grown increasingly irrelevant as the United Nations and the two superpowers, Russia and America, directed most of the meaningful debate on world affairs. Within five years, global politics would change to a degree that the kings, queens, presidents and prime ministers meeting in Zimbabwe could not have imagined.

In the old Soviet bloc, the Berlin Wall had already been torn down and Russia was about to have a new, democratic government. The despots of Eastern Europe, a major source of support for Third World tyrants, would all be gone within a year.

In South Africa, FW de Klerk had taken the reins of government from the bumbling PW Botha, and in February 1990 would release Nelson Mandela from prison after twenty-seven years. At the same time, liberation movements such as the ANC and PAC, as well as the South African Communist Party, would be unbanned, and all-party talks would pave the way for a new, liberal constitution and a democratic election.

Mandela became South Africa's first black president in May 1994, and Mugabe's influence in the region collapsed. World leaders now deferred to Mandela for advice, and South Africa, with one of the most democratic constitutions in the world, was held up as the new example of what African states should and could be.

# 6

# Fortress ZANU

Perhaps the most important thing to understand about Zimbabwe's electorate is that most people did not switch their vote from ZANU-PF.

Until the formation of an organised opposition in 1999, they simply didn't vote.

Participation in local, general and presidential elections was consistently low after independence, with less than 10 per cent of registered voters bothering to cast their ballots in some constituencies.

'There was a sense that nothing was going to change, and also, things were not that bad anyway,' according to Marcia Katsande, who was a teacher in Masvingo before moving to Johannesburg.

'There was no organised opposition, though there was usually a choice on the ballot papers. But the ZANU-PF candidate was the only one from an organised political party; the rest were independents who were unknown to the people and who usually did little by way of campaigning.'

Marcia, who moved to South Africa in 2000 when election violence got out of hand in her home area, told me that Zimbabweans had always been sceptical of candidates for public office.

'There is a suspicion that independent candidates want to get into parliament to enrich themselves, and they don't take time to tell people otherwise. And radio and TV were all controlled by ZANU-PF, so it was hard for anyone else to get a campaign message across through the media.'

Even in the 1980s and early 1990s, she said, candidates were victims of intimidation.

'It would have been hard for anyone to really campaign, really hold meetings and rallies, because the police would tend not to give permits and, if they did, ZANU-PF would visit the candidate with warnings to stop making a noise. The usual line was: "You are embarrassing the president and we will not stand for that."

'It was nothing like the blatant intimidation that came later, and the police and army were not involved, though CIO may have been. ZANU-PF knew it was untouchable, so there was no need for the kind of violence evident from 1999, but those in office didn't make it easy for anyone to stand against them.'

Until 2000, ZANU-PF held 148 of the 150 seats in Zimbabwe's parliament, 30 of which were filled by non-elected members appointed by the president.

In 1980 the labour movement, like most social structures, was taken over by ZANU-PF, and Robert Mugabe's cousin, Albert, was appointed president of the Zimbabwe Congress of Trade Unions (ZCTU). After a series of strikes that embarrassed the government, Albert fell out of favour with the party, and one morning his wife found him dead in the swimming pool of their suburban home.

In 1988, a former mine worker, Morgan Tsvangirai, was appointed secretary general of the ZCTU. Born in 1952, he had no formal education and had not even finished high school. Most of his working life had been spent underground, and after ten years with Bindura Nickel he had risen to a senior post in the mining union.

As with most of the nation's office bearers, he had good credentials within the party and was referred to in the state-owned press as Comrade Tsvangirai.

Under his leadership the labour movement remained under ZANU-PF control, but in 1991 the International Monetary Fund (IMF) convinced Mugabe to accept an Economic Structural Adjustment Programme (ESAP), which put an end to the payment of state subsidies inherited from the Rhodesian era, and introduced fees for government services, including health and education. At the same time, the price of basic goods such as maize meal began to rise.

Having a member of parliament in the family was almost a guarantee of a job, and the system kept MPs loyal to Mugabe. If a backbencher stepped out of line, he or she could be called in and reminded of the brother who worked for Air Zimbabwe, the two cousins at home affairs, and so on.

The IMF demanded that the government payroll be slashed, and that import controls be relaxed to allow foreign goods to compete against local products, thus raising domestic industrial standards. Regulations governing the start-up of small- and medium-sized businesses were streamlined, reducing the notorious red tape that could see a foreign investor waiting two or three years to get a project off the ground.

The public service was bloated and incompetent, and the mentality of business had changed little since the days of UDI. The economy had not opened up under ZANU-PF rule, and exchange controls discouraged investors from bringing capital into the country.

A perpetual shortage of goods – especially imported items – created a commercial culture in which the seller was always right. Shop assistants were courteous enough, but customers were left with the clear impression that attendance was tantamount to a favour. And, in many cases, it was. If you needed a refill for your Parker pen and there were none on the shelves, you would have to chat up the owner of the local stationery store before he'd pull one out of the stash he kept for special clients.

With most large companies being run by accountants rather than salespeople, the business ethos became rigid and unimaginative. One of the best examples was that of a greeting card manufacturer, who produced a new range in 1997 and printed the retail price of Z$10.01 on the cellophane packaging. There was no thought of making it Z$9.99 to attract sales.

Zimbabwe's largest pharmacy chain, QV, applied a similar policy, relying on computers to calculate the sales price based on cost plus profit and 15 per cent sales tax; if the result came out at Z$1 401.06, so be it.

'We can't do anything else, it's how the prices are calculated,' the QV manager in Borrowdale, one of Harare's posher suburbs, told me. 'The customers just have to buy at that price.'

This take-it-or-leave-it approach, coupled with a limited choice of products, led to a poor relationship between manufacturers, retailers and the buying public, already harbouring suspicions that those who sold the goods were – at least in part – responsible for the high prices that confronted consumers from 1991.

ESAP produced ever-increasing hardships and was especially tough on poor families, where four or five people depended on the income of one worker. Adding to a growing sense of despair in the mid-1990s was the baby boom that followed independence. From a black population of only six million in 1977, the number had doubled to more than twelve million by 2000.

A glance at a population graph by year of birth shows a bulge between 1980 and 1982. By 1997, those children were in their teens and at high school. While Mugabe had introduced free primary education in 1980 (though parents were still faced with the cost of books and uniforms), high schools demanded tuition fees, and these jumped with the introduction of ESAP. The squeeze on family budgets was tight enough to push the children of poorer families out of school prematurely, and added to public anger.

'There was talk, a lot of talk,' Marcia Katsande recalled. 'People were distressed by how little they were able to buy when they got paid at the end of the month, but compared with how things became, it was paradise. There was no shortage of basic goods but they were becoming expensive, and people started skipping meals. But the real anger started when people could no longer afford to go *kumusha*.'

The issue of transport is central to understanding the revolt against Mugabe.

If you ask a black South African working in Johannesburg where he comes from, the answer will most likely be Soweto, Alexandra or one of the other satellite townships around the city.

Ask a Zimbabwean the same question, and he will tell you about his *kumusha*

– his rural family seat and spiritual home – and he will say the word with the reverence a devout Catholic might use when talking about the Vatican.

Phillip Kuleti was born in Mozambique and moved to Rhodesia as a child when his father went there to work. The family settled in Rusape, 120 kilometres east of Harare. His name gives him away as a foreigner, because the Shona language has no 'L'. In 2000, he was one of dozens of black wage earners who spoke to me about their life in Zimbabwe.

'No one really lives in Harare,' Phillip explained. 'Everyone comes from some other part of the country and works in town, but their parents and young brothers and sisters will stay in the rural areas.

'Although I was born in Mozambique, if someone asks me, "*Unobva kupi kumusha?*" [Where is your rural home?], I will tell them about Rusape, because that is where my family settled. I have lived very little time in Rusape because I worked mostly as a hotel chef in Bulawayo and Harare, and even, for a few years, in South Africa. But people want to know where you come from, and by that they mean your rural home in Zimbabwe.

'It is one of the first things black people ask when they meet each other.'

Going home is a regular pilgrimage for city folk, and it is not surprising that few people have roots in urban areas, because industrialisation only began in earnest after UDI in 1965. Thus, where black residents of Johannesburg or Durban may be fourth of fifth generation city dwellers, urban Zimbabweans have not yet developed that sense of belonging.

Which is not to say that large numbers of them yearn for a permanent return to country life. On the contrary, working the land is seen as the lowest job of all, with less status than a street sweeper. The greatest insult among urban dwellers is: *Dzokera kumusha unorima mbambaira!* It means 'go back to the rural areas and grow sweet potatoes', and implies that the target does not have the know-how to make a decent living in town.

Coupled with inflation, the scrapping of subsidies on rural bus fares caused not just physical hardship because it left less money for other things: it became an emotional issue. People working in town could not see their parents as often as before, and those living *kumusha* could not visit the city to catch up with family and buy a few luxuries.

But the real pain is rooted far more deeply in Zimbabwe's culture. Among the Shona, no one ever dies of natural causes. If your aunt is ninety-five, blind and bedridden, her death will still be attributed to the fact that someone hated her enough to bump her off with a spell or by sending an evil spirit to do the deed.

The closest relatives will then consult a *n'anga* [spirit medium], who will help to identify the culprit, though only in the most general terms. Often, the *n'anga* does little more than confirm that someone in the extended family or inner circle was the culprit. At other times, the medium will absolve everyone and state that the death was just an act of God, but in most cases the verdict is a broad accusation, such as 'one of your neighbours was to blame'.

In a village where each hut is part of a cluster containing a dozen or more dwellings, there are many neighbours to choose from, and there is rarely any finger pointing, but consulting the *n'anga* is part of the Shona mourning process.

The visit takes place after the funeral, which gives the family a chance to see who has attended the ceremony and how much grief they showed. If a close relative does not make it to the graveside, he or she might be regarded with suspicion.

A year after the burial, another ceremony, the *nyaradzo*, takes place. The word means to comfort or console, and this is the final letting-go of grief, a ritual beautiful to behold. It is usually held in the dead person's hut, and the emphasis is very much on the immediate family, helping them over the final stages of their loss.

In April 1998, Tawanda Chinoshava was working in Harare as an office clerk when both his parents were struck and killed by lightning at Buhera, about 200 kilometres south-east of Harare.

'The funeral and the *nyaradzo* are so central to our culture that to miss either one is not just painful, but it tears into your mind and causes you not to sleep for many weeks,' he told me.

'When my parents died, it was the family and my friends who helped me to carry on, and if anything happens to one of their loved ones, I would travel as far as I needed to in order to be there for the funeral and *nyaradzo*.

'But I know that it may not be possible, because nowadays most of us don't even have enough money to travel home more than once a year,' he said.

'I can remember that in 1995, when I started working in Harare, I used to go home every month. Then it became once in three months, and in 2000 I managed it only twice. The year after that the bus fares were so high, I could not go *kumusha* even once, and that filled me with sorrow in a way I cannot explain.'

In 1997, the cost of food, school fees and rural bus fares was disrupting people's lives in ways they had never experienced before, and in Phillip Kuleti's view, by the middle of that year, 'the talk had turned to rage'.

'In 1977, I was working in Harare and I earned Z$20 a month. The bus fare from Harare to Rusape was 40 cents, stewing meat was 30 cents a kilogram and bread 20 cents a loaf. Although I had four children, three of them at school, we were never short of money.'

By 1997, the bus fare to Rusape had risen to Z$180, or 450 times the cost twenty years before, but although Phillip's salary of Z$600 a month was double the minimum wage, it was only thirty times as much as he earned in 1977.

The IMF adjustment programme can be blamed for some of the problems, but government inefficiency, a still bloated yet stagnant public service and corruption at high levels meant that any economic policy was doomed.

It was all very well to advocate opening up the country for investment, but when installing a telephone line took up to two years and invariably involved a bribe (in some rural areas there was a fourteen-year backlog), and obtaining residence permits for foreign staff could take just as long (if they were issued at all), Zimbabwe was not a business-friendly environment.

Botswana and South Africa were much more attractive propositions, and many companies that did set up operations in Zimbabwe during the 1980s, moved to South Africa once Mandela became president.

In December 1997, Morgan Tsvangirai explained the failure of ESAP as follows in an interview with the South African *Mail & Guardian* newspaper: 'At the stage we had reached [in 1991] some form of structural adjustment was needed. The general vote was thumbs down for structural adjustment. But it was a failure of administration, not policy. It was a failure of the government, not the strategy.'

Rising prices did not curb government spending. On the contrary, towards the end of 1997, Mugabe announced that each of his ministers would receive a new Jeep Grand Cherokee, imported from the USA.

Sally had died of kidney failure, and Mugabe married his secretary, Grace Marufu, despite the forty-year age gap between them. The first couple took frequent shopping trips to London, where they spent small fortunes at Harrods, and even toyed with the idea of buying a long-haul private jet. For the average Zimbabwean, these were not signs that the government was concerned about their suffering, or that a plan was being developed to make things better.

As Tsvangirai said in 1997: 'The problem is that Mugabe doesn't have an economic strategy. He has this huge bureaucracy, which is used for patronage. But the economy is not growing and he is spending more and more money. We are not living within our means.'

Organised opposition came from the last source Mugabe would have expected.

Zimbabwean author Shimmer Chinodya was perhaps the first person to raise the plight of war veterans in his 1989 novel, *Harvest of Thorns*, which I commend to anyone who wants to understand the origins and passions of the civil war of the 1970s.

Whether they had been in the front lines or peeling potatoes in the barracks, members of the Rhodesian armed forces, black and white, qualified for a government pension. Mugabe inherited this obligation at independence, and to his credit, never shirked it.

However, his own fighters, and those of ZIPRA, received no such consideration, and were left to fend for themselves after the war, without so much as government health care. Economic decline affected them no less than any other Zimbabwean, and in some instances the veterans were actually worse off than those who had remained civilians, because many had joined the armed struggle before finishing school and were qualified to do only menial and low-paying work.

This applied especially to non-voluntary combatants, who had been abducted from schools in the rural areas and marched at gunpoint to training camps in Mozambique, Botswana or Zambia, from which they returned as guerrilla fighters. Two decades after the war, while the ruling elite grew rich and fat, they were abandoned to eke out an existence in town or on the land.

The war veterans began talking among themselves about this inequality, and a retired CIO officer told me that he had reported the danger signals in a briefing to senior members of the intelligence service.

'No one listened. The war had become irrelevant. Twice a year, on the anniversary of independence and on Heroes' Day, Mugabe would talk about the sacrifice made by the veterans, but for most of the time, they were forgotten.'

He believed that this was part of a wider problem of marginalisation.

'The greatest number of war vets were from Masvingo province and belonged to the Karanga tribe. And there were many Korekores from Mount Darwin, some Manyikas from the east, and, of course, the Matabele.

'But Zimbabwe was being run by Mugabe's tribe, the Zezurus, who were also dominant in business. Their origins were the districts around Harare, and because they had better access to the capital and knew their way around, they tended to find work fairly easily. The destitute were mostly in other parts of the country, and had few lines of communication to senior levels of the party.'

In 1992, Mugabe set up a fund to help people who had sustained injuries during the war. However, few front-line fighters benefited; a total of Z$450 million (at that time worth US$40 million) went missing, and a list of the alleged payouts read like a ZANU-PF who's who, as the following examples show:

- Robin Shava: former Zimbabwe Broadcasting Corporation employee – 100 per cent disability, Z$483 535.
- Vivian Mwashita: MP for the Harare suburb of Hatfield – 94 per cent disability, Z$579 091.
- Perence Shiri: Air Force chief and the man who led the Fifth Brigade massacres in Matabeleland – 50 per cent disability, Z$90 249.
- Joyce Mujuru: cabinet minister and wife of former army commander Solomon Mujuru – 55 per cent disability, Z$389 472.
- Augustine Chihuri: police commissioner – 20 per cent disability, Z$138 664.

There wasn't even an attempt to create credible injuries. Commissioner Chihuri got his money for dermatitis on his feet, while senior politicians claimed for blisters, aches and stress, though many had spent the war in the safety of Maputo or Lusaka.

In the five years after the fund was set up in 1992, a total of Z$1.5 billion was handed out, but the majority of the war vets got nothing.

The anger surfaced in December 1996, when a former ZANLA guerrilla, Brigadier Gibson Mashingaidze, commanding officer of the army's Fourth Brigade based in Masvingo, delivered the eulogy at the funeral of a friend with whom he had served during the war. Mukoma Musa had died in poverty, and Mashingaidze told the mourners he had paid Z$10 000 from his own pocket to give Musa a decent burial.

In an unmistakeable reference to Mugabe and the ZANU-PF leadership, the angry officer continued: 'Some people now have ten farms and luxury yachts and have developed fat stomachs, while ex-combatants like Comrade Musa lived in poverty.

'Is this the ZANU-PF I trusted with my life? The party that promised to care for us in our old age?'

Even though he was still a loyal member of the party, he said, he believed that the leaders had abandoned their most faithful supporters.

The state media castigated Mashingaidze, and the *Herald* ran an editorial about the need for the military to stay out of politics. Defence minister Moven Mahachi relieved him of his command in Masvingo, and issued a statement warning soldiers to either keep their own counsel on controversial issues, or resign.

'Army officers are not supposed to take a political stance,' he said. 'They pay their allegiance to the people and government of this country.'

But the die had been cast. Mugabe had ignored the people who had not only fought his war, but intimidated voters in the 1980 election, ensuring his victory at the polls.

Worse was in store. In 1995 another former guerrilla, Margaret Dongo, had been dumped as the ZANU-PF candidate for the Harare seat of Sunningdale. She decided to run as an independent, and despite a media campaign against her, she won.

As more information came to hand on how extensively the war pension fund had been looted, Dongo tabled a motion calling for the Auditor-General to mount a full investigation. Although Dongo herself had been a beneficiary, a number of ZANU-PF backbenchers voiced their support for her cause, and in the end more than 100 defied party discipline and voted with her.

The president was patron of the War Veterans' Association (WVA), a group that represented fighters from both ZANLA and ZIPRA. Their leader was a medical doctor called Chenjerai Hunzvi, who had spent the war in the safety of Poland, where he finished his studies and married a citizen, abandoning her and their two children when he returned to Zimbabwe at independence. When Hunzvi became a household name due to his leadership of the increasingly violent land seizures by war veterans, his former wife told a London newspaper that her marriage had been a nightmare. 'He was a cruel and vile man who took delight in beating me,' she said. 'And as for the war, he never fired a shot. He saw no action at all.'

But Hunzvi was a born orator with a gleam in his eye, and he was able to whip up his comrades and press them to take action against the government.

His rise to power began in 1995 when, because of his medical qualifications, he was employed to assess the injuries suffered by people claiming compensation.

'He suddenly found himself in the role of Father Christmas,' I was told by Gibson Mhlanga, a ZIPRA war vet who was shouted down by his colleagues in 1997 when he tried to speak out against Hunzvi, and later moved to Johannesburg.

'With his nod, you got some money. Without it, your claim was turned down. It was because of this that the mighty in the land sought favour with Hunzvi, and he rose to some position of importance. It was ridiculous for him to be leading the protest to demand money for the war veterans – he was a main player in the theft.'

But Mhlanga's voice was a lonely one, and Hunzvi was duly elected chairman of the WVA.

At that stage, Mugabe still had a chance to regain control by bringing his backbench into line, but he dithered. Military action against the war vets was not an option, because former guerrillas led Zimbabwe's army, air force and police.

In July 1997, Hunzvi demanded a meeting with Mugabe, who refused, and instead asked Judge Godfrey Chidyausiku to head an inquiry into the looting of the compensation fund, promising that the treasury would consider allocating more money for the veterans.

Hunzvi could smell blood, and he took his WVA members to the streets for three days of rowdy but non-violent protest. On the second day, they chanted war slogans outside the main government building before marching on a convention centre where Mugabe was meeting with African-Americans, but he still refused to see Hunzvi.

In the days that followed, the protestors turned up at any meeting where Mugabe was due to make a speech, even disrupting events over the long weekend in August set aside to honour those who had died in battle. When Mugabe tried to make a speech at Heroes' Acre outside Harare, the war vets shouted and banged iron bars on the bonnets of ministers' Mercedes, making such a din that the president folded up his notes and left. The protestors moved to the ZANU-PF building near the Harare Sheraton and ran from floor to floor, overturning furniture and filing cabinets. Ten days later, Mugabe agreed to meet with their representatives.

By then, it was too late. Although there were only 32 000 guerrillas at the end of the war, and it could be assumed that a fair number of them would have died over the intervening twenty years, Hunzvi claimed to have 50 000 veterans on his books. They would settle for nothing less than a pension for life, an immediate payment of Z$50 000 and a piece of arable land each.

Their representatives made it clear to Mugabe that unless the cash was paid to them by the end of the year, and their plots allocated within six months after that, they would invade white farms and take the land by force.

Shortly after the meeting, Judge Chidyausiku's inquiry into the looting unearthed the perfect weapon with which to destroy Hunzvi and discredit him in the eyes of both his followers and the nation. The WVA chairman had received more than half a million dollars from the fund for loss of hearing and a leg wound. If one added up his claims, Chenjerai Hunzvi was 117 per cent disabled.

But that wasn't the only revelation.

Grace Mugabe's brother, Reward Marufu, had been classified 95 per cent disabled by Hunzvi, and was paid Z$821 668 shortly before being posted to the Zimbabwe high commission in Canada in April 1997. It was checkmate.

The report sparked furious debate within ZANU-PF on how best to handle the affair. Some felt that Hunzvi's fraud could be used to bring him to book and lock him away, but the majority feared he would go down fighting, taking Mugabe's family and much of the cabinet with him.

So they decided to pay.

By Christmas 1997, all 50 000 of the people calling themselves war veterans – and many had suspect credentials – would receive a one-off sum of Z$50 000, followed by a monthly pension of Z$2 000 each, which would be subject to future review in line with inflation.

It was one thing for cabinet to capitulate, quite another to find the money. Zimbabwe's ruling party had always lived well, with luxury cars and fat salaries for ministers and the well connected who ran the parastatals, a large army and a growing foreign debt.

When the decision was announced, a World Bank task force flew in for consultations, but they might as well have stayed at home. The government ordered the Reserve Bank to print enough money to cover the payouts and the endgame was set in motion.

The government decided to fund part of the war vet compensation by raising sales tax from 15 to 17.5 per cent, increasing the tax on electricity and imposing a fuel surcharge of 20 cents a litre.

Tsvangirai called a general strike for 9 December, and as I drove into town from my home in the northern suburbs that day, I noticed that every access road was filled with thousands of people heading for the city centre, not quite sure what form their protest would take, but keen to make their feelings known.

I dropped in to see Robert Cutty, owner of a safari company and one of the most astute businessmen I've ever known, who always had his ear to the ground. He was alone in a triple-storey office block, and when I rang the doorbell, he ushered me in nervously.

'You shouldn't be wandering around,' he said, as we walked to his office. 'If people think you're going to work, they'll beat you up.'

We both made several telephone calls to contacts and shared our reports on what was going on. That afternoon, I typed the following note to Nick Russell, a friend in Melbourne:

What a day it's been. Lots of phones off around Harare because the exchange has closed down. The post office, public service and all the shops and restaurants are also shut. Meikles, Sheraton and the other hotels are on skeleton staff.

This morning at 9 am about 500 protesters gathered in Africa Unity Square in the centre of town and began a peaceful demonstration. The local police unit did the worst thing and fired tear gas into the crowd and began chasing them around the square. Word of the police action spread, and within an hour demonstrator numbers had swelled to 3 000 as workers poured out of the few shops and offices that were open and came to join the demo at the square.

By 10 am the police had lost control of the situation; despite attempts to close the city centre and erect roadblocks on all streets leading to town, people still streamed into the city. More tear gas, a BBC reporter was beaten with a truncheon and riots started in Southerton, Mbare and Chitungwiza. Cars were overturned, buses stopped and emptied of their passengers, who then joined the riots, and the police turned their efforts towards stopping the crowds from entering town.

The Zimbabwe dollar has tumbled and is reported to be 40 to the US$ (from 21). The government has reportedly seized all remaining forex accounts, but as always in Africa, rumours are more common than news and I can't confirm this until banks open again tomorrow – if they do.

There's a strong mood for change, and even ZBC-TV gave reasonably impartial coverage of the riots. Police commissioner Augustine Chihuri said his officers would do everything they could to control the riots, because there was such a high level of resentment towards government that the police could not risk allowing demonstrations to proceed.

Last week, the government declared the protest illegal, but yesterday, the ZCTU obtained an injunction from the High Court which effectively allowed them to proceed with the demo as long as it was peaceful. I suspect that this led to the police tear-gas attack this morning. They had to turn it into a non-peaceful event before they could intercede.

The main gripe is the 2.5% sales tax hike and 20 cents a litre jump in petrol – plus an increase in the sales tax on electricity bills from five to 10%. In true Zim fashion, storekeepers have used the sales tax hike to raise prices well above 2.5%, and if I was living 10-to-a-room in Mbare, I guess I'd also be on the streets.

The government tried to say that white employers had incited the strike, but on ZTV the rioters dismissed this as an attempt to divert attention from the real issues. Mugabe was supposed to address the nation at 2 pm, but hasn't done so. The road to the airport was impassable at 11 am. Tourism will be stuffed for a while. The people have tasted people-power and they know now that they can outnumber and outpace the police. Mugabe could bring out the army, but that would do even more damage to his image as head of the OAU.

Thankfully, there's been no trouble in the suburbs, except for gangs moving through the shopping centres enforcing the stayaway, and giving people 10 minutes to send their staff out and close for the day. It's going to be an interesting week.

As the day wore on, mobs smashed shop windows and the looting began. Police fired tear gas and restored order as best they could, but, like Hunzvi and his war vets, the people had found their voice.

Mugabe blamed 'whites and foreigners' for inciting the riots, and a gang of eight men visited Tsvangirai at his office in the CBD, beat him up and tried to throw him out of a window on the tenth floor before the arrival of a co-worker scared the thugs and they ran away. The labour leader was shaken when he addressed a media conference later that day, but vowed to continue the fight.

'We have been strengthened,' he told reporters, 'and there is no going back now. You can remove leaders, but not the cause. This is class warfare, between the haves and have-nots.'

A source in the CIO told me privately that the gang that had attacked Tsvangirai had nothing to do with the government, but had been settling a personal score. I never believed the story, because if it was true, no effort would have been spared to find the culprits and parade them in court to back up the claim that ZANU-PF was not a violent party. Nothing of the kind happened, and no one was ever arrested for trying to kill Tsvangirai.

After the riots, most town-dwellers went *kumusha* for Christmas, but when they returned after the holidays, they were far from merry.

On Sunday 7 January 1998, the privately owned *Standard* ran a front-page story detailing imminent rises in the cost of basic goods. Cooking oil would jump from Z$12 to nearly Z$20, and soap, sugar and most essentials would rise sharply in price as well. But the hardest blow was maize meal, which the newspaper reported would cost 36 per cent more.

Within a week the first increases took hold, and the government announced a further 21 per cent rise in the price of maize.

Tsvangirai seized the initiative and called a three-day strike from 19 January. This time, the ZCTU presented the government with a set of demands in advance:

- remove the recent 2.5 per cent increase in sales tax to pay war veterans;
- abolish the 5 per cent 'development levy' on salaries;
- end the 15 per cent tax on profits from pension investments; and
- meet with the ZCTU for broad negotiations on the economy.

The union also released figures showing that salaries had lost 75 per cent of their real value since 1980, that food prices had escalated by 500 per cent, and that at 38 per cent, Zimbabwe had one of the highest average personal income tax rates in the world.

As dawn broke on the first day of the strike, the black commuter suburbs of Chitungwiza, Tafara and Kuwadzana were cordoned off by police who deployed in force, armed with batons and ready to beat the crowds into submission. Instead, their vehicles were set alight and the law enforcers fled on foot.

A pall of tear gas hung over the CBD, and the staff of British Airways, who had gone to work as usual on the eighth floor of an office block near Meikles Hotel, were trapped in the building overnight, not for fear of being attacked by the crowd, but because of the gas. A canister was also fired into the foyer of Meikles by mistake and guests had to take refuge in their rooms.

Labour minister Nathan Shamuyarira called for calm, and announced that a proposed second price rise of 21 per cent on maize meal would be dropped. But the crowds were in no mood to stop. The ZBC accused the rioters of 'looting, killing and raping', but only the first claim was true, with many stores being forcibly entered and emptied of their stock.

I went into town on the second day and found a war zone. There was broken glass everywhere, and I had to keep my car windows closed and breathe through a handkerchief to avoid the tear-gas fumes, but none of the rioters showed any hostility towards me.

That night, Mugabe withdrew the police from the townships and deployed the army. Most of the rioters had gone home to eat, sleep and ready themselves for a third day of action, and the soldiers, armed with whips, batons and assault rifles, went from house to house.

Douglas, a fruit vendor, had served in ZANLA during the war but rejected Hunzvi's doctrine. The weekend after the riots he was back at his stall near my local shopping centre, and told me what had happened near his home in Tafara.

'We noticed that the police had gone and things were suddenly quiet. Then the army vehicles came in around seven o'clock and there were many of them, all full of soldiers.

'The men jumped off the trucks and began running from house to house, pushing or breaking open doors and pulling people out into the street. Some families were eating dinner and the soldiers dragged them all out, mother, father and children, and began beating them with whips and sticks.

'The beat me and my family, and at my neighbour's house they broke the arm of his twelve-year-old daughter. They didn't care if you were part of the riots or you had stayed at home. Everyone was beaten equally.'

The hard line ended the riot, but could not quell the anger, especially when the main story in the *Independent* at week's end revealed that the government had just imported fifty Mercedes Benz cars for ministers.

Mugabe's reaction to the display of grass-roots anger was to play the race card, ranting about how whites were behind ZCTU. He also belittled Tsvangirai, scorning his lack of formal education and the fact that he had not taken part in the war.

'You have the misplaced belief,' he said in the state media, 'that you are more powerful than the government. People must weigh themselves and see what they are good at. Some drive trains, some are foremen, but people who witnessed the liberation struggle will not accept you.'

Tsvangirai's response was brief but to the point: 'At least a train driver keeps the train on the tracks.'

The battle for Zimbabwe had begun.

# 7

# MDC – ready for a fight

The success of the strikes showed not only that people no longer supported ZANU-PF blindly, but – worse still from the government's viewpoint – they had lost their fear of Mugabe.

The war vets had challenged him and won, the masses had defied the power of the state, and despite the reprisals meted out by the army, the voice of dissent had not been silenced.

While people like Tsvangirai were old enough to remember the war (though he himself was a non-combatant), those engaged in street battles during the strike were in their late teens or early twenties, products of the post-war Mugabe era and his extended programme of free education. Mugabe needed a new cause that would rally young and old alike behind him, and in the absence of a real battle, he would create one.

Just before Christmas 1997, the government announced that 1 471 white farms had been earmarked for compulsory acquisition. A list of properties was published in the *Herald*, but there was no word on how landowners would be compensated, as required by the constitution.

Food experts cautioned that any move towards wholesale nationalisation could render the country vulnerable to shortages of maize, the staple diet, especially in drought years, but Mugabe would not be swayed. He accused white farmers of holding onto the best farms in the country – mostly stolen by their ancestors who had arrived with the Pioneer Column – while the black majority remained poor and unable to feed itself.

The argument was full of holes:

- Less than 5 per cent of the white population could trace its ancestry back to 1890, most having been born of parents who had moved to Zimbabwe after the Second World War.
- More than 80 per cent of farms had been bought from previous owners since 1980. At independence, the government had passed a law giving itself first refusal on any rural land offered for sale. If the farm was not required for resettlement, a 'Certificate of No Current Interest' was issued, and the owner was free to place his property on the market.

• In 1981, a land redistribution programme had been set up with funding from donors – notably Britain – but this aid was halted when it became clear that most of the farms were being given to ministers and their extended families.

Mugabe was correct in stating that the black majority was growing poorer, but Zimbabwe had become an increasingly urban society, with towns and cities experiencing a population explosion, and rural areas losing most of their young people. There were few jobs in the outlying regions, and many school leavers had older brothers and sisters living in an urban environment who would provide accommodation until the youngsters found their feet.

Urban growth is a global trend, and according to one United Nations report, the number of people living in cities and towns throughout the Third World jumped from 650 million in 1975 to more than 1.6 billion in 2000, a rise of 146 per cent. In Africa, the swing over the same period was even higher at 160 per cent, with the greatest migration in the fifteen to twenty-four age group, which included many with a secondary education.

Far from Zimbabwe being a special case, it mirrored the situation in countries such as Thailand or Mexico, and the issue was more about the lack of jobs than a shortage of land.

Despite the listings, no farms were expropriated immediately, and the issue dropped out of sight for a few weeks in August 1998, when Mugabe announced that troops would be sent to shore up the government of President Laurent Kabila in the Democratic Republic of Congo, or DRC (formerly Zaire), where Ugandan-backed guerrillas had launched an attack in the east of the country. As with the proposed land seizures, there was no word on how Zimbabwe's participation in the war would be funded.

In the wake of the strikes, the government had scrapped the 2.5 per cent increase in sales tax and dropped a range of other surcharges designed to meet the cost of paying pensions to the war vets. Mugabe also conceded that the people should have a greater say in how the nation was run, and to this end proposed that a new constitution be drawn up with a focus on human rights and a finite term for the presidency.

The views of the nation – regardless of colour, tribe or leaning – would be recorded by a commission made up of the 150 MPs (all but two of whom were ZANU-PF), plus a team of academics and business people chosen by the president.

It was a huge exercise, conducted in a superb manner. Commission members travelled to the furthest corners of the country with their notebooks and tape recorders. I gave my views on tape at the Borrowdale Shopping Centre and, over the months, encountered different teams in Bulawayo, Beit Bridge, the farming district of Mutorashanga, 100 kilometres from Harare, and on a dirt road past Mount Darwin.

In every town and hamlet, more than two million people had their say, but they needn't have bothered. When the first draft was produced, it was clear that, while on paper Zimbabwe had a system of one person, one vote, in practice Mugabe *was* the one person, and his word was law.

The new constitution was similar to the old one and still left the president with more power than parliament. In future, he or she could serve only two consecutive five-year terms, but Mugabe's tenure would be reckoned from the 2000 election, allowing him to rule for another ten years, or thirty in all.

There was another clause, which had not been raised in the millions of words carried by the state media during the months that the commission was doing its work. Under the new constitution, the government could seize any piece of farmland, and the onus for compensation would rest with the British government. The clause further stated: 'If the former colonial power fails to pay compensation … the Government of Zimbabwe has no obligation to pay compensation for agricultural land compulsorily acquired for resettlement.'

It was a piece of chicanery worthy of a Monty Python sketch, but my contacts in government told me that Mugabe's cabinet was convinced it would work, and that if the farmers sided with Mugabe, Tony Blair's government would give in and pay up.

A referendum – the first since 1978 when Smith had asked the Rhodesian electorate to vote on the concept of majority rule – was set for the weekend of 12 and 13 February 2000 to determine support for the new constitution. Had the exercise been undertaken in the late 1980s, there is little doubt that the government would have carried the day, but these were different times.

As the final constitution was being prepared, a number of senior officials working at the National Oil Company of Zimbabwe (NOCZIM) embezzled more than a billion dollars of the nation's fuel funds. NOCZIM was a parastatal with the sole licence to import crude oil, which was then refined in Zimbabwe and sold as petrol, diesel or paraffin.

The Minister for Energy, Enos Chikowore, assured the nation that there was nothing to panic about, and that the so-called scandal was a lie made up by 'enemies of the state'.

The day after his speech the country ran dry, and Chikowore resigned. The fraud involved not only the NOCZIM board, but also several cabinet members. However, there were no successful prosecutions, presumably because, as with Hunzvi, the guilty parties would have implicated too many other people.

To make matters worse, yet another new fleet of Mercedes had just been imported for ministers and their acolytes, and shortly before Christmas 1999 there was another round of price hikes on basic goods.

Inflation had risen to 50 per cent, unemployment was at its highest level in half a century and many people faced the prospect of not going *kumusha* for Christmas. Even if they could afford the fares, a large number of long-haul buses were stranded with empty fuel tanks.

In the past Zimbabweans had suffered quietly, but this time their anger had a voice.

In February 1999, the ZCTU had approved the formation of a union-based political party, the Movement for Democratic Change. Morgan Tsvangirai and his colleague, Gibson Sibanda, resigned from the union executive to lead the new movement, along with a well-known constitutional lawyer, Professor Welshman Ncube.

'The primary objective of this whole process is to create a political party that is going to contest elections,' Tsvangirai told the inaugural meeting. 'There will still be mass action, but now there is a chance for the public to do something about their anger by voting ZANU-PF out of power.'

Public response was enormous, and when the new party launched a recruitment drive, the first batch of membership cards sold out in one weekend.

'We are surprised by the level of support,' Tsvangirai admitted. 'But people are ready for change. Things are falling apart and the government has no economic plan to get us out of the mess.'

As for the referendum, he called on the nation to reject it. His party, he said, was ready for a fight.

The timing was perfect. On 31 March 1999 a new daily newspaper was launched, with my old colleague, Geoff Nyarota, as editor. By the end of the year, it had eclipsed the *Herald* in circulation and was carrying news that the state media would not touch.

The *Daily News* denounced Mugabe's rule as a disaster for the working class, pointing out that social conditions were far worse than they had been at UDI, real wages had fallen 75 per cent since 1980 and 700 000 workers had lost their jobs since 1991.

For a few days at the end of 1999, Zimbabwe, in common with the rest of the world, was distracted by the Y2K bug and the new millennium, but by the first week of January the *Daily News* was leading a campaign against the referendum, which it described as a ruse to keep the ruling party in power.

Mugabe recruited one of his former critics, Professor Jonathan Moyo, to lead the state-funded 'yes' campaign. Previously, while a lecturer at the University of Zimbabwe, Moyo had spoken out against the government's abuse of power, but with the promise of a ministry in the next government, he threw himself into his new role.

The CIO sounded clear warnings that the electorate was going to reject the constitution, but Mugabe ignored their assessments and went ahead with the poll. Opposition advertisements were banned from radio, television and the state-owned newspapers, a command centre was set up at the Harare Sheraton, and trucks buzzed in and out of the hotel gates to flood the townships with pro-government fliers, posters and stickers. Towards the end, ZANU-PF party vehicles were being used as well, and advertisements urging a 'yes' vote became increasingly desperate, with claims that the referendum was being sabotaged by white farmers and the British government, and that anyone who voted against the constitution was a sell-out.

In truth, most people had not even read the draft document, but used the opportunity to send a message to the government. Rodwell Tapfuma, a thirty-two-year-old security guard at my local shopping centre, summed up the feeling when I interviewed him an hour after he had voted.

'In the morning I have a piece of dry bread and a cup of tea,' he said as he lit a cigarette. 'I smoke because it stops me feeling hungry, and tobacco is cheaper than food.

'I can't afford bus fare, so I walk to work, which is more than five kilometres. There is no money for lunch because I am paying school fees for my two children, and I walk home when I finish work at 6 pm. When I get home, we have a family meal, but most of the food is kept for the kids, and I am always hungry.

'How can I vote "yes" when my life is so harsh?'

But when I asked him who he thought would win, he cast his eyes to the ground. 'It's obvious. Mugabe always wins.'

The turnout at the polls was the biggest since 1980. Gone was the apathy that had marked general and presidential elections, and a sense of carnival prevailed among the queues of people waiting to cast their ballots.

On Valentine's Day, Monday 14 February 2000, the first results leaked out. Some rural areas had voted 'yes', some 'no', but in Harare and Bulawayo, the vote against the constitution had topped 70 per cent. The following night, Mugabe addressed the nation, but this was not to be one of his long, drawn-out speeches accompanied by beating drums and stirring music. He announced the results, thanked the people for voting peacefully and ended with a plea for unity. 'Let us all, winners and losers, accept the referendum verdict and start planning our way for the future.'

The next morning, the effects of what had happened in the townships overnight were plain to see. Everyone, from bank tellers to pump attendants manning the fuel queues, seemed to be nursing a hangover. My local fruit vendor, Douglas, who was usually there from 8 am, staggered to his stall at noon.

'We thought at first that soldiers would come and punish us,' he said, when I stopped off after lunch to buy a box of mangoes.

'Then we saw the president on TV and we knew that he had accepted the result. Straight away people rushed to the beerhall to talk about what had happened. There were parties in the streets and people played music from speakers in their windows. Today my kids did not go to school, because they did not sleep last night.'

'Did you think the "no" vote would win?' I asked as he handed me the change.

'Ah, never,' he replied, and then he smiled. 'But maybe this is a fresh start. Maybe we can really see something new in the future.'

A general election was due later in the year, on a date to be set by the president. By extrapolating the voting pattern of the referendum across the nation's 120 constituencies, analysts predicted that ZANU-PF would take fewer than 40 seats. Elections were still held at five-year intervals, with the president being chosen in a separate poll every seven years. But the 1987 constitution, which gave Mugabe his sweeping powers, had been drawn up on the assumption that ZANU-PF would never face a serious challenge.

All legislation had to be signed into law by the president, who could, in theory, reject anything he didn't like. And he had the sole power to appoint ministers, so even if his party was reduced to forty or fifty seats, he could still create an exclusively ZANU-PF cabinet.

If an MDC majority in parliament refused to approve budgets or government expenditure, Mugabe could declare a state of emergency and rule by decree. The situation would then have to be referred to the High Court for resolution, and the judges were presidential appointments. Muddying the waters even more was the tricky question of the police and the army, which were increasingly being expected to show allegiance to the ruling party ahead of parliament.

Mugabe called a meeting of the ZANU-PF executive and took personal responsibility for the outcome of the referendum. One MP, Dzikamai Mavhaire, suggested he should retire, and was promptly suspended. But the rest pledged their fawning support and predicted that the election would bring a better result. The president gave a morale-boosting speech, but no one believed it would be easy to win back public support.

'They knew that there was a problem,' one of the presidential secretaries told me privately. 'And I think that many would have liked to jump ship, but ZANU was the only party they had ever known, and they felt tied to it. I saw the same thing when I studied in the UK – people habitually supporting Labour or the Conservative Party because that was what they had always done.

'Here there is an added strain. Many party loyalists lost family during the war and believe that they owe it to those who died to stay with ZANU. Others, of course, have done well from the party and are worried about losing favours if they defect.'

When Tsvangirai announced that the MDC would field candidates for all 120 seats and predicted the end of ZANU-PF's twenty-year rule, privately owned newspapers published photographs of MDC officials briefing white farmers on their manifesto, which guaranteed the rights of all Zimbabweans, regardless of colour. The MDC also promised that any redistribution of land would be done transparently and in keeping with the law. Farmers wrote out cheques to the party and many became members.

The MDC was also allowed to campaign among farm workers, who signed up in droves.

After ZANU-PF's general executive met, Mugabe called a closed session of his inner circle. The first task, he told them, was to regain control in the rural areas, where it was easier to conduct a campaign of intimidation away from the media's prying eyes. The cities would be dealt with later. And if the war vets were going to get a pension, they might as well earn it.

Within days of the constitutional referendum, a rag-tag army of former guerrillas invaded white-owned farms and occupied land throughout the country in a coordinated operation. The government provided Z$20 million (US$500 000) to fund the war vets, and the severity of attacks ranged from courteous negotiation to total occupation of the farmer's home, forcing him and his family to withdraw to a neighbouring property or the safety of the nearest town.

In the first few days of the crisis, the police responded to calls for help and turned the veterans away. Then police commissioner Augustine Chihuri sent out the word that his officers should not intervene in 'political matters', and rural communities were left to fend for themselves.

Chenjerai Hunzvi made regular appearances on radio, TV and in the *Herald*, vowing that WVA members would not rest until all the land was taken.

'Those whites who believe they are Zimbabweans will be marched to the airport and sent home to Britain,' he frothed in one interview.

On any weekday, dozens of men and women would sit outside the gates of factories in Workington, a large industrial estate south of Harare, hoping to gain employment. Now state-owned buses prowled the area and party men offered the unemployed Z$50, a meal and a plot of land in exchange for joining the war vets. They would be transported to a rural area close to town, where the real veterans would tell them what to do.

The Commercial Farmers' Union (CFU), a prehistoric structure that had made little effort to attract black members, set up a special task force to monitor the invasions. Within days, their office on Nelson Mandela Avenue, near the Harare Club, was swamped with calls from farmers whose land was being pegged by well-organised teams of veterans and city youths. Jerry Grant, vice-president of the CFU, made one of the first public statements on the issue.

'I'm shell-shocked. I just can't believe a government can behave in this manner,' he told a reporter from the French news agency, Agence-France Presse.

'The word is out that this is punishment for the whites for rejecting the constitution, and it is orchestrated at the highest level. Government and party vehicles are being used to transport the invaders. Farmers are being intimidated and the police are aware of this, and they're still doing nothing about it. They've had an instruction from the top not to interfere.'[1]

Information minister Chen Chimutengwende, a large, bumbling man who had spent the war raising funds for ZANU-PF in London, responded in the state media, denying that the government was involved.

'It is absolute rubbish,' he said on television news. 'The government has had no hand in this, but the blame lies with those who voted "no" in the referendum. It's now leading to these invasions, and I can only see more of the invasions.'

Mugabe echoed this when he was interviewed by CNN a few days later.

By the middle of March, 500 farms had been occupied, and the CFU had opened a dialogue with government. Union members would hand over a total of five million hectares for resettlement, without payment of any compensation. The offer was rejected.

The farmers went to court and were granted an order evicting the war vets, but Hunzvi simply ignored the order and the police refused to enforce it, saying they didn't have the manpower to remove the squatters and, in any case, it was a political issue.

Party heroes were created overnight. Former guerrilla Joseph Chinotimba became a prominent figure and was soon leading groups of war vets into factories and even company boardrooms, terrorising the bosses and forcing them to take back fired staff and increase the wages of the lowest-paid workers.

Border Gezi, the bearded governor of Mashonaland East, declared his province a 'one-party zone', warning that no MDC election material would be allowed in the region, and adding: 'We have also banned the *Daily News* and if we find it on sale in any shops, we will confiscate the copies and burn them.'

His followers did just that.

The newspaper ran pictures of government officials delivering bags of maize meal to occupied farms and paying the invaders a weekly wage. Hunzvi said the photographs had been staged, and warned that Nyarota would be 'dealt with sooner or later'.

An art gallery on the ground floor of the *Daily News* building in Harare was bombed late one night, and the next day the *Herald* claimed that the MDC had carried out the attack to vilify the government.

But Nyarota was undeterred.

'They can bomb the building, I suppose they could even kill me,' he said when we spoke on the phone the day after the attack. 'But they will not silence the newspaper, and they will never be able to stop the people from demanding change – it's too late for that.'

The Reserve Bank of Zimbabwe gave Mugabe a confidential report criticising the farm occupations and predicting major fall-out on three fronts:

- All foreign investment would disappear.
- There would be no further money from the IMF.
- Many farmers had mortgaged their properties, and unless they could grow and sell crops, they would default on their loans to the commercial banks, creating a financial crisis.

They might as well have told him that Elvis Presley was staying in the penthouse suite at Meikles Hotel.

While the farmers could retreat to the safety of nearby towns (though most chose to defy the invaders and stay on the land), their two million workers had no such option. The war vets were convinced that farm labourers – many of them descended from Malawian or Zambian parents or grandparents – had pushed up the rural 'no' vote in the referendum, and were determined to get even.

Graphic images on BBC television showed mobs setting fire to entire farm compounds and beating the fleeing occupants with sticks, pick handles and lengths of hose.

Meetings of ZANU-PF were convened throughout the rural areas, with the message that anyone who didn't attend would be killed. The rallies attracted huge crowds of people who raised their fists in support of the party and sang songs that dated back to the war.

At a peace march in Harare on 1 April, the police stood by as war vets arrived in government vehicles and beat up the marchers, after which several of the victims were arrested. In any other country, people recounting the events of that day would have been accused of making up an April Fool's joke, but this was no laughing matter.

By the middle of April, two black MDC members and five white farmers had been murdered, the police either refusing to respond to their distress calls or setting up roadblocks so that medical help could not get through.

Mugabe blamed the problem squarely on the British government and the farmers. London had reneged on the land reform programme started in the 1980s, he said, and the farmers had sided with the opposition and attended their rallies in the rural areas, encouraging a 'no' vote in the referendum.

The corridors at the high commission in Harare were packed with whites begging for British passports on the basis of some or other ancestor whose roots could be traced back to the United Kingdom. But the greater exodus was among blacks. Air Zimbabwe had four flights a week to Gatwick, and with no visas required and no passport control on flights out of London, British authorities had no way of checking whether Zimbabwean 'tourists' stayed on in the UK or returned home.

'The place was becoming chaotic,' twenty-eight-year-old Magdalene Musonza recalled when I interviewed her in London in February 2003. 'I came here in May 2000, and after a long battle I managed to get permanent residence.

'Our family lived in Bindura, where my father was a mechanic who specialised in tractors. He was at a farm repairing an engine when the war vets arrived with their youth militia and beat up the farmer, accusing him of allowing the MDC to hold a rally on his land.

'My father tried to explain that he was only there to do a job, but the men were drunk and they knocked him to the ground. They poured motor oil on his body and smashed one of his kneecaps with a wrench. Then they beat him with a chain.

'He came home that night covered in blood and oil, and we got him to the hospital. Luckily for him, I knew one of the doctors, because at many government hospitals the staff refused to admit people who had been beaten up by ZANU-PF. They were scared of losing their jobs.

'My parents now live in the London suburb of Croydon, but my father still walks with a limp.'

But on television, Mugabe claimed that his people were simply reacting to provocation. 'They [the MDC] started the violence,' he ranted. 'Now they are getting more than they bargained for!'

Gangs of party thugs had started terrorising the black townships around Harare, descending on the homes of suspected MDC supporters and either taking them away to be tortured or committing atrocities on site. The *Daily News* was filled with reports of people who had been beaten, subjected to electric shock, stabbed and raped. The police would not intervene unless the victims ganged up and beat their tormentors, in which case *they* would be arrested, and beaten again in the cells.

In the three months following the referendum, twenty people had been killed and human rights groups recorded more than a thousand cases of torture.

Hunzvi had spent the Z$20 million the government had given him, and was seeking another Z$80 million.

In private briefings with the business community, cabinet ministers admitted that the farm seizures were a political strategy that would continue until the elections, after which there would be a lawful effort to allocate land to the people. The plan was to 'shake up the white community' because of its support for the MDC.

'The trend will carry on until after the elections, at which point we can sit down and talk,' an unnamed minister told the weekly *Financial Gazette*. 'By then we also hope to have passed in parliament an amendment to the constitution regarding land acquisition.

'The whites have chosen to be political on the issue, and we will match them on this one. What we are doing is not a random exercise, but a systematic and orderly takeover of the farms. This will be our strategy up until election time,' he said.

In the same story, however, Mugabe's official spokesman, George Charamba, said the invasions were not an election strategy, but an issue of 'redressing the historical imbalance' of land allocation.

'There is a link between the historical land imbalance in the country and the actions of the war veterans, which have been interpreted as chaotic. You don't solve a problem by cracking down on the effect,' Charamba said.

Either way, the government was determined to amend the constitution to allow the seizure of land without compensation, and a special session of parliament was convened so that the relevant clauses could be approved. This required a two-thirds majority vote, which some in the party believed they might not be able to muster after the election.

On 19 May, the CFU executive met with Mugabe, who told them that the occupations were hard to curtail, but promised nevertheless to ensure an end to the violence. CFU director Dave Hasluck even joined Chenjerai Hunzvi on a tour of affected properties, but ended the exercise lamenting that, far from subsiding, 'the violence is spiralling out of control'.

By then, 1 477 farms had been occupied, and on 990 of them the invaders had started parcelling out land.

The British government had largely been caught on the hop. In Commonwealth circles, many black leaders bought the argument that it was all about London previously having reneged on genuine land reform. British newspapers were filled with reports about the horror unfolding in Zimbabwe, but for the most part, diplomats in Harare were outmanoeuvred by Mugabe's rhetoric and the speed of events.

High commissioner Peter Longworth was a quiet-spoken man who, before the trouble, had travelled the length and breadth of the country, visiting schools and the communities they served, personally handing over aid to needy groups. Formerly consul general in Johannesburg, he had been posted to Harare pending retirement, and was not adept at handling a diplomatic crisis.

His deputy, Ian Hay-Campbell, a former broadcaster with the BBC, spoke fluent Russian thanks to a spell in Moscow, but was more an expert on Europe than Africa.

The Americans were in an even worse position. Ambassador Tom McDonald was a political appointment, a lawyer and Clinton Democrat whose loyalty had been rewarded in 1997 with a four-year stint in what should have been a comfortable posting.

Tom was affable, had been an election observer in both Uganda and South Africa, and was a good PR man for Washington, but when the trouble started, he appeared to be out of his depth, refusing to be drawn on Zimbabwe's plight, and insisting as late as 2000 that it was still a good place for Americans to invest.

There was a further quandary in both London and Washington. The respective ruling Labour and Democratic parties had been staunch Mugabe supporters since the 1970s, and had never criticised his tyranny prior to the referendum.

Britain's Minister for Africa, Peter Hain, was born in Kenya and grew up in South Africa, escaping to Britain in his teens to avoid compulsory military service. He became a leading light in the anti-apartheid movement, but had not spoken out against Gukurahundi or human rights abuses anywhere else in Africa. To criticise Zimbabwe for the first time at this late stage could be construed as a racist response to the plight of the white farmers.

In May, the British tried to buy their way out of the problem. 'We have put £36 million on the table,' Hain announced at a media conference, 'but this can only be provided if President Mugabe ends the illegal farm occupations, restores law and order and stops the violence which is devastating the country.'[2]

Reaction to what had become truly horrendous human rights violations in Zimbabwe was pathetic. American president Bill Clinton ignored the issue, British prime minister Tony Blair cancelled some of his country's aid, and, in South Africa, Thabo Mbeki refused to say a word against the head of a neighbouring state.

Only Nelson Mandela, who had retired after just one term as president, called on Mugabe to step down, and infuriated the ANC by saying that black tyrants deserved to have their people take up arms and overthrow them by force.

Privately, diplomats made it clear that their governments were extremely concerned. As far back as 1998, the South African high commissioner, Kingsley Mamabulo, had told me that things in Zimbabwe were not looking good for the future.

In 2000, Peter Longworth went further and suggested that there would be a total economic meltdown if the chaos continued, and even the Botswana and Zambian high commissioners were willing to tell journalists, off the record, that their governments were deeply disturbed by the effect Mugabe's actions were having on the tourist industry and on investors' perceptions of the region. If they were saying the same things in private to Mugabe and his cabinet, their words were falling on deaf ears.

Commonwealth secretary general Don McKinnon paid a visit to Harare, but was so bent on not being seen as a white New Zealander attacking a black head of state that he delivered no criticism at all.

In neighbouring Zambia, the government was offering farms to anyone who had lost property across the river, and Zimbabwean landowners made trips to Uganda, Malawi and Mozambique in search of a stable political dispensation where they could start again.

'We would like to see genuine farmers coming here,' the president of the Zambian National Farmers' Union, Ajay Vashe, told one newspaper. 'And we would especially welcome those who would like to invest in tobacco and horticulture.'

The CFU predicted that if the problem continued, there would be a 30 per cent drop in the winter crop of barley and wheat, and that maize yields could be so badly affected that Zimbabwe would have to import supplies to feed the nation. But the Central Statistics Office in Harare denied the reports, predicting a surplus instead.

In an interview with *Time* magazine, Tsvangirai supported the concept of land distribution, but attacked the way it was being handled.

'The land invasions have nothing to do with race,' he said. 'It is all about intimidating the opposition.

'Most Zimbabweans agree that a program of orderly land reform is needed, but few back Mugabe's chaotic land grab. In the past, land distribution has failed because poor subsistence farmers were given small plots without training, money for equipment or access to urban markets.'

He also claimed that the government had already bought 400 000 hectares of white-owned land, which was now lying idle.[3]

Mugabe announced that the election would be held over the weekend of 26 June, and both parties tendered candidates in all 120 constituencies. However, many of those standing for the MDC in rural areas found it hard to campaign. War vets and their youthful legions would descend on meetings and beat all those present, while several prospective MPs were abducted and tortured.

The Amnesty International report for the period leading up to the elections reads like a horror novel, as the following extract shows:

There is evidence that the Government of Zimbabwe is either instigating or acquiescing in serious violations of human rights, including extrajudicial executions, torture and other cruel, inhuman or degrading treatment or punishment. There appears to be a deliberate and well-thought out plan of systematic human rights violations with a clear strategy, constituting state-sponsored terror, in the run-up to the June elections.

Specific cases dealt with in the report included the following:

- ZANU-PF agents murdered David Stevens, a white farmer from Macheke, east of Harare, after abducting him from his home and taking him to the small town of Murewa. Another man who was abducted with Stevens managed to escape and sought refuge in the Murewa police station, but the gang arrived a few hours later and removed him from the building without any resistance from the police. No arrests were made, and the man who allegedly shot Stevens at point-blank range continued to live in Murewa.

- Chenjerai Hunzvi set up what he called a 'surgery' in the satellite town of Budiriro near Harare, from where he ran a torture centre. Over a period of nearly two months, hundreds of people were dragged to the building by gangs of party youths, and once inside they were beaten, burned and electrocuted, and suffered sexual abuse. Groups of thugs took it in turns to torture suspected MDC members around the clock, holding some of their captives for up to four days. Police only intervened when an abductee managed to escape and was beaten to death near the surgery, but Hunzvi was never questioned over the matter.

- In an attack at a bus station on 9 May, Blessing Chebundo, the MDC candidate for the town of Kwe Kwe, between Harare and Bulawayo, was beaten, stabbed and doused with petrol. He managed to wrestle a box of matches from one of his attackers or he would almost certainly have been set alight. On 15 May, petrol bombs were tossed into the Chebundo home, burning it to the ground. While the fire raged, ZANU-PF youths attacked the candidate and his family, and were only driven back when MDC supporters arrived at the scene. Blessing phoned the police, who were stationed only 500 metres away, but was told they had no transport and could not respond. They arrived at the scene after the attack, by which time the house had been reduced to ashes.

- In Buhera in the south-east of the country, two MDC members, Tichaona Chiminya and Talent Mabika, escaped death on 15 April when a petrol bomb was thrown into their car. They reported the matter to the police, identifying the culprits as members of Mugabe's CIO who had harassed them in the past, but no arrests were made.

The report continued with pages of other violations, and Amnesty International concluded that: 'The government has failed to ensure that all Zimbabweans are able to exercise their rights to freedom of expression, association, assembly and movement in the run-up to the election.'[4]

And if the people did vote for the MDC, Mugabe made it clear that he reserved the right not to accept the election results. His powerful party chairman, John Nkomo, went even further. 'ZANU-PF will form the government whatever the results,' he told a press briefing. 'There will be no opposition in government.'

In South Africa, the MDC held rallies at which they encouraged supporters to return to Zimbabwe over the election weekend to cast their votes. Although Mugabe had changed the law to exclude postal votes, people could cast their ballots in any constituency, and have the outcome recorded in the area where they were registered. In theory, this meant that Zimbabweans living in Johannesburg had to make their way only to the polling station at Beit Bridge, though the MDC urged them to travel all the way home in order to reduce the risk of inter-constituency votes going astray.

I travelled to South Africa several times in the months leading up to the election, and it was clear to me that feelings in the exile community were even stronger than in Zimbabwe itself, and that anyone suspected of supporting ZANU-PF could expect to be beaten up, possibly even killed.

A limited number of foreign observers were allowed to enter Zimbabwe for the poll, and with their arrival there was a marked drop in the level of violence. War veterans now occupied almost half of the country's 4 000 commercial farms, but the worst they did was force labourers to attend all-night 'political education' sessions.

On the Thursday before the vote, fourteen of the MDC's election monitors were abducted in Matabeleland and one polling station was burned down, but the madness of the previous four months had subsided. The weekend of the election was even quieter.

'The difference of the process prior to and on election day is like night and day,' Swedish observer Pierre Schori told Reuters.

The polls closed on Sunday 27 June, and on Monday the first results were made known. Many of the most powerful in the land had lost their seats. In Bulawayo, Joshua Nkomo's former deputy commander, Dumiso Dabengwa (the minister responsible for the police), had won 3 644 votes, while Tsvangirai's former ZCTU colleague, Gibson Sibanda, polled 20 380.

Blessing Chebundo, who had been so harassed by the militia that by the end of the campaign he and his family were in hiding, took 15 388 votes in Kwe Kwe, while Mugabe's heir apparent, Emerson Mnangagwa, managed only 8 352.

Five white MDC candidates had thrashed incumbent black members of

ZANU-PF. The MDC took every urban seat and all but two in Matabeleland, but in the rural areas of Mashonaland the terror had done its trick.

Nationwide, ZANU-PF won 48.4 per cent of the total ballot, or 1 205 580 votes, while the combined opposition parties gained 51.6 per cent, or 1 285 407.

But not all these votes went to the MDC. There were more than a dozen small contenders – including some funded by government to split the vote – that mopped up 114 086 votes, but the only one to gain a seat was the remnant of the late Ndabaningi Sithole's original ZANU, which won in his home area of Chipinge in the south-east.

The MDC, which was less than a year old, had won 57 of the 120 seats with a total of 1 171 321 votes, or 47.2 per cent – not enough to form the next government, but a strong enough weapon to bloody the nose of the ruling party in parliament, and block any further changes to the constitution.

The perception was that, with the referendum and the election over and Mugabe and his party still in charge, life would return to normal. The war vets could come off the farms, the militia gangs would be disbanded and the real problems of inflation and unemployment could be tackled.

But Mugabe's seven-year term would expire at the beginning of 2002 – little more than eighteen months away – and his own future would hang in the balance with the next poll. The system of 'persuasion' he had introduced all over the country had served him well, and, if anything, it needed to be strengthened.

With the benefit of hindsight, and compared to the terror that lay ahead, it could be said that by June 2000, the people of Zimbabwe had merely been roughed up.

# 8

# Publish and be damned

'The so-called private media never have anything nice to say,' ZANU-PF MP Walter Shamu told me in 1998 when we found ourselves at the same table one evening at a party hosted by the Egyptian embassy in Harare.

Walter had spent some time at the ZBC and now edited the party's own tabloid, *The People's Voice*.

'Why can't they run a headline that says, "Mugabe is a Great Leader"'? he asked, as though I represented some corps of unfriendly writers.

'Well, that would be an opinion rather than a story,' I ventured.

'It's all opinion, all their news is just opinions, and nasty ones at that,' he said. 'It's a shame, because they could play a role in building this nation, but all they want to do is break it down.'

Later that year, Walter was interviewed for a documentary film on Zimbabwe's media, and defended the way that state-owned broadcast channels had been turned into a party mouthpiece.

'We knew the danger of cosmetic change,' he told the interviewer, 'and that if we did not move in a revolutionary fashion and ensure that we truly took over the reigns of power at the broadcasting commission, we would have sold the revolution down the drain.'[1]

But if people such as Walter Shamu, Jonathan Moyo and previous information ministers and propaganda chiefs like Chen Chemutengwende hoped to rival Nazi Germany's propaganda minister, Joseph Goebbels, in silencing the truth, a few brave souls would deny them victory, though some paid a heavy price for their courage.

In 2000, Zimbabwe's government passed laws banning citizens from owning a radio transmitter, and requiring that any privately owned radio stations (of which there were none) pay an annual licence fee far beyond the means of most people. Stations would be required to transmit ruling-party material whenever asked to do so by the information ministry.

All journalists were later required to obtain a licence from the same ministry in order to ply their trade, and the only daily newspaper in private hands was bombed twice, the last attack destroying its printing press. A CIO agent was also sent to murder the former editor, Geoff Nyarota, in his own office, but Nyarota managed to talk him out of it.

The BBC office was shut down, CNN's journalists were rarely granted permission to enter the country and the Minister of Information, Professor Jonathan Moyo, had become one of the most powerful men in Zimbabwe. Originally an outspoken critic of the government, he had gone much further than any of his colleagues since being appointed to the cabinet in justifying the terror that had become part of daily life for the average person. In his arguments, all acts of aggression were laid at the door of the opposition, which was financed by foreign interests, while ZANU-PF was trying hard to keep the peace.

Every day, journalists at state-owned newspapers and the Zimbabwe Broadcasting Corporation sold their souls for a monthly pay cheque, presenting Mugabe as a hero and denouncing as a liar anyone who claimed to have been tortured or abused.

A Media Monitoring Project, financed by non-governmental organisations, concluded that in the state media, MDC victims of violence were either not identified as such or were accused of provoking violent reaction by their harassment of ZANU-PF. In some cases, it was both.

Over a one-week period leading up to the election in June 2000, the monitors recorded all television broadcasts and analysed the incidences of violence reflected in political news. They found that 96 per cent of political stories were about ZANU-PF, and that 'each story harangued the MDC as sell-outs, colonialists and traitors'. There was not a single positive news item on the opposition.[2] A good example of the biased reporting was the way ZBC dealt with an incident at Kariba, where a ZANU-PF gang stormed a meeting of the opposition, leaving two people dead and fifteen injured.

According to the ZBC reporter at Kariba, 'It was apparently a question of retaliation as ZANU-PF members, fed up with continued harassment by MDC youths, sought help from their counterparts in Karoi to stop the intimidation.

'Members from the two parties continued to harass each other, but events turned tragic when ZANU-PF members gained the upper hand on Tuesday with the help of the Karoi youths, and rounded up the youths. The ensuing fighting resulted in the deaths of two unidentified men and injury of supporters who were reportedly severely beaten up.'

The two dead men and the injured were all from the MDC, and the reporter filed his story from a ward at the Kariba Hospital, the injured victims clearly visible in a row of beds behind him, but he interviewed none of them.[3]

A favourite trick of the *Herald* was to use the words 'alleged' or 'possible' in order to cast doubt on reports. When opposition leaders were quoted, the newspaper would have them 'allegedly' saying this or that, even when the statement was made in response to a question from one of its own journalists.

This aberration of style even crept into headlines, such as one *Herald* classic: 'Alleged Politically-Induced Assault Claims Life'. An MDC supporter had been beaten to death when a group of ZANU-PF youths attacked his village near Shamva, assaulted the residents and set fire to their homes. The police detained five of the youths for questioning, but the *Herald* took the position that the five were 'assisting police with investigations into possible allegations of arson, malicious injury to property, assault, public violence and murder'. No reference was made to the political allegiance of either the victims or the perpetrators.

Government interference in the media is common in most developing countries, and until the mid-1990s, Zimbabwe was no worse than, for example, Zambia, Tanzania or Pakistan. Journalists did as they were told, and contentious stories were killed at birth.

But with the end of the Cold War, the spread of democracy saw a new defiance of authority. In Kenya, for example, privately owned newspapers played a major role in forcing former president Daniel arap Moi to accept multiparty rule. However, while the media was being liberated elsewhere in Africa, ZANU-PF was losing popularity, and the press came under fire.

To Mugabe's credit, more private newspapers were established under his rule than at any other time in the country's history. The challenge was how to control them.

The *Financial Gazette*, originally set up by the Rhodesian government and later bought out by Clive Wilson and Clive Murphy, had been owned by black investors since 1988. Printed on pink paper, like the *Financial Times* in London, it carried a mix of business and politics and was edited by the head of the Zimbabwe Union of Journalists (ZUJ), Basildon Peta, until he was forced into exile in 2002 and joined *The Star* in Johannesburg.

The *Independent*, founded by Wilson in 1996 in opposition to the *Gazette*, came out on Fridays and carried more hard news and fewer finance stories. Also in Wilson's stable was the *Standard*, a Sunday tabloid first published in 1997 and edited, until 2001, by Mark Chavunduka, son of a former ZANU-PF member of parliament. It was Mark who became the first casualty of the new-style repression that began in the late 1990s.

On 10 January 1999, the *Standard* ran a front-page story alleging that several officers from units of the Zimbabwe National Army (ZNA) fighting in the Congo had been arrested for plotting a coup. Journalist Ray Choto had written the story and Chavunduka had passed it for publication after checking the facts with his reporter.

'The military started looking for me on Monday the 11th,' Chavunduka told the now defunct *Horizon*, a monthly news digest published in Harare.[4]

'As a Sunday paper, we did not work on Mondays, so there was hardly anyone at the office, but three military vehicles were parked outside our building.

'The following day at 7.15 am, I received a call at home from Major Mhonda of Military Intelligence at the King George VI barracks. He said he wanted to discuss the story with me and I should pass through his office before going to work.'

At the barracks, soldiers were waiting for the editor, and Mhonda informed him that the story was not true, and that defence minister Moven Mahachi was furious. Mhonda also demanded to know the source of the information, but Mark said this was something he could not divulge.

He was escorted first to the Ministry of Defence in the same building as Mugabe's office, and then to the military's Cranborne Barracks on the road to the airport. There he was ushered into a small room, where twelve members of the CIO and army intelligence were waiting to question him.

'They said they had nothing against me, my newspaper or the staff, but that the story had tarnished the image of the army and the country. I said that if I was wrong, I would publish an apology.'

The offer was refused, and for two hours Chavunduka faced repeated demands to name his sources.

'I asked if I was under arrest,' he later recalled. 'They said I was not, but that I could not go anywhere.'

At 6.40 pm, Chavunduka was told that he had been formally charged with 'publishing false information likely to cause alarm and despondency'. The Zimbabwe army has no powers of arrest, which, in terms of the constitution, can only be carried out by a police officer, but Chavunduka was nevertheless held overnight. He was given food but was not allowed to wash or sleep, and at 7.15 am the next day, soldiers escorted him to his office and searched it before returning him to Cranborne.

Meanwhile, the army had been hunting down Ray Choto, and on Thursday morning they told Chavunduka that his colleague had been arrested while crossing the border into Botswana. But Choto was still in Harare and in contact with the newspaper's management, whose view was that they didn't need two staff in custody, and that he should not hand himself over to the police or army.

Clive Wilson had also been arrested, and was moved from one police station to another during three days of detention. His lawyers obtained an order from the High Court requiring that Mark be released, but the army ignored it and the police refused to intervene. On Thursday, Chavunduka's captors turned nasty.

'Different teams would come in and interrogate me. I was asked to write, on about 120 sheets of paper, my autobiography and give details about the newspaper and its directors. That afternoon, I was beaten up.

'The first assault took place in the office. They brought studio lights and forced me to look into them. If I turned away, they beat me. Then I was stripped naked and forced to do all sorts of exercises.'

The interrogation continued until Saturday, when Mark was blindfolded and driven to a basement forty-five minutes away from Cranborne. There he was tied up and the blindfold removed.

'They told me that President Mugabe had already signed my death warrant. They asked me what I could see on the walls and I told them it was the blood of other victims, and then they beat me with planks and applied electric shocks to my genitals.'

On Tuesday 19 January, a week after Chavunduka had been detained, Choto handed himself over to the police and was taken to Cranborne Barracks, where he was blindfolded and handcuffed. He was stripped naked and electric shocks were applied to his feet and genitals.

'They told me "we are going to torture you until you tell us", but I refused to disclose my sources,' Choto said later.

While Choto was being tortured, Chavunduka had been brought back to the barracks and was in another room, where his head was repeatedly plunged into a bucket of water. When he passed out, his interrogators laid him on the ground and applied pressure to force the water out of his lungs. As soon as they had revived him, the process began again.

Having obtained no answers, the soldiers brought Mark and Ray together for the first time since their arrest and forced them to roll naked on the grass at the barracks while they were beaten with whips, sticks and lengths of wire cable. Finally, they were placed in adjoining rooms and tortured within earshot of one another.

Mark recalled hearing Ray's cries while he himself was being abused.

'They tortured us in a marathon session, and Ray screamed so much, and then suddenly went quiet. I thought he had died.'

In the High Court, Justice James Devitte threatened to issue a warrant for the arrest of Moven Mahachi if the men were not handed over to the police, but the minister's permanent secretary, Job Whabira, scoffed at the idea. 'The judge cannot direct us,' he told Wilson, who had meanwhile been released. 'We are moving at our own pace. Any civilian who meddles in military matters is subject to military law.'

The MDC had not yet been formed, but its future office bearers were ready to comment on the matter, though none of what they said appeared in the *Herald* or on ZBC.

Morgan Tsvangirai, still head of the ZCTU, suggested that the security forces – including the police – were out of control. But Welshman Ncube went further. 'If indeed the government authorised the detentions,' he told the *Standard*, 'then we are not only under a police state, but under the worst kind of dictatorship imaginable.'

Basildon Peta launched a campaign to publicise the issue as widely as possible in South Africa and abroad. 'We are also taking up the matter of torture with the International Federation of Journalists,' he told the ZUJ executive, 'and we must do everything to spread the word around the world.'

In London, Zimbabwe's high commissioner, Ngoni Chideya, was called to Whitehall and asked to explain what was happening at Cranborne, and foreign journalists and their organisations sent letters of protest to Mugabe.

On Thursday 21 January, Choto and Chavunduka were handed over to the police, neither having revealed any information about their sources, and taken to hospital for treatment, and then kept in separate cells. They finally appeared in court the next day, and were released on bail of Z$10 000 each and told to surrender their passports. Their case was marked down for later in the month, but all charges were eventually withdrawn by the state.

In terms of Zimbabwe's constitution, anyone detained by the authorities must be charged within forty-eight hours or be released, but police minister Dumiso Dabengwa's only comment on the Chavunduka affair was that new laws should be introduced.

'We will not sit idly and do nothing while the security of the army is being undermined,' he said in Bulawayo while addressing mourners at the funeral of two soldiers who had been killed in the Congo.

Mahachi appeared on television and laughed when asked about claims that the men had been tortured. 'They just fell and hurt themselves while in our care,' he said.

But Mugabe was well aware of what had happened, and sounded a warning to others who might want to cross his regime.

'This is not the worst the army can do,' he said. He also made a speech on television condemning the *Standard*.

'The story was blatantly untrue,' he said, 'and their heinous objective was to instil alarm and despondency. If the *Standard* had not behaved in such a shameful and unethical manner, the army would not have behaved as it did.'

Then he proceeded to attack private weekly publications in general, claiming that they were owned and controlled by people, mostly white, whose aim was to undermine his government.

'They are filthy tabloids of the gutter type and are edited and run through fronts, using young blacks who have been employed [by the owners] as editors and reporters. In some cases, these are also their homosexual lovers.'

Mugabe provided no evidence for the latter claim, and was clearly not in a mood to be questioned about it.

But why the anger about this particular article on the alleged coup, when far worse had already been written about Mugabe and his government?

A contact in the South African intelligence service told me that Pretoria had received information on the coup story before it appeared in the *Standard*, and it is possible that their source inside the ZNA was the same person who told Ray Choto.

'My own view,' she said, 'is that they knew that we knew, and they wanted to know who was leaking information to us. They couldn't torture anyone in the South African government, so the next best thing was to try to beat a name out of the journalists.'

The story of how Choto and Chavunduka had been treated made headlines around the world, and while journalists are expected to remain impartial as a rule, there is little doubt that this case created a media bias against Mugabe. This in itself was not unique: the apartheid government in South Africa had suffered a similar fate through its oppression of the media, as did General Sani Abacha of Nigeria when he executed the author Ken Saro-Wiwa.

But if the government in Harare thought that the *Standard* would temper its editorial stance, they were wrong. Chavunduka published a full account of the treatment and torture he and Choto had suffered, and his newspaper continued to carry damning stories about government theft, corruption and abuse of human rights.

Unfazed by the actions of his soldiers, Moven Mahachi was interviewed on ZBC news and showed no remorse.

'Journalists who distort information and in the process cause anarchy by misleading the nation and the international community, will be dealt with within the law,' he said. 'Such reports are bent on tarnishing the image of the country, and they drive away potential investors and cause general despondency.'

And he forecast new measures, which were indeed introduced in 2002.

'If this distortion of information about Zimbabwe is not stopped by incarcerating those who perpetrate it,' he said, 'then the Minister of Information will work on a bill that will enable government to bar some private media organisations from operating in Zimbabwe.'[5]

In September 2000, Trevor Ncube – editor of the *Independent* and no stranger to detention and state harassment – bought both this newspaper and the *Standard* from Clive Wilson, and under his ownership both journals became even more outspoken.[6]

The launch of the *Daily News* in 1999 was a major blow to the government, because the cover price was lower than that of the *Herald* and the new paper was able to penetrate both high-density urban areas and rural ZANU strongholds throughout the country.

'This was a paper very different to anything published before,' Geoff Nyarota told me. 'Existing independent weekly newspapers tended to circulate within the upper bracket of income earners, whereas a daily had to sell itself on bread-and-butter issues to the masses in the towns as well as to country dwellers.'

The paper was less than a year old at the time of the 2000 referendum, but its effect on public opinion had already been massive. When the land invasions and rural terror campaigns began in March 2000, one of the first actions of the war veterans and the youth militia was to ban the *Daily News* from areas under their control, assaulting anyone who was found with a copy in their possession.

Nyarota was forty-nine when he founded the paper, and had a lot of media experience as well as a long history of upsetting Mugabe.

After taking his degree at the University of Rhodesia he became a teacher, and was posted to a school at Inyanga, on the border with Mozambique. In 1977, after a gun battle in the school grounds between ZANLA guerrillas and the Rhodesian army, the pupils were sent home and the school, like many others in the country at the time, was closed. That brought Nyarota's career as a teacher to an end.

'Soon afterwards, the *Herald* advertised vacancies for cadet journalists,' he recalled. 'For the first time, they were accepting blacks into what had previously been a white domain. Of the twelve trainees, four were black, and I qualified in 1978.'

Nyarota then joined the *Herald* as a cadet reporter. The newspaper's owners, Rhodesian Printing and Publishing Company, acquired a new title, the *National Observer*, and Nyarota was transferred to join the staff of a publication aimed specifically at a black readership.

At independence in 1980 he was transferred back to the *Herald*, and became the municipal reporter at a time when many white journalists, along with other professionals, were leaving Zimbabwe. The flight of whites had also thinned the ranks at the Ministry of Information, and Nyarota was invited by the government to join the staff. Six months later, he was appointed press secretary to Zimbabwe's first president, Canaan Banana.

When Jean Maitland-Stewart was fired after the North Korean story, Geoff was appointed editor of the *Manica Post* and brought the weekly more in line with the new style prescribed by ZANU-PF. For example, whereas Jean – and Stan Higgins who was acting editor for a while – refused to use the term 'comrade' for members of the government, Geoff adopted the style which was already in use in the other government-owned papers.

He gave the newspaper a wider reach among the black community, and circulation more than doubled from 5 000 copies to just over 11 000.

I remember having a conversation with him when we both worked on the *Post*, and he told me that Zimbabwe's 'new breed of journalists' was less inclined to publish stories that might embarrass the government. But he clearly did not subscribe to the idea himself, and proved as much in 1988, by which time he had been promoted to editor of the *Chronicle* in Bulawayo.

'We had information from the Willowvale motor assembly plant, which was 51 per cent government-owned, that politicians were abusing a scheme that entitled them to get Mazdas and Toyotas ahead of ordinary people. At that time there was a tremendous shortage of vehicles, and politicians were given priority because they needed transport to visit their constituencies. But some were buying a new vehicle from the plant in the morning, say a Toyota Cressida for Z$30 000, and then selling it in the afternoon for Z$115 000.

'Many of them had effectively ceased to be politicians and become full-time car dealers. We knew of MPs and even ministers who had already sold more than a dozen cars each. One of the major culprits was Enos Nkala, who was then Minister of Defence and also the Acting Minister for Home Affairs. Nkala reacted very sharply when we published our first story. He told me, "shelve the investigation immediately or I'll have you arrested", and referred to me publicly as "little Nyarota".'

It was unthinkable that a journalist working for a government-controlled publication would run such a story, and both the ZBC and other newspapers in the group refused to touch it. But in spite of Nkala's threats, Nyarota published more details.

Mugabe set up an inquiry, and five ministers were found to have been involved, including Nkala, who was sacked from the cabinet. But the greatest casualty was Maurice Nyagumbo, who as Minister for Political Affairs was allocated a budget by parliament, which he used to extend the party's stranglehold on Zimbabwe.

Nyagumbo was born in Manicaland in 1924, and in 1940, with only a Standard 4 education, moved to South Africa, where he met James Chikerema and was introduced to radical black politics. Like Chikerema, he was deported back to Rhodesia, and after stints in both ZAPU and ZANU, he was imprisoned in 1964, released under the détente initiative in 1975, jailed again in the same year for 'recruiting young men for terrorist training outside the country', and only released for the Lancaster House talks in 1979.

Nyagumbo's stature within the party was enormous, and the inquiry placed him at the centre of what became known as 'Willowgate'. He was also the only culprit who appeared to show genuine remorse, and talked in private about the need to clear the air with a full account of what had happened. Instead, he committed suicide by swallowing poison.

Even Sally Mugabe was said to have received some of the profits from Willowgate, though her name never appeared on any documents and she was not named in the *Chronicle* reports.

'We published only the proven facts,' said Nyarota, 'and while there were rumours about Sally, there was no evidence.'

The thieving ministers were all found guilty by Mugabe's inquiry, headed by Justice Sandura, but the president decreed that they be pardoned, adding credence to the popular belief that *someone* living at State House was involved.

The government found itself in a difficult position. The people saw Nyarota as a national hero, but if he was left at the *Chronicle*, it would send the message that editors could stand up to the highest in the land, and survive. So instead of being dismissed, he was 'promoted' to the previously non-existent position of group public relations manager at the Zimbabwe Newspapers head office in Harare.

Asked at a press conference on Willowgate about Nyarota's 'promotion', Mugabe couched his response in classic doublespeak.

'He played quite a part in revealing the information he had as a journalist and which he published in the *Chronicle*. But he went a bit far in lumping together everyone who had bought a car from Willowvale under the headline "Willowgate".

'And he has been upgraded. I understand he has been promoted and is receiving more money than before.'

Nyarota's boss at ZimPapers was group chief executive Elias Rusike who, having tired of the government's constant interfering, had set up a consortium in 1988 to buy the *Financial Gazette* from Murphy and Wilson. Rusike's partners were Fanuel Muhwati and Eric Kahari. I worked briefly with Kahari in the late 1990s, when I was a guest lecturer at Zimnat Insurance, of which he was managing director at the time. Kahari was a lawyer and a man of great integrity, who had spent the 1970s working in the United States and returned to Zimbabwe at independence.

'In 1980, we were thrilled at Mugabe's victory,' he told me. 'But then we saw the truth behind the façade.'

With Rusike at the helm and a good board to guide him, the *Gazette* became the principal voice of conscience in Zimbabwe, and Nyarota was poached from ZimPapers to become the editor. If the government thought that black ownership would tone down the newspaper's strident criticism of its actions, disappointment lay in store. The battle was on once more, with journalists trying to uncover the truth, and ministers and their staff working just as hard to stop them.

Many of Zimbabwe's most respected media personalities built their reputations on the *Gazette*, including Bill Saidi, who would later be appointed assistant editor of the *Daily News* by Nyarota, Iden Wetherall, who went on to edit the *Independent*, and Trevor Ncube, who was Nyarota's deputy before becoming editor of the *Independent*. Alan Dryden, who founded Africa Travel News, perhaps the continent's best travel industry publication, spent many years as advertising manager of the *Financial Gazette*.

Rusike admitted that during his time at Zimbabwe Newspapers, he had done the bidding of Nathan Shamuyarira, the Minister of Information, who insisted that any speech by Mugabe should always appear on the front page. As owner of the *Gazette*, however, he and his staff exposed a series of scandals, including vote rigging, corruption and embezzlement of foreign aid.

Despite increasing the cover price, Nyarota managed to lift the circulation from 10 000 to 18 000 in his first year as editor. This initial success spurred Rusike to launch the *Daily Gazette*, funded by a loan from the Zimbabwe Banking Corporation. The bank had originally entered southern Africa as the Bank of the Netherlands, but when the Dutch government disinvested in the 1970s, the South African branch was bought out and relaunched as Nedbank, while in Salisbury the government bought the shares and traded as Rhobank.

After 1980, all that changed was the name, which placed Rusike in the awkward position of criticising the government while depending on a parastatal to fund his business. In June 1991, while Nyarota was out of the country, Rusike dismissed him, saying that the staff was not happy with their editor.

Nyarota denied the allegation, claiming that Rusike wanted to buy a new printing press and needed to obtain funding from the government-controlled bank.

'Their condition was that I should be fired,' according to Nyarota. He sued for unfair dismissal, and two years later, Rusike settled out of court.

In 1992, facing high interest rates and poor support from advertisers, the *Daily Gazette* and another spinoff, the *Sunday Gazette*, closed down.

From 1994 to 1996, Nyarota taught journalism courses throughout southern Africa, all the while developing the idea of creating a truly independent daily that would challenge the *Herald*, and in March 1999, with a small board of investors and limited funds, he launched the *Daily News*.

When I was working for Rupert Murdoch, he told me that journalists can sometimes be the worst people to set up new publications, because they don't pay enough attention to advertising. Murdoch and his senior executives make a huge fuss of their key advertisers, and his corporation's US$13-billion annual turnover is testament to the success of this philosophy. Advertising is the fuel that powers any freestanding publication, and on some large newspapers, ad sales can make up 70 per cent of total company revenue.

It wasn't long before the demand for advertising space in the *Daily News* began to fall off, the novelty of a new paper having waned. Management had clearly not paid enough attention to the courtship of clients, and the sales representatives were largely ignorant about their craft. Some of them had been poached from the *Herald*, where they were little more than order clerks, manning telephones and waiting for customers to call. But the *Herald* was more than 100 years old, and both clients and advertising agencies had got used to spending most of their print budgets on its badly written pages.

Nyarota called and asked me whether I could give his people a talk on how they might increase the advertising revenue of the *Daily News*. I was happy to oblige, and he told me later that my lectures helped motivate his staff to go out and canvass business by knocking on doors.

About a year after the launch, the newspaper hired new sales executives and won over a significant number of clients. One of the section managers, Wilson Choto, became a powerful player in the marketplace, but it was the referendum and general election in 2000 that really allowed the *Daily News* to turn the corner.

'Our circulation rocketed,' Nyarota told me. 'You could see it on the pavements where the vendors stacked their papers: by mid-morning ours was sold out, and there was still a great pile of *Herald*s with no one buying them. But, with our paper surpassing the government daily's circulation, the threat of drastic action by the state became a horrifying reality.'

In April 2000, a bomb took out much of the ground floor of the *Daily News* building, destroying a curio shop and ethnic art gallery situated directly under Nyarota's office. Apart from a large crack on one wall in the editor's suite, the newspaper's offices, on the first to fourth floors, were unscathed.

Three months later, CIO agent Bernard Masara was sent to assassinate Nyarota, but developed cold feet and made a full confession about the plot to his would-be victim.

The *Daily News* published the story and installed Masara in a safe house, but when he threatened to carry out the murder unless he was paid a considerable sum of money, he ended up being arrested and charged with extortion. However, the newspaper was now firmly in the government's sights, and on 28 January 2001 the printing works was bombed and the press destroyed. The attack came just days after both information minister Jonathan Moyo and war veterans' leader Chenjerai Hunzvi had made public threats against the *Daily News*.

'Thanks to the exceptional efforts of our staff, we did not miss a single day's issue after the blast,' said Nyarota. 'But we were using someone else's press and could only print a maximum of 24 pages and 70 000 copies. Before the bomb, we often ran 48 pages and sold up to 120 000 copies.'

No one was ever charged with the bombings, and in time the *Daily News* acquired its own printing press – but Nyarota and many of his staff members and directors were arrested over and over, only to be released without any charges being laid against them. Theirs are among hundreds of individual cases of harassment against journalists from all the non-government papers, and the following are but a few examples of the tactics employed in the last few months of 2001:

- On 8 September, Mdudzi Mathuthu of the *Daily News* and Loughty Dube from the *Independent* were arrested for trespassing in a police station. They had gone to Bulawayo Central Police Station seeking comment on the arrest of bodyguards working for MDC member of parliament David Coltart.[7]
- A few days later, Mathuthu and three colleagues were attacked by ZANU-PF youth militia while covering an attack by war veterans on farm workers. The four were beaten with sticks and bicycle chains while police at the scene watched, but made no attempt to help them.[8]
- Early in November, a CIO officer threatened to kill freelance photographer Philemon Bulawayo for taking pictures outside a government building.[9]
- On 28 November, a journalist from the *Daily News* was charged under the Law and Order Maintenance Act for 'causing alarm or despondency' by reporting that people had walked out of a rally where Vice-President Joseph Masika was guest speaker. The story had appeared in August, but it apparently took the police three months to decide that it had alarmed anyone or made them despondent.
- Vendors selling non-government papers on street corners were regularly harassed or rounded up, and their stocks confiscated either by police or the party militia.
- On 1 December, the *Daily News* building was stoned by ZANU-PF supporters, who broke windows and beat photographer Chris Nhara when he tried to take pictures of the mob. The police ignored the attack.[10]

The arrests and harassment continued, and the level of persecution grew worse over the next two years, causing many members of the media to emigrate or change jobs. Journalists on all publications critical of the government were routinely dubbed 'enemies of the state', had their mail intercepted, telephones tapped, e-mail delivery disrupted and their personal affairs, including tax returns, scrutinised by agents of the state.

Foreign correspondents, including Zimbabweans working for international publications or news agencies, were singled out for special treatment. In February 2001, Jonathan Moyo expelled Joseph Winter, a BBC correspondent – who was forced to flee his home with his terrified family after it was attacked by a group of thugs at 2 am – and Mercedes Sayagues, of the South African *Mail & Guardian*. The next target was one of Britain's top journalists, David Blair of the *Daily Telegraph*, who was expelled in July 2001 after simply being informed by Moyo that his temporary work permit would not be renewed 'on administrative grounds'.[11]

On 23 November 2001, the *Herald* ran a front-page story and photographs of six other foreign correspondents: Basildon Peta of the *Independent* (UK), Bumisani Muleya of *Business Day* (South Africa), Jan Raath of *The Times* (UK), Peta Thornycroft of the *Daily Telegraph* (UK), Andrew Meldrum of the *Guardian* (UK) and Angus Shaw of Associated Press.

It was little more than two months since Osama Bin Laden's disciples had attacked the World Trade Center in New York, and President George W Bush had vowed in a speech that America would not distinguish between the actual terrorists and those who befriended and supported them.

The *Herald* took up the theme.

'We, too, will not make any difference between terrorists and their friends or supporters,' it thundered, accusing the writers of 'media terrorism' because they had written stories critical of Mugabe.

'For these reporters to continue aiding and inflaming is morally wrong, because journalists are ethically bound to tell a complete, balanced, fair and accurate story. That is what is lacking in all their reports, and this is unacceptable.'

The idea of the *Herald* pontificating on the subject of fair reporting was laughable, but in the mad world of Jonathan Moyo, rational thought always was a rare commodity.

A few months later, Basildon Peta was forced into exile in South Africa, fearing for his life, and other foreign correspondents continued to be harassed.

If the government was scared of the press, it was terrified of the electronic media, which allowed people to access and share information on a scale no one could have imagined in 1980. As more Internet service providers entered the market, a law was introduced that allowed the authorities to install filtering software through which all e-mail messages could be monitored. The directors and management of service providers not only had to cooperate, but also faced fines and prison sentences if they informed subscribers that their e-mail was being tapped.[12]

Mobile phones – known in southern Africa as cellphones – were another target, and the government tried hard to prevent the establishment of private networks that would cut across the CIO's ability to tap lines at will.

After 1980, landline equipment used by the old Post and Telecommunications

Corporation (PTC) had been stretched well beyond its capacity to cope with thousands of new black subscribers. Additional equipment was installed, but in some districts the backlog meant a wait of up to fourteen years for a new landline connection.

On average, sub-Saharan Africa offers one landline for every seventy people, compared to a one-to-one ratio in Europe, and by the early 1990s, it was clear that the PTC was losing the telephone battle in Zimbabwe.

In 1993 Strive Masiyiwa, who had studied engineering in Wales before returning home in the 1980s to join the PTC, decided to establish a mobile phone network. He was able to raise the funds, but when he proposed a joint venture with the PTC, he was told there was no demand for cellphones in Zimbabwe, and that in any event, the government had a monopoly on telecommunications.

When Masiyiwa went to court to test that monopoly, the judges agreed that it was in conflict with the constitution, which guaranteed freedom of speech, but Mugabe simply issued a presidential decree making private cellphone networks illegal.

Undaunted, Masiyiwa went back to court and challenged the very powers that had been given to Mugabe in 1987, including his right to issue binding decrees. Legal advice suggested that this conflicted with the constitution, and if the court agreed, not only this latest decree, but all others issued previously, would be rendered null and void.

But Masiyiwa never got the chance to strike a blow for freedom. He told me this was one of his major regrets. 'On realising that we would win, Mugabe pushed through separate legislation that allowed him to stop us from operating, which meant we had to mount a fresh case, based on the new law.'

By that time, the PTC had set up its own cellphone system, NetOne, but tenders were also called for a private network licence.

'Our argument to the court was simply that the government was not acting in good faith to get a private operator licensed and, in response, the court then gave communications minister Joyce Mujuru six weeks to go to tender and licence an operator. The judgment said if she did not do so in that time period, our company, to be known as Econet, would be deemed licensed by the court.

'Mujuru then went to tender, and awarded the licence to a firm called Telecel. Apart from the involvement of Leo Mugabe, the president's nephew, the chairman of the company was James Makamba, who at the time was the business partner of the minister's husband, former army general Solomon Mujuru.

'We challenged the award to Telecel as being irregular, and the judge ruled that we were correct, which meant that Mujuru had failed to licence an operator in the six weeks given by the court, so we were therefore deemed licensed.'

Even the vice-president, Joshua Nkomo, had questioned Joyce Mujuru's actions in parliament, and the government offered Masiyiwa a generous deal, including shares in Telecel, but he refused.

Dragging the matter through the courts delayed the launch of his Zimbabwe network by a year, but in the meantime he had established a cellular phone service in Botswana in February 1988. Five months later, Econet began operating in Harare, and after just three months had captured 60 per cent of the market.

Telecel eventually also obtained a licence, but it is Econet's numbers – with the 091 prefix – that are most in demand, because the CIO finds them hardest to tap.

But Masiyiwa had made powerful enemies in government, and over the next few years he and his staff were harassed to the point where he relocated to Johannesburg.

'I can't even travel to Zimbabwe these days,' he told me.

By the end of 2002, Econet had branched out into eight countries, including Nigeria and New Zealand, and that year Masiyiwa, aged forty-one, was named by *Time* magazine as one of the most influential people on the planet.

While the battle against the Internet, cellphones and the independent press continued, the government faced another threat. In 2000, a group of radio presenters had asked the courts to determine whether the ZBC had a legal monopoly on broadcasting.

The woman behind the move was veteran journalist Gerry Jackson, who had been fired from ZBC radio after warning listeners on 9 December 1998 to stay away from the centre of Harare, where food riots had sparked running battles between police and demonstrators.

'I was doing my usual shift when listeners started calling the studio,' she recalled. 'These people were in town and stuck in their cars in the middle of the chaos, and I put some of the calls on air.'

The government's view was that Jackson had caused alarm and despondency by even acknowledging that riots were in progress, whereas radio news bulletins had chosen to ignore the issue.

Her boss, Admire Taderera, told her she would not be able to return to Radio 3 because of her 'insubordination and total disregard for authority'. Taderera later confirmed that there had been pressure from both the president's office and the then Minister of Information, Chen Chemutengwende, to get rid of her.

This was not surprising, given that the minister regularly told reporters at the ZBC that it was their duty to support the ruling party 'even if this means stretching the truth'.

I also had a slot on ZBC radio in those days, a weekly programme called *Another Country*, in which I interviewed ambassadors and high commissioners, soliciting their views on a wide range of topics. My guests frequently made provocative comments, but although the series was pre-recorded, none of my tapes was ever doctored.

John Masuku, the head of radio who had recruited me for a part-time position with ZBC, explained that the government was not too concerned about what interviewees said on air, 'but when our own staff make comments, they get upset'.

Gerry Jackson resolved to set up her own radio station, but the prevailing wisdom, dating back to the 1950s, was that the state had a monopoly, though there was no specific legislation to this effect.

'I challenged the ZBC monopoly in court and the case was eventually heard in September 2000, after the parliamentary elections and when the country was in a real crisis. And we won the right to set up the first independent radio station,' she recalled.

The government had obviously not envisaged that anyone would attack the status quo and seek to compete against the existing radio services, and the court concluded that as there were no laws governing broadcasting, anyone could do it, especially as Section 20 (1) of the constitution guaranteed freedom of expression.

Jackson's lawyers had told her they expected the judges to mull over the problem for some months, but the decision was handed down swiftly on a Friday.

'The lawyers took me aside and told me that Jonathan Moyo had been sabre rattling, and was preparing to table restrictive legislation at the end of the next week, so I had better be set up and broadcasting by then, because it was easier to defend a reality than a theory. If the radio station was a fact, it would be a lot harder for the government to act.

'I had four working days to find staff, equipment, premises and a transmitter, which had to be sourced from Johannesburg, and the Monday was a public holiday in South Africa. I also had to find a huge amount of money – much of it in foreign exchange – and I called in every favour from everyone I knew. By the following Thursday, we were ready.

'There had been a panic that afternoon when the engineer who was supposed to install our equipment called at the last minute and said he thought what I was doing was illegal and he wasn't prepared to help, but I found someone else.

'Because there were no statutory regulations, there was no government authority to give us a frequency, so we chose one of our own, and at about 11.30 on Thursday night, we broadcast our first signal as Capital Radio.

'We had set up in temporary premises at the Eastgate Shopping Centre next to Meikles Hotel, but the next day we took a suite at the Monomatapa Hotel and raised the transmitter on the roof. We could actually see the ZBC mast from our window.

'Six days later, Mugabe decreed that it was illegal for anyone to own a transmitter. The first I heard of it was while I was at a production company, and someone asked me whether I knew that paramilitary officers were at my home with automatic rifles. Moments later, armed police broke down the door of our hotel room and seized the equipment.'

Jackson went back to court and was granted an order instructing the police to return the equipment, but they defied the ruling. The Capital Radio team realised they would have to beam their signal into Zimbabwe from another country.

Regional governments were reluctant to entertain the idea, so Jackson looked further afield.

'We needed a country with a good communication system, preferably English-speaking and where we would be allowed to work unhindered.

'I found a shortwave provider in England with a licence to relay programming from independent stations. All you had to do was assure them that you would not be transmitting hate speech, they would monitor broadcasts for a while, and that was it.

'At that time I was still funding the whole exercise myself, and from a personal point of view the project was a financial disaster. Then came the problem of recruiting staff. I approached the best Zimbabwean broadcasters I knew and made up a team. Some pulled out, others stayed, and eventually we settled down with a stable crew.

'It was vital that the broadcasters were known to the target listeners, preferably already had a radio audience in Zimbabwe and especially that they were unlikely to be used as ZANU-PF spies.

'The whole thing was hugely expensive, and when we first moved to England we had no idea how long we would last. I had assumed we could rent space in London, but the costs were horrendous and there were licensing rules imposed by the different councils. So I found a licensed business centre that already had the blessing of the council, and we set up shop.

'In addition to our start-up costs, we had to find the money to advertise in Zimbabwe, though of course the state-run newspapers refused to sell us space. The shortwave provider had a hub in London and our signal had to be sent there, and then transmitted to a footprint in southern Africa. Our signal could not be picked up in London, not even with a shortwave transmitter, but it could be accessed through our twenty-four-hour Internet streaming.'

The station was named Short-Wave Africa, but its call sign was SW Africa, and despite intimidation in Zimbabwe, it quickly built up a chain of correspondents across the region.

In Mugabe's home area of Zvimba, ZANU-PF youths assaulted an elderly couple in December 2002 and threatened to burn down their house because they had been caught listening to the station, but no official action was taken by the authorities to clamp down on people tuning in during the daily broadcast times of 6 pm to 9 pm.

Presenters included Georgina Godwin, who used to present the breakfast show on ZBC Radio 1, Mandy Mundawarara, the first black newsreader with the old Rhodesian Broadcasting Corporation, Tererai Karimakwenda, Violet Gonda, John Matinde, Richard Allfrey and Gerry Jackson herself.

Thousands of Zimbabweans at home and living in South Africa tuned in nightly to the independent service bent on breaking Mugabe's control of the airwaves. Shortwave bands increase in strength once the sun has set, and the signal from Hertfordshire, north of London, came through almost as clearly as the propaganda put out by the ZBC.

It is amazing that as late as January 2000, ZBC Radio still had independent broadcasters doing part-time shifts, and whose programmes management did not regulate beyond the guideline that they should contain no political content.

For several years, I hosted the Friday drive-time show from 4 pm to 8 pm that became known as *The Mile Long Club*, because most of my listeners were stuck in petrol queues. So, the joke ran, many people claim to have had sex in an aircraft, thus qualifying for membership of the Mile High Club – but have you ever done it in a fuel queue?

The show was lighthearted, with an easy mix of music ranging from rock to country and western, and a liberal dash of comedy by the likes of the Goons, Monty Python, Dudley Moore, Bill Cosby and old BBC shows including *Round the Horn* and the audio versions of *Yes, Minister* and *The Good Life*. Surveys revealed that I had an audience of close on half a million, the biggest late afternoon listenership of the week. I was also the only white presenter who switched between English and Shona on air, and since there were only 80 000 whites left in the country, at least 420 000 of my listeners were black.

John Masuku had been transferred to Bulawayo not long after recruiting me for the ZBC, but I worked well with the head of Radio 1, Petros Masakara, who lived in terror of being called upstairs to explain himself to the directors, but always tried to defend his staff. When Petros left to join a non-governmental organisation, Phatu Manala took over. She came from the minority Venda tribe near Beit Bridge, and even though her partner was a CIO officer, Phatu was not always a fan of ZANU-PF.

Georgina Godwin was still on air when I joined, and I took my cue from her by playing songs with a political message so subtle that the significance simply sailed over the heads of Moyo and his commissars. When a senior party thug died, I would slip in Queen's 'Another One Bites The Dust', and on the eve of any by-election, listeners would get Europa with 'The Final Countdown'.

My listeners, black and white, would phone in to let me know that *they* had got the message, and their favourite tracks were John Lennon's 'Power to the People' and the Dylan classic, 'The Times They Are A-Changin'.

And indeed they were.

ZBC Radio was a challenge for Moyo, because the station had no money, a library full of old, cracked vinyl records (announcers had to bring their own CDs) and a staff made up mostly of part-timers who were paid a mere Z$300 per shift – enough for a few cans of cola. But all three stations, Radio 1, 2 (Shona and Ndebele) and 3 (heavy rock music) were hugely popular.

Moyo tried to solve the problem by relocating Radio 1 to Bulawayo, 2 to Mbare and 3 to Gweru, which meant that new managers and staff could be recruited under his watchful eye and the stations could at last become twenty-four-hour propaganda machines. Moyo commissioned three double albums of anti-white and anti-MDC hate music, and presenters were instructed to play the tracks at twenty-minute intervals.

In our last days at ZBC, presenters were all given copies of the first album, and one of my colleagues was in a surprisingly good mood – and grateful to Moyo – on distribution day.

'Cassettes are expensive,' he told me with a laugh. 'As we speak, I am recording some R&B over the tracks, and when that's done, I'll gladly play the minister's "tapes" on my show.'

Phatu was initially tasked to set up a station in Harare for the minority languages, including Shangaan, Xhosa, Tonga and her own Venda, but like most ZBC employees she was eventually retrenched. My final programme was on 6 January 2002, and I received more than 130 calls. Some listeners even came into the studio to say goodbye, but they were not just bidding farewell to a broadcaster or a specific show – it was the death of a national radio service that had existed for more than eighty years. On the replacement stations, presenters with scant experience would be given instruction sheets and told not only what music to play, but what to say.

My old boss, John Masuku, was a true radio hand, a man of both wisdom and compassion and the only manager at ZBC who really understood the medium. He had been with ZBC since before independence and had seen censorship applied by both white and black governments, though he told me that nothing had ever matched Moyo's brand of tyranny.

When the country was still Rhodesia, his family, who were Matabele from the Bulawayo area, had been forced to move off their land to make way for white farmers, yet he had forgiven the disgraceful act and bore no bitterness.

In 2000, like Gerry Jackson, he tried to start a private radio station. When it became clear that the government would not allow him to do so, he set up a studio where programmes could be taped and sent to Holland, from where they were beamed to Zimbabwe on transmitters rented from Radio Netherlands.

Masuku was rightly proud of his achievement. 'After years of a staple diet of rationed or distorted information from state radio, Zimbabweans were finally able to receive objective news coverage that canvassed all viewpoints and opinions,' he told me.

The fledgling station, Voice of the People (VOP), was guided by a board of trustees headed by a leading psychiatrist, Dr Faith Ndebele, and her deputy, Professor Masiphula Sithole, a political science lecturer at the University of Zimbabwe. VOP broadcast two one-hour programmes – one in the morning and the other in the evening – on 7120 Khz, shortwave, and covered politics, the economy, health, the law and community development issues in Shona, Ndebele and English. But the government would not leave Masuku alone, and in July 2002, police raided VOP's offices in search of transmitters, and took away with them some tapes and files which they did not return until three weeks later.

After that, they got serious.

Shortly after midnight on 29 August, two explosions destroyed both the studio and VOP's office at 32 Van Praagh Avenue in Milton Park, Harare. John, a tough customer, was close to tears when he told me the story.

'Three men overpowered the guard and gained entry to the premises. Two held the guard while the third went to plant the bombs, which went off soon after. No culprits were ever brought to book.'

Undeterred, the VOP team rebuilt their studio and went back on air, but the toll of victims in the battle between ZANU-PF and the media continued to mount.

Towards the end of 2002, Mark Chavunduka died of causes related to his torture. Ray Choto went to live in America, one of dozens of journalists, advertising executives, public relations consultants and others associated with the information industry who either left Zimbabwe voluntarily or were forced out.

Perhaps the greatest casualty was Geoff Nyarota, who parted company with the *Daily News* at the beginning of 2003.

The reasons for his departure are complex, and depending on whose version one believes, were either the result of ZANU-PF spies infiltrating the management echelon, or Nyarota's own shortcomings in running the business side of the newspaper.

It would be no exaggeration to say that Nyarota *was* the *Daily News*, and that without his courage and vision the newspaper would never even have got off the ground editorially, let alone eclipse the *Herald* and become a major factor in the opposition's success in both the referendum and the 2000 election.

Should a future government establish a truth commission in Zimbabwe – one of Morgan Tsvangirai's most solemn promises during his election campaigns – and should certain ZANU-PF luminaries be tried for crimes against humanity, much of the recorded testimony would come from the pages of the *Daily News*. But the newspaper was never a viable business proposition, and in the weeks preceding the 2000 election, it came close to financial collapse.

When Trevor Ncube bought the *Independent*, he asked Strive Masiyiwa to 'warehouse' the shares. This meant that Masiyiwa, living in Johannesburg, would pay Wilson the full asking price and hold the equity in trust until Ncube could raise the money to cover the deal.

Perhaps it was with this precedent in mind that Nyarota and the board of Associated Newspapers Zimbabwe (ANZ) approached the Econet boss.

'They came to me in the middle of 2000, before the election,' Masiyiwa told me. 'The *Daily News* needed Z$100 million urgently, and it would have been a tragedy for our democracy in Zimbabwe if the newspaper shut down, so I agreed to help.[13]

'I bought into the paper, thus joining Derek Smail, who had provided much of the original funding and still owned 38 per cent of the shares. But I made it a condition that the other new investors and I would control the business side of the newspaper.'

Smail, a wealthy British businessman and OBE, had financed Nyarota in 1999 through a company called Africa Media Investments, though on more than one occasion ZANU-PF incorrectly claimed that the money came from the British government.

After the election, according to Masiyiwa, the new investors wanted to re-organise the board to reflect their equity.

'There was no suggestion of interference with editorial control, but a newspaper is also a business, and I asked a friend in Harare to find someone who could act as a non-executive chairman. One of the names that came up was that of Sam Nkomo, and we ended up appointing him, while Much Masunda retained his role as chief executive and Geoff remained editor-in-chief.'

It seems that this was where the trouble started. After a few months, Nkomo told the new owners that the business side of the paper was a mess. Accounts were not processed in accordance with standard practice, and decisions to hire and fire people were taken on a whim, often by Nyarota.

Masunda was asked to leave, and Nkomo took over as executive chairman.

Nkomo had crossed swords with the *Daily News* in 1999 while chief executive officer of the wealthy Mining Industry Pension Fund, which was financing a new building called Angwa City in Harare's CBD. Allegations were made that Nkomo had bypassed the usual tender process and awarded some of the construction contracts to a personal friend, and after the *Daily News* and other newspapers ran the story, Nkomo was forced to resign.

He was duly arrested, but before he was asked to enter a plea, the charges against him were withdrawn. The Minister for Home Affairs, under whom the police fell, was Sam's cousin John Nkomo, but there was never any evidence that he intervened in the matter.

Despite their recent history, Sam Nkomo and Geoff Nyarota seemed to get on well, according to Masiyiwa.

'They used to come to my office in Johannesburg and discuss things with me, and in the early days of the relationship there was no evidence of a clash. But Geoff wanted no interference in the way he ran things and was not consulting Sam, even on the hiring of staff. Naturally, Sam complained to me that as the person legally responsible for actions taken by the company, he needed to know what was going on.

'I dared not set foot in Zimbabwe, so I asked Derek Smail to go to Harare from London, and get an undertaking from Geoff that he would follow Sam's direction. Geoff agreed to this, but there was still a huge personality clash between him and Sam. And then there was the strike.'

The staff of the *Daily News* walked out shortly before Christmas 2002, after being told that their next pay rise would be only 10 per cent, while inflation was running at close on 200 per cent. The newspaper's executive committee decided that none of the striking employees would be paid during the stayaway, and according to Nkomo, Nyarota was at the meeting and agreed with the decision.

Nyarota's own recollection of events is more complex.

According to him, the executive agreed unanimously that the no work, no pay rule would be applied only in respect of actual days lost, and that the December pay packets of only those employees who had gone on strike would be docked.

'Sam Nkomo then asked heads of department to furnish his office with two lists: one containing the names of those who had stayed away, the other the names of those who had continued to turn up for work or were on legitimate leave.

'He sent the names of striking employees to the bank, with instructions that their full December salaries should be frozen. The bank was expected to go through the entire ANZ payroll and effect the separation, a task that was simply beyond their capacity at the time.

'The bank was unable to carry out Sam's instructions for purely logistical reasons. All banks were under pressure because of the Christmas rush, with endless queues of clients, and at times they even ran out of cash due to the demand.

'So the bank did the next best thing – froze *all* ANZ salaries. Sam had not shown the courtesy of informing anyone of the pending freeze, so workers were actually punished twice: they were not paid for the days they had been on strike *or* the rest of the month. And staff who had not even been part of the strike, but had rendered a crucial service during the crisis, had *their* salaries stopped as well!

'I became aware of this when I failed to access my own salary at the bank. I checked with our company finance manager, who said he was not aware of any problem, but would look into the matter and get back to me.

'When he did, it was to say he'd been informed by the bank that an instruction was received from ANZ to freeze all December salaries. By that time, Sam had disappeared to enjoy his Christmas holiday, leaving staff high and dry, to spend Christmas with their families and nothing in their pockets.'

When I put these claims to Nkomo over the telephone, he denied them.

'Staff who were working, including Geoff, received their salaries in full, and it is nonsense for anyone to suggest otherwise,' he said.

Nyarota raised the money privately, and paid the employees a total of Z$4 million. According to Nkomo, it was Z$9.6 million, but he acknowledged that the money did not come from the *Daily News*.

Nyarota made the staff agree to certain conditions before paying them.

'I arranged that they would return to work on Monday 30 December, to produce the newspaper that had been suspended due to their strike action, and that they would repay the money as soon as their salaries were secured.

'That was how the *Daily News* appeared on the streets on 31 December. Unfortunately, the lead story on the front page was that I had been dismissed, though I have never received any official communication to that effect.

'The first I heard of my fate was on ZBC news, and I have still not received my termination benefits. Not a word has ever been said, and legally I am still a member of the newspaper's staff.'

The *Herald* had lost no time capitalising on the strike, publishing their customary Moyo-speak version of events on Christmas Day under the headline 'Daily News Makes History, Fails to Publish'. The story claimed that the *Daily News* had 'become the first daily paper in the history of Zimbabwe which has failed to hit the streets owing to industrial action'.

That was a blatant lie, because the *Herald* had been hit by strikes and failed to publish several times.

The report also stated that 'irate advertisers and subscribers complained bitterly and felt robbed after the paper, which claims to command the largest circulation in Zimbabwe, failed to reach its readers', but neglected to name any of these angry individuals.

'Insiders say there was more to the problems bedevilling the *Daily News* than meets the eye,' trumpeted the *Herald*.

'It is understood that there were serious differences between the editor-in-chief of the *Daily News*, Geoff Nyarota, and the chief executive of the holding company – Associated Newspapers Zimbabwe – Mr Sam Siphepha Nkomo.

'When Mr Nkomo assumed his new post, he relieved Nyarota of his roles to be in charge of circulation, sales, advertising and the editorial as he tried to lead the paper in a professional manner.

'Nyarota was reported to be meeting with reporters whom he was urging to carry on with the industrial action. "He is actually blessing the strike, he is having secret meetings with reporters and telling them that he has never failed to produce a paper and the current management was failing," said a source.

'Nyarota, who could not be reached yesterday, has throughout the week referred all questions relating to the strike to Mr Nkomo who in turn has been very hostile.'

At no point did the *Herald* name its sources or quote anyone in management, but the idea that Nyarota was secretly encouraging the strike makes no sense, since it was he who paid the staff and persuaded them to return to work.

Nevertheless, the state media attacked Nyarota at every turn, belabouring the point that Nkomo was doing his best under difficult conditions.

The soft take on Nkomo inevitably gave rise to conspiracy theories, and Nyarota remained convinced that his former boss was influenced by his cousin, the Minister for Home Affairs, and that the plot to oust him as editor had originated with Jonathan Moyo.

'Moyo had achieved the major aim of his agenda, with a little help from Sam Nkomo,' he told me. 'Moyo must have been kicking himself for failing to think of such a simple strategy earlier – destabilisation through infiltration.'

Nyarota's unilateral action in paying the staff placed Strive Musiyiwa in an impossible position.

'The management at the paper were furious,' he said, 'especially the head of personnel, who was responsible for salaries. I phoned Geoff and asked him how he would feel if personnel secretly published an edition of the newspaper without his consent, because this is the way they felt when the editor interfered with their work.

'But he would not listen. He said it was now a simple choice: either Sam would have to go, or he would leave. I asked my other shareholders what they thought because, between us, we owned 98 per cent of the stock, and it was unanimous that Geoff should step down.'

It was a hard decision, said Masiyiwa, because Nyarota was a close friend who had laid his life on the line time and again in the paper's daily fight with the government.

Almost as soon as he was fired and no longer able to use the newspaper to expose harassment by agents of the state, the police started looking for Nyarota, and he had to leave the country. Not surprisingly, he took with him a deep bitterness about the way his dream had ended.

'The problem with the story of my departure from the *Daily News* was that nobody – not the board of directors to whom I reported or the media – ever bothered to ask for my side of the story. I realised everyone had been mesmerised by Nkomo's "charm". Even the *Daily News* failed to tell it like it was. Suddenly, I was without a friend. I had been used and discarded like toilet paper, and that was that.

'I left Zimbabwe because I valued my life. I did not want to die in the front line fighting for a cause in which I was almost the only soldier, subjecting myself (and members of my family, in some cases) to harassment, endless arrests, threats of death, pain, embarrassment and deprivation. I became seriously diabetic as a result of the stress caused by the *Daily News*. I left Zimbabwe because I no longer had the support of the newspaper, the police were hunting for me day and night and they could have killed me by simply withdrawing medication for my diabetes.'

On 7 January 2003, the *Daily News* published a report headed 'Why Nyarota Was Fired'. The only person quoted was Sam Nkomo, who said: 'We painfully avoided parting ways with Geoff for some time, but the paralytic effect that the strike had on the company, and Geoff's unfortunate decision to support this action … left us with no option but to let Geoff go.'

In a style more usually associated with the *Herald*, no alternative view was offered, and Nyarota was not invited to put his case.

Sam Nkomo admitted to me that Nyarota was the key ingredient of the early success achieved by the *Daily News*.

'There is no question about his bravery or his editorial abilities,' Nkomo said, but insisted that neither his cousin John nor the ruling party had influenced his own work at the newspaper in any way.

'It is true that I have a cousin who is a senior member of the ruling party and a minister. We are related through our fathers, who are brothers. But whereas Geoff Nyarota might have been a member of ZANU-PF in the early days, I myself never belonged to that party. I was a ZAPU member in the sixties and spent time in jail for it, but when the split came, I knew that black politics was going in the wrong direction. I never supported ZANU or became a member, and I was never even close to my cousin. We see each other at funerals or other family gatherings, but we never talk politics because it would only lead to an argument, and John knows that.'

The *Daily News* continued to live up to its masthead promise to 'tell it like it is', but it had lost its former spark. Nyarota was offered a prestigious Nieman Fellowship at Harvard University in the US, and launched a new career by lecturing widely on Zimbabwe.

That he was difficult to work with is a matter of record, verified by several people who spent time under his editorship at various publications. As for his dismissal, it was probably true, as Masiyiwa said, that the shareholders were left with little choice.

But even in a true democracy like Britain or America, an editor's job is never easy. Dozens of stories vie for attention, some true, others merely rumour, and as the daily deadline ticks ever closer, it is the editor who must decide to publish or abandon a particular story. Often these decisions are based on courage, experience and gut feel, and one has only to read accounts of how the *Washington Post* exposed the Watergate scandal in the early 1970s to understand the pressure under which any editor works.

In a country like Zimbabwe under Mugabe, where the government would stop at nothing – including murder – to safeguard its position, a genuine editor's job would be that much harder, with no room for weakness or vacillation. And it was, after all, Nyarota's authoritarian style that gave the *Daily News* its strength, and allowed it to break stories that charged the most powerful people in the land with murder, torture, corruption and fraud. It was truly a case of publish and be damned.

The media battle in Zimbabwe raged on long after Nyarota's departure. The next step required journalists to be licensed by the state, with a panel appointed by Jonathan Moyo deciding who would or would not be permitted to report for both the local and foreign media.

By late 2003, few foreign correspondents had survived. Peta Thornycroft and Jan Raath were still in Harare reporting the facts, but Andrew Meldrum of the *Guardian*, who had been covering on Zimbabwe for twenty years, had his residence permit withdrawn and was manhandled onto an aeroplane and deported to London.

Despite the increasing repression, indomitable veterans such as Iden Wetherall, editor of the *Independent*, remain as resolute as ever.

'We are all just going to carry on doing our work,' he told me when the licensing regulations were introduced.

As pressure on the media continues to mount, a small corps of men and women at the *Independent*, the *Standard*, the *Daily News*, John Masuku's studio in Harare and Radio SW Africa north of London, continue to hold the front line in the battle for Zimbabwe, determined to ensure that the truth will out.

# 9

# Die another day

Before the general election in June 2000, cabinet ministers had suggested – off the record – that once their party was returned to power, the war vets would leave the farms, factory invasions would be halted and things would go back to normal. But, with Mugabe facing a presidential election during the first half of 2002, the opposite happened. By the end of 2001, 90 per cent of Zimbabwe's 4 000 commercial farms had been occupied or were under threat of imminent seizure by war veterans and the youth militia, while political violence in its many guises had claimed more than 120 lives across the country, mostly at the hands of ZANU-PF.

Many more had been assaulted, and it was from these people – the survivors – that evidence about both the nature and scale of atrocities poured into the offices of non-governmental organisations and human rights watchdogs.

According to one report produced by Radio Netherlands,[1] more than 40 000 people were tortured and abused in 2001. Amnesty International (AI) recorded that 70 000 farm workers had been chased off the land by the invaders, leaving many of them homeless, and that there were 'forced evictions, arbitrary arrests, beatings, torture and political killings amounting to a pattern of deliberate state-sponsored repression of opposition to government policies'.[2]

In many cases, according to AI, 'the police not only stood by and failed to intervene in assaults by war veterans and the militia, but actively took part in a number of attacks alongside ZANU-PF supporters'.

The organisation's 2001 report is extensive, but a few cases stand out for their brutality:

- In April, an MDC supporter abducted by ZANU-PF militia in the Dzivaresekwa township near Harare had an X burned into his back with red-hot chains as punishment for distributing MDC membership cards.
- In the same month, Tawanda Hondora, chairman of the Zimbabwe chapter of Lawyers for Human Rights, was kicked, whipped and beaten by ZANU-PF supporters while visiting Chikomba, north of Harare, to consult with witnesses in another case of intimidation that was about to go to court. Police watched the attack but took no action, and when Hondora reported the incident at a

charge office in Harare, the police at Chikomba denied that it had ever taken place.

- On 8 April, black students at the University of Zimbabwe were set upon by police while staging a peaceful campus demonstration against a cut in college grants. One student, Batanai Hadzidzi, was beaten to death, and twenty-eight others were injured. The next day, when Hadzidzi's friends mounted a fresh protest to draw attention to his death, police opened fire on them with live ammunition.

- In June, Zondiwa Dumukani, a thirty-two-year-old driver working on a farm near Harare airport, was beaten to death by a group of eight war veterans while police watched and failed to intervene. The killers alleged that he had not shown up for a ZANU-PF meeting. When Dumukani's employer, a white farmer, reported the murder to the police, they took no action against the war veterans, arresting the farmer and thirty of his employees instead for 'assaulting members of the ruling party'.

- In August, Douglas Chapotera, MDC deputy chairman for Makoni West, had his home set on fire by fifty ruling party supporters who arrived just before midnight, brandishing pick handles. While Chapotera and his wife, niece and four children hid inside, their assailants smashed the doors and windows, doused the house with petrol and set it ablaze. The family fled, then realised that their baby son was still in the building. As they tried to fight their way back inside, the mob beat them so badly that Mrs Chapotera was later admitted to hospital and her baby had to be treated for severe burns. The attack was reported to police, but by the end of the year they had neither arrested anyone nor gathered any evidence.

In August 2001, the worst violence yet occurred in the Chinhoyi area, 100 kilometres north of Harare, when war veterans, youth brigades and police ransacked more than twenty white-owned farms, while gangs moved through the town beating up white residents and those blacks perceived to be sympathetic to the MDC.

Instead of stemming the violence, the police arrested the white farmers, whom the *Herald* accused of hiring gangs to raid their own properties in an effort to discredit the militia.

Following this spate of attacks, South Africa's president, Thabo Mbeki, said in a television interview that Mugabe was 'not listening' to his words of caution, but in Lagos, Nigerian foreign minister Sule Lamido took a tougher line.

'The [Zimbabwe] government must not give the impression that it, directly or indirectly, acquiesces in forcible land takeovers,' he told the media. 'Nigeria is very concerned about the threat the situation poses to regional peace and security in southern Africa.'[3]

A month later, in September, the foreign ministers of seven Commonwealth countries – Australia, Britain, South Africa, Nigeria, Jamaica, Kenya and Zimbabwe – met in Abuja, where Nigerian president Olusegun Obasanjo made it clear that he wanted Zimbabwe to sign an undertaking that the government would end farm invasions, restore law and order, uphold court rulings and judgments, show due regard for human rights and guarantee freedom of the press.

Mugabe's foreign minister, Stan Mudenge, phoned Harare and sought permission to sign the document.

'They were serious, dead serious,' one of Mudenge's assistants told me later. 'We thought we could get some slack from black countries like Jamaica and Kenya, but they said that what was going on in Zimbabwe was affecting the world's perception of Africa as a whole, and my boss is a very practical man who knows when the game is up. He phoned the president and told him he would have to concede, or risk losing what little support we had left in the Commonwealth.'

Mudenge signed the so-called Abuja Accord, but the violence continued as Mugabe stepped up his campaign to win back the electorate by force. Nigeria and South Africa had pledged to ensure that the agreement was honoured, but within weeks it was clear that their efforts had failed.

Two months after the accord was signed, Zimbabwean author Cathy Buckle, whose book *African Tears*[4] deals extensively with the land question, sent me a story describing the naked terror of a farm invasion that had just taken place, and which is reproduced below in full:

One afternoon this week, I sat in a civilised Marondera restaurant and listened to an elderly couple relate the events of a night of barbaric terror. A mob of 40 youngsters stormed a farmhouse and left a trail of utter destruction.

As is often the case, the invaders claimed to be war veterans and they came at night. Shortly after 7 pm there was frantic barking at the back of the house and desperate knocking on the front door. One farm worker had raced to warn his employers that a rabble was approaching. The farmer's wife heard the roar of a mob at the gate, and barely had time to lock the back door.

The invaders broke the garden gates and swarmed towards the house, roaring, shouting and bellowing. The elderly woman and her husband had nowhere to run, no way of getting out of their own home, because in moments the house was surrounded.

Windows were rattled, gutters banged and a steady and incessant thumping began on the back door. The noise was overwhelming. 'It was just a great roar,' the farmer's wife told me, and they had to shout as they called for help

147

from neighbours via the radio and from the police on the telephone. The situation was deteriorating by the second, but the police did not come.

The couple heard the back door being broken down and they retreated down the passageway, closing and locking an interleading door behind them. The noise escalated; someone was on the roof, smashing a hole into the asbestos, and windows were shattering all over the house.

Then the thugs started on the interleading door, banging and hammering, and the couple were forced to leave the farm radio and retreat to their bedroom. They heard the second door being broken down and could only communicate with their cellphone. Still the police did not come.

The bedroom windows were smashed and a burning torch came through as the mob attempted to set the curtains on fire. For three hours this went on: banging, shouting and smashing as 40 men rampaged through the farmhouse.

When at last help came at 10 pm, there were no sirens, arrests or handcuffs; instead the situation was 'defused' by political intervention. The couple came out of their bedroom and, in deep shock and thankful to be alive, saw the ruin that had been their home.

A plug had been put into a sink and the taps turned on. The lounge, pantry and dining room were completely flooded, carpets and furniture stood in five centimetres of water. The contents of the fridge and deep freeze – meat, milk, fruit, vegetables and bread – were gone. Plates and glasses were smashed and there was broken glass everywhere. Cutlery had been taken from the drawers, tools from the garage and someone had attempted to drain petrol from the car.

Two dozen geese had been stolen from the garden and for that three men were arrested the following morning. For the destruction amounting to nearly half-a-million dollars worth of damage, no one was arrested. For the empty fridge and deep freeze, the missing cutlery and tools, no one was arrested. For the breaking and entering, smashed windows and doors, flooded property and extreme intimidation, no one was arrested.

The words that this couple used as they told of their horror, are ones that are being echoed by farmers all over Zimbabwe. 'It could have been worse,' they said. 'At least we are alive.'

When I asked them what they were going to do, the couple were united. 'We haven't got a Plan B. That farm is 40 years of our life. We haven't got anywhere to go.'

ZANU-PF had lost two prominent figures in a row in 2001, when the Minister for Employment, Border Gezi, and defence minister Moven Mahachi were killed

The ruins of Great Zimbabwe – the largest stone structure in
sub-Saharan Africa – fuelled speculation that the country was rich in gold

Lobengula's kraal at Bulawayo

On 11 November 1965, Ian Smith – here signing the document – became the first leader since George Washington to unilaterally declare his country independent from Britain

The election of Abel Muzorewa as president in 1979 was the first democratic change of government in Africa in 25 years. He abolished discrimination, but could not end the civil war

Sally Mugabe, Robert Mugabe's first wife,
in Copenhagen, 1980

Edison Zvobgo supported Mugabe throughout
the war, and drew up the Act that vastly increased
the president's powers. Later in life, he denounced
both Mugabe and the Party as failures

Despite a 40-year age gap, Mugabe married his secretary, Grace Marufu,
with whom he had two children prior to the death of his first wife, Sally

Former president Nelson Mandela (right) was never on good terms with Mugabe,
and is on record as saying that all African dictators should be overthrown

Morgan Tsvangirai, recently elected president of the Movement for Democratic Change,
reads the headline story on the government's shock defeat in the constitutional referendum, 2000

War veterans' leader Chenjerai Hunzvi forced Mugabe to accept that former ZANLA and ZIPRA guerillas had been treated shamefully after independence

The farm invasions by war veterans were coordinated at the highest level, although Mugabe claimed the occupations were spontaneous

A young resident of Mabvuku township in Harare runs across a road blocked with rocks used by protestors as a barricade on 16 October 2000, during a demonstration against hikes in bread prices

Zimbabwean information minister, Professor Jonathan Moyo, at the Hilton Hotel in Sandton, Johannesburg, for the World Summit on Sustainable Development, 2002

In the 2002 presidential election, Tsvangirai presented himself as
relaxed and friendly, while Mugabe went for a show of strength

*Daily News* editor Geoff Nyarota waits in line to
cast his vote in the 2002 presidential election

The future is uncertain
for young Zimbabweans

At every level, the South African government has been tolerant of black Zimbabwean protestors, seen here setting up outside President Mbeki's office in Pretoria

A wanted poster used by the pressure group in London, which lists 94 people allegedly murdered by the state

in car crashes within weeks of one another. Beerhall gossip had it that they had been deliberately bumped off because Gezi, who had set up the youth militia, was becoming too powerful, and Mahachi knew too much about Mugabe's plunder of the Congo, where thousands of troops were fighting to prevent the collapse of Laurent Kabila's government. The Congo was bankrupt, but paid for the help by allowing companies owned by senior ZANU-PF officials to take out timber and diamonds worth millions of dollars.

Then, in June, the leader of the war veterans, Chenjerai Hunzvi, died in hospital. Sources, including a nurse, leaked the news to the media that he had been diagnosed with full-blown AIDS, and had died as a result of contracting malaria.

The three fallen comrades had served ZANU-PF well, and their reward was burial at Heroes' Acre, but no further honours were accorded Hunzvi and Mahachi, not even a street or park bearing their names. However, Mugabe announced at Gezi's funeral that the militia system he had set up would be expanded into a voluntary national service scheme, with the original pilot programme near Bindura to be named the Border Gezi Training Camp.

There were already other training centres across the country, and more sprang up in quick succession. Young people either joined of their own free will in exchange for regular meals, or were grabbed by gangs of older recruits and taken to the camps for training. There they were kitted out in the distinctive olive drill trousers that earned them the nickname 'Green Bombers'.

But even in the midst of the most severe crisis, the Zimbabwean sense of humour is irrepressible, and this had soon been shortened to GB, which in colloquial slang translates as 'garden boy', regarded by many as the lowest form of employment. As mentioned earlier, the youth squads later underwent another name change, and were known on the streets as the Talibob.

From the bases, thousands of youths, male and female, were sent out daily to terrorise every school, store and village in the district. Unlike the war vets who were middle-aged and cantankerous, or the soldiers who had to be paid, the youngsters were inclined to follow orders and came cheap at the price – a pair of trousers and one meal a day.

With the advent of Christmas, calm fell over the land, and even the Talibob were allowed to go home and spend time with their families. The urban population went *kumusha*, and it was hard to believe that Zimbabwe was at war with itself.

But the New Year would show that this had merely been the eye of the storm.

Following a meeting of the ZANU-PF executive, the war vets and militia leaders about the need to escalate intimidation of the masses, the weekend of 12 and 13 January was designated for a campaign of terror.

In those areas previously unaffected by violence, camps were set up and Talibob were bused in and told to await further orders. One group of war vets near Centenary in central Mashonaland jumped the gun and chased twenty-three white families off their tobacco farms in the first week of January, providing an ominous warning of what lay ahead.

But on Saturday 12 January, I had no inkling of the scheduled campaign as I drove to a small village about ninety minutes from Harare.

For several years I had supported a community of about fifty men, women and children, most of whom were related to people who had worked for me at one time or another. The village is a typical small settlement where life is hard and luxuries are few. I had left Harare at about 10 am after packing the boot of *Ernie* – my Toyota Corolla hatchback – with clothes and toys collected from neighbours, and food that my housekeeper had bought that morning.

My wife, Hope, and I had brought the car with us when we moved from Sydney to Harare in 1997. Originally it was a company car bought for my business partner, Nick Russell, whose children had named it after a character in *Sesame Street*. But with three children the Russells needed a station wagon, and I took over the Corolla. *Ernie* was almost ten years old in 2002, and had notched up 400 000 kilometres in Australia and Africa.

The effects of the land invasions were clearly visible on supermarket shelves in Harare, items such as cooking oil and margarine having long since disappeared. But I had always taken food to the village, and my housekeeper had managed to find cans of corned beef, margarine, bread, tomato sauce, powdered milk and bottles of jam and soft drink, all of which would go down well with people who rarely enjoyed such treats.

In previous years, the government had made sure that shops were well stocked ahead of elections, but this time the economic collapse had become a calamity, and the United Nations was predicting that by the end of the year, 60 per cent of the population would be living on handouts.

But these were not thoughts for a day in the bush.

January is mid-summer in Zimbabwe, and it was already 27°C and rising. Beyond where I was headed, the good single-lane tar road continued to the border, and from there, heavy trucks used to push on to neighbouring countries to the north and east, laden with Zimbabwean produce such as milk, cheese, maize and beef,[5] or goods in transit from South Africa.

At the roadside, groups of black women sold potatoes, mangoes, guavas, tomatoes, butternut squash and spinach to passing motorists, and when the traffic was sparse, practised hymns for the Sunday service. If your car engine was well tuned, you could hear their singing on the breeze as you rounded a bend. On seeing the car they would smile and wave, trusting that their friendly demeanour would draw another customer.

I passed a homemade sign advertising potatoes at Z$600 a pocket – less than half the price in town – and I made a mental note to stop on the return journey.

One thing that strikes you outside the towns in Zimbabwe is the sparseness of the population. There are old people and children of school-going age and some young women who either care for their children while their husbands work in the city or help their parents in their old age.

Before the farm invasions, there were large numbers of workers on the land but they lived in special villages on the farms. Beyond that, the young adult population was dwindling as people sought a better life in town. When I was a child, I used to see a lot of people walking along the roads in rural areas but now it was just the young women sitting at their stalls, practising their songs and selling the tomatoes, potatoes and maize cobs they had grown.

I had heard on the BBC that morning that war veterans and youth brigades were setting up roadblocks on several routes, and had checked with the police before setting off. They assured me that the road I was travelling was clear and that it was safe to proceed.

I turned right onto a narrow tar strip just past a small growth point, a collection of stores and grain merchants supported by local farmers. It is beautiful country, with flat-crowned acacias, fertile soil and formations of balancing rocks that reach 100 metres or more into the air. This was always tribal land, part of the settlements reserved after 1923 for the exclusive use of the Shona, which had become known as communal areas.

It would be nice to stay at the village overnight, I though as I braked for a pothole.

Having spent some of my childhood in the bush, I was not averse to rural life, be it on a commercial farm or in a black village where I would sleep on a mat in one of the huts.

There's a sense of welcome in the Zimbabwe bush that I have found nowhere else, not even in South Africa, and I had told my housekeeper to pack me an overnight bag, 'just in case I break down'.

A few kilometres from the turnoff is a store flamboyantly named Cantata, and as usual I stopped for a cold drink – though I use the term lightly, because the shop fridge had not worked for years and the drinks were tepid.

In Africa, every rural store has a cool, wide verandah where people with nothing better to do pass the day, and Cantata is no different. Two unarmed policemen, out on foot patrol, were sitting on the porch. I bought them both a drink and we chatted about nothing in particular. When I asked about the road ahead, they said they hadn't been that far yet, but there were no reports of trouble.

It was only five kilometres to the next shops at Chikuyu Centre, but the tar road had given way to a dirt track that looked like a moonscape, and it took half an hour to cover the distance. Corruption and nepotism had virtually shut down the rural councils, giving rise to an oft-repeated joke: What looks like two red lights on a dark road? The eyes of a giraffe that has fallen into a pothole.

Finally, I parked next to the elevated verandah that ran along the front of five or six stores that all sold the same products at much the same prices, except for one at the end, which had a liquor licence. A former headmaster, long since retired and one of the world's true gentlemen, owned the first shop. Business was brisk in the morning and late afternoon, but in the heat of noon on a Saturday, people were relaxing at home, and when his shop was empty, the headmaster (I never learned his name) used to sit on a chair in the doorway and snooze.

But the place seemed deserted.

I left the keys in the car and went inside, and was about to jump the counter and go in search of the headmaster when a voice called out behind me.

'Give me money or I will kill you.'

I turned to see a middle-aged man urinating in the corner near the door. His shirt was hanging out and he spilled some beer from a bottle while he struggled to do up his fly. Leaving his zipper undone, he walked to the middle of the shop and stood with his eyes closed for a few seconds before repeating his threat.

'I am in charge of the war vets in this area,' he slobbered. 'I need money for beer. Give me Z$500 or I will call my other veterans and we will kill you.' He closed his eyes again and stood quite still.

In such circumstances, it was best to pay off a drunk and let him continue imbibing until he fell over or moved on to harass the local residents, so I went over, placed some notes in his hand and walked him out of the shop.

From my elevated position on the verandah, I looked down in horror to see my car surrounded by a group of perhaps 100 youths.

They had opened the door and one young man was standing with my keys in his hand.

Then things happened quickly.

One of the gang saw me and shouted '*Murungu!*' [white person], and the crowd turned and stared in my direction. Some were wearing ZANU-PF T-shirts, and the bottles of beer and smell of marijuana told me I was in real trouble.

It's amazing how much detail you absorb when adrenalin hits the brain. Even now I can picture the faces looking at me. There were four or five older men, who turned out to be genuine war vets, a handful in their late twenties, and I estimate that the rest were aged between fourteen and eighteen. Almost all of them appeared confused, each waiting for someone else to make the first move.

Instead I made the move, marching confidently from the porch, and the crowd parted as I walked up to the car. My idea was to simply get in, start the engine and drive off before anything else happened. I recognised a number of youngsters from the village, which told me the mob had been forcibly brought together, because most of the people in the area supported the MDC.

The man with the keys pushed the ignition key in the door lock and twisted it, breaking off the tip then he held it up for me to see and he laughed. 'Not going anywhere now!' he said, and I cursed myself for leaving the spare at home.

One of the older youths, wearing a black shirt with a dirty white collar and brown trousers stained with beer, pushed the younger children out of the way until he stood with his face ten centimetres from mine.

Then he bellowed like a sergeant major.

'You are trespassing here! This is ZANU-PF land, you fucking shit. And we can see a copy of the *Daily News* on the back seat of your car. You are here to put up posters for the presidential election.'

I had indeed brought some newspapers for the villagers, both the *Herald* and the *Daily News*, but as luck would have it, the opposition paper lay on top.

'The car is now ours. Open the door so we can search it.'

The youths murmured and shuffled their feet in the sand as they moved closer, those at the back standing on their toes and peering through the car windows like a jury trying to get a glimpse of Exhibit A.

The young man's spittle had sprayed across my face and I wiped it off with my sleeve before extending my hand.

'I'm Geoff Hill from the ZBC,' I said. 'And what is your name?'

He stood silent, then dropped his shoulders and lost all authority.

'I am James Makore,' he said. 'I am from this area and we are organising a new branch of the ZANU-PF youth league to help fight the presidential election.'

In that moment, had I brought the spare ignition key, I might have got away. But I was stranded, and I could do nothing but stand and wait for someone to speak.

The crowd parted and a man in his fifties came through. He was dressed in a pink shirt that clashed with his yellow checked trousers, but he was sober and spoke with a sense of authority.

'I am Winston Mukaka,' he said. 'I am chairman of the war vets in this area.'

He told me that when I had arrived, they were at the back of the shops, organising their new wing of the Green Bombers. Now they would need to interrogate me and discover my real purpose in the area. First, they would need to see my ZANU-PF membership card and some identity from the ZBC. I said I had neither because they were both at home (which was at least half true), so he looked at my Zimbabwe driver's licence, then handed it back to me.

Makore tried to tell me to open the car, but Mukaka cut him off.

'Be quiet,' he said. 'We are going to do this properly.'

Then he turned to the crowd.

'Over there!' He pointed to a clearing under some trees about 100 metres from the shops. 'Let us gather and sort this out.'

The teenagers and their leaders cheered and whooped and moved quickly across the road, some shouting ZANU-PF slogans and punching the air with their fists.

I leaned over towards Mukaka. 'Please, look after me,' I whispered in his ear, but as I spoke some of the older boys shoved me away from the car, and through the driver's window I could see my cellphone in its mount between the two front seats.

'Can I lock the car?' I asked, hoping to retrieve the phone.

'We are ZANU-PF,' said Mukaka as he waved me away. 'We are not thieves. Only the MDC are criminals.'

I was dragged over to the clearing and made to sit in the centre of a bare patch created by the combined shade of a dozen giant acacias.

The five or six bona fide war vets, all in their forties and fifties – including one plump woman – sat in a group near the edge of the clearing on some wooden tomato boxes that served as makeshift chairs. Tribal custom dictates that the elders must always sit in an elevated position in relation to the minions. I was on the ground, which left no doubt as to my place in the hierarchy.

Five Green Bombers, probably from the Border Gezi camp in Bindura, were left at the store, and whenever youngsters arrived to buy a soft drink or do shopping for their mothers, they were told to join the meeting under the trees. None dared refuse.

Mukaka gave a signal and James Makore stood up. He spoke in Shona, unaware that I could understand what he was saying.

'Today we are here to make sure that no enemies of our revolution sneak into this area and hand it over to the sell-out puppets who call themselves the MDC.'

He raised his fist.

'We fought for this land and many of us died. It is ours!'

He brought down his arm like a judge wielding a gavel, but in his drunken state almost lost his balance. Some of the youngsters tittered, but quickly fell silent under the chastising stare of Mukaka.

'We spilled our blood,' screamed Makore, who, aged perhaps twenty-eight or thirty, would have been six or eight years old when the war ended. 'Now we will spill the blood of those who try to take our birthright,' and he pointed his beer bottle in my direction.

There was a cheer from the other men of Makore's age, and the teenagers joined in.

'If any of you see any posters for the MDC, you will tear them down,' said Makore. 'And if you find anyone speaking in favour of the MDC or handing out their lying papers, you will bring them to the war vets to be punished.'

For the next three hours, songs were sung about ZANU-PF, the glory of Mugabe's rule, and how whites and the MDC should be hounded out of the country or killed. Makore introduced two other men of his age, Robert Nyakudya and Simon Chirume, and said they would lead the youth militia.

Several times I was made to stand and repeat some of the slogans, but when passions rose and it seemed that Makore and his thugs might assault me, Mukaka walked over and told his comrades to lead the crowd in song again. Despite the fact the he was directing this circus, it was Mukaka who saved me, and I remain grateful to him for that.

Marijuana was being passed around, and even the youngest boys and girls were encouraged to smoke it.

By 4 pm, I was worried. I knew that if I stayed there overnight, the beer would flow and the drugs would make people crazy, and I would not see another sunrise. But even if I was released, there was no way I could start the car. After a spate of thefts in our street, I had my mechanic weld a small steel box around the ignition, so hot-wiring was out of the question.

By 5 pm, the crowd under the trees had swelled to more than 300, and the female war vet came over and asked me if I would like a drink. I wondered if this was a ploy to drug me and declined, but in retrospect I think she was just a good soul.

Makore was on his feet again.

'Are you thinking about your parents in England, white man? They will cry for you when you are gone.'

He threw back his head and crowed like a rooster, spilling some of his beer – he had drunk at least five bottles since I had arrived – and the teenagers laughed at him.

'No,' I said, my first words in several hours. 'My mother and father are both dead.'

Mrs War Vet was standing near Makore and she stepped over and smacked him hard on the ear. 'Don't make jokes about those who have died,' she said.

African people are deeply respectful of the dead, and Makore did not mention my parents again, but since I now had the floor, so to speak, I decided to continue.

'My father's family came to Africa in 1795, more than 200 years ago.'

'But where did they come from?' asked one of the war vets.

'From Scotland,' I replied.

'Ah, then you cannot be Zimbabwean,' he said. 'You are Scottean.'

I left it there, because my attention was drawn to some digging that was taking place under one of the more distant trees. In other abductions, people had been forced to watch their own graves being dug while they awaited execution. To add to my growing concerns, a beefy youth arrived with an axe and swung it in an arc over my head, the blade tipping my hair. Then he retired to a nearby tree and stared at me.

Makore began chanting in Shona: 'We will kill all sell-outs!' The crowd took up the cry, over and over, ever louder in my ears.

'Kill all sell-outs. Kill the traitors. Death to the enemy.'

Up to this point, I had showed no fear. I had said a few silent prayers, but as a Buddhist I was ready to go forward to the next life, and felt a deep sense of calm. But there was anger, too, over the fact that my death would go unpunished. Just as not a single conviction for murder had resulted from the scores of deaths in the run-up to the referendum and general election, James Makore and his thugs could kill me with the axe and would not even be taken into custody. Law and order had broken down so completely and the police were so politicised that my death would simply be one more statistic on the list of Mugabe's victims.

Winston Mukaka rose and waved his arms to silence the mob, then walked over to where I was sitting.

'Stand up!' he said quietly, but at first I didn't register what he was saying. 'Stand up now,' he repeated, without raising his voice.

My legs were cramped from sitting for so long, and as I wobbled he placed a hand on my shoulder.

'You have heard our African songs,' he said, smiling, 'even if you did not understand them. Now we are going to hear one of your English songs to show us how a Scottean sings. Come, sing for us one of your music.'

He winked at Makore and pushed me forward. I had never faced a command performance and I looked around at the audience. Even in the fading light under the trees, I could see the youthfulness of their faces, people who should have been at high school or starting jobs in the city. Some, no doubt, had come home for the weekend, as their smarter clothes indicated, but it was the childlike innocence that struck me most. There is something obscene about people so young having their values warped by a regime that acts with impunity to murder and torture its enemies, real or perceived.

I only ever sing in the bath, and anyone who has heard my voice knows why, but now I took a deep breath, and sang for my life.

*Inindadzoka kumusha, Baba n'dadzoka,*
*Tamba nudzai mahoko enyu,*
*Inindadzoka.*

It was from the current Shona hit parade, and the lyrics told of a young man returning to the rural areas and calling on his father to embrace and welcome him to back to his spiritual home. The song also had a religious connotation in the sense of a person going to heaven and calling on God to lead him into paradise.

There was a long silence as jaws dropped. Makore tried to stand, but fell down again as 300 pairs of eyes stared at me in disbelief because – disgracefully – a white person who can speak Shona is a rare beast in Zimbabwe.

Of the whole seven-hour ordeal, it is that silence I remember most vividly. Even the digging had stopped, and the scene was frozen as I waited for the shock to break into violence or laughter.

The female war vet was the first to laugh, a deep rumble from her belly that exploded in her mouth and swept out over the heads of the crowd. Soon everyone was laughing, clutching others in mirth and clapping their hands together, and I began to think I might get out of my predicament unscathed.

I started singing the next verse, and when I came to the chorus, the children and even the war vets joined in.

The song went on for three or four minutes, and when it was over, it was as though a school bell had rung and the class was out. Mukaka, who was still standing next to me, suggested that we all stretch our legs.

'You sing well,' he said in Shona, the first (and probably last) person to pay me such a compliment. 'Now the people are hungry and thirsty and we would like to buy them bread and beer at the store, but we have no money.'

I had about Z$5 000 (US$20) in my wallet and figured that it would be taken if I didn't offer.

'These are young people,' I said. 'Let us not waste good beer on them. The headmaster's store has orange squash and I'm sure they would enjoy that.'

'Much better,' said Mrs War Vet, and over the next thirty minutes the girls diluted the juice concentrate in buckets, and a limited number of tin cans were found and washed out for use as mugs. The bread was broken and we all sat on the ground and shared a meal that had cost me Z$3 200.

The headmaster didn't look up as he took my money, and I could only guess at the pain he felt in seeing children abused by the government he used to work for.

Back in the middle of the circle, I was given bread and juice. When I had finished, I went over to Mukaka and asked if I could now go home.

'Yes, you are a good man,' he said. 'And you can come back here any time you like.'

'Thank you,' I said, and he smiled and nodded.

I was about to ask whether anyone knew how to start the car when another five war vets arrived from a neighbouring area with some fifty youngsters in tow.

The oldest of the guerrillas seemed to outrank Mukaka, and when he was told that I was being released, he shook his head.

'No. I have not heard this case and I am not releasing any traitors before I am satisfied,' he said.

At that moment, the two policemen I had encountered at Cantata walked into the clearing and asked what was going on. Within minutes they had negotiated my release, and said they would take me to their station for questioning.

The war vets agreed, on two conditions: I was not to drive, and Winston Mukaka would accompany me to hear what I said at the police station.

I scrabbled in the dust and found the tip of the key, and with some difficulty managed to get it into the ignition, followed by the broken shaft.

Only the war vets came to the car, while the teenagers stayed under the trees. But as I was about to leave, James Makore, now hopelessly drunk, lumbered over and held out his hand.

I ignored it.

'Don't worry,' he grinned. 'You have survived this time. But you can die another day.'

And so I sat squashed in the back of my own car next to a policeman, with Mukaka in the passenger seat and the other policeman at the wheel.

My cellphone had been stolen, of course, and on arrival at the police station I had to give my statement to the inspector in charge in the presence of Mukaka, who would decide whether or not I should be released.

'Do you have any complaint about your treatment?' asked the inspector. I could see by the ribbons on his chest that he had served in both the Rhodesian and Zimbabwean police. I shook my head, and Mukaka insisted the car be searched. There was nothing to be found, though my portable radio was tuned to SW Africa in London. Mukaka turned it on, but blessedly the reception was awful and all we heard was a hissing sound. He handed it back to me but confiscated the copies of the *Daily News*, and said I was free to go.

As one of the constables repacked the car, Mukaka went to relieve himself and the inspector leaned in close.

'You are so fucking lucky,' he said. 'Some of the people who held you also killed a white farmer and we are not allowed to arrest them.[6] These war vets even come to my station sometimes and harass my officers, and there is nothing I can do. Thank God my retirement is soon.'

The pain in his eyes said everything. The law he had sworn to uphold was in tatters, and he was taking orders from thugs and criminals. Without a word, he patted me on the back and I got into the car and drove home.

On Monday 14 January, under the headline 'Zanu-PF Goes On Rampage', the *Daily News* reported a spate of violent attacks by war vets and Green Bombers over the weekend. Near Dande in the north, the militia had uprooted cotton and maize plants in fields owned by black farmers they accused of supporting the MDC. One farmer, who declined to be named for fear of reprisals, told the newspaper how 500 youths had descended on his home.

'They told me that all land in Zimbabwe belongs to President Mugabe and that members of the MDC should not plant crops on it,' he said.

In Buhera in southern Manicaland, war vets attacked the local MDC office and beat the workers so badly that seven of them had to be hospitalised and transferred to Harare for further treatment. The militia then proceeded to break up ten MDC meetings in the constituency, declaring that opposition rallies were now illegal in Zimbabwe.

In Mutare, thirty-two MDC members were arrested at a meeting and denied access to their lawyer while in custody. In Harare, two MDC members of parliament, Tichaona Munyani (Mbare East) and Gabriel Chaibva (Harare South) were attacked, and in Mbare the Green Bombers carried out a stop-and-search campaign and beat up people who could not produce ZANU-PF party membership cards.

There were also several reports of attacks by the militia at random points around the country, and I realised anew how lucky I had been in my encounter with the war vets.

# 10

# Fighting for the vote

In terms of Zimbabwe's constitution, a presidential election has to be held within ninety days of a head of state retiring, and since a normal presidential election was already scheduled to take place during the first half of 2002, the end of 2001 would have been the perfect opportunity for Mugabe to step down without losing face.

But in October 2000, a national opinion poll financed from South Africa by the Helen Suzman Foundation had shown that 62 per cent of Zimbabweans favoured Morgan Tsvangirai as their next president. In Harare, support for Mugabe was a mere 7 per cent, and though Tsvangirai had failed to win the parliamentary seat of Buhera South in the general election, he remained leader of the opposition and had made it clear that he would stand against Mugabe in the presidential poll.

If Mugabe won another seven-year term, he might face the prospect of dying in office without nominating a successor. But there were problems when it came to handing over power to anyone else within ZANU-PF:

- There was no heir apparent, and Mugabe had never allowed his colleagues to talk openly of succession. The divisions that characterised black politics in Zimbabwe during the 1960s and 1970s had left their scars, and he was aware that the emergence of an alternative leader could cause the party to fracture as supporters lined up behind their man. In no time, Mugabe would have become a lame duck president, possibly even forced out of office, instead of being able to go with dignity.

- There was no guarantee that another ZANU-PF leader would shield him from prosecution. All the senior officials had blood on their hands, and any one of them might be tempted to seek personal immunity by doing a deal with the international community that would see Mugabe tried for crimes against humanity. Britain's highest court had set a precedent by ruling that General Augusto Pinochet of Chile, arrested while in London for medical treatment, could be extradited to Spain to face charges of killing his own people. Slobodan Milosevic had gone on trial in The Hague for the same reason, and those who had led the genocide in Rwanda were in the dock in

Arusha, Tanzania. In Europe, banks had taken a tough line on blood money and were freezing fortunes hoarded by tyrants who had died or been overthrown. Even safe havens such as Switzerland and Jersey were publishing details of funds stashed away by the late Mobuto Sese Seko of the Congo, Sani Abacha of Nigeria and the Indonesian dictator Thojib Suharto, who was still alive and under house arrest in Jakarta.

• Mugabe saw himself as the only person strong enough to defeat the opposition. If he retired and his successor lost the election, an MDC president would almost certainly authorise a criminal investigation against him.

After working in Zimbabwe from 1981 to 1983, Australian teacher Madelaine Laming maintained a lively interest in the country, and corresponded with Mugabe for many years.

'All his life, Mugabe has believed he is special,' she wrote in early 2002, 'but lately he has undergone an apotheosis. He sees himself as more than the elected leader of his people these days. He is their ruler, their chief. His mandate comes not from their will, but from his vision of himself as somehow appointed by God or the ancestral spirits or by his own manifest destiny.'[1]

By September 2001, it was clear that Mugabe was out of control, and the effects of the deepening crisis in Zimbabwe were starting to be felt by other countries in Africa.

The value of South Africa's currency was declining, regional tourism had fallen off and Thabo Mbeki was finding it hard to garner support for his New Partnership for African Development (NEPAD). The initiative would bring together a dozen or so African states, including South Africa, Botswana, Senegal, Ghana and Nigeria, that had demonstrated both good governance and sound financial management. Armed with US$75 billion from developed countries, NEPAD would launch what Mbeki called the African Renaissance.

The theory was that as the original member states prospered from the new deal, less progressive regimes would be persuaded to meet the criteria for participation, including full democracy, lack of government corruption, recognition of human rights and, crucially, willingness to accept a system of 'peer review' that allowed members of NEPAD to police one another for violations.

But none of the potential investors had put any money on the table as yet.

As one British banker told me: 'The issue is not Zimbabwe, because the country is not currently a member of NEPAD. It's more about Africa's response to Mugabe. Once the donor money is on the ground, what happens if another Mugabe emerges in Botswana or Ghana or even Pretoria? What steps will other African states take to deal with renegades and protect our investment? Zimbabwe has provided them with a chance to show us how serious they are, and they have failed the test.'

In the dying days of 2001, the ZANU-PF executive met at Victoria Falls, and one speaker after another complained that in every electoral district people were hungry, unemployed … and ready for change. In short, the presidential campaign was in jeopardy.

The meeting agreed that the war vets and militia, backed by the police and even the army in serious cases, would have to work much harder to subdue the rural areas and reduce the MDC's enormous lead in the urban townships.

Having made it clear that he would be ZANU-PF's sole candidate, Mugabe announced that the presidential election would be held over the weekend of 9 and 10 March 2002. Committees were set up to deal with every aspect of the campaign. The state-controlled media would have to pump out even more propaganda, and a plan would be needed to increase the rural vote as much as possible, while limiting the turnout in the cities, where Tsvangirai was sure to win the majority vote.

Parliament was recalled in the second week of January 2002, and two bills were passed along party lines.

The first, known at the Public Order and Security Act (POSA), made it an offence to criticise or 'engender hostility towards' the president, which meant that MDC campaign material could not question his track record. The bill also outlawed criticism of the army and police, declared public gatherings illegal without prior consent, and made it compulsory for all citizens to carry metal identity tags that had been in use since 1979. There was a special reason for the latter, but it would only become apparent in the months ahead.

The second bill created new laws for the election. Voters would not only have to be on the roll, but would be allowed to cast their ballots only in the constituencies where they were registered. They would also be required to prove that they had been resident in those constituencies for a period of at least twelve months.

This meant that urban workers registered in rural areas could not vote in town, and would fail the residency clause in their home electorates, so, in practice, they would not be able to vote at all. The law also disenfranchised more than a million exiles living in South Africa, many of whom had previously crossed the border at election time and voted at Beit Bridge. Legislation passed prior to the 2000 general election had already outlawed postal votes for anyone except diplomats and soldiers serving abroad.

In addition, non-governmental organisations, church groups and even charities were forbidden from carrying out voter education campaigns. This would be the exclusive domain of government.

A third piece of new legislation tabled that day in January would have given

Jonathan Moyo the sole right to license both newspapers and individual journalists, but when senior ZANU-PF members of parliament protested that this was too much of an assault on freedom, the bill was shelved.

While the special parliamentary session was in progress, General Vitalis Zvinavashe, supreme commander of the armed forces, caused a stir by stating publicly that he and his officers would not accept a win by Tsvangirai.

'The highest office in the land,' he said, 'is a straitjacket whose occupant must observe the objectives of the liberation struggle. We will therefore not accept, let alone support or salute, anyone with a different agenda that threatens the very existence of our sovereignty.'

Attorney-General Patrick Chinamasa, whose portfolio included upholding the constitution, tried to play down the general's comments.

'As far as the Zimbabwean government is concerned,' he told parliament, 'there is no concern whatsoever over the statement in the country. The statement by General Zvinavashe was long overdue. It was intended to put the record straight.'[2]

But in Pretoria, the ANC said it was disturbed by the general's words, which also provoked widespread condemnation in the South African and foreign press.

In the week following ZANU-PF's terror campaign on 12 and 13 January, Southern African Development Community (SADC) presidents met in Malawi for talks about the ongoing war in the Congo, but during a closed session they told Mugabe to rein in General Zvinavashe. With the exception of Botswana and South Africa, all SADC countries have their share of state-sanctioned intimidation at election time, but the threat of a coup in Zimbabwe could not be left unchallenged.

Two days before the meeting, British prime minister Tony Blair telephoned Thabo Mbeki and made it clear that Britain wanted to see a 'more robust approach' on Zimbabwe, even if only in private talks with Mugabe. But a spokesman for Downing Street later denied that there had been any difference of opinion.

'Both leaders take the issue seriously,' he said, 'and it is clearly deteriorating in a way that is giving everyone cause for concern.'[3]

One of Zimbabwe's leading political analysts, Dr Brian Raftopoulos, predicted that whatever Mbeki might have promised, there would be no condemnation of Mugabe outside the SADC forum.

'The crisis in Zimbabwe has worsened to a level where SADC should have no problem finding a strong voice,' he said. 'But I don't think we are going to get the kind of strong statement suggesting that Mugabe is totally isolated in the region, which he is.'[4]

Behind the scenes, though, the talk in Malawi was tough, and Mugabe was left in no doubt that while his fellow presidents would not break ranks and condemn him publicly, they expected to see some change, if only because their own economies were being affected.

But ZANU-PF was on a roll, and more violence took place the following weekend.

The MDC had informed the police, as required by the new legislation, that a rally would be held on Sunday 20 January at the White City Sport Stadium in Bulawayo. On the Saturday, they staged a vehicle procession through town, playing music and using megaphones to call people to the meeting.

Party members spent the afternoon setting up loudspeakers and a stage at the stadium, but as soon as they left, ZANU-PF deployed 200 militia inside the arena, and when MDC youths arrived that evening to guard the equipment, they walked into an ambush.

The Green Bombers were armed with batons, irons bars and bicycle chains, and it was a one-way fight. The MDC youths fled back to the party office, and some of the injured were taken to the police to ask that the militia be removed from the stadium, but no action was taken.

Afterwards, the *Daily News* suggested that the troublemakers had been ferried to the city with the express purpose of stopping the rally.

'Most of the ZANU-PF supporters who caused the disturbances came from Harare, Marondera and Buhera,' the newspaper reported. 'Two trucks full of ZANU-PF supporters from Buhera, led by a war vet called Chapirwa Munyire, were seen in the city on Saturday.'[5]

When MDC workers tried to ready the stadium on Sunday, they, too, were beaten, and the police cordoned off White City. By 9 am, thousands of people had arrived to attend the rally, but they were refused entry and began singing protest songs, at which point the police fired tear gas into the crowd.

One MDC member had a video camera and filmed the incident. The footage might have been of a 1980s anti-apartheid riot in Soweto. People could be seen running in all directions, some collapsing from the tear gas and being dragged along by their friends, others scrambling over walls, jumping fences and clambering over cars to escape the fumes.

The rally was called off, and the next day Mbeki and Nigerian president Olusegun Obasanjo arrived in Harare for talks. Obasanjo insisted on meeting Tsvangirai as well, which he did in private. There was no public statement on the situation as the two visiting heads of state smiled for the cameras, hugged Mugabe and each other, then flew back from whence they came.

The beatings and violence began taking their toll on the MDC, and by the end of January the party could not campaign in 40 of the country's 120 constituencies.

Apart from the growing political crisis, the lack of food was becoming a problem. More than a thousand white farmers had left the land, and those who stayed were unable to plant crops because of imminent seizure or the presence of war vets who threatened their workers.

Across the country, thousands of hectares lay barren, stocks of maize and wheat ran out, and the World Food Programme warned that 500 000 people were facing starvation.[6] The subsistence farmers who should have started tilling the plots that had been pegged for them, failed to materialise, since many of the recipients had jobs in urban centres. In order to feed itself, Zimbabwe needed at least 2 million tons of maize annually, but poor rains in 2001, compounded by the invasions, had led to a 40 per cent drop in the harvest and a shortfall of 800 000 tons. The government conceded that 150 000 tons were required immediately, and almost twice as much again by April.

Since December 2001, when a law was passed making the state-owned Grain Marketing Board (GMB) the sole body authorised to buy, sell or stockpile maize and wheat, hunger had become the newest weapon in ZANU-PF's arsenal.

At the end of January, raids were mounted on farms where tons of corn were held to feed pigs or poultry, and the contents of entire granaries were confiscated. GMB manager Justin Mutasa told government-controlled newspapers: 'There is so much maize in the country that we may not even need to import if we manage to impound all the maize from commercial farmers.'

The story was seized upon by the ZBC, and white farmers were accused of creating an artificial shortage by secretly filling their barns – and even empty dams – with hundreds of tons of grain in an effort to bring down the government. It was like a Monty Python skit, but no one was laughing.

The price of beef, pork and poultry plummeted as farmers, unable to feed their animals, sent them to slaughter, and by mid-year there was a chronic shortage of meat and eggs. Meat and milk production was already in trouble because, on farms seized from white owners, the war vets killed the livestock at will in order to feed their own people and the youth militia. The national cattle-breeding herd fell from 508 000 animals in 1999 to 378 000 in 2001. By 2003, the number had dropped to below 200 000.

The GMB legislation, which also barred anyone except the government from importing maize, meant that ZANU-PF could control food aid in areas where their own policies had caused famine, and so coerce people into joining the party in exchange for a meal.

In southern Matabeleland and around Binga near the Zambezi River, the lack of rain had left thousands with little or no food. Aid agencies began reporting that when donated maize was handed out, GMB officials and Green

Bombers were on hand to make sure that each recipient produced a ZANU-PF membership card.

Some organisations protested and others withdrew their assistance from the areas, but since they could not import any grain without government approval, there was little they could do. According to the Canadian branch of Oxfam, which had been active in Zimbabwe for several years, numerous families in rural areas had been reduced to one meal a day by the second half of 2001. One aid worker told a reporter from the *Sydney Morning Herald* that medical teams were starting to see the effects of malnutrition, and that children were at serious risk of stunted growth due to hunger.[7]

Both in Africa and abroad, the clamour for change grew louder. On returning to South Africa from his talks with Mugabe, Mbeki addressed the media and, for the first time, made clear his own feelings about Zimbabwe. 'The instability,' he said, 'has gone on for far too long. The levels of poverty and conflict are increasing, and if you add to that a fraudulent election, this has to be avoided.'

In West Africa, Ghana's foreign minister, Hackman Owusu-Agyemang, issued a direct warning to Mugabe. 'Attempts to pass laws which seek to suppress the legitimate aspirations of Zimbabwe's opposition, muzzle the media and outlaw international observers, will undermine the credibility of the presidential elections,' he told the BBC.[8]

In Washington, Congress had passed the Zimbabwe Democracy and Recovery Act, which provided for extensive sanctions against the country, bans on travel by Mugabe and his ministers, and the freezing of any personal assets they held in America. It also contained punitive clauses against companies that sought to gain from doing business directly with the Zimbabwe government. All that remained was for President George W Bush to implement the sanctions at a time of his choosing.

The US secretary of state, General Colin Powell, had never disguised his contempt for Mugabe, but said America would act in tandem with the European Union, which was threatening to impose sanctions unless two key demands were met: there would need to be an immediate end to the violence, and the Zimbabwe government would have to allow international monitors to scrutinise every aspect of the presidential election.

Foreign minister Stan Mudenge sent the EU a four-page letter in which he ignored the issue of violence entirely and insisted that he alone would decide who should be invited to monitor the poll.

Straight-talking Euro MP Glenys Kinnock (UK Labour) reacted strongly. 'This four-page letter,' she told the European parliament in Brussels, 'is further evidence that the government of Zimbabwe has no intention of meeting the two most important criteria. They have failed to undertake that violence and intimidation must end and have not given us a clear timescale for the entry of election observers.'

In anticipation of sanctions, authorities in America, Britain and Europe began searching for bank accounts held in the names of Mugabe and his ministers, their wives and family members, and in the tax haven of Jersey, the Financial Services Commission ordered banks to scour their records for funds held by prominent Zimbabweans.

In Britain, opposition foreign affairs spokesman Michael Ancram demanded that the Labour government abandon what he called its 'softly-softly approach' on the crisis in Zimbabwe, and another Tory MP, Julian Lewis, accused Mugabe of running a 'racist and fascist regime', equating Blair's response to Neville Chamberlain's policy of appeasement towards Adolf Hitler in the 1930s.[9]

During a heated parliamentary debate, junior minister Ben Bradshaw's response was that Britain would take up the matter at the forthcoming CHOGM in Australia.

The biennial gathering of leaders of former British colonies and dominions should have taken place in October 2001, but because of security fears after Al-Qaeda's attack on the World Trade Center in New York on 11 September, it had been postponed to 3 March 2002, the weekend before the presidential election. Bradshaw said the British government would push for Zimbabwe's suspension from the organisation.

Tony Blair was in a difficult position. If he took any steps that were not in concert with those envisaged by the EU and the US, he risked upsetting African members of the Commonwealth, which would condemn his action as 'post-colonial interference'.

At media conferences where I heard Blair address various issues, he came across as a man who cared deeply about injustice. Historically, however, his party's record on fighting for human rights in Africa was less than impressive. In the 1960s and 1970s, Harold Wilson had done nothing to stem the rush towards one-party states in Africa, and in 1984, when the Matabele massacres were at their height, the party – then in opposition and led by Neil Kinnock, husband of Euro MP Glenys – had not attacked Margaret Thatcher's inaction.

Blair's government supported President Moweri Museveni in Uganda, where political life was far more oppressed than in Zimbabwe, and maintained good relations with dictatorial regimes in Saudi Arabia and other countries in the Middle East. More than once, Mugabe and Moyo had slated Britain publicly for applying what they viewed as double standards in its dealings with Harare.

Adding to Blair's dilemma was the fact that Britain's intelligence service, MI6, was telling foreign secretary Jack Straw that Morgan Tsvangirai's support would be strong enough to absorb a 25 to 30 per cent 'margin of fraud'. This assessment was probably correct, but the British underestimated Mugabe's determination to rig the poll. As in 1980 when the foreign office believed that Muzorewa would win, they fell prey to their own optimism.

In London and Washington, some intelligence officers even suggested that in the event of an obviously fraudulent election, a 'Belgrade scenario' could present itself, with hundreds of thousands of blacks taking to the streets and making the country ungovernable. But the British and Americans failed to take into account the inherently placid nature of the Shona.

They did get one thing right, however. From my discussions with the intelligence community in Britain and the USA, I gathered that both MI6 and the CIA predicted – correctly – that if Mugabe was returned to power, neighbouring countries, and especially South Africa, would be swamped by wholesale black emigration.

Inexplicably, the South Africans themselves seemed unable to grasp the magnitude of the human wave that was likely to engulf them. A senior intelligence agent in Pretoria told me: 'There has always been a healthy flow across the border, and we have little reason to think that this will increase just because Mugabe wins or loses the election.'

In Harare, ZANU-PF was starting to show the strain of its own tyranny.

On Monday 21 January, Jonathan Moyo's Access of Information and Protection of Privacy bill (AIPP) had gone back to parliament where, instead of the four or five amendments that were the norm, it was hacked to pieces by both the opposition and the house committee responsible for media, led by veteran MP Edison Zvobgo, and ended up with thirty-six alterations.

Zvobgo, who had been with Mugabe in the war and at Lancaster House, and had reworked the constitution in 1987 to give the president his new powers, publicly denounced the bill as an assault on freedom. Once viewed as a possible successor to Mugabe, Zvobgo was old, sick and perhaps intent that history should not portray him as a villain, and had launched several open attacks on the government. He had even fallen out with the war vets by declaring that the land invasions had 'tainted what was a glorious revolution, reducing it to some agrarian racist enterprise'.[10]

The amended legislation allowed journalists to criticise Mugabe, even though this was still outlawed by the Public Order and Security Act. Other concessions were that media licences would be issued not by Moyo himself, but by a commission he appointed, and that existing investors in media companies would be exempt from a clause requiring new ventures to be 51 per cent Zimbabwe-owned.

Parliament passed the new law, but Mugabe waited until after the election to ratify it. The delay made no impression on the Americans, with State Department spokesman Richard A Boucher describing the legislation as 'another tragic example of President Mugabe's increasingly authoritarian rule, and his govern-ment's apparent determination to repress freedom of speech and dissent'.

Boucher also warned that Washington was consulting friendly governments on a plan to impose sanctions. 'We're still talking to other countries. We're still considering what we can do, and we're watching developments in Zimbabwe very closely.'[11]

Like the former government of Ian Smith, ZANU-PF was deaf to the warnings that were being sounded clearly by friends and critics alike, and Patrick Chinamasa dismissed American concern as part of a campaign to destabilise his government ahead of the election.

Meanwhile, the *Daily News* reported a new strategy to disenfranchise potential MDC voters. In rural areas, the militia were confiscating the national identity discs of any person who could not produce a ZANU-PF membership card. It now became clear why the new election laws had made it compulsory to carry the metal tags, as without them no voter could prove his or her identity.

In a telephone interview, Tsvangirai told the BBC that the the new election laws were was 'not in the spirit of maintaining law and order and the spirit of free campaigning', but that he remained confident. 'It's now up to the people of Zimbabwe,' he said, 'to see what they can salvage from this situation.'[12]

Amazingly, all this activity – Mugabe's attendance of the SADC meeting in Malawi, the visit by Mbeki and Obasanjo, the violence in Bulawayo, Mudenge's rejection of independent monitors, the passing of the new media bill and the threat of sanctions – had taken place over the space of just ten days since my encounter with the war vets.

On Sunday 1 February, both Mugabe and Tsvangirai were set to address their first campaign rallies. The contrast between the two rallies could not have been sharper. Mugabe chose a small settlement in a ZANU-PF stronghold in rural Mashonaland and arrived in a screaming motorcade, surrounded by armoured vehicles and troop carriers loaded with soldiers who had bayonets fixed to their rifle barrels.

He wore a three-piece suit over a shirt printed with photographs of himself, a white baseball cap and an armband emblazoned with the words 'Land for Economic Empowerment'. Mugabe's speech was fraught with rhetoric, and he led the 8 000-strong crowd in chants of 'Down with the British' and 'Down with the whites'.

'We are in a war to defend our rights and the interests of our people, and the British have decided to take us on through the MDC,' he told supporters.

While the ZBC cameras focused on the president, shots of the crowd showed war vets and Green Bombers prowling the perimeter like wolves circling a flock of sheep, waiting to pounce on anyone who tried to leave.

Tsvangirai held his rally in the southern Matabeleland town of Gwanda, and arrived in a small convoy of modest cars, looking relaxed in an open-necked shirt. The state media largely ignored the gathering, but police estimated the crowd to be about the same size as Mugabe's, and a British journalist recorded a jubilant atmosphere.

'The people came of their own free will,' she wrote, 'singing spontaneously and laughing loudly.'[13]

Earlier that week, scores of women in Gwanda had been beaten up in a maize queue when war vets discovered that they were not carrying ZANU-PF membership cards, and Tsvangirai vowed that this type of violence would end.

'After we've won the election and the results have been announced and I am inaugurated, violence and anarchy will be a thing of the past,' he said to cheers from the crowd.

He also tried to pacify the armed forces.

'There will be no revenge, no one will indulge in a witch-hunt,' he promised. 'We will not create a new army. It is a national institution. Those not prepared to serve will be free to resign.

'But, in the meantime, I ask you to brave ZANU-PF's campaign of violence.'

Tsvangirai also touched on the question of land reform, acknowledging that redistribution was necessary. 'But we want a land reform programme that benefits the whole country, that recognises that farming is a commercial venture and not just about pieces of land for peasants,' he said.

In a different part of Africa, another politician was garnering support for the forthcoming CHOGM in Australia. Tony Blair and his wife Cherie made a lightning tour of West Africa, and on 7 February in Ghana, he sent out a warning that the days of ruthless leaders were numbered and called on African states to bring dictators to book. Promising aid to Britain's former colonies, Blair made it clear that only those who upheld a culture of human rights would qualify, and that future assistance would not take the traditional form of large sums of money being handed over to governments to do with as they pleased.

'It must be a partnership between us,' he said. 'Not aid as a handout, but aid as a hand-up, to help people to help themselves.'

The EU, meanwhile, had decided to push the issue of independent election monitors, and was incensed by Stan Mudenge's announcement on state television that no invitations would be sent to the EU as an organisation, and that he would not accept observers from member countries regarded as hostile to Zimbabwe. These included Britain, Denmark, Finland, Germany, Holland and Sweden. Ironically, with the exception of Britain, these were all countries that had backed ZANU throughout the civil war.

The EU defiantly appointed Sweden's ambassador to the UN, Pierre Schori, as head of its delegation and packed him off to Zimbabwe, but when he landed at Harare on Sunday 10 February, the authorities refused to recognise his diplomatic status and issued him with only a tourist visa.

Schori had covered the 2000 election and been highly critical of the government, and it was clear that Mudenge had no intention of recognising him as an official observer. 'There is no invitation to the EU as an organisation,' he reiterated, 'but I have written to them that Zimbabwe has formally invited nine members of the EU in their individual national capacities.'

A statement was issued in Brussels giving Zimbabwe forty-eight hours to accredit Schori or face sanctions, but Mudenge would not be moved and the unwelcome Swede left the country.

By the middle of February, a majority vote in the European parliament approved 'smart sanctions' against a lengthy list of Mugabe's ministers and advisers.

The EU move made it easier for Blair, because his government no longer needed to impose sanctions of its own, though it was the British who drew up the list of those who would be subject to the EU measures. The US, Canada, New Zealand and Australia followed suit, freezing bank accounts and banning an extensive list of ZANU-PF members from entering their countries.

Jonathan Moyo immediately went on the offensive, telling the *Herald*: 'We will never allow in our country a situation where our sovereignty is hijacked under the guise of election observation.'

But refusal to accredit Schori was merely the trigger, and the tougher international stand on Zimbabwe had been a long time coming, as Tsvangirai pointed out when welcoming the move.

'This will send a strong signal to Mugabe and his cronies that the international community will not accept an election whose result does not reflect the will of the people of Zimbabwe,' he said.

However, if the EU and its partners thought their action would change anything inside Zimbabwe, they were disappointed. Within seventy-two hours of the announcement in Brussels, the privately owned media reported that voter registration was being carried out on a party-political basis, and the MDC chairman for Mashonaland West, Gift Konjana, complained that in Chinhoyi, electoral officers were registering only those who could produce either a ZANU-PF membership card or a letter of introduction from a member of the party executive.[14]

Inside ZANU-PF, the sanctions aroused suspicions about party loyalty because, mysteriously, some of the heavyweights had been left off the list. Whether the omissions were intentional or accidental is unknown, but those who had escaped included Mugabe's two vice-presidents, Simon Muzenda and

Joseph Musika, finance minister Simba Makoni, water affairs minister Joyce Mujuru (whose husband, a retired army commander, *was* on the list) and former party treasurer Herbert Murerwa, who had become Minister for Industry.

'You know what Zimbabweans are like when it comes to rumour,' one permanent secretary told me over a beer. 'Makoni was suspected of receiving some protection from the EU because he is known for his moderate views.'

But, he revealed, one of the vice-presidents was incensed at being left off the list!

Apart from cabinet ministers, the list included all the armed services chiefs and police commissioner Augustine Chihuri.

The South African government had accepted Mudenge's invitation to send fifty election observers, and an advance team of thirteen, led by successful businessman and former ambassador to Saudi Arabia, Sam Motsuenyane, arrived on 14 February. Motsuenyane immediately held a press conference and expressed concern about allegations that the police had stood by while MDC members were attacked by war vets and the militia in various parts of the country.

'We have received reports about the existence of "no-go areas" for some parties, and we are taking up this matter. We have already deployed our observers to some of these areas,' he said, adding that members of his team would increase their visibility to ensure that the election took place in an environment free of intimidation and violence. Motsuenyane also announced that additional teams would arrive in Harare on 20 February and 3 March, and that they would include representatives of trade unions, business, agriculture and government, as well as religious groups, youth and women's organisations.

The South Africans didn't have long to wait before experiencing the violence at first hand. On Friday 22 February, a gang of about 200 youths attacked the MDC office in Kwe Kwe while two South African observers, Eleazer Maahle and Bethuel Sethai, were inside holding talks with the opposition. The mob threw stones at the building, breaking windows and damaging the observers' car, which was parked outside.

That same day, police used tear gas to break up a rally in Masvingo, which was due to be addressed by Tsvangirai. He arrived while his supporters were fleeing, and the police opened fire on his car. No one was injured and the MDC leader returned safely to Harare, but the incident prompted the foreign office in London to warn British citizens not to travel to Zimbabwe except on 'essential business'. Motsuenyane described events in Kwe Kwe as reprehensible, and said he was 'very disturbed about the reported clashes and violence'.

What lay ahead would be 'a daunting task', and while the withdrawal of EU observers was unfortunate and regrettable, Motsuenyane said his group would not be deterred by their absence.

'Zimbabwe will need a stable political and economic environment after the elections, irrespective of who wins,' he pointed out.

Motsuenyane was a safe choice for the ANC, a man who could be depended on to brief the South African government on the real situation in private, while treading carefully with public statements.

In fairness, the South African team also included members of both the opposition Democratic Alliance (DA) and Mangosuthu Buthelezi's Inkatha Freedom Party (IFP), and provision was made for those who might disagree with the final report to record their personal findings in the official documents.

One of Motsuenyane's first challenges was to seek accreditation for the South African media. Jonathan Moyo had issued permits for the state broadcaster, SABC, and the privately owned television channel e.tv, but barred the Independent newspaper group (publishers of *The Star*), the *Sunday Times*, the Afrikaans newspapers *Die Burger* and *Beeld*, online news service *Media24* and the influential talk radio stations 702 and Cape Talk.

I had been the Australian correspondent for Radio 702 for eleven years from 1986 to 1997, and agreed to cover the election for them and their sister station, Cape Talk.

It was a year since I had been commissioned to write this book by Steve Connolly of Struik Publishers, and my interviews with both government and opposition figures had begun to draw attention. A contact in the CIO had already warned me that my phone was being tapped and my mail intercepted. Now I faced imprisonment by working for a news organisation that had been banned by the all-powerful Moyo. So I assumed the nom de plume of Chris Cutsunday and used a gravelly voice when I phoned through my daily reports.

Motsuenyane pulled few punches regarding Moyo's gag orders. 'We believe that the media should be given access to the electoral process in a free way,' he said at one of his regular press conferences.

'We are optimistic that the problem of accreditation will be resolved amicably and speedily with the Zimbabwean authorities.'

Moyo ignored his optimism and accused South African journalists of 'demonising Mugabe'. None of the banned organisations was allowed to enter Zimbabwe, and along with the BBC and CNN had to report from Beit Bridge.

But official concern over the situation was singularly lacking from Pretoria. While on a visit to Sweden, Mbeki brushed off an interviewer's questions about the ongoing violence by pointing out that more than 1 000 people had died in the run-up to South Africa's first democratic election in 1994.

'There was a great deal of violence, a great deal of instability,' he said, 'but the elections took place and everybody said they reflected the will of the people of South Africa and were free and fair.'[15]

It was a specious comparison because, in South Africa, the ruling National Party was not a serious contender in its own right, media coverage was unrestricted, thousands of monitors were deployed throughout the country, and the security forces had acted swiftly against anyone who tried to disrupt the election process. But Mbeki had very little room to manoeuvre when it came to Zimbabwe.

A South African intelligence officer in Harare told me that the president might have welcomed an MDC victory in the election, but could say or do nothing that might be seen as steering the process of change.

'It was hugely difficult for him and the more progressive forces in the ANC,' she said, 'due to the party's left wing believing that, as a former liberation movement, the ANC won the right to rule South Africa in perpetuity, making them fellow travellers of ZANU-PF. The issue was both sensitive and strong enough to split the ANC if not handled with care.'

Zimbabwe's sensitivity to Pretoria's pulse was illustrated when South African Airways cancelled late afternoon and early morning flights between Johannesburg and Harare.

The airline offered a sound explanation for the decision. 'We did the same thing during the 2000 election, and the reason is simple,' a spokesman told the *Standard*. 'The plane comes into Harare at 8.30 pm and stays on the apron overnight, ready for take-off the next morning. During elections and potentially stressful events, we prefer not to leave our aircraft out overnight.'

No sooner had the report appeared than the Zimbabwe government contacted the South African high commissioner, Jeremiah Ndou, and expressed strong dissatisfaction with the move, which was seen as a vote of no confidence. The decision was duly reversed.

But when a group of SADC observers arrived in Harare under the leadership of Duke Lefoko, he spoke out strongly against ZANU-PF's brand of electioneering.

'It is vital that the political situation changes to remove fear and allow people to freely exercise their political rights,' he told journalists.

Lefoko was from Botswana, the only African state to have enjoyed un-interrupted democracy since independence, and whose president, Festus Mogai, had made clear several times that he did not approve of Mugabe's tactics.

On Sunday 24 February, fragments of glass hit Lefoko and several members of his delegation when ZANU-PF youths stoned their minibus en route to an MDC rally in Chinhoyi. Recounting the attack afterwards, Lefoko did not mince words.

'I watched it as it happened. I saw these youths with stones at the side of the road. We passed them. I was looking through the back window at our other vehicle, which was following us, and they started smashing the windows.

'I am overwhelmed by what ZANU-PF youths have done,' he said.[16]

Another observer mission slipped quietly into Harare under leadership of a former Nigerian president, General Abdusalam Abubakar. He had been a high-ranking member in military dictator Sani Abacha's government, but when the president died under suspicious circumstances in 1998 and Abubakar assumed office, he released scores of political prisoners, initiated investigations into the embezzlement of more than US$3 billion by Abacha, and lifted restrictions on the press.

Under Abacha, Nigeria had begun to resemble Idi Amin's Uganda, and Abubakar was no stranger to rigged elections. When Nigerians went to the polls in 1993, veteran politician Moshood Abiola almost certainly won the largest number of votes, but he was not the man the army wanted to see in power, so they refused to announce the result and installed Abacha, who ruled by decree until his death.

Abiola was jailed and, tragically, when Abubakar announced his release in July 1998, he suffered a heart attack and never made it out of his cell. His supporters, mainly from the Yoruba tribe in the oil-rich south, took to the streets, and the riots were quelled only after several days of violence. Abubakar could have clung to power through the army, using the uprising as a pretext to cancel the election he had already called, but instead he went on national television and promised an even faster pace of reform.

Nigeria had been suspended from the Commonwealth under Abacha, but Abubakar quickly restored order, set up an independent electoral commission trained by UN, EU and Commonwealth representatives, then invited them to monitor the poll, which was won by Olusegun Obasanjo.

Now Abubakar was heading twenty teams of two people each that made up the Commonwealth observer group in Zimbabwe, and was perhaps the person best qualified to make a judgment on whether the election was free and fair.

'Our concern will be purely with the electoral environment and the process rather than the outcome,' he told journalists on 24 February. 'We will be impartial and objective, we will give an honest assessment.'

Abubakar proved as good as his word and took a special interest in campaign violence.

At his press briefings in Harare, I got the impression that the sixty-year-old general had seen so much terror and violence in his own country – from the Biafran genocide of the late 1960s to the wanton killings under Abacha – that he literally felt ill at the mention of physical abuse. This is a syndrome familiar to psychologists who have found, for example, that the mere sight of blood or carnage in a film can trigger panic attacks in someone who has witnessed a gruesome road accident.

At a meeting in Bulawayo, which was open to the press, Abubakar heard the testimony of two opposition supporters who had been abducted by the militia and beaten with whips for six hours. There was a collective gasp from both the observers and the media when the victims lifted their shirts to show the welts on their backs.

Abubakar winced, looked down and then back at the victims before turning away and shaking his head.

A month away from the election, it looked as though Tsvangirai had it in the bag. Opinion polls published in the *Daily News* confirmed earlier surveys by the Helen Suzman Foundation, even though the majority of respondents were too scared to even talk to pollsters. Those who did, however, gave Tsvangirai a comfortable lead.

Then an obscure Australian television channel dropped a bombshell. On Tuesday 13 February, *Dateline*, a weekly current affairs show on SBS TV, alleged that Tsvangirai had conspired with a Canadian public relations firm, Dickens and Madson, to assassinate Mugabe.

At the centre of the saga was an alleged Israeli confidence trickster, Ari Ben-Menashe, who claimed to have worked for his country's intelligence service, Mossad, at one time. His name had previously been linked to the Iran-Contra arms scandal that rocked American president Ronald Reagan's administration in the 1980s, after which Ben-Menashe sought refuge in Australia.

SBS journalist Mark Davis and *Dateline* presenter Jana Wendt claimed they had obtained a videotape of a meeting between Ben-Menashe and an MDC delegation in Montreal on 4 December 2001. They alleged that both Tsvangirai and his deputy, Welshman Ncube, attended the meeting, at which the 'elimination' of Mugabe was discussed.

Davis said he had been researching a story on Ben-Menashe when he became aware that the Israeli was dealing with Tsvangirai, and further investigations had led to the tape.

The recording had been made using cameras hidden in the ceiling, and only the tops of speakers' heads could be seen. The soundtrack was so inaudible that subtitles had to be added to explain what was being said. But even these shortcomings could not mask the fact that at no time did Tsvangirai suggest that Mugabe should be murdered, though Ben-Menashe tried several times to lead him in that direction.

Newspapers in Australia and elsewhere dismissed the tape as a fraud, and disclosed that Ben-Menashe and his public relations consultancy were on the Zimbabwe government's payroll. But the day after SBS broadcast their story, the state media in Zimbabwe accused Tsvangirai of treason and – amazingly – ZBC television already had a copy of the Dickens and Madson tape.

Tsvangirai initially denied that the meeting had even taken place – a serious blunder on his part, as it turned out – but later claimed that he *had* gone to Montreal to talk to Dickens and Madson about representing the MDC in North America.

A week after the broadcast, Davis defended his story.

'Unquestionably, many people have branded Ari Ben-Menashe a liar,' he told *Dateline* viewers on 20 February. 'In this case, his evidence is corroborated by others, by various documents and recordings and, most importantly, a video of the Montreal meeting. Probably the very reason he recorded it is that he felt he may not otherwise have been believed, and that brings us back to the tape and what was said in Montreal on December 4.'

He then conceded that Ben-Menashe had been contracted by ZANU-PF and had sent a copy of the tape to the government in Zimbabwe.

But how did SBS obtain the tape?

Davis was in Harare shortly before the first programme was broadcast, and the rumour around town was that Mugabe's personal spokesman, George Charamba, had given him the video. If that was true, he should not only have realised he was being set up, but ought also to have weighed the moral issue of journalists accepting material from despotic regimes and presenting it as news.

On the telephone from Sydney, Davis told me this was 'absolutely not the case'.

'We got the tape through a contact in Canada,' he said.

Since being established in 1980, SBS had waged a constant battle to be taken seriously. The station took its name from the Special Broadcasting Service, formed in 1975 by the Labour government of Australian prime minister Gough Whitlam.

It was originally a multilingual radio station, but in 1980, Malcolm Fraser's conservative government added a television unit as an outlet for foreign-language films aimed at the burgeoning immigrant community.

The station was always underfunded and, as a result, could only afford to buy box-office failures, and it became the butt of jokes in Australian comedy shows.

'And tonight we have a wonderful premiere for you,' one comedian would say in her weekly sketch on commercial television in which she parodied an SBS presenter. 'We begin our eight-part series on the life of the fourteenth-century Icelandic folk hero, Olaf the Hairy.'

The other state-funded channel, Australian Broadcasting Corporation (ABC), largely offers a diet of documentaries and reruns, and its programmes rarely feature in the top fifteen ratings in any given week.[17] SBS is lucky to get one spot in the top fifty shows.

Whereas in a typical week commercial television programmes will capture up to 20 per cent of the national audience during prime time, the ABC often struggles to draw half that number, while SBS viewers account for 4 or 5 per cent, and some of its slots carry an asterisk in the ratings, which means the audience sample was too small to be measured.

The official Australian television ratings for 2002 charted the audience share of the country's five national free-to-air networks over a twelve-month period as follows: Channel Nine 30.2 per cent; Channel Seven 26.4 per cent; Channel Ten 23 per cent; ABC 15.5 per cent; and SBS 4.9 per cent.[18]

It was the known weakness of SBS that first made me question the credibility of what became known as the 'treason tape'. If the content was genuine, it would have been worth a fortune and could have been sold to one of the global news networks for a six-figure sum. Instead, it landed on a poorly funded network, in a country far removed from the centres of world power.

What most discredited SBS and *Dateline* was the closing voice-over on the first programme, during which excerpts of the tape were screened and suggestions made that Tsvangirai was plotting to kill Mugabe.

'So far in Zimbabwe, a lot of property has been lost, but not a lot of lives,' a disembodied voice commented.

'There's still some chance of reconciliation here. The honour of smashing that chance, starting the mass bloodshed so long predicted, may not belong to the supposed dictator, but to the democrat and his friends …

'For millions who dreamt of a new era in Zimbabwe, a new style of government through Morgan Tsvangirai, it is not just his principles that he has betrayed.'

Davis and Wendt should never have referred to Mugabe as a 'supposed dictator', given the twenty-two years of evidence against him. But worse still was couching the closing statement in words that implied Tsvangirai had already been found guilty as charged. The Australian show's indictment was immediately mirrored in Zimbabwe, where the state-owned press, radio and television assumed the roles of judge and jury, condemning Tsvangirai even as they called for his arrest.

On Monday 25 February, the MDC leader was interviewed by police for two hours and charged with treason, then released on the understanding that he would not face trial before the presidential election.

Mugabe could have pressed for an expedited prosecution or even had Tsvangirai remanded in custody, but the Commonwealth heads of state were due to meet in Australia that weekend, and had he jailed his opponent ahead of the election, CHOGM – which already had Zimbabwe high on the agenda – would almost certainly have suspended the country's membership.[19]

The ZBC edited and spliced the videotape so selectively that, in the six-minute extract screened on television news bulletins around the clock, it sounded as though the MDC leader had indeed been party to a plot of some kind. After being told he would face treason charges, Tsvangirai made his first public statement on the affair and categorically denied any wrongdoing.

'The whole thing has been contrived to damage me politically,' he told reporter Peta Thornycroft. 'It is intended to distract and confuse people, but the people will see through this whole ploy.'[20]

Tsvangirai followed these comments by launching a defamation suit against SBS, which remained unresolved at the time of writing.

At the Commonwealth conference there was a split along racial lines, with Britain, Australia, New Zealand and Canada calling for Zimbabwe's suspension, and leaders from Africa, Asia and the Caribbean expressing concern but demanding that the election be allowed to run its course before any decision was taken.

A compromise deal saw Australian prime minister John Howard and the presidents of South Africa and Nigeria appointed to what became known as the 'troika' to assess what action, if any, should be taken. It was agreed that the verdict of General Abubakar's Commonwealth observer group would guide the troika, and in the spirit of black solidarity that had marked African politics for forty years, Mugabe's supporters doubtless expected that the Nigerian would at least be gentle in his criticism.

A week before Zimbabweans were due to cast their ballots, the government office responsible for running the election – whose senior staff were appointed by ZANU-PF – had still not announced the number and location of polling stations, making it impossible for observer teams to plan their strategy.

The MDC mounted an eleventh-hour legal challenge against the regulations that required voters to exercise their franchise in the constituencies where they were both registered and could show proof of residence. The High Court declared the restrictions unconstitutional, but Mugabe used his presidential decree to reinstate them.

On Tuesday 5 March, the BBC reported that 40 000 regular soldiers and 35 000 police were being forced to lodge absentee votes ahead of the election and in the presence of their commanding officers. A policeman in Masvingo province – whose name was withheld for fear of reprisals – had allegedly told the BBC: 'We are busy casting our votes. The ballot papers were sent to individuals in envelopes and our bosses were presiding officers.'[21]

The report also carried a denial by defence minister Sydney Sekeramayi, who said the allegations were part of a disinformation campaign against Mugabe.

Voter registration had officially closed on 27 January, but the registrar general, Tobaiwa Mudede, continued to enrol residents of ZANU-PF strongholds after that, and the Chinhoyi branch of his office was still adding the names of party supporters to the roll less than twenty-four hours before polling stations opened.

I set out early on the morning of Saturday 9 March to do my first report for Radio 702 and Cape Talk. In previous elections, virtually every primary and secondary school had served as a polling station, and sure enough, at Chisipite High, across the street from my house, a small queue had already assembled and things seemed to be going well.

I went to another school, about a kilometre away, but it was closed. So were the next four schools I passed, and it was not until I reached Highlands, three kilometres away, that I found another polling station.

A quick tour of Tafara township and Chitungwiza revealed the same situation, and by lunchtime the MDC was crying foul.

The number of polling stations in all urban areas had been slashed by 40 per cent, based on statistics for the general election in 2000, while an additional 644 had been set up in ZANU-PF's rural strongholds.

Rural voters found no queues, but by 3 pm that Saturday the lines at some schools in Harare stretched for up to three kilometres, with tens of thousands of people waiting to cast their votes. At several schools, members of the electoral supervisory commission, handpicked by Mugabe, were assaulted as they tried to manage the queues.

In Chitungwiza, police fired tear gas when people who had been waiting in the sun all day pushed into a building where officials were taking up to twenty minutes to process each voter.

When the doors closed at 7 pm, people refused to go home. Those who had voted earlier in the day brought food and blankets, and the waiting throngs slept in their places along the line.

The late summer night was warm, but I have no doubt that even if the election had been held in mid-winter, when Harare's night temperature can slip to −2°C, it would have made little difference, so strong was the determination to vote.

By the end of the second day, the queues in Harare were longer than ever and the MDC brought an urgent High Court application for voting to be extended by another day. The government vigorously opposed the request, but after Judge Ben Hlatywayo flew over Harare in a helicopter and saw the extent of the problem for himself, he granted the order.

However, no one told the polling agents, so it was not until noon on the Monday that stations opened again, and by then thousands of would-be voters had been forced to abandon the election of their president in favour of going to work. The MDC sought another twenty-four-hour extension, but this time they lost, and the election was declared officially over at 7 pm on Monday 11 March.

In the days that followed, reports of violence, intimidation and outright cheating poured in from all over Zimbabwe. A number of non-governmental organisations had pooled their resources to form the Zimbabwe Election

Support Network (ZESN), and briefed the media from their base in Harare. Irregularities included the following:

- Both the MDC and ZANU-PF had placed polling agents at each ballot station to observe the fairness of the exercise and be present when ballot boxes were sealed and later opened for the votes to be counted. But according to both the ZESN and Amnesty International, more than 1 400 people – mostly MDC agents – had been arrested over the three-day election and prevented from performing their duties.

- The voters' roll was in a shambles, and many people registered in areas where MDC support was strongest had not been allowed to vote, because their names could not be found.

- In the area north of Mount Darwin, MDC polling agents had not manned the booths because they had been kidnapped by the militia and held at Katarira Primary School, which was turned into a detention centre. The agents were repeatedly beaten and tortured until police from Mukumbura, on the Mozambique border, rescued them.

- When MDC officials arrived at nearby Muzarabani on Friday 8 March, police stopped their vehicles, confiscated the keys and then watched while the local ZANU-PF member of parliament, Nobie Dzinzi, and a group of war vets set fire to the cars. In the same area, twenty-seven other polling agents were arrested and their vehicles impounded before they reached the polling station.

- At stations across the country, ballot boxes went missing for hours at a time, and when MDC officials asked why, they were either chased away by police and militia or arrested and held in custody until after the election.

- At Shamva, near Harare, the ZANU-PF member of parliament and minister responsible for the CIO, Nicholas Goche, was seen handing out ID cards to people who then proceeded to vote. It was presumed that the metal identity discs had been confiscated from local residents and that CIO members used them to cast multiple ballots.

- At some polling stations, up to 50 per cent of voters claimed to be illiterate and asked an electoral officer to accompany them into the booth. In a country with a literacy rate of more than 90 per cent, this was highly unlikely, and the MDC alleged that people were being paid to plead ignorance, and that electoral officers were then filling in their ballot forms in Mugabe's favour.

- Intimidation was so heavy in some districts that before dropping their ballot papers into the box, voters asked for a ZANU-PF polling agent to witness that they had drawn an X next to Mugabe's name.

- When counting began, hundreds of boxes from virtually all districts were found to have broken seals. When an MDC agent lodged an official complaint at Bindura, police threatened to arrest him and he was chased away by the militia.

- When the ballots were counted, there were widespread discrepancies between the recorded number of voters at particular stations over the three days, and the number of ballot papers in boxes from those stations. In Mount Darwin South, for example, a total of 21 000 people voted, but 29 000 votes were counted. At nearby Rushinga, 19 000 recorded voters produced 27 000 ballots.
- The MDC alleged that the registrar general had printed an additional 500 000 ballot papers, which, they said, were unaccounted for.

On Wednesday 13 March, the official results were announced. Mugabe had received 1 685 212 votes, while Tsvangirai took 1 258 401, giving the president a margin of more than 400 000, but his support was concentrated exclusively in Shona-speaking rural areas.

Tsvangirai won by a slim majority in Matabeleland South, but took 61 per cent of the vote in Matabeleland North, compared with Mugabe's 35 per cent. In Bulawayo, the split was 79/17 in Tsvangirai's favour, while in Harare it was a staggering 75/24.

But in all these areas, little more than half the registered voters had either turned out or made it to the front of the queue amid the congestion created by limiting the number of polling stations.

In Mugabe's strongholds – which were also the areas where MDC agents had been unable to function – voting levels ranged from 56 to 70 per cent, and Mugabe took 75 per cent of the votes on average.

Post-election criticism was damning. Elphas Mukonoweshuro, professor of political science at the University of Zimbabwe, said the poll had been designed 'to produce a predetermined outcome' and had been 'effectively and thoroughly rigged from all angles'. It could not be called a 'normal' election 'by any stretch of the imagination', said the professor.

Mugabe lost no time in consolidating his position. On Monday 18 March, he was inaugurated for another seven-year term during a ceremony at his official residence in Harare. Although the usual crop of ambassadors and dignitaries had been invited, more than a hundred chairs stood empty on the lawn.

'We have dealt a blow to imperialism,' the president ranted for the benefit of the ZBC cameras. 'And we have said loudly to those in Europe, no, no, never – never again shall Zimbabwe be a colony.'

But it was a hollow victory. Virtually the entire Western world refused to accept the result or recognise Mugabe as the legitimate president of Zimbabwe, and Tsvangirai insisted that he would be satisfied with nothing short of a fresh election, ruling out talks with the government on any other subject.

As for the official observers, their conclusions differed so widely that it was hard to imagine they had all witnessed the same election. Mugabe's staunchest supporter in sub-Saharan Africa, Sam Nujoma of Namibia, had sent a team that said the process had been 'watertight, without room for rigging'.

I spoke with several members of the South African team prior to their departure, and all dismissed the election as a farce. But in their final report, the ANC members claimed that while the outcome was 'credible', they could not describe it as 'free and fair'. Members of the DA and IFP slammed the whole thing as a sham.

The OAU declared that, in general, the election had been 'transparent, credible, free and fair', and the official Nigerian team delivered a similar verdict, though Obasanjo himself sounded a word of caution.

'Whatever the ordinary people of Zimbabwe have done, voted or not voted, they need to be assisted,' he said the day before Mugabe's inauguration. 'That help may not come unless the leaders of Zimbabwe put their arms together and work together in a way that brings hope to this country.'

The largest European delegation, which was from Norway, said that while there had been reports of violence from both sides, the evidence was 'extremely clear' that the majority of incidents had been the work of the ruling party.

The presidents of Ghana and Senegal also condemned the poll, but the harshest censure came from General Abdusalam Abubakar.

His preliminary report covered just three pages and came straight to the point, listing his reasons for recommending that the Commonwealth should not accept the election results:

- There was a high level of politically motivated violence and intimidation before the election.
- Most acts of violence were perpetrated by members or supporters of the ruling party.
- Graduates of the National Youth Training Programme (Green Bombers) led a systematic campaign of intimidation.
- There was a climate of fear and suspicion.
- The observer team had serious reservations about the rule of law in Zimbabwe.
- The new election laws were flawed.
- Restrictions on freedom of speech, movement and association had prevented the opposition from campaigning freely.
- Restrictions had been imposed on civil society groups as well as independent domestic observers.
- Thousands of Zimbabwean citizens were disenfranchised by the lack of transparency in the voter registration process and the wide discretionary

powers of the registrar general in deciding who would be included on or omitted from the voters' roll.

- ZANU-PF used state resources to fund its election campaign and had a virtual monopoly in the broadcast media.
- On polling days, many who wanted to cast their ballots could not do so because of a significant reduction in the number of polling stations in urban areas.

Abubakar's conclusion was that 'conditions in Zimbabwe did not adequately allow for a free expression of will by the electors'.

Unfortunately, most of the worst cases of abuse never came to the attention of independent observers, because the victims were held in camps by the militia until the election was over. In the first three months of 2003, in preparation for this chapter, I interviewed seventy-three black Zimbabwean exiles in Johannesburg and London, who had been subject to violence both before and after the election.

Of the twenty-one women who spoke to me, nineteen had been raped while in the camps or police custody. Of the fifty-two men, thirty-eight had been sexually assaulted.

I soon established that rape of men and women alike had been used as a weapon to break the morale of MDC supporters.

In the militia camps, MDC prisoners were often forced to perform sex acts with each other: men with women, and, all too frequently, men with men. Full penetration was ordered, while war veterans, militia leaders and sometimes soldiers, police and CIO agents watched and cheered.

The testimony of those subjected to such abuse is shocking in the extreme. I was so profoundly disturbed after bearing witness to the victims' stories that I had to seek counselling, and rather than including them in this chapter, I have chosen to publish only four of the accounts as an appendix at the back of this book. I earnestly caution anyone of a sensitive disposition *not* to read them.

The Media Monitoring Project Zimbabwe (MMPZ), which had analysed all print, radio and television coverage, found that pro-Mugabe reports accounted for 13 hours and 34 minutes of the total of 14 hours and 25 minutes devoted to the election by ZBC TV. The remaining 51 minutes had been used to denigrate Tsvangirai. Furthermore, the ZBC had refused to run any campaign ads for the MDC.

Radio had fared no better. The most popular station, which broadcast in Shona and Ndebele, carried 275 campaign-related reports, of which 237 (86 per cent) favoured ZANU-PF. The remainder either criticised the MDC or dealt with obscure issues unrelated to either party.

The day after Mugabe's inauguration, Tsvangirai was summoned to court to face charges of treason, and ordered to post bail of nearly US$80 000 and surrender his passport. Welshman Ncube and four other members of the MDC executive who were alleged to have attended the meeting in Montreal were also charged and later acquitted.

In Pretoria, Thabo Mbeki faced a new headache. With an illegitimate regime on his doorstep and few black leaders willing to criticise Mugabe, his dream of an African Renaissance could become a nightmare.

In a guest editorial for the *New York Times*, American political analyst David J Simon summed it up as follows:

'The OAU has long been perceived as a club for corrupt, authoritarian leaders distinguished primarily by tolerance for each others' misdeeds. However, the past decade has been one of political liberalization across the continent ... and Africa's new democratic leaders have called for a continent-wide commitment to democratic principles.'

Then Simon pinpointed the key issue for Mbeki. The OAU, he said, had launched NEPAD as a new initiative that would bring capital and development to Africa in a climate of true democracy and a commitment by all member states to 'free, open, fair and democratic elections'.

'Africa would have a new resolve to deal with conflicts and censure deviation from the norm.

'But the failure to criticize the way the Zimbabwean elections were conducted demonstrates that the new resolve and the confidence to censure deviation have yet to be found.'[22]

Within two weeks of the election, the Commonwealth's troika – Mbeki, Obasanjo and Howard – met in London to decide on a course of action against Zimbabwe. Mbeki was confident that Obasanjo would band with him and oppose any steps that could further internationalise the crisis, but instead the Nigerian leader voted with Howard for Zimbabwe's suspension from the Commonwealth.

Archbishop Desmond Tutu supported the decision.

'I am deeply, deeply distressed and deeply disappointed,' he said when commenting on South Africa's acceptance of the election as 'credible'.

'When democracy is not being upheld, we ought for our own sakes to say it is not so,' he pointed out, adding that he supported the decision to impose sanctions 'with a very heavy heart, hoping that President Mugabe and his government, elected in a flawed election, will draw back from the precipice'.[23]

While there is no doubt that the election was rigged and that turnout in Harare and other MDC strongholds was hampered by the long queues, it was still surprising that less than half of the more than five million legitimate voters cast their ballots, and that percentage polls in Matabeleland were so low.

At least one explanation for this anomaly should have set alarm bells ringing in Pretoria. Many of those who had registered as voters in recent years had since left the country.

In the crucial presidential election of March 2002, Zimbabweans were not afflicted by voter apathy – it was just that between one and two million of them were now living in South Africa.

By the middle of the year, it had become clear that I would not be able to write and publish this book while continuing to live in Zimbabwe, and I, too, moved to South Africa.

# 11

# Exile!

After Tsvangirai's defeat, the mood in Zimbabwe changed. The violence, empty shelves, long queues for petrol – even hyperinflation that saw the price of goods doubling every two or three months – could be written off as part of the pain that comes with change. But when change didn't happen, the focus shifted, and instead of discussing what they might be doing in a few years, people under the age of forty were talking about where they would be twelve months later.

Austrian psychiatrist Victor Frankl (1905–97) defined misery as 'to suffer without meaning', and for young, skilled people the idea of staying in Zimbabwe in the hope that things would improve no longer made any sense.

Judging by those I interviewed in Johannesburg and London, the typical emigrant was unmarried, aged between eighteen and thirty, had a high school education or better, and was willing to take any job just to get started in a new country. The human stream into Botswana, South Africa, Mozambique, Germany, Holland and Britain became a flood, and for the first time since 1980 the British government imposed visa restrictions on Zimbabweans travelling to the United Kingdom.

In 2002, according to official statistics, 26 717 Zimbabweans were deported from Botswana, and 26 408 from South Africa (excluding thousands intercepted or turned back at the border). But in Gaborone and Pretoria, both governments admitted they were only picking up a fraction of the total number of illegal immigrants.

South Africa had long required visas for Zimbabwe passport holders, and the high commission in Harare was inundated with applications for 'holiday permits' that allowed a stay of up to three months, after which the bearer required one or other residency permit. But, for a bribe of R1 500, this was easily obtained from the South African Department of Home Affairs.

My research suggested that the department was corrupt at many levels – especially at Beit Bridge and in Johannesburg, where most Zimbabweans were processed – and that the South African government was fighting a losing battle against illegal immigrants. Human rights groups estimated that in the six months after the 2002 presidential election, more than 150 000 people had crossed the

Limpopo from Zimbabwe with the intention of staying on despite the absence of legal documents allowing them to do so.

The majority of black Zimbabweans I interviewed in South Africa had 'jumped' the border – one of the most closely monitored boundaries in Africa, patrolled day and night by a special police unit. The South African media put the daily influx of permanent foreign residents at between 1 000 and 1 500, though probably half of these arrived with legitimate visas and simply stayed on when their permits expired.[1]

In every enterprise – public or private – there are many honest and dedicated people trying to achieve the best possible result, and the border police are no different. But they are understaffed, poorly funded and not paid enough to stop the junior ranks – who do most of the legwork – from taking bribes. It is easy to criticise, but I suspect that most of them know their efforts are in vain, and that illegal immigrants using the so-called A Route are buying their way across the official border post.

In Johannesburg, people from elsewhere in Africa are known as *kwerekwere*, which translates roughly as 'gobbledygook', and stems from the fact that the locals can't understand what the foreigners are saying.

But in Zimbabwe, people who carried their possessions on their backs and slipped out of the country became known as *girigamba* – slang for a dung beetle – and the term has also made its way across the border and gained currency in South Africa.

The flightless African dung beetle is an industrious insect that eats the droppings of large herbivores, including cattle, buffalo and even elephant. First it forms the waste into a sphere, then rolls it to a place of safety, where the dung can be stored and eaten. The journey may cover several kilometres and the beetle will collect more droppings along the way, and a single ball of dung can reach the size of an apple.

Calling the refugees *girigamba* has nothing to do with dung, but refers to the fact that everything they own is packed into one piece of luggage, which they carry with them.

Among the border jumpers I interviewed were Patrick Pindura, thirty-two, and his cousin Raymond, twenty-four.

Patrick had run a fruit stall in Harare before being forced into one of the militia camps, from which he managed to escape, but Raymond had lived in South Africa for four years and been spared the violence of the general and presidential elections. He was an economic refugee who had seen the writing on the wall, and I found his advice invaluable because he had gone back and forth across the Limpopo River more than twenty times, returning to Zimbabwe at Easter, Christmas and for various marriages and funerals.

The three of us met several times, and they told me about the ways people slipped into South Africa illegally.

'It's easy once you know the system,' said Patrick.

'From Harare, Bulawayo and Masvingo, there are cars and minivans owned by people who specialise in moving Zimbabweans in and out of South Africa, and you have three choices.

'If you have a lot of money[2] you go the A Route. No passport, no documents, you just get into the vehicle, and when you reach the border the driver pays a bribe to the immigration and customs authorities on the Zimbabwe side, and crosses Beit Bridge without anyone checking the car.

'He does the same thing on the South African side, and your next stop is Jo'burg, where you are dropped near the rail terminus at Park Station.

'I'm not sure why the police don't just wait for the cars at the station and demand to check people's passports, but they don't.

'For about 80 per cent of that price you get the B Route, which is the same, except that the car stops in Musina, just across the border, and you make your own way to Jo'burg from there.

'But the most popular is the C Route, which can be less than half price if you shop around among the drivers. This one happens mostly during the day, and your vehicle drops you off on the Zimbabwe side of the bridge, where you wait until dark and then make your own way across the river. The transport is waiting for you near Musina and they either drop you in Pietersburg [now Polokwane] or take you all the way to Park Station. Part of the deal is that if the vehicle is stopped at a roadblock along the way, the driver will do his best to bribe the police to make sure they don't ask for your documents.'

But Raymond had not travelled by any of these routes.

'The first time I came here I was broke,' he said, 'so I just took an ordinary bus to Beit Bridge. I got there around lunchtime and bought a few rand from the currency traders who hang out near the post office, and they put me in touch with one of the guides who will take you across the river.

'There are many at Beit Bridge; mine was an old woman, and that night she took me and about ten other "clients" to a spot east of the bridge, maybe five or six kilometres down the river, and we crossed into South Africa without any problems.

'She walked fast and led us as far as the highway on the South African side. From there, she said, we could make our own way to Musina, and she turned back. But she even gave us her phone number and said she meets people north of Musina for the journey back home. She claimed she had been stopped a few times, but she always carried money to bribe the police or home affairs.'

Although Raymond's story dated back four years, more recent migrants also told me about the 'gadding granny', who was reportedly from the Venda tribe that straddles the river. According to one account, she was originally from Musina and used to lead South African exiles into Zimbabwe in the days of apartheid.

One man who had crossed with her several times said she always carried a gun for fear that one of her clients would hold her up and steal her bribe money.

In spite of the fact that dozens of people told me how easy it was to move between the two countries, I still found it hard to believe, and asked Patrick and Raymond if it would be possible to witness some of the action at first hand.

So, at 11 pm on a summer night in October 2002, *Ernie* was parked in a glade of trees next to a dirt track two or three kilometres from the river on the South African side of the border.

With Patrick and Raymond, I stood in silence next to the car and sipped a plastic mug of tepid coffee, poured from a flask the motel in Musina had prepared for us four hours earlier.

Just north of Musina we had turned east and followed a narrow road for a few kilometres, then turned onto the track, which appeared to be quite well used and was possibly an access route for staff maintaining the fence running along the border. About 100 metres from our hiding place, the road rounded a bend and disappeared into the trees.

If people were really coming across as brazenly as I had been led to believe, I wanted to see it for myself, and as luck would have it the moon was almost full and the landscape stood out clearly in the light.

In daylight our eyes can see detail, but at night we pick out the shape of things. Even under the brightest moon there is no colour, and the bush and trees, the scrubby grass fringing the track, even the road itself, were all defined in shades of black.

Patrick had broken some branches and packed them around the sides of the car, and had made up a code of signals. Three taps on the roof meant someone approaching from the front, two taps would alert me to an approach from the rear and one would mean that we had been spotted. Any other sound, he warned, would scare people away.

Earlier that day, the four of us had driven 320 kilometres from Johannesburg on the Great North Road, through the resort town of Warmbaths and on to the provincial capital of Polokwane, where we stopped for lunch. I had been toying with the idea of buying a small farm in the area, and an estate agent showed me over the property.

Polokwane is a delightful city, with warm summers and temperate winters. Just south of the tropic of Capricorn, it is the first major centre on the route from Beit Bridge to Johannesburg, and a hub for northbound traffic as well. A string of new platinum mines had created a boom in property prices, but I decided against the farm, and we continued on our way.

It was another 200 kilometres to Musina, where we had time to check into a motel, bath and eat before setting off for the spot where Patrick and Raymond said we might well have some luck.

At midnight the tropical air was still warm and mosquitoes started buzzing around my head. I made a mental note that if I ever came this way again, I would bring a cooler box instead of coffee, and a large can of insect repellent.

Mosquitoes generally don't seem to like the taste of me, but these were different, and my neck was tingling from the bites. I'd brought a small bottle of brandy and thought of rubbing some on my skin to stop the itching, but if I'd taken the bottle out my companions would have wanted a sip, and I wanted to keep the brandy for later. Besides, the mosquitoes would probably have enjoyed it!

A lone jackal howled in the distance, an unmistakable call, somewhere between a laugh and a cry for help, creepy enough to make us smile at each other for comfort.

Then a bushbaby or lesser galago bawled from a nearby clump of trees – 'whaah, whaah, whaah' – and when the cry died down a pair of owls hooted. I looked at Raymond and pointed in the direction of the sound.

On the journey from Johannesburg we had talked about African magic, and despite having three O-levels, Raymond had insisted that owls were really witches who, like the werewolves of Eastern Europe, could change from human to animal form, and back again. He laughed silently and hugged himself, pretending to shiver.

The night fell quiet, except for the buzzing of the insects, and I was about to take out the brandy when Raymond touched my elbow and I looked down the track to see two people walking towards us. Patrick had seen them too, and hunched up his shoulders the way some people do when they are excited or nervous. I didn't move, but I could feel a pulse throbbing in my neck.

I'm not sure how I had expected people on the run to behave: maybe some nervousness, glancing around and darting from bush to bush, but there was none of that. They both carried backpacks and moved with a slight swagger, and for a moment I thought they might be soldiers or police. But as they drew closer I could make out their clothes, and put their gait down to fatigue.

Patrick put a finger to his lips and made a gesture with his hands as though he was smoothing a tablecloth in mid-air. This was not one of our agreed signs, but it clearly meant that we should let these people pass. Although I wasn't sure why, I was happy to take his advice.

The pair walked so close to the car that I could smell the tobacco smoke on their clothes, and when they had gone Patrick put his face to my ear.

'We would have scared the hell out of them,' he said. 'And if one of them was armed, there could have been an accident.

'I'm going to move down the road,' he whispered. 'When I see someone, I will make as if I am also on my way, and I can maybe talk to them before they reach the car.'

I nodded and he slipped out of the trees, walked down the track and disappeared around the bend.

In less than five minutes he came back towards us, with two other people. As they approached, I could make out a couple in their early twenties.

Patrick was talking to them in Shona.

'*Hapana chekutya,*' he said. 'There is nothing to worry about. No, we are not linked with the police, but I have with me one white guy who would like to hear your story.'

The three stopped within two metres of the car and, in keeping with custom, the woman stood slightly back from the men.

'Is this white man in Musina?' asked the man at almost the exact moment that the woman spotted us and let out a cry of disbelief.

Five minutes later we were sipping brandy, using the car's roof as a table, while Ena and Crisis (yes, that really was his name) told us their story.

This was their third crossing into South Africa, and they were headed for Durban, where Crisis had a job as a cleaner. He was Ndebele, she was Shona, but they were equally fluent in both languages and spoke perfect English.

'The first time, I came on my own,' said Crisis. 'Ena was working at a hotel at Vic Falls and we were both supporters of the MDC. That was after the 2000 election, and it was time to move. I had a brother in Durban, so I went to join him, and I got a tourist visa in my passport.'

Crisis was granted a two-week stay in South Africa but remained for six months, and knew he would have problems when he tried to leave.

'So I used a guide to go back to Zim. I spent three weeks at home near Bulawayo and Ena came to join me. By this time I had a job in Durban and had brought enough money to take us both on a bus to Jo'burg without going through immigration.'

In Durban, Ena found work at a bed and breakfast, but when her mother died in September they went home for the funeral.

'We went as far as Musina, and on the afternoon we arrived we met some other Zimbabweans who were going home, and we all went across that night.

'Coming back now, we used the same route and got through a hole in the fence.'

They had left Beit Bridge as part of a larger group, but some had decided to wait until the early hours of the morning and were still on the opposite bank of the river. More people would come across that night, but I had seen enough to confirm that the border was leaking, just the way I had been told.

Crisis told me that while Ena visited friends in Musina, he would be meeting some of the other *girigamba*, and I invited him to bring as many of them as he could find to the motel for breakfast. I offered the couple a lift, but they wanted to wait for friends who had yet to cross, and we left them there and drove back to town.

Patrick and Raymond had the room next to mine, and it was after three when we turned in. I told them to sleep as late as they liked and come down to breakfast when they were ready.

I was in the dining room by seven, half expecting to find a dozen people waiting for me, but only Crisis was there. While I ordered coffee, he told me that most of the people he had invited were too scared to come, in case I was linked with the authorities. But he had found two men willing to talk to me, and he went outside and called them in.

Phineas was a stocky Ndau from Chipinge who had worked as a labourer in Kimberley for the past three years, but had gone back to Zimbabwe on leave to see his family. He was only twenty-two, but his Rambo-like build made him look older. Clement was twenty-eight and a teacher from my old stomping ground of Mutare. This was his first time in South Africa. They had not known Crisis before meeting him on the road earlier that morning.

One of Clement's cousins worked with Phineas in Kimberley, and had asked him to help Clement come to South Africa. Their journey had not been easy, and the older man was clearly shaken and barely said a word. But over fried eggs, bacon and toast, Phineas told their story.

'I have made the journey many times, and I have only been stopped once on the South African side, about two years ago,' he said. 'In those days it wasn't so bad if they caught you, and I only paid them R20 and they let me go.

'But this time, we left Beit Bridge too early. We should have waited until midnight, but I had got used to coming through without problems. At around 8.30 last night we were stopped on the Zim side by an army unit who asked where we were going.

'I told them that we did not have papers to cross the bridge, and they said we needed to pay them if they were going to let us pass. We gave them Z$500 each and they escorted us to a point on the river which we know as Crossing Number 10. They turned back, and we went through.'

He didn't know why the crossing point was called 'Number 10', but said there was private land on the South African side, and the name might have something to do with the farm address.

'It was a long walk to Musina and we were tired, and I should have been watching the path. Instead, we walked into a South African patrol and they arrested us.

'They asked how much we could pay, but these days they are greedy. The only bribe they will accept is to take all your money. I pulled out R50 from my pocket and they searched me and found nothing more, and let me go.'

Phineas broke off his narrative and looked at Clement. 'I had forgotten to tell him to hide most of his cash in his shoes. He had nearly R1 000 in his pocket, and they took it all. He is left with nothing.'

I asked Clement about the experience and he started crying.

'For R500 I could have bought a ticket on the bus that takes you through without papers,' he said. 'That was all the cash I had saved for more than a year. I have nothing to start life in South Africa.'

I wondered whether Crisis had told Clement to weave a hard-luck story in the hope that I would take pity on him and hand over some cash that they would split between them as soon as I was gone. But, when you look into someone's eyes, there is a difference between sadness and misery. I believed Clement was in real trouble, and gave him R200, which would at least cover his fare to Kimberley.

Patrick and Raymond joined us for the rest of our meal, and we talked about the country we all loved and the hope that, some day soon, things would be different. It was mid-morning before we began driving back to Johannesburg.[3]

On 5 December I was back at the Limpopo to photograph a demonstration staged by Zimbabwean exiles from the shanty towns around Johannesburg.

Jay Jay Sibanda, a thirty-something teacher who had been forced out of the government school system for refusing to join ZANU-PF, had already organised a number of anti-Mugabe protests by angry exiles who were living ten to a room in rundown suburbs such as Hillbrow, Berea, Yeoville and Malvern.

In September 2003, it was at Jay Jay's initiative that about 150 black Zimbabweans took over a busy intersection near the posh suburb of Sandton, north of Johannesburg. They arrived at 6 am and erected a banner that read 'Hoot If You Want Mugabe To Go!' As the morning traffic built up, thousands of motorists honked their horns.

When a listener alerted Radio 702 to the gathering, journalists around town began tipping one another off. By 8 am I was there, along with representatives of Reuters, Agence France Presse, CNN, BBC and the daily newspapers.

On the approaches to the junction men waved Zimbabwe flags, and at the traffic lights volunteers handed out badly printed leaflets accusing the Mugabe government of torture and brutality, calling on Thabo Mbeki to take a tougher stand on the issue.

Others moved through the traffic with plastic jugs, asking people for donations to fund future protests. South African drivers are used to being plagued at intersections by vendors selling everything from soft drinks to cellphones, and rarely wind down their windows. But that morning, I saw black and white hands dropping coins and notes into the jugs.

I had first met Jay Jay a month earlier at the UN World Summit for Sustainable Development in Sandton, where he attended several press conferences called by the MDC. He had a religious commitment to his cause, spurred on partly, I think, by a sense of injustice at having been forced out of teaching.

The summit ran for a fortnight, and halfway through, on Saturday 31 August, the anti-globalisation lobby staged a huge march from the neighbouring township of Alexandra to the Sandton Convention Centre. Protestors included a pro-Palestinian faction, homeless South Africans and a rag-tag army of pressure groups, including the MDC.

A fracas broke out at the start of the march, when members of the ANC confiscated placards calling for Mugabe to be put on trial. Apparently it was acceptable to call for justice in Israel – 8 000 kilometres away – but not in a neighbouring state. The Zimbabweans were eventually allowed to march, but most of their visual aids had been destroyed.

Jay Jay told me later that he had learned from an American journalist about apartheid-era protests in New York, where students held up banners that read 'Hoot If You Want To Free Mandela'. He adapted the idea to his own cause, and following the success of the Sandton protest, the 'hoot' banners were used again and again at intersections all around Johannesburg.

Jay Jay and his group called themselves Concerned Zimbabweans Abroad, and in October they wanted to mount a demonstration outside Thabo Mbeki's office at the Union Buildings in Pretoria. This time, the message was 'Hoot If You Want Mbeki To Act On Zimbabwe', but because the Union Buildings is a high-security area, permission had to be obtained from both the police and Mbeki's staff.

It was granted immediately, and Jay Jay told me that one of the president's aides had said: 'This office wishes you well with your protest.'

It made me wonder whether the South African government secretly enjoyed the idea of Mugabe being publicly lambasted by his own people, or perhaps even saw the protests as a way of putting more pressure on ZANU-PF. Then again, perhaps this was just the 'new' South Africa paying homage to the freedom of expression entrenched in its constitution.

Some of Jay Jay's people travelled by bus from Johannesburg and were joined by Zimbabweans living in Pretoria to form a group of more than 200. Motorists responded with hooters and cash donations, both the BBC and CNN covered the story, and it was clear that a new front had opened up in the struggle.

But the media soon tires of a cause, and although public support for the demonstrations remained strong, newspaper and television coverage began to wane. Interestingly the *Sowetan*, a daily that caters almost exclusively for the black working class, reported on the protests regularly and always sympathetically. I managed to sell stories and pictures to several newspapers in Australia, Britain and the USA, including a daily in Washington, but it was clear that the anti-Mugabe movement needed a new angle.

In early November, Jay Jay telephoned me one afternoon, so excited that I could barely make out what he was saying, except that it had something to do with the forthcoming eclipse that was being punted around the world as a major tourist event. He had a plan, and based on my experience as a journalist in both Zimbabwe and abroad, he wanted to know if I thought it would draw attention.

A total eclipse had taken place over the Zambezi River in 2001, and the next one – over the Limpopo in December 2002 – would be the last in southern Africa for at least twenty-five years.

Over breakfast the next day, Jay Jay could scarcely contain his enthusiasm.

'Some hotels in the path of the eclipse have been booked out for more than a year,' he read from a tourist brochure, 'and the world's media will be on hand to cover this heavenly phenomenon, when the shadow of the moon falls across the sun and plunges the day into darkness.'

Jay Jay gulped his orange juice and looked at me as though he had just discovered the password to Mugabe's Swiss bank account.

'You see,' he said, 'you see how great our chance will be?'

Then he ran through the idea point by point:

- More than 60 000 people – many of them from abroad – were expected to converge on the northern region of Limpopo Province to view the eclipse.
- Local and foreign press would cover the event.
- It would happen on Zimbabwe's border.
- Besides the eclipse, his would be the only story in the area competing for media attention.

Then he produced a tatty piece of A4 paper on which he and his colleagues had penned suggested slogans for their placards and banners: 'Mugabe Casts A Shadow Over Southern Africa'; 'The Lights Have Gone Out In Zimbabwe'; 'See The Light And Tell Mugabe To Go!'

They were good, and I told Jay Jay while I thought his idea was a winner, the story might get lost amid coverage of the eclipse itself, especially in the local newspapers. But, I reckoned, the foreign press would rush to reproduce the slogans as a way of giving their stories a different angle.

However, it turned out not to be that easy. Jay Jay and his lieutenants, Jairos and Philemon, travelled to Louis Trichardt (also known as Makhado), a town between Polokwane and Musina, and obtained the permits needed for a public demonstration. The day before the eclipse, a number of Zimbabweans arrived by bus from Johannesburg and set up base near a series of tunnels on the road to the north.

Waving banners and placards, they sang and danced at the side of the road, and passing traffic responded with a symphony of hooters. Cars, trucks, freight carriers bound for Zambia and Malawi, even students on motorcycles, black and white, all joined in, and twenty minutes after arriving to photograph the scene, I was giddy with the noise and had to retreat 500 metres up the road to clear my head.

But the demonstrators seemed to have no such problem, and performed for the passing parade for five hours straight. Then the police arrived.

The authorities had withdrawn the permits, and the protestors were told to board their bus and leave. They obeyed, returning to town for lunch while their leaders went to the local government offices. A spokesman for the council told them that several of the town elders had driven past the protest, and although they had no problem in principle with the message being conveyed, the ANC-dominated council had concerns over the sensitivity of the issue, especially in light of the national government's stated policy of quiet diplomacy in dealing with Mugabe and the situation in Zimbabwe.

It was a classic case of small-town paranoia, and although Jay Jay's deputy, Jairos, explained that a similar demonstration had been allowed right outside Mbeki's office, it made no difference. Finally, a compromise was reached. The protest could continue, a few kilometres north of the tunnels and thus beyond the council's jurisdiction. An hour later, the show was back on the road.

I spent the night in Musina, where the only accommodation available was in a converted school hostel. For miles around, every lodge, cottage and private game reserve was fully booked, but the mood was far from festive. As night fell the clouds rolled in, and when I ventured out at five the next morning there was not a patch of blue sky to be seen.

The grounds around the hostel and every park, pavement and sports field in Musina were packed with people hoping for a miracle. But the heavens were blanketed in white, though the clouds were moving in swirls, which meant a wind was blowing somewhere high above, offering some reason for optimism.

I interviewed a few of the tourists who had come from Germany, Holland, Australia, one family from Russia and others from Britain and America. All had seen the demonstration and had positive things to say about it. Clearly, Jay Jay's strategy had worked, but for now, all eyes were on the sky.

Then it happened.

'It was amazing,' said John York, a visitor from England, whom I quoted in one of my reports. 'Up to ten minutes before the moment of totality, the sky was white. Then, a minute before climax, a miracle. It was as though the hand of God brushed away the mist, and we saw a ring of fire as the shadow of the moon covered the sun. And the world around us went as dark as night. Then it was gone, and we couldn't believe our luck.'

The peak of the drama lasted only eighty-seven seconds, but I was awe-struck, and those who have seen one of these heavenly events will know what I mean.

Authorities in Limpopo Province estimated that the visitors had spent more than R100 million, but in Zimbabwe, bad press and a shortage of fuel left hotels and lodges with rooms to spare.

When I drove back to Johannesburg later that morning, the protesters were still at it. As I had predicted, the South African media concentrated on the eclipse, mentioning the demonstration in passing, but it was a different matter abroad. German and Swiss radio, Voice of America, Danish television, a Dutch weekly and even a newspaper in Uruguay highlighted the way the Zimbabweans had drawn attention to their plight.

Full of confidence and with ample funds collected during the eclipse, Jay Jay mounted a massive protest in Johannesburg on 30 December, with a four-metre banner that read 'Happy 2003 – The Year Mugabe Goes'. He chose a busy inter-section again, this time near the SABC's headquarters in Auckland Park, and the newspapers lapped it up, with one daily making it the lead story on New Year's Eve.

The exiles kept up the pressure in 2003 with campaigns around Johannesburg and Pretoria. In May, when Grace Mugabe tried to take a weekend break at Caesar's Resort and Casino near Johannesburg International Airport, they protested in front of the hotel, and the first lady checked out the same day. Later that month, a demonstration was staged outside the five-star Westcliff Hotel in Johannesburg's northern suburbs, where Mugabe himself was staying while in South Africa for the funeral of ANC elder statesman Walter Sisulu.

The media reported both incidents, as well as details of Grace's R100 000 shopping spree at some of Johannesburg's finest stores during her stay at Caesar's.

In June – having borrowed the idea from the MDC's protest wing in London – Jay Jay hired an old double-decker bus and took a group of exiles on a tour of Pretoria's diplomatic belt, where they hung banners with tailor-made slogans at various embassies. In front of the Congolese ambassador's office, the sign read: 'Pres. Kabila, Tell Your Friend Bob His Time Is Up!' The French were chided for having allowed Mugabe to visit Paris four months earlier, while the message for the White House was: 'Bush, Give Mugabe 48 Hours!' – a reference to the ultimatum the American president had sent Saddam Hussein on the eve of US and British armed forces invading Iraq in March.

When the Zimbabwean exiles made the rounds of the foreign missions, the regime in Baghdad had been toppled, but Saddam's fate remained unknown. At the Iraqi embassy they left a sign reading: 'Saddam Hussein, Wherever You're Hiding, Mugabe Will Be Joining You Soon'.

At each stop, group leaders left the bus to hand over a letter to the respective ambassadors, calling on their governments to do whatever it could to end Mugabe's rule. A special version of the letter, urging Mugabe to resign, was taken to the Zimbabwe high commission, but staff refused to accept the envelope and it was thrown at the protestors' feet in plain view of media cameras.

No longer was the story just about white farmers, but about ordinary black Zimbabweans who had fled their homeland and were vocal in demanding that something be done to end the tyranny in their country.

But while the exiles danced and waved at the cameras during their demonstrations and charmed the public with their own versions of 'Homeless' and protest anthems such as 'We Shall Overcome', the reality of their life in South Africa was nothing to sing about.

In conducting the many interviews that provided background for parts of this book, I visited several of the dwellings in poverty-stricken suburbs where these people were crammed eight or ten to a room.

In one case, reminiscent of a scene from the Nazi-era ghetto in Warsaw, I was led through a hole in the back wall of a building that had been condemned and boarded up, and found a dozen people sharing a bundle of blankets in the basement.

They were all in their twenties, new arrivals who had no family to stay with in South Africa. They cooked on one paraffin stove, drew their water from a single tap across the road and huddled together at night for warmth.

Their greatest problem, they said, was the corruption of both police and immigration officials.

Among the basement dwellers were Joyce Makore, twenty-eight, and her brother Philip, twenty-four. Her husband, previously a ranger at a small private game reserve in Zimbabwe that had been overrun by war vets, had gone to look for work near the Kruger National Park.

Joyce and Philip were destitute because, although they had both been granted asylum – and were given the papers to prove it – the police had picked up Joyce the previous week when she left the building to use a public telephone. They had confiscated her papers and taken her to the police station, where they demanded R100 before she could be released.

She was allowed to phone Philip, who had to borrow some of the money from fellow exiles, and now they had nothing left.

I found many members of the exile community who had either been held to ransom in similar fashion or knew someone who had gone through the experience. If no one paid, the refugee would be sent to the Lindela deportation camp near Johannesburg, where the going rate for release was a R600 bribe. Those who could not pay would be deported – a virtual death sentence for anyone on the run from the CIO.

Asylum permits had to be renewed every month at a government refugee centre in Jorissen Street, not far from Park Station, but the queues were so long that applicants had to sleep on the pavement overnight if they were to have any chance of being attended to the next day. When the doors opened at 8 am, the crowd would surge inside, only to be beaten back by security guards with whips. However, payment of a R150 bribe to one of the touts moving brazenly up and down the queue would secure entry and service without delay.

I visited the centre early one morning in May 2003 and photographed the impossibly long queue, the touts, even the guards whipping the people. The pay-for-entry racket was run by a number of Nigerians and a few burly men from the Democratic Republic of Congo, who threatened me when I tried to photograph the money changing hands. I withdrew to a balcony across the street and carried on taking pictures with a telephoto lens.

One man from the former French colony of the Comores off the coast of Mozambique told me openly that if he had enough money, he would no longer have to go through the monthly bother of standing in line to renew his permit.

'The Nigerian gangs can get you anything,' he said, and others in the crowd agreed. 'You can get a work permit, a South African ID, anything you want. And at the top of the range is a deal that costs R10 000, which gets you a South African passport in any name you like, plus an air ticket to Britain or any other European country.'

The air ticket intrigued me. Why could the 'client' not make his or her own travel arrangements? But over the next few days I verified the story with a former home affairs official, who said she left the service because she could no longer stand the rampant corruption.

'I have seen some of the passports myself,' she told me. 'They are totally genuine, but of course there is no documentation on record to back them up.

'The air tickets are for specific flights on certain days, and the middleman takes the passenger to the airport and makes sure there is no problem at check-in or immigration. They have contacts everywhere, and the flights they use are never direct to London but always via another country, sometimes in East Africa, but I have seen some that went through Egypt and Dubai.'

I had heard that even the American authorities had expressed concern about the problem after they picked up two suspected Al-Qaeda members in Kenya. Both allegedly had genuine South African passports, even though neither of them had ever set foot in the country.

The US State Department had also warned Pretoria that, given the flow of refugees from Zimbabwe, it was likely that professional human traffickers from South-East Asia might well set up shop in the region, and that such operations could, in turn, be exploited by international terror networks.

In December 2002, Kathleen FitzGibbon, senior reporting officer in the State Department's human trafficking division, predicted an escalation in the already high number of people entering South Africa from Zimbabwe.

'There will be a huge increase when Zimbabwe blows. Traffickers take advantage of situations where there are large concentrations of people,' she said, adding that Johannesburg served as a hub for refugees fleeing civil wars in central Africa, particularly the DRC, Burundi and Rwanda.

'It's easy to move people through [South Africa]. This could easily be exploited by the bad guys, and we wouldn't like to see a terrorist attack because someone transited South Africa.'[4]

In February 2003, I raised some of these issues with Dr Mangosuthu Buthelezi, the South African home affairs minister, whose portfolio included passport control and immigration.

We sat on the couch in his Pretoria office, and he talked frankly about illegal immigrants, Mugabe, corruption, and a South African cabinet that did not give him enough money to do the job.

His political career spanned nearly half a century, and while he chose not to go into exile during the struggle against apartheid, his Inkatha Freedom Party became a force for change in the old South Africa.[5]

Throughout the liberation struggle, the ANC viewed him with suspicion bordering on hate, fuelled largely by Buthelezi being his own man and refusing to go along with the slogans and ideology of either the white or black nationalists. In his book on the Zulu leader, Ben Temkin[6] relates how, in November 1986, John Nkadimeng, then secretary general of the South African Congress of Trade Unions and a member of the ANC national executive, condemned Buthelezi in a broadcast on Radio Freedom, a shortwave station beamed into South Africa from the Zambian capital of Lusaka.

'It is clear,' said Nkadimeng, 'that the puppet Gatsha [a nickname Buthelezi detests] is being groomed by the West and the racist regime to become the Savimbi of a future, free South Africa. The onus is on the people of South Africa to neutralise the Gatsha snake, which is poisoning the people of South Africa. It needs to be hit on the head.'

When the ANC came to power in 1994, instead of bludgeoning Buthelezi as Nkadimeng had suggested, they gave him enough rope to hang himself. The IFP was brought into a government of national unity, and he was given a cabinet post that made him responsible for the issuing of identity documents and passports, immigration, and registration of births and deaths.

Under apartheid, and in a climate of civil disobedience, many blacks had refused to apply for ID documents, and since few of them had the financial means to travel abroad, there was little demand for passports.

When people realised that democracy had come to stay, however, they flocked to regional home affairs offices to obtain ID documents. The situation was aggravated when the government announced that only the latest, bar-coded ID books could be used by voters in the 1999 general election, and millions of South Africans of all colours had to join the queues for both these and the new, supposedly forgery-proof passports that were also introduced.

Then came the crisis in Zimbabwe and a flood of new people seeking documentation, but still the department's budget was not raised to a level at which it could reasonably be expected to cope with demand.

Buthelezi was an interviewer's dream, picking up the question before I'd finished framing it and answering with a frankness that almost restored my faith in politicians.

At the outset, I told him what I had learned about widespread corruption in his department:

- A visitor's visa for twelve months (instead of the usual twelve weeks) cost R800.
- Residence permits cost R1 500.
- South African passports were up for sale.
- Many Zimbabweans had obtained passports that gave Johannesburg as their place of birth, and when they went home, South African immigration officers at Beit Bridge knew full well that these documents had been obtained by foul means, because neither their surnames nor their accents were South African. So, before the passports were stamped, the officers required that a R50 note be slipped between the pages.[7]

What made Buthelezi so special was that he had the balls to concede that there was a problem, and even allowed me to tape the interview.

'Corruption is everywhere in this country, and my department has serious problems, because staff are handling money and they have opportunities,' he told me.

'It is very serious, and we are doing our utmost to overcome it. We have excellent relations with the police and the Scorpions [special investigations unit], but I know that where there is temptation there will always be some corruption, even at the highest levels of government.'

But, he said, underfunding made it even harder to deal with the problem.

'The baseline of the treasury is too low,' he said diplomatically. 'We have 1 500 vacancies in this department that cannot be filled, because we don't have the money. The government has chosen to give me a portfolio in which I am condemned, whatever I do. It is an unwinnable situation.'

As for the flow of illegal immigrants, he said this was by no means limited to people from neighbouring states such as Zimbabwe and Mozambique.

'There is a perception in Africa that this is a very rich country. But we have a high rate of unemployment, and there are not even enough jobs for South Africans. Every year, more of our own people graduate from colleges and high schools, and we cannot afford to have illegal immigrants take what jobs we can offer our school leavers.

'If you go to a flea market, you will hear French being spoken and find people from West and even North Africa selling their goods. If people are here illegally and we can round them up, we do it, but to think that we will ever solve the problem is a dream.

'We have a very serious problem, and it extends well beyond the difficulties of our region.'

It was, according to the minister, the proverbial vicious cycle. There was not enough money to employ the right number of staff, so procedures were slow and backlogs built up, which encouraged people to offer bribes so that their applications would go to the top of the pile. And once payments for quicker service gained a foothold in the system, the problem spread like a cancer into other areas, and in no time at all officials simply expected to make extra money on the side.

As for the future, Buthelezi was not optimistic. Large-scale immigration, he pointed out, was a symptom of problems in the source countries, and Zimbabwe was a good example.

'One solution would be to change the situation in Zimbabwe, so that people would not want to come here in the first place,' he said, reminding me that his party had voted against an ANC-sponsored parliamentary motion that sought to legitimise the result of the 2002 presidential election.

'Mozambique's government must create jobs for their people, or they will continue to come here looking for work. And in Zimbabwe the current crisis would have to be solved before we might expect the number of people crossing the border to slow down.'

Our time was up, and Buthelezi had to leave for a cabinet meeting. But I wanted to ask just one more question, and took a risk on an issue that went to the heart of South Africa's status as the continent's superpower.

Should Pretoria be concerned about the internal affairs of countries where bad governance resulted in an exodus of people to South Africa?

'We don't have a choice,' said Buthelezi. 'There is no question of our right to do that.'

The meeting left me with a lasting regard for the minister, and in the months following our interview I read press reports that things were being tightened up in his department. But right until September 2003, I was still interviewing people who had chosen or been forced to pay bribes, and I never found out why, with corruption so widespread and blatant, so few of the culprits have been brought to book.

Two weeks after interviewing Buthelezi, I went to London to see how exiled Zimbabweans were faring in Britain. The story was different, but no less tragic.

Entry to Britain used to be easy for Zimbabwe passport holders, who did not require visas until 2002. As their number swelled, the Home Office adopted a new approach. Because of the violence in their homeland, no Zimbabweans would be deported from the UK, but they would need visas to gain entry, which was an effective way of limiting the number of new arrivals.

It was hard to get figures on how many people from Zimbabwe have moved to Britain. Many began their journey in a third country, some travelled on South African passports, and others – mainly older whites – had British passports, even though they were born in Rhodesia.

The conventional wisdom is that around 500 000 UK residents are originally from Zimbabwe.[8]

Whereas the highest concentration of exiles in South Africa is in Johannesburg, in Britain they are spread out, with sizeable communities in Manchester, Birmingham, Liverpool, Norwich and York. Even in London, where the largest group has settled, there doesn't seem to be the sense of togetherness one finds in Johannesburg.

'It's the climate and the high cost of living that does it,' Jabu Ncube told me over a beer late one Friday afternoon in Piccadilly. Jabu had left Bulawayo in 1999, and spent a year in Durban and another in Ireland before moving to England.

'I don't think that people who come from the tropics ever really adapt to cold weather,' he said. 'So we tend to spend a lot more time indoors – especially those with young families – and when we do go out, we have to think about what we're going to do, because everything is so expensive and you don't have cash to go larking about with your friends. People get very cut off, and this fragments the community.'

But those who have sought the company of others, especially in London, play a role in turning British opinion against the ZANU-PF government.

'Tomorrow is Saturday, and if you go to the Zimbabwe high commission in The Strand, you will find our people demonstrating outside the building. They do it every week,' said Jabu.

Zimbabwe House, as it is known, is a beautiful building that served as the Rhodesian foreign mission until UDI in 1965, when Harold Wilson's government shut it down. It was fifteen years before it reopened in 1980, but in the intervening period black and white demonstrators would assemble near the front door with posters denouncing Ian Smith and calling for the country to be handed over to ZANU.

Sure enough, just as Jabu had said, when I arrived at noon on Saturday there was a crowd of black and white Zimbabweans who had set up banners denouncing the rulers in Harare as a 'regime of killers', and for hours they sang and danced and asked passers-by to sign petitions calling for tougher action against Mugabe.

They even nailed posters to the door (something the South African police would never tolerate), demanding that the high commission be closed because it did not represent a legally elected government.

I spent the next few hours tape-recording their views, which generally indicated that while they did have problems as political refugees or asylum seekers, Britain at least had a system that guaranteed their human rights.

Givemore Chindawi went to London in 2001 after a stint in Johannesburg, but said he had never felt safe in South Africa.

'I was worried that the CIO would still be after me,' he said, as he handed out fliers to the never-ending flow of pedestrians. 'Everyone knows that Mbeki and Mugabe are friends, and I did not feel safe there, but here the CIO is powerless.'

Standing next to him was his wife Enika, who was encouraging people to sign the petitions.

'Our problems started in April 2000,' Givemore continued. 'Both my wife and I supported the opposition. I was an organising secretary in the men's wing at district level, while my wife helped in the women's division.

'We were easy targets because we sold membership cards, gave out T-shirts, recruited new members and organised party meetings.

'And of course it wasn't long before I was visited by war veterans – a gang of ten – who accused me of treason and warned me to mind my own business and leave politics to ZANU-PF. I tried to reason with them, hoping I could find a chance to escape and alert my wife to contact other MDC members.

'They wanted to take me to their offices, but I knew if that happened, I would disappear forever. Luckily, Enika was nearby and saw that I was surrounded, and she quickly phoned other MDC members who came to my rescue, and the men ran away.

'A few days later, war vets abducted Patrick Nabanyama, the campaign manager of David Coltart, who is now our MP for Bulawayo South. As you may know, Patrick's body has never been found.

'On the night of 27 June 2001, four members of the CIO visited my wife at home and pretended to be MDC members who had come to collect me for a meeting in town. Enika was suspicious, and told them I had already left. Two days later, the same men returned in the middle of the night and broke down our door.

'They assaulted my wife and searched the house, but I had taken to sleeping in different places every night and was not there. But they confiscated all my MDC papers. Luckily, our passports and other documents had been hidden.

'That was the turning point in my life. I packed a small bag and kissed Zimbabwe goodbye, and after a short stay in South Africa, I flew to London.

'Back home in Zimbabwe, Enika was in worse trouble, because those CIO men were still terrorising her. They kept asking for my whereabouts, but she told them she didn't know. Finally, in November 2001, I told her to sell everything that we owned, take all the money that was left in our bank accounts and join me in London. She also came via South Africa.

'Now we are both working for the cause of change in Zimbabwe, and sadly, at home, many others are still being tortured and harassed by the same people who forced me out of the country.'

In July 2002, Givemore and Enika Chindawi were granted leave to remain in the United Kingdom indefinitely.

I interviewed more than twenty exiles that afternoon, and heard many tales of tragedy. One man had fled when his father, who was also working for the opposition, was abducted and murdered and his body hanged from a tree outside the family home. Others had scars from their own encounters with state-sponsored thugs.

One of the white MDC youth leaders, Tom Spicer – also known as Tawanda – was among the protestors, having recently left Zimbabwe after being tortured by the police. He had been abducted several times, spent weeks in jail and suffered numerous beatings at the hands of both the authorities and ZANU-PF's henchmen.

His father, Newton, a fourth-generation Zimbabwean, was a leading environmentalist, and his British-born mother, Edwina, was a filmmaker whose documentaries on Zimbabwe had won international acclaim.

Tom struck me as a very special person who could play a major role in the country's future. He spoke fluent Shona, and at only nineteen displayed a deep understanding of Zimbabwe's problems. I hope that in future many other whites in both Zimbabwe and South Africa will follow his example and become fluent in at least one indigenous language.

Many of the exiles I spoke to had neither sought nor been granted official refugee status, but travel to and from Britain was so poorly controlled that the government had little idea who was in the country at any given time.

British passport holders had only to show their documents at a point of entry, and no record was kept of their movements. Foreign citizens had to obtain an entry stamp and their arrivals were logged in a computer database, but there were no controls on outbound travel, and people didn't even have to present their passports when exiting Britain. So the authorities had no way of knowing whether short-term visitors had overstayed their welcome.

Some Zimbabweans had been in Britain for several years, others for only two or three months, but there had been few new arrivals since the introduction of visas. A small number had travelled via the Republic of Ireland, from where they would make their way to Northern Ireland, which was part of the UK, then complete the journey as domestic travellers. In an effort to close this loophole, Dublin had also begun demanding visas for Zimbabwe citizens, and these had become even harder to obtain than those issued by the British authorities.

Most of the exiles were well educated, yet many were doing menial work. Employers demanded work permits before granting job interviews, and there was a rising intolerance against foreigners, especially those perceived to have entered Britain as refugees. So the majority of exiles were forced to take casual jobs from unscrupulous employers, who saw migrant workers as cheap labour: people who could be paid well below the legal minimum wage, and fired at will.

The issue of asylum was a hot topic in Britain, though the focus was on refugees entering from North Africa and Eastern Europe, most of whom travelled via France, either by boat or on the train linking mainland Europe with England through the Chunnel.

While British immigration officials themselves did not appear to be corrupt, there was a mafia-like network of forgers who provided illegal immigrants with the documents needed to open bank accounts, qualify for social security benefits, and even obtain residence permits and passports.

The problem came to the fore after the attack on the World Trade Center and Britain's support for the US-led wars in Afghanistan and Iraq, the argument being that if refugees could gain access to Britain so easily, there was nothing to stop international terrorists doing the same thing.

Harriet Sergeant, a researcher who has written extensively on the subject, caused a furore in the British parliament with her best-known work, a discussion paper titled 'Welcome to the Asylum'. After the UK Centre for Policy Studies published the paper, she became a popular guest on radio and TV talk shows, and pulled no punches.

'Our immigration policy is a mess,' she said bluntly, quoting figures showing that the budget for welfare assistance to asylum seekers doubled from £475 million in 1999 to more than £1 billion in 2000.

And, she insisted, the government could not even produce accurate statistics for the number of people flooding into Britain.

'We have no idea who is entering this country, in what numbers, how they live and how they get here, how many leave and how many come and go. The policy is to let in an unlimited number of immigrants, then treat them badly or pretend they do not exist.'⁹

Forgery and corruption had made the problem even worse, said Sergeant.

'In just one raid on the home of a Nigerian couple, police found some 13 000 forged documents, including blank electricity and gas bills, British and Nigerian birth certificates, driving licences and even nursing qualifications.'

According to Sergeant, the only genuine document in the house was an official letter informing the woman that she had been granted indefinite leave to stay in Britain.

'While we have been pretending that an immigration problem does not exist, a criminal world has grown up in which the terrorist can thrive and operate,' she warned.¹⁰

Patience Gondwe, who had been living in Britain for two years when we spoke and had managed to legalise her status, told me that in her experience the British people had little sense of geography and a poor grasp on world affairs, and as a result lumped all immigrants together.

'I think they see all foreigners as lazy, dishonest people who have come to England to live off social welfare. And what makes it harder for us is that we don't really want to be here anyway, and would go home if we could. But for now, that is not an option,' she said.

But I got a different view from an immigration official who was willing to speak to me on condition of anonymity. Her personal belief was that, without the influx of well-educated young migrants, Britain would have a problem.

'Young black people, especially those from Zambia and Kenya, and both black and white migrants I've met from Zimbabwe and South Africa, are actually more employable than many Brits in the same age group,' she said.

'They are intelligent, speak good English, are well mannered and sail through interviews, whereas some of our own people stammer and stutter at the questions. We have produced a generation that, despite ten or twelve years of schooling, is nowhere near as lucid and literate as the Africans, who also have a better work ethic.'

Then there was the question of working conditions. In 2001, Britain had to recruit 473 nurses from Zimbabwe, because more than half the British nurses who had qualified in the past thirty years had left the profession. For the new arrivals, a stressful, low-paid job with long hours was infinitely better than staying at home.

Unlike South Africa, where the MDC and Jay Jay Sibanda's pressure group are separate entities, in London the party leads the way, and every Monday night exiles meet in a lounge above the bar at the George Hotel opposite the Royal Court of Justice in The Strand.

'It's an open forum,' Patson Muzuwa, one of the leading lights in the movement, told me at the Saturday rally. 'It is an MDC initiative, but anyone can come, and we always welcome journalists. There should be at least sixty people, maybe more.'

'Sixty!' I exclaimed. 'So where are the thousands of Zimbabweans who are reportedly living in the UK?'

'They don't come,' said Patson. 'If you meet them, they talk about deposing Mugabe and how we must all do our bit, but you never see them at meetings. They hang out together and give each other support, but they are too busy rebuilding their lives, and the struggle is left to those of us who care enough to come here every weekend and protest.'

Another young Shona, Clifford Mahembe, offered to take me to some of the hostels where many exiles started out in London, and on the Monday morning we met at Brixton Station and walked down to one of the biggest refugee centres, a place called the Eurotower, in the borough of Lambeth.

There was a time when this was a posh area. Brixton had some of the first streets in Britain to get electricity, and before the Second World War it was a good address. And Lambeth is where successive Archbishops of Canterbury have based themselves for more than 700 years.

In the 1950s, immigrants from the Caribbean moved into the area and, as their numbers grew, Brixton in particular became a ghetto. In 1980, and again in 1985, the infamous Brixton race riots erupted, with running battles between police and black demonstrators, who claimed they were being treated as second-class citizens.

Today, the average Londoner's advice would be to steer clear of the area, which many see as a danger zone rife with muggers and criminals on the run. After the 11 September attacks in New York and Washington, Brixton gained further notoriety because a British cell of Osama Bin Laden's terror network had based itself there, one member being Zacarias Moussaoui, who was later arrested in America on suspicion of planning the attacks.[11]

The only impression I had gained of the down-and-out side of British life had come from watching a BBC police drama series, *The Bill*, set in the fictitious London precinct of Sunhill, near a sub-economic zone called the Jasmine-Allen housing estate. When I visited Brixton, I realised how accurately the TV show had portrayed the real thing: drab, featureless blocks of flats, two or three storeys high, some with broken windows and all crying out for a coat of paint.

We passed some rough-looking teenagers and a few women pushing prams, but no men. Maybe they were out working, though on *The Bill* this kind of environment was typically home to single mothers.

'There are many asylum seekers here,' Clifford told me as I picked up my step to try to get warm. 'But nobody wants to stay long, and they only use it as a place to get started.'

'What kind of refugees?' I asked.

'All kinds. People from Africa, Sri Lanka, India and Romania, and many from countries in the Middle East like Afghanistan and Iraq. But they find it very rough, and the British people who still live here are not easy to get on with.'

It was a pale spring day with wispy clouds and a wind that sliced through even the warmest clothes. All the features that add colour to a suburb – pets, flowers, the sound of laughter – were lacking, and a sadness crept over me, as though I were on my way to the funeral of a friend who had killed himself.

In less than ten minutes we had crossed from Brixton into Lambeth, but nothing changed, except that there seemed to be more graffiti on the walls.

The last row of flats leading up to the Eurotower lay on a stretch known as Paradise Road, and I wondered how anyone could have been moved to give the street such a name. But, with London being such an old city, I supposed that when the area was first laid out, it was probably just a village with thatched cottages, and a green where cows would graze and children play.

I had heard that the 'gentrification' of the inner suburbs, which saw young professionals buying slum blocks and turning them into townhouses, had changed the face of some sections of Brixton and Lambeth, but this area was clearly not among them.

We were refused access to the Eurotower, but an Iranian man in charge of the foyer told me there were only a few Zimbabweans in residence. 'We used to get them here, but I think they now have such a large community that the new arrivals have usually got someone to go and stay with,' he said.

It must have been quite a place in its day, big and self-important in the swinging sixties when it first opened as a hotel. It was then turned into a youth hostel, and even now, I guessed, the upper rooms would command a good view of the city.

It wasn't so much the building that depressed me as the rundown flats and houses surrounding it, the graffiti, a couple of stripped cars on a vacant lot and the general sense of decay.

'There have been a few suicides here,' Clifford told me as I took photographs from across the street. 'People spend so long hoping to get into Britain, and then they end up here, with no money, no job and no way of getting home.'

But, he said, the Zimbabweans soon found either legal or informal employment, after which it was just a matter of time before they moved on to better surroundings.

The meeting that night kicked off at seven in a small function room over the pub, set out in schoolroom style, with rows of straight-backed chairs facing a table from where the committee addressed the audience.

I counted just over eighty people, all of whom listened attentively while the treasurer went through a statement of funds and the local chairman talked about how the MDC would hand over its petition of 15 000 signatures to the Minister for Development, Clare Short, on Wednesday. Short had been informed, and her office had said she was looking forward to the ceremony, which would take place in the public hall next to the House of Commons.

Before that, they planned to hire a double-decker bus and do a grand tour of London with banners and fliers on a circuit that would include Downing Street, Piccadilly, Mayfair, Buckingham Palace and The Strand.

A speaker from one of the NGOs involved with asylum issues talked about the problem of visas and what was being done to convince the British government that more Zimbabweans should be allowed into the UK.

But it was the close of the meeting that really moved me. A group of men I had seen at the Saturday demonstration walked to the front of the hall and performed a rendition of 'Homeless'[12] in harmonies that had some of the audience in tears. The song was written jointly by Paul Simon and Joseph Tshabalala, the lead singer of Ladysmith Black Mambazo, and the melody is from an old Zulu wedding song:

We are homeless, we are homeless …
Somebody cry, why, why, why?

The song is written in both English and Zulu, and tells of a strong wind destroying homes, leaving many dead, and the fear that tonight it might be one of them who dies.

The English translation of the Zulu words is more or less as follows:

The cold has almost killed me,
I wish the nation would talk.
But what can we do?
Happy are those who love us,
Even though we are homeless.

People got up and danced, while others hugged each other. If not exactly homeless themselves, they were certainly homesick in that cold city that is so far removed from Africa, in so many ways. Perhaps this is the major difference between exiles in Johannesburg and London.

South Africa is not Zimbabwe, but even for those who cannot go home for fear of persecution there is the knowledge that the country they have left is only a few hours away. And many of the birds, trees and flowers are the same as those at home, and I think this familiarity tempers the pain of exile to some extent.

In London, white and black Africans alike feel like foreigners, not just because they speak and think differently from the people they encounter every day, but because of the climate and lifestyle. Physically, mentally and spiritually they are a long way from home, the only compensation being that they are safe, and, notwithstanding all the criticism of government policy, refugees in Britain do receive some financial assistance, whereas in South Africa they get none.

But among all the exiles I interviewed in both Britain and South Africa, there was not one who referred to either of these adopted countries as home.

# 12

# The money trail

When Zimbabwe gets its first truly democratic government, one of the hardest jobs will be tracking down the millions – some say billions – of dollars allegedly embezzled by Mugabe, his ministers and their cohorts.

In February 2002, the London *Financial Times* estimated that Mugabe's personal wealth could be as much as U$100 million, though there was no indication of how the newspaper had arrived at this figure.[1] But whatever money he might have abroad was unlikely to be sitting in an account under the name of Mr and Mrs RG Mugabe.

An elaborate network of companies and trusts had been set up by ZANU-PF under the guiding hand of Emerson Mnangagwa, the man Mugabe favoured to succeed him as president. Mnangagwa was in charge of state security during the Matabeleland massacres in the 1980s. Later, as justice minister, he did not intervene when Chenjerai Hunzvi and his war veterans began occupying farms in 1999. He was also the party's financial secretary.

But, before examining the structure of ZANU-PF Inc., it is worth looking at the scale of embezzlement that takes place around the world, especially in developing countries.

Transparency International, a worldwide NGO that spends its time exposing corruption, publishes a yearly report on governmental and corporate theft. Their 2003 survey listed some of the funds identified or recovered in 2002, and the numbers are staggering. All figures are in US dollars.

- Retired admiral Mansur ul-Haq, former chief of the Pakistani navy, handed back $7.5 million stolen while in office. The money was enough to pay the salaries of the entire navy for two years.
- A parliamentary inquiry in the Philippines estimated that the country lost $1.9 billion a year through corruption, enough to build half a million new homes.
- Relatives of the late Nigerian dictator, Sani Abacha, agreed to hand back $1 billion looted from the country's central bank during his four-and-a-half years in power (November 1993 to June 1998). In exchange for the cash, the government agreed to drop some criminal charges against the Abacha family.

- Former Zambian president Frederick Chiluba was stripped of his immunity ahead of a trial in which he was accused of stealing more than $80 million.
- Nicaragua moved to charge its former president, Arnoldo Alemán, with the theft of $100 million during his term of office.
- A leaked IMF report estimated that $1 billion went missing each year from the state treasury in Angola. The amount was four times larger than the sum the United Nations was trying to raise in 2003 to help more than a million Angolans who were facing starvation.

To keep these figures in perspective, it should be remembered that in 2002 corporate fraud at the American media company WorldCom was estimated at more than $7 billion.

When the Mugabe government first came to power in 1980, it was not overtly corrupt, though there were some noticeable changes to the way things had been done in the past.

Aid money given to ZANU-PF in exile by Scandinavian countries was used to buy homes in Harare for the party leaders. The modest official cars driven by both the Rhodesian Front government and that of Bishop Muzorewa were dumped in favour of a new fleet of Mercedes Benz, along with some Peugeot sedans, but the salaries of MPs and senior public servants were not increased. The role of city mayors – traditionally an unpaid position – was changed, and the new 'executive mayors' were each provided with a car, a rent-free house and a salary.

A system of patronage developed, and major contracts were awarded to friends or companies in which ministers and party chiefs held shares. In 1983, government funds were channelled to ZANU-PF to help build the party office block, which stands next to the Harare Sheraton Hotel.

Once the press had been nationalised in 1982, the coast was clear to embark on a 'get-rich-quick' programme.

An early example of ZANU-PF's foray into business occurred shortly after independence, when the party took over the catering at Harare International Airport. A company called Catercraft was established to supply in-flight food and beverages to all airlines flying to Zimbabwe. ZANU-PF took 51 per cent and brought in a long-time Omani contact, Kamal Khalfan, as the junior partner and managing director.

When the war ended in 1980, a slew of long-haul airlines introduced flights to Harare, including Lufthansa, Alitalia, British Airways, Qantas, Air France and KLM, along with regional carriers such as Kenya Airways, Air Tanzania, Egypt Air and Ethiopian Airlines.

Since Catercraft had a monopoly on airline food, ZANU-PF made money every time an aircraft landed in Harare.

It should be noted, however, that Kamal Khalfan ran an excellent operation and offered world-class catering to the airlines, and there was no apparent effort to exploit the monopoly by employing a take-it-or-leave-it approach.

Kamal made his home in Harare and cut a dapper figure around town. Whenever possible, he tried to source products locally, contributed money to Zimbabwean charities and worked hard to maintain a good relationship with his clients.

Within fifteen years of taking power, ZANU-PF had a stake in more than 100 local companies, and Mnangagwa was on the board of more than a dozen enterprises.

But the Zimbabwe economy was small pickings, and the party started casting around for regional opportunities.

The programme to integrate ZANLA, ZIPRA and the Rhodesian Army had gone smoothly and produced the Zimbabwe Defence Force (ZDF). But, although the war was over, little effort was made to downsize the armed forces, which gobbled up a sizeable chunk of the national budget.

Then, in 1982, Mugabe received a cry for help from his closest ally, President Samora Machel of Mozambique, without whose help ZANU could not have pursued the war.

The Renamo rebel movement, originally supported by the Rhodesians and subsequently funded and supplied in secret by the South African Defence Force, was in control of much of rural Mozambique and had begun laying siege to towns in the north. The country was in the grip of a full-scale civil war, and Machel refused to accede to Renamo leader Afonso Dhlakama's demand for multiparty elections. Since independence from Portugal in 1975, one national poll had been held, but Machel had decreed that his ruling Frelimo party would be the only one allowed to field candidates, and all other political activity had been banned.

Machel had also allowed the ANC to set up guerrilla training camps in his country as part of their battle against the apartheid government in South Africa, and Pretoria responded by increasing aid to Renamo.

Machel asked Mugabe to send in troops, and by 1983 Zimbabwe had been dragged into the war.

The next year, the government in Harare set up a company called Zimbabwe Defence Industries (ZDI), which had the sole task of procuring equipment for the army by circumventing the usual tender process. Through ZDI, goods could be purchased from companies owned by ministers and their families, and with the war in Mozambique escalating by the week, supplies worth millions of dollars were required.

In 1984, South Africa and Mozambique signed the famous Nkomati Accord, in which both countries agreed to withdraw all military support for guerrilla movements and ban them from their soil. Machel kept his word and closed down the ANC training camps, but the South Africans continued to covertly arm Renamo.

By 1996, the war in Mozambique was costing Mugabe US$1 million a day (at that time equivalent to Z$1.6 million), and was eroding funds that should have been used to build infrastructure, create jobs and pay for land redistribution. Instead, the money was spent on rifles, bullets, landmines and jet fuel. Britain was Zimbabwe's main supplier of military equipment and also a major aid donor, but, as with the massacres in Matabeleland, the Thatcher government took a decision not to comment publicly on what was happening, and even supplied instructors to train the Zimbabwe army.

When Machel died in 1986, his successor, Joaquim Chissano, realised that he could never win militarily, and began searching for ways to accommodate the rebels. In 1988 he asked that the ZDF be withdrawn from Mozambique, but the adventure had cost Zimbabwe more than Z$1 billion.

Four years later, Chissano accepted Renamo's demands and held elections, which saw Frelimo returned to power and Dhlakama installed as leader of the opposition. Machel's Marxist doctrines were discarded in favour of a free-market system, but, as investment dollars poured into Mozambique, it was South African and Portuguese firms that snapped up deals in tourism, construction and farming.

However, Mugabe and his inner circle had learned from their mistake, and when a request for help later came from Congolese rebel leader Laurent Kabila, the response was very different.

Kabila had been fighting for thirty years to free his country from the rule of US-backed dictator Mobutu Sese Seko, who had turned the former Belgian Congo into his private fiefdom and was estimated to have accumulated a personal wealth of more than US$3 billion.

Kabila had taken part in a number of uprisings, starting with the Battle of Stanleyville (now Kisangani) in 1964, when Mobutu crushed the rebels and forced them to flee to the Uvira district in the east of the country. There they formed an enclave of resistance among the Tutsi people, whose population was spread across Burundi, Rwanda and the Congo.

According to Gerard Prunier, a French expert on the region, in order to raise money 'Kabila and his supporters killed elephants and did mining. Then they smuggled the ivory and diamonds and gold through Burundi.'[2]

With the end of the Cold War, the US withdrew its support and money from Mobutu, and Kabila saw his chance. The Congo's infrastructure was in ruins, there were no all-weather roads, the security forces were demoralised and had not been paid for months, and with luck and some good backers, it would be possible to move through the country and take the capital, Kinshasa.

Kabila approached Mugabe, who allegedly provided US$5 million to help fund the assault. As the rebels closed on Kinshasa, senior officers from military intelligence in Harare were helping to plan the attack.[3]

The Zimbabweans were not the only ones taking an interest. According to a 2002 report compiled by the Center for Public Integrity in Washington, South African mining giant De Beers sent one its senior officials, Nicholas Davenport, to meet Kabila ahead of the final push against Kinshasa. Though the report made clear that no money had changed hands, it claimed that De Beers had 'long backed and supported Mobutu', and was keen to maintain good relations with his potential successor.

The same document alleged that Kabila was being flown around the Congo in a Lear Jet owned by American Mineral Fields (based in Hope, Arkansas), that a delegation of potential US investors met with him a week before Mobutu was deposed, and that one company even paid for a NASA satellite study of the Congo that identified possible mineral deposits.[4]

In May 1997, what was left of Mobutu's army deserted and the ageing dictator fled into exile. Laurent-Desire Kabila was sworn in as president, and in the same month Zimbabwe Defence Industries was given a contract to supply dried fish, corn meal, uniforms and boots worth US$53 million to the new government. Zvinavashe Transport, owned by Mugabe's army chief, General Vitalis Zvinavashe, was commissioned to convey the goods from Harare to Kinshasa via Zambia.

It was the start of what would become a multi-billion-dollar venture that would bankrupt Zimbabwe, but enrich the ruling elite to a degree that not even they themselves had thought possible.

In 1998 a new company, Congo-Duka, was set up in Harare and entered a joint venture with ZDI and a Congolese firm to supply consumer goods to Kinshasa. The Zimbabwean directors of the new enterprise included Charles Kuwasa, permanent secretary in the ministry of finance, Zvinavashe, and Air Marshal Perence Shiri.

The main liaison between Kinshasa and Harare was the then Minister of Justice, Emerson Mnangagwa.

The government underwrote guarantees of Z$1.6 billion (then US$90 million) against political risk, and Zimbabwe became the Congo's major supplier, with the majority of goods being sourced from companies in Harare that were owned by well-placed business people, ministers or the military.

What made the deals even sweeter was that the DRC paid in foreign exchange, and the US dollars were passed on directly to the suppliers in Harare. But not all the high-level transactions were quite as successful.

In November 1998, on a state visit to Zimbabwe, Kabila announced that one of Mugabe's local supporters, Billy Rautenbach, was to be made chairman and chief executive of the Congo's state-owned cobalt mining company, Gécamines.

Rautenbach had a long association with both ZANU-PF and the DRC. In 1997, one of his companies had been involved in building a 300-kilometre road from Kinshasa to the regional capital of Matadi, and his transport company, Wheels of Africa, had operated in the Congo for several years.

Under the new deal, Rautenbach's company in the British Virgin Islands, Ridgepoint Overseas Development Ltd, won the rights to extract cobalt from a mine near the southern town of Lukasi.

In 1999, however, one of Rautenbach's South African companies fell foul of its creditors and the courts ordered the seizure of his Congolese cobalt, which was stored in Durban awaiting export. As a result, Kabila cancelled the deal with Rautenbach, citing irregularities in the management of the operation.

But the Congo president had bigger problems to deal with. After taking power, he had fallen out with his Tutsi backers and with the governments of Rwanda and Burundi, which had supported him during his long years in Uvira. A new rebel group known as La Rassemblement Congolais por la Democratie-Goma emerged, and with military backing from Rwanda and Uganda applied Kabila's own strategy and began moving on the capital.

At a meeting of ZANU-PF's inner circle in 1999, the party leaders agreed that they would do whatever it took to protect their investments, and over the next year Mugabe sent more than 10 000 troops and military advisers to shore up Kabila's position.

The operation was impossibly expensive and fraught with difficulty. The Zimbabwean soldiers were well trained but they spoke no French, and few of the Congolese could speak English. The distance from Harare to Kinshasa was more than 1 500 kilometres – across Zambia's bad roads – and re-supply was both slow and costly, with much of it eventually having to be done by air.

Kabila agreed to pay the bill, but the DRC was bankrupt. So, instead of cash, he offered an equivalent value in mining, timber and farming concessions.

As Zimbabwe's military role in the DRC expanded, tension arose between defence minister Moven Mahachi and Mnangagwa, who, in 1998, demanded that senior officers in the army and air force should report directly to him regarding their activities in the Congo. In 1999, Mugabe made this an official order.[5]

According to the United Nations panel investigating the exploitation of mineral resources in the Congo, Kabila wielded a highly personalised control, avoiding any semblance of accountability. 'Management control over public enterprises was virtually non-existent and deals granting concessions were

Central African Republic

DEMOCRATIC
REPUBLIC OF
CONGO

Uganda

Rwanda

Burundi

Uvira

Kinshasa

Angola

Mbuji-Mayi
Mining concession

Tanzania

Katanga Province

Cobalt Mine

Lubumbashi

Zambia

made indiscriminately in order to generate quickly needed revenues and to satisfy the most pressing political or financial exigencies,' the UN report found.[6]

American firms that had courted the future president in the days before he took Kinshasa found themselves sidelined, and Robert Stewart, the former chairman of American Mineral Fields, which had worked so hard to forge bonds with Kabila, complained that his contracts in the DRC had been cancelled. At the Non-Aligned Movement conference in Durban in 1998, Stewart told the media: 'The country is dead as long as he is running it. Every mining project in the country is stalled.'[7]

Kabila also terminated a deal with De Beers for the export and sale of Congolese diamonds, and in 2000 sold a monopoly export licence to an Israeli company, International Diamond Industries, for U\$20 million. According to the UN, the company's twenty-seven-year-old owner, Dan Gertler, agreed to arrange, through his connections with high-ranking Israeli military officers, the delivery of arms, as well as the training of Kabila's troops.[8]

But the DRC's Lebanese community, which had dominated the diamond industry during Mobutu's rule, refused to accept what they regarded as low prices offered by Gertler, and by the end of 2000 the Belgian Diamond Office, which monitors international trade in the stones, estimated that of diamonds worth US$1.02 billion exported from the DRC that year, close on 85 per cent – valued at US$854 million – had been smuggled out of the country, with some gems being routed through Harare.[9]

A new company, Osleg Pvt Ltd, was formed in Harare with a board that included Zvinavashe, Job Whabara – the permanent secretary in the defence ministry – and Onesimo Moto, director of the Minerals Marketing Corporation of Zimbabwe. The army commander's brother, Colonel Francis Zvinavashe, and two retired military officers represented Osleg in Kinshasa.

Under the Osleg banner (the name was an acronym of Operation Sovereign Legitimacy) there were several other companies: Osleg Enterprises, Osleg Ventures, Osleg Mining and Exploration, and Osleg Mines.

But forming companies and maintaining troops in the DRC did not automatically generate wealth, and the actual business of extracting diamonds, cobalt, timber and other resources was slow, and the ZANU-PF elite was becoming impatient.

In early 1999, Kamal Khalfan arranged a dinner in Harare for a visiting Omani trade delegation that included Thamer bin Said Ahmed Al-Shanfari, the son of Oman's former oil minister. Mugabe was the guest of honour and sat next to thirty-two-year-old Shanfari – a graduate of the Colorado School of Mines – and told him about the problems with the DRC deal.

After that, things moved quickly. On 16 July 1999, one of Shanfari's companies, Oryx Natural Resources, based in the tax haven of the Cayman Islands, joined forces with ZDI's subsidiaries to form Oryx-ZimCon (Pvt) Ltd.

Osleg then put forward a proposal to form a joint venture with Comiex-Congo, a company in which Laurent Kabila was the majority shareholder. According to documents outlining the Zimbabwean offer, Osleg would 'protect and defend, support logistically, and assist generally in the development of commercial ventures to explore, research, exploit and market the mineral, timber, and other resources held by the state of the Democratic Republic of the Congo'.

The amalgamation of Osleg and Comiex-Congo produced Cosleg, which was granted mining rights to a state-owned diamond deposit in Kabila's home region of Katanga, with Oryx-ZimCon as the technical partner. Together they formed Sengamines, which would handle the day-to-day work of extracting the stones.

On 6 January 2000, Cosleg established a forestry arm called Socebo (Société Congolaise d'exploitation du bois) with its headquarters at 195D Colonel Ebeya Avenue, Kinshasa.

Cosleg controlled 98.8 per cent of Socebo's shares, with the remaining 1.2 per cent held by Mawapanga Nanga (DRC finance minister); Abdoulaye Ndombasi (DRC foreign minister); Godefroid Tchamlesso (DRC defence minister); and two Zimbabweans, Colin Phiri (project coordinator, Zimbabwe Forestry Commission) and Francis Zvinavashe.

Parastatals, including the Zimbabwe Forestry Commission, railways and Air Zimbabwe, were used to either ferry goods or provide expertise, all at taxpayers' expense, but the proceeds of the venture did not show up in the national accounts.

In January 2000, Zimbabwe's finance minister, Dr Simba Makoni, admitted in parliament that the country's military costs in the DRC had exceeded Z$10 billion, then equal to around US$240 million. But Michael Quintana of the *Africa Defence Journal* disputed Makoni's figures, and estimated that a further Z$14 billion (US$330 million) had been poured into maintaining an air bridge to ferry supplies between Harare and Kinshasa, pushing the total figure to more than half a billion US dollars, at a time when Zimbabwe's health budget had been slashed to the point where hospitals and clinics had run out of all but the most basic drugs.

Although Sengamines was expected to produce more than a billion dollars worth of diamonds from its concession, events elsewhere in Africa got in the way. Wars in Sierra Leone and Angola were being funded by sales of illicit gemstones, and under political pressure from America and the EU, international dealers agreed that they would no longer trade in so-called blood diamonds. In future, all stones would have to carry a certificate of origin.

On 16 January 2001, Laurent Kabila was gunned down by his bodyguards. The Congolese ministers and military chiefs, deeply distrustful of each other, could not agree on who should succeed him, so they appointed his thirty-year-old son, Joseph, who had been educated in East Africa and was more fluent in English and Swahili than French, the DRC's national language.

The change did not stop the rebels backed by Uganda and Rwanda, who redoubled their efforts to take the country, and the new president had to rely on military help from Zimbabwe and, to a lesser extent, Namibia and Angola, which had also sent troops to his aid.

In private, Joseph Kabila made clear that he wanted to clean up the corruption that had ruined the Congo since independence from Belgium in 1960, but he was smart enough to know that any hasty moves would simply see him ousted in favour of a more pliable successor.

Instead, he sought help from South Africa's president, Thabo Mbeki, to broker a peace deal with the rebels. After repeated attempts, endless all-party meetings in Pretoria and a peace conference at the Sun City resort north-west of Johannesburg, an agreement was hammered out requiring withdrawal of all foreign troops involved in the conflict.

There were regular breaches of the agreement, but the negotiations drew the world's attention to the DRC where, by 2002, the United Nations estimated that more than three million people had died in the civil war.

As efforts to build a lasting peace intensified, international agencies began to unravel the activities of Osleg, Cosleg, Oryx-ZimCon, Sengamines and Socebo, and at the end of 2002 the UN published its report of an investigation into looting that had taken place in the DRC.

Between them, politicians and their accomplices in Uganda, Rwanda, Zimbabwe and the DRC had stolen billions of dollars worth of diamonds, minerals and timber, and it is worth reading the complete report to gauge the full scale of the crime. However, the following extract focuses on the UN's accusations against Zimbabwe, and shows how successful ZANU-PF and the army were in their ventures:

**Final Report of the Panel of Experts, appointed by the UN Secretary General, on the Illegal Exploitation of Natural Resources and Other Forms of Wealth of the Democratic Republic of the Congo.**[10]

- An elite network of Congolese and Zimbabwean political, military and commercial interests seeks to maintain its grip on the main mineral resources – diamonds, cobalt, copper, germanium – of the Government-controlled area. This network has transferred ownership of at least US$5 billion of assets from the State mining sector to private companies under its control in the past three years with no compensation or benefit for the State treasury of the Democratic Republic of the Congo. The network benefits from instability in the Democratic Republic of the Congo. Its representatives in the Kinshasa Government and the Zimbabwe Defence Forces have fuelled instability by supporting armed groups opposing Rwanda and Burundi.

- Even if present moves towards peace lead to a complete withdrawal of Zimbabwean forces, the network's grip on the richest mineral assets of the DRC and related businesses will remain. Zimbabwe's political-military elite signed six major trade and service agreements in August 2002 with the Government of the DRC. Reliable sources have told the Panel about plans to set up new holding companies to disguise the continuing ZDF commercial operations in the Democratic Republic of the Congo and a ZDF controlled private military company to be deployed in the country to guard those assets.

- The key strategist for the Zimbabwean branch of the elite network is the

Speaker of the Parliament and former National Security Minister, Emerson Dambudzo Mnangagwa. Mr Mnangagwa has won strong support from senior military and intelligence officers for an aggressive policy in the DRC. His key ally is a Commander of ZDF and Executive Chairman of Cosleg, General Vitalis Musunga Gava Zvinavashe. The General and his family have been involved in diamond trading and supply contracts in the DRC. A long-time ally of President Mugabe, Air Marshal Perence Shiri has been involved in military procurement and organizing air support for the pro-Kinshasa armed groups fighting in the eastern DRC. He is also part of the inner circle of ZDF diamond traders who have turned Harare into a significant illicit diamond-trading centre. Other prominent Zimbabwean members include Brigadier General Sibusiso Busi Moyo (Director General of Cosleg); Air Commodore Mike Tichafa Karakadzai (Deputy Secretary of Cosleg, directing policy and procurement); Colonel Simpson Sikhulile Nyathi (Director of Defence Policy for Cosleg); Sidney Sekeramayi (Minister of Defence and former Security Minister who coordinates with the military leadership and is a shareholder in Cosleg). The Panel has a copy of a letter from Mr Sekeramayi thanking the Chief Executive of Oryx Natural Resources, Thamer Bin Said Ahmed Al-Shanfari, for his material and moral support during the parliamentary elections of 2000. Such contributions violate Zimbabwean law.

- In June 2002, the Panel learned of a secret new ZDF diamond mining operation in Kalobo in Kasai Occidental run by Dube Associates. This company is linked, according to banking documents, through Colonel Tshinga Dube of Zimbabwe Defence Industries to the Ukrainian diamond and arms dealer Leonid Minim, who currently faces smuggling charges in Italy. The diamond mining operations have been conducted in great secrecy.

- Among the businessmen in the elite network, a Belgian national, George Forrest … owes his commercial ascendancy to his long-standing ties to the establishment in the Democratic Republic of the Congo. One of his companies also makes and markets military equipment. Since 1994, he has owned 100 per cent of New Lachaussé in Belgium, which is a leading manufacturer of cartridge casings, grenades, light weapons and cannon launchers. He has built up the most wide-ranging private mining portfolio in the DRC. He benefits from strong backing from some political quarters in Belgium where some of his companies are based.

- The techniques used by Mr Forrest have since been replicated by Zimbabwean-backed entrepreneurs John Arnold Bredenkamp and Mr

Al-Shanfari. Mr Bredenkamp, who has an estimated personal nett worth of over $500 million, is experienced in setting up clandestine companies and sanctions-busting operations. Mr Al-Shanfari has gained privileged access to the Government of the DRC and its diamond concessions in exchange for raising capital from some powerful entrepreneurs in the Gulf such as Issa al-Kawari who manages the fortune of the deposed Amir of Qatar. Also working with ZDF is a convicted criminal based in South Africa, Nico Shefer, who has arranged for Zimbabwean officers to be trained in diamond valuation in Johannesburg. Mr Shefer's company, Tandan Holdings, has a 50 per cent stake in Thorntree Industries, a diamond-trading joint venture with ZDF.

- Highly placed [DRC] government officials provide mining licences and export permits in return for private gain. The Panel has compiled extensive documentation of such facilitations. For example, in its attempts to buy rights to the Kolwezi Tailings, First Quantum Minerals (FQM) of Canada offered a downpayment to the State of $100 million, cash payments and shares held in trust for Government officials. According to documents in the possession of the Panel, the payments list included the National Security Minister, Mwenze Kongolo; the Director of the National Intelligence Agency, Didier Kazadi Nyembwe; the Director General of Gécamines, Yumba Monga; and the former Minister of the Presidency, Pierre-Victor Mpoyo.

- The Panel has documents showing that three 'clans' of Lebanese origin, who operate licensed diamond businesses in Antwerp, purchased diamonds from the DRC worth $150 million in 2001, either directly through Kinshasa or through comptoirs in the Republic of the Congo (the former French Congo, the DRC's neighbour). The three 'clans' – Ahmad, Nassour and Khanafer – are distinct criminal organizations that operate internationally.

- The richest and most readily exploitable of the publicly owned mineral assets of the DRC are being moved into joint ventures that are controlled by the network's private companies. These transactions, which are controlled through secret contracts and offshore private companies, amount to a multi-billion-dollar corporate theft of the country's mineral assets. Some 30 businessmen, politicians and military officers are the main beneficiaries of the arrangements. The elite network has been trying to legitimize such corporate theft and market these assets to legitimate international mining companies.

- The Panel has now obtained documentary evidence that Mr Al-Shanfari's company, Oryx Natural Resources, is being used as a front for ZDF and its military company Osleg. Sengamines claims an 800-square kilometre concession, just south of Mbuji Mayi, carved out of the concession of the Société Minière de Bakwanga. According to company officials, Sengamines' diamond concessions would be worth at least $2 billion if they were put into full production.

- Tremalt Ltd, represented by Mr Bredenkamp, holds the rights to exploit six Gécamines concessions containing over 2.7 million tons of copper and 325 000 tons of cobalt over 25 years. Tremalt paid the Government of the DRC just $400 000, but the estimated worth of the six concessions exceeds $1 billion. Like Oryx, Tremalt insists that its operations are not linked to ZDF or the Government of Zimbabwe. However, the Panel has obtained a copy of the confidential profit-sharing agreement, under which Tremalt retains 32 per cent of nett profits, and undertakes to pay 34 per cent of nett profits to the DRC and 34 per cent to Zimbabwe. This profit-sharing agreement was the subject of a confidential memorandum from the Defence Minister, Mr Sekeramayi, to President Mugabe in August 2002. Tremalt also undertakes to provide the Congolese and Zimbabwean militaries with motor vehicles, trucks, buses and cash payments as necessary. These are to be subtracted from the two countries' part of the profit share. A forum has been established between Tremalt and ZDF to plan strategy in the DRC and 'look after the interests of the Zimbabweans'. Meeting monthly, the forum's main members are General Zvinavashe, Brigadier Moyo, Air Commodore Karakadzai, Mr Bredenkamp, the Managing Director of KMC, Colin Blythe-Wood, and the Director of KMC, Gary Webster.

Because of his mention in the report, John Bredenkamp was pursued by the media after its publication, and it seemed that journalists found the idea of a white businessman being involved with Mugabe more interesting than the story itself.

Bredenkamp had played rugby for Rhodesia in the 1960s before starting his own tobacco-buying firm in Antwerp, Belgium, from where he helped the Smith government circumvent UN sanctions that had been imposed after UDI.

He dabbled in the arms trade, selling rifles for the Belgian company Fabrique National (FN), the weapons used by Rhodesian forces during the war. In 1993, Bredenkamp sold his tobacco interests, and by the time the UN report was published he had moved to Britain. With a personal fortune estimated at between £300 million and £500 million, he was rated one of the wealthiest people in the UK.[11]

He also owned the Masters Group of Companies, which managed some of the world's biggest names in sport, including South African golfer Ernie Els.

Always charming and highly approachable, Bredenkamp staunchly denied any wrongdoing in the DRC and also dismissed claims in the British parliament that he had supplied aircraft spares to the Mugabe government after Britain imposed an arms embargo on Zimbabwe. The truth of his involvement will have to wait until the proposed MDC justice commission launches a full investigation into business dealings that took place under ZANU-PF rule.

After the release of the UN document, Joseph Kabila dismissed several of his ministers who had allegedly been involved in illicit deals, including Mwenze Kongolo, Denis Kalume and Augustin Mwanke, but the Zimbabwe government simply scoffed at the allegations made against it.

In parliament, the MDC proposed the setting up of a special committee to investigate the matter, but justice minister Patrick Chinamasa refused to entertain the idea. 'We have no time to waste to clear malicious rumours targeted at our people,' he said.[12]

In 2002, the same year as the UN report, the British-based NGO, Global Witness (GW) released a paper on ZANU-PF's logging concessions in the Congo. Like Amnesty International, GW has no political affiliation, and investigates the environmental and human impact of business activities around the world.

Their fourteen-page report was called 'Branching Out: Zimbabwe's Resource Colonialism in the DRC', and the contents were almost as damning as the UN dossier.

GW claimed that Cosleg and Socebo had 'effectively created the world's largest logging concession by gaining rights to exploit 33 million hectares of forests in the DRC'.

If this was true, it meant that an area almost the size of Zimbabwe would be denuded of trees.

Socebo had an export arm in the UK via a British company called African Hardwood Marketing Limited (AHM), based at 2 Millwood Street, London, W10 6EH, and run by Elkin Pianim.

Pianim hailed from one of Ghana's leading families and had excellent connections in business and politics. In 1994, he and his wife Elisabeth, daughter of media tycoon Rupert Murdoch, had been the toast of the business press when, using a $31-million loan from Murdoch, they bought a television station in California and sold it sixteen months later for a profit of $12 million.

In 1996 they moved to London, where Elisabeth was appointed general manager of her father's Sky TV network, while Elkin invested their money in a black community newspaper called *New Nation*. The venture failed, and although Elisabeth was pregnant with their second child, the couple parted and eventually divorced.

But Pianim had found new friends in Zimbabwe.

## The Congo Logging Concession

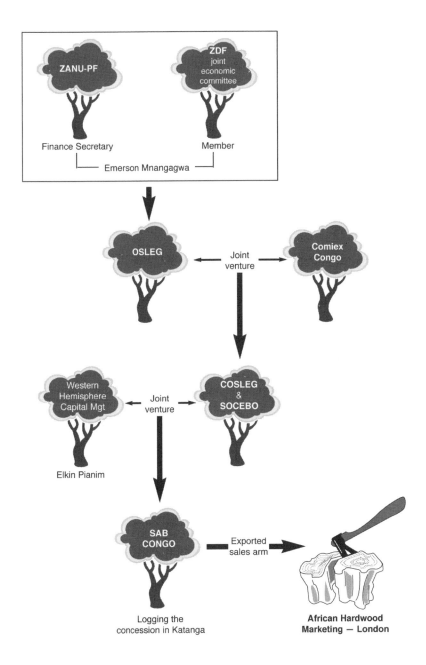

Information courtesy of Global Witness (UK)

In the documents obtained by GW, Pianim claimed that, 'The timber [sold by AHM] has all been harvested using current best practice in forestry management,' but in a letter obtained by GW, he admitted that his company was the export arm of 'SAB-Congo, a forest products firm with concessions in the Democratic Republic of Congo'.

'The logs,' he wrote, 'are converted into planks by on-site sawmills, air-dried and then exported by road and rail to ports in South Africa and Tanzania.'

GW investigated the firm SAB-Congo and discovered that it was jointly owned by the Cosleg subsidiary, Socebo, and Western Hemisphere Capital Management – controlled by none other than Elkin Pianim.

GW claimed that the hardwoods were being bought by end-users in France, Germany and South Africa.

Socebo had estimated that it would make a profit of US$300 million in its first three years of operation, but GW disputed these figures, saying they were optimistic and underestimated the set-up costs.

Whatever the case, as with the diamonds, the potential existed for a small number of people inside ZANU-PF and the Congolese government to make huge personal fortunes.

The UN and Global Witness reports also cited evidence that Harare International Airport had been used as a transit zone, and that the functions of the Zimbabwe Customs Service had been undermined by senior members of the government, allowing diamonds and other contraband to move through the facility unchecked. This created a potential conduit for the movement of guns, bombs and terrorist weapons, drugs, ivory, rhino horn and other goods derived from endangered wildlife from sources beyond the DRC.

In November 2002, South African police uncovered a racket in which perlemoen, an endangered shellfish also known as abalone, was being poached off the coast near Cape Town, trucked to Manzini in Swaziland and then flown to Harare, from where it was airfreighted to clients in the Far East.

Perlemoen is a tightly controlled product in South Africa, but since Swaziland is a member of the Southern African Customs Union, there are minimal checks on road transport between the two countries. In Harare, airport staff were told to look the other way as the crates were allegedly loaded onto cargo flights to Hong Kong.

The racket was exposed when a light aircraft crashed on the South African side of the Limpopo River while flying from Manzini to Harare. It was overloaded with 800 kilograms of perlemoen, worth close to R1.5 million in Asia. The pilot, Tony Robinson, died when the heavy crates shifted in flight and crushed him.

Another aircraft on the Manzini–Harare route was intercepted when it had to make a forced landing in South Africa, and police recovered 890 kilograms of perlemoen.

Investigations led to a spate of arrests in Cape Town and the province of Limpopo in late 2002 and the first few months of 2003, but some South African analysts believed that the movement of shellfish was only one facet in a major smuggling operation that ran through Harare.[13]

But, if Zimbabwe's political and military elite were raking in millions from their nefarious activities, the question had to be asked: Where were they stashing the proceeds?

After the EU imposed financial sanctions on prominent members of ZANU-PF, British banks located and froze a total of twenty-eight accounts held by named leaders of the Zimbabwe government. But, by November 2002, the total sum of money that had been traced amounted to only £513 000.[14]

Mugabe had become a regular visitor to Malaysia, and it was rumoured that he and other senior members of ZANU-PF kept their wealth in government-owned banks in Kuala Lumpur. Senior party figures, including Philip Chiyangwa and Jonathan Moyo, made frequent shopping trips to Johannesburg, and some of them paid their bills with money transferred from bank accounts in the Namibian capital of Windhoek. With the Namibian dollar fixed at par with the rand, there was no risk of currency fluctuation, and banking in Namibia would make sense, since the president, Sam Nujoma, was Mugabe's staunchest ally in the region. Holding money in South African accounts would have been risky, because investigative journalists might well have uncovered them.

If the state coffers have been looted by ZANU-PF luminaries, their family members and associates, it will be up to a new government to track down and recover money that will be sorely needed for the reconstruction and normalisation of Zimbabwe.

The Congo plunder had generated a fortune in hard currency, but those on the take in Zimbabwe were not fussy, and profited from a series of domestic self-enrichment schemes as well.

Details of how the War Veterans Compensation Fund was looted have already been dealt with (see Chapter 6), but there were many other opportunities.

In the late 1990s, a fund set up to provide low-cost housing loans to public servants was hijacked and millions of dollars went into building homes for, among others, police commissioner Augustine Chihuri, Grace Mugabe and a string of ministers and MPs.

In April 2002, the *Daily News* claimed that Z$96 million raised by a tax levy to assist AIDS sufferers had been embezzled, and that there were virtually no accounting procedures in place to control the distribution of funds.[15]

Sometimes, 'reallocation' of resources was done through the proper channels. Hardly a year went by without a new fleet of luxury cars being imported for ministers and senior public servants. In May 2001, Mugabe decided that he needed a new limousine, and cabinet approved his request for Z$250 million (then worth US$4.5 million) to import a top-of-the-range armoured sedan from Cloer International GmbH in Germany.

The vehicle was bullet-proofed and fitted with the highest level of bomb protection – known as the B7 Draganov standard – and was airfreighted to Harare at an additional cost of Z$4.4 million.

The bill included another twenty-three vehicles for use in the presidential motorcade, among them two more armoured Mercedes Benz. In 2001, a total of Z$469 million (US$8.5 million) was spent on vehicles for the president, ministers, MPs and judges. In the same year, the UN estimated that one out of two Zimbabweans were living on or below the world poverty line of just US$1 a day.[16]

In 2003, Brian Kagoro, coordinator of the Crisis in Zimbabwe Coalition, a collection of civil society groups, summed up the situation when he wrote: 'The state was captured by a corrupt, self-seeking and authoritarian political elite.'[17]

Eventually, the toll of all the embezzlement, the huge expenditure in the Congo, payouts to war vets and mismanagement of the economy became too much, and the 'economic meltdown' that some South African economists had predicted, came to pass.

In June 2003, Zimbabwe literally ran out of money. Banks and building societies limited withdrawals to Z$5 000 per client – enough to buy a 100-gram bottle of instant coffee – and although the government was printing new notes as fast as possible, with inflation touching 300 per cent the crisis showed no sign of easing.

Other shortages that had seemed so inconvenient when they first began in 2000 had become a way of life. It was accepted that you cooked without oil, drank tea without milk or sugar, ate bread without margarine (assuming you could find bread) and walked when there was no petrol.

But, in a country where fewer than 20 per cent of people had cheque accounts, the absence of cash meant that even when goods were available the majority of people could not buy them.

Most garages demanded cash for fuel, and it cost around Z$40 000 to fill the tank of an average family car. But with hardly any supplies, there *was* no fuel at the pumps, and petrol and diesel were only available on the black market at three or four times the official price … and always for cash.

In 1999, cabinet had pegged the exchange rate at Z$55 to the US dollar, and when agricultural exports fell because of the farm invasions, Mugabe insisted that the currency should not be devalued.

There were two forces at work, pulling in opposite directions. Although foreign income had been slashed, the demand for forex continued at normal levels, and even rose when unemployment topped 70 per cent in 2000 and cross-border trading became the only source of income for thousands of men and women.

Falling crop levels meant that essential goods such as sugar, maize, cooking oil, salt, margarine, flour and milk powder disappeared from supermarket shelves. Yet they were plentiful in neighbouring Botswana and South Africa, and a roaring trade developed at Plumtree and Beit Bridge, where hawkers would cross the border in the morning and return fully laden a few hours later, either paying duty on the goods or bribing customs officers to look the other way.

At the end of 2001, in a laughable effort to check inflation that was heading for 100 per cent, the government introduced price controls on hundreds of products – from baked beans to building cement – but many of the goods were already unavailable in shops. In some cases the gazetted price came in below cost, forcing manufacturers to discontinue the lines.

This led to more shortages, which boosted both the black market and the cross-border trade that fed it.

The economics of supply and demand took over, and rands, pula and US dollars started changing hands away from banks at well above the set rates. Anyone lucky enough to be paid for a service in what people started calling 'real money' would try to sell it at the street or parallel rate, and the Reserve Bank of Zimbabwe (RBZ) found that the foreign exchange coming in from banks was dwindling.

But ministers and those with connections in government used their political muscle to force banks to sell them – at the official rate – what little forex there was, and fortunes were made reselling the money on the black market.

Traders bringing goods in from abroad sold only for cash and demanded anything up to ten times the official price, thus fuelling inflation, which, in turn, made it even less viable for manufacturers to sell their products at controlled prices. Some decided to export them instead, thus compounding the shortages. By August 2003, inflation had topped 400 per cent.

As if the situation wasn't bad enough, the government pegged interest rates, which meant that banks paid virtually nothing on call accounts and less than 40 per cent on long-term savings. And loans were available from as little as 50 per cent. But holding money in the bank was pointless, since inflation meant that Z$100 invested on fixed deposit in January 2001 and left untouched for twenty-four months would only grow to Z$164 by December 2002. Over the same period, the consumer price index (CPI) rose by more than 500 per cent. Even with interest, the total amount of Z$164 would purchase only what Z$42 would have bought in January 2001.[18]

Public savings and corporate investment in government bonds – the safety net of any free-market economy – collapsed, and at the same time there was an escalation in the demand for loans to buy houses, cars and consumer items, the purchasing of which did little to lower the unemployment rate.

A loan at an interest rate of 60 per cent in the face of inflation that saw prices doubling more than once a year meant that any item could be bought and sold at a profit, even after the loan had been paid, and slowly the banks ran out of money.

'Anyone who did even some basic research could have seen the problem coming,' John Robertson, one of Zimbabwe's leading economists, told me in July 2003. 'In 2000, the RBZ released a Z$500 bill, and should have printed Z$1 000 and even $10 000 notes in quick succession, but they either didn't see the inevitable, or the people in the finance ministry who *did* have some foresight, were too afraid to tell their bosses the bad news.

'At the start of 2002, notes and coins worth Z$30 billion were in circulation, and in the face of rampant inflation the government's answer was simply to print more money. By the end of the year they had minted a further Z$60 billion, and still it wasn't enough. By that time the ink and paper used to produce a single Z$500 note cost somewhere around Z$1 250.'

By the middle of 2003, the country's biggest source of income was money remitted by Zimbabweans working abroad, but virtually none of it went through formal channels.

Before the cash crisis, a young woman working in London might send her parents £100 a month, either by telegraphic transfer if they had a bank account or in cash, the notes folded into the pages of a letter.

Either way, the couple would convert the currency into Zimbabwe dollars and the bank they used passed the hard currency on to the RBZ, where it went into the pool of money used by the government to pay for imports.

By mid-July 2003, the official exchange rate against the South African rand was Z$105:1, but the street rate in Harare or Bulawayo was 250:1. However, the fuel shortage had brought mail deliveries to a halt and looting had become rife in the postal service, so it was no longer viable for exiles to send money with their letters.

Enter the moneychangers, hundreds of men and women across South Africa who offered a rapid and reliable service for switching rands into Zimbabwe dollars at rates that were close to the parallel market. In Johannesburg, for example, the sender would hand over rands along with the name and telephone number of the person to whom the funds would be paid back home. The moneychanger then called a contact in Zimbabwe, who in turn telephoned the recipient and arranged that the cash be collected.

A similar system sprang up in London, and while there are no figures available on the scale of the trade, it doesn't require an accountant to work out that huge sums were changing hands.

Let's start with the rough figure of three million Zimbabweans living abroad, and a conservative estimate that only one in ten of them was sending money home. If each person remitted only the equivalent of R400 a month (approximately US$50 or £35), some R120 million was flowing into private Zimbabwean pockets every month. The parallel exchange rate in July 2003 was 250:1, but let's assume a moneychanger offered only 200:1. The total of Z$24 billion a month constituted more than 25 per cent of all Zimbabwe dollar notes in circulation, and since my calculations are based on the most conservative figures, the actual amount of money remitted from outside Zimbabwe could well have been two or three times more. No wonder there was no cash left in the banks.

The government's response was to bar citizens from carrying or hoarding large bundles of cash, but the regulations were unenforceable.

John Robertson told me: 'The transfer of money from abroad is certainly responsible for a large part of the demand for cash. Once the currency swap has been done, the person receiving the Zimbabwe dollars will engage in mostly cash transactions.

'Depositors get hardly any interest on call accounts, and with inflation at 300 per cent we all find the interest offered insulting. Hoarding cash does not carry a severe financial penalty, and besides, having banked your money, you would have a terrible time trying to get it out of the bank again. So it is best not to bank cash in the first place.

'The financial institutions are so desperate that supermarkets depositing cash at the end of the day are getting the banks to compete for the money. Banks are offering a bonus of 10 to 15 per cent to attract deposits! That rate of return can be as high as the mark-up on the supermarket's goods, so it is not to be taken lightly. Some retailers are refusing to take cheques now because these are excluded from the bonus schemes.'

The situation had become so grave that people were paying a premium for local bank notes. One businessman, recently returned from a trip to Harare, told a Johannesburg newspaper that he had written out a cheque for Z$200 000 to a friend who gave him Z$160 000 in cash.[19]

Another factor in the meltdown was the subsidised fuel price. In Rhodesian times, a parastatal had been set up to bypass sanctions and import petrol, diesel and paraffin, and after 1980 the organisation was turned into a regular government-purchasing agency called NOCZIM – the National Oil Company of Zimbabwe.

The system was straightforward enough. Fuel companies in Zimbabwe such as BP, Shell and Mobil placed their orders with NOCZIM, which imported the required quantities and paid the foreign supplier. In the early 1960s, Rhodesia had built its own refinery and a pipeline to the Mozambican port of Beira, which meant that oil tankers could offload their cargo into bond and it would flow directly to Harare via Mutare.

In Harare, the fuel companies paid NOCZIM, then delivered the product to their service stations, most of which had to pay cash on delivery, and the garage owners added their profit before selling the fuel at the pumps.

There were no lengthy credit lines and cash flowed continuously from the retailers to the fuel companies to NOCZIM, which used the RBZ to obtain the forex with which to pay the international fuel brokers, who made sure there was a constant supply to Beira.

In 1979, a system was developed for the production of ethanol from sugar cane and this was mixed with petrol to produce a blend that made Zimbabwe partly self-sufficient in fuel. But when the farm invasions resulted in a collapse of the sugar industry, unblended petrol went on sale ... but the price was still pegged at less than half the international spot price.

In 1998, a series of thefts, bribes and embezzlements at NOCZIM saw the company robbed of well over a billion dollars, and although the government commissioned an inquiry, only junior employees were caught in a net that might well have scooped up some of the most powerful people in ZANU-PF.

The treasury made up the deficit by printing more notes, but NOCZIM never recovered from the loss.

After the referendum in 2000, inflation demanded a fuel price increase, but Mugabe could not risk upsetting the electorate. While a few small rises were allowed, the pump price slipped further and further behind the real cost that NOCZIM was having to pay offshore.

From September 2001 to February 2003, the fuel price remained unchanged, while the consumer price index rose by around 325 per cent.

But, while the RBZ could print money to cover the difference inside the country, there was no foreign currency available to buy fuel on the open market. By December 1999, unpaid bills had forced suppliers to cut off Zimbabwe's credit. Mugabe flew to Libya and arranged a deal with Colonel Muammar Gaddafi for a line of credit. When the government couldn't pay the debt, state assets, including newly seized farms, were transferred to Libya to cover the bill.

When the treasury could no longer afford to subsidise the pump price of fuel, a series of massive increases went into effect. In February 2003, petrol doubled in price, and two months later another 210 per cent increase followed. But it was all hypothetical, because by then even the Libyans had cut off supplies and service stations throughout Zimbabwe had run dry. Petrol, diesel and paraffin became three more commodities that could be found only on the black market.

Economists gauge a country's foreign reserves by how much money the reserve bank has to cover the nation's daily foreign currency requirements, and in Zimbabwe this had fallen from reserves covering several months in the mid-1990s to less than three weeks in mid-2002. A year later, it was down to a single day.

For those fortunate enough to be earning foreign currency, anything was available at a price. Late model vehicles were on display in the Mercedes Benz showroom on Third Street near Meikles Hotel, and stores catering to the high end of the consumer market had good supplies of diamond and emerald jewellery, cosmetics, whisky, even Belgian chocolates.

And, amazingly, in US dollar terms, between 2002 and 2003 Harare went from being the world's twenty-sixth most expensive city to live in to the second cheapest, according to an international cost of living survey.

Using New York as its benchmark, the 2003 report by Mercer Human Resource Consulting said Harare had recorded the 'biggest drop in the rankings this year, falling from position 26 to 143'.

Johannesburg, the cheapest city in 2002, dropped down to number nine.

The report attributed Zimbabwe's freefall to the 'drastic depreciation of its currency'. In mid-2002, the street rate for US dollars was 550:1, but a year later, it cost Z$2 700 to buy a single greenback, and locally priced goods had not yet caught up with the change, which translated into greater spending power for those on foreign salaries.

Elizabeth Nerwande, executive director of the Consumer Council of Zimbabwe, told a South African newspaper: 'We only have two classes now. There is no more middle class; you either have it or you don't.'[20]

Many people, she said, could not afford even the average Z$30 000 monthly bus fare needed to get to work. And if they did make it to the office, they were often hungry, unable to come up with the Z$141 000 a month a family of six needed to buy basic commodities.

At the beginning of July, Mugabe flew to Libya again, to beg Gaddafi to extend him further credit, but the colonel refused. Even so, on 4 July, shortly after the president arrived home, the unstoppable Jonathan Moyo told the *Herald* that petrol would soon be available.

A week later, the country was still dry.

The UN and other agencies have compiled huge dossiers on the looting that has reduced Zimbabwe to a ruin of its former self, and a new government will have a great deal of information to go on *if* it should decide to investigate the crimes, prosecute the culprits and recover the money. The key word, however, is 'if'.

During the presidential poll in March 2002, mayoral elections were also held in Harare, Bulawayo and several other urban centres, and the MDC won all the posts.

In Harare, there had not been a mayor for more than two years. The Minister for Local Government had sacked the last incumbent, Solomon Tawengwa, after he spent Z$75 million (then almost US$2 million) on building a mayoral mansion in the northern suburbs and furnishing it with antiques. What really angered his own ZANU-PF party was not the extravagance, but the fact that he had not used building contractors owned by any of the ministers.

After Tawengwa's dismissal the mansion stood empty, and Harare was run by a government-appointed commission.

In the week leading up to the poll, the MDC candidate, Elias Mudzuri, made a speech in which he promised not to move into the mayoral residence and solemnly pledged that he would not follow ZANU-PF's example and expect the council to provide him with a Mercedes Benz.

Less than two months after taking office, Mudzuri was ensconced in the guest wing of the mansion – and had taken delivery of a new Mercedes.

Morgan Tsvangirai tried to intervene, ordering the mayor to move out of the house, but Mudzuri refused and stayed put until the Minister for Local Government suspended him in April 2003 on grounds of alleged incompetence.

In his defence, it should be said that during his brief term of office, Mudzuri was one of the most effective and approachable mayors in the history of Harare, and had made a start at repairing more than twenty years of neglect suffered under a succession of ZANU-PF councils. But his penchant for the good life raised a question never asked before: If Morgan Tsvangirai and his MDC became the next rulers of Zimbabwe, would they honour their promises and cut government spending, or was Mudzuri a taste of things to come?

# 13

# Killers on the loose

By 2003, political observers agreed that change in Zimbabwe was no longer an 'if' but a 'when'. And, in non-governmental forums and even at meetings of regional leaders, people talked about the WHAM factor: *What Happens After Mugabe?*

The big unknown is how long Mugabe can resist the force of change, a point emphasised by US secretary of state General Colin Powell, in a piece he wrote for the *New York Times*: 'Mr Tsvangirai wages a non-violent struggle against a ruthless regime. President Mugabe and his Politburo colleagues have an absolute monopoly of coercive power, but no legitimacy or moral authority. In the long run, President Mugabe and his minions will lose, dragging their soiled record behind them into obscurity. But how long will it take?'[1]

But a change of government would only mark the start of a long journey back to reality in a country where the accepted understanding of right and wrong has been warped, and where, for forty years, successive regimes have acted with impunity against their real or imagined enemies.

There are rapists, torturers and killers on the loose, people who have acted, for the most part, on the ruling party's instructions, and have never been held to account. And for every perpetrator there is a victim, hungry for justice or even revenge. After the change, it would take the wisdom of Solomon to put the country back together again, and Tsvangirai has promised, during both the general and presidential election campaigns, that an MDC government would appoint a judicial commission to lance and heal the wounds inflicted over a period of almost four decades since 1965.

But what if, on taking power, a new MDC president discovered that his own supporters have transgressed as well? Would the proposed inquiry push ahead with no holds barred, or be watered down, as with South Africa's Truth and Reconciliation Commission (TRC)? Headed by Archbishop Desmond Tutu, the TRC fell short of examining some of the ANC's abuses, especially the murder and torture of its own members at camps outside South Africa. Or would a new president get cold feet and scrap the idea of a commission altogether?

Judging by reports issued by neutral groups such as Amnesty International, more than 90 per cent of the violence has been perpetrated by ZANU-PF members or agents of the state.

The idea that the ruling party should be able to act against its opponents in whatever way it pleases dates back to Rhodesian times, and has been endorsed by several pieces of bad legislation:

- The Emergency Powers (Maintenance of Law and Order) Regulations of 1965;
- The Preservation of Government Act; and
- The Indemnity and Compensation Act 45 of 1975.

Mugabe added to these the Emergency Powers (Security Forces Indemnity) Regulations of 1982, which decreed that people caught acting for or on behalf of the state 'in good faith', including the police, army and civil servants, could not be held liable for their conduct, either under criminal or civil law.

And, whenever it looks as though someone might have a case against the government, there is the presidential power of pardon, which means the ruler can indemnify anyone from just about anything.

The idea of pardon was introduced to the Rhodesian constitution in 1953 (it had previously been exercised by the British monarch on the advice of the Rhodesian prime minister), and was based on noble precedents in democratic countries. It was a safety valve, to be used only when a case cried out for justice, and the state might, for example, pardon a woman found guilty of murdering a husband who had beaten and abused her over a period of many years.

But it doesn't work that way in Zimbabwe.

A blanket amnesty was declared in 1980 for all acts committed by ZANLA, ZIPRA and the Rhodesian forces during the civil war, and it could be argued that this was a pragmatic way of getting the country off to a fresh start.

In 1983, the Fifth Brigade murdered an off-duty army officer, his wife and another couple in Lupane, Matabeleland. At an inquest in October 1984, the magistrate found that the murders had been 'exceedingly cruel' and that the four had been 'repeatedly stabbed with bayonets, much as a hunter slaughtering a wounded animal with a spear'.

The victims were found in a shallow grave, with their hands tied behind their backs, and the women showed evidence of rape. The suspects were released from custody pending their trial, which took place in 1986. On being found guilty of first-degree murder without extenuating circumstances, they were granted a presidential pardon.

Also during the Matabeleland campaign, a member of the CIO, Robert Masikini, shot a detainee at point-blank range in a police cell in front of witnesses. He was found guilty of murder, and pardoned.

On 18 April 1988, Mugabe granted a general amnesty for all political crimes committed since 1980 up to that date, including Gukurahundi. Only 122 ZAPU dissidents sought and were granted immunity, whereas thousands of soldiers, police and CIO members were absolved of their crimes.[2]

In the 1990 election, a candidate for the newly formed Zimbabwe Unity Movement, Patrick Kombayi, survived an assassination attempt, while an official from the Catholic Commission for Justice and Peace, who was acting as an election monitor, was beaten and almost killed. In both cases the attackers were arrested, found guilty and pardoned.

There was less violence in the 1995 election because there was effectively no opposition, and only 26 per cent of registered voters cast their ballots. But the president nevertheless pardoned all those who had been convicted of political violence.

After the 2000 election – at that time, the most violent in the country's history – Mugabe granted a blanket amnesty for all politically motivated crimes, excluding rape and murder. Although members of both the main political parties qualified, most of the culprits were from ZANU-PF.

After the presidential poll, the state simply didn't bother to pursue or charge those ZANU-PF members who had broken the law, and towards the end of 2002 the situation was starting to mirror conditions in Uganda under Idi Amin. A good example of this emerged when the two parties went head to head in a by-election in the Insiza constituency, around the village of Filabusi, south-east of Bulawayo, where the local MP, Joe Ndhlovu (MDC), had died.

He had won the seat in 2000 with 12 049 votes to ZANU-PF's 5 304, giving the MDC a comfortable margin of more than 65 per cent.

The by-election was set for the weekend of 25 and 26 October 2002, with Andrew Langa standing for ZANU-PF and Siyabonga Ncube for the MDC.

By the end of September, the area was in a state of anarchy. Hundreds of Green Bombers had been trucked in to 'soften up' the voters, and the police took no action as people were beaten in the streets, at bus stations, in the market and at their homes.

'Fear has gripped the district,' said an MDC spokesman, Albert Mkhandla, in a telephone interview with a human rights group. 'The youth militia is preventing the MDC from holding rallies, yet ZANU-PF can hold their meetings without any problems.'

From Lupane, 220 kilometres to the north, the government had brought in back-up teams of war veterans, some of whom walked around with firearms, but no effort was made to disarm them.

Instead, the police alleged that the MDC was bent on 'unleashing violence', and conducted a raid on the local party office, where they found a few catapults and two containers of petrol, which, they alleged, was to be used for making bombs.[3]

On 11 October, matters came to a head when an MDC party car carrying funds for the Insiza campaign was ambushed by a group of armed men outside Filabusi. The robbers made off with Z$5 million in cash, 1 000 party T-shirts and other campaign material, suggesting that the attack had been organised by ZANU-PF.

According to Maxwell Zimuto, the MDC's national information officer, who was in the car, he and his colleagues proceeded to Filabusi and went to Andrew Langa's home to plead for the return of their property. But, when they confronted the candidate, he produced a handgun and fired shots into the air, at which point the group dispersed and ran to the safety of the local police station.

As they were filing their report to the officer in charge, an Inspector Shoko, Langa arrived and opened fire again, hitting one MDC member, Darlington Kadengu, in the spine.

With gun in hand he walked calmly out of the charge office, while the police called an ambulance and proceeded to place the injured man and the other MDC members under arrest for provoking the attack.

The charges were eventually withdrawn, but Langa went on to win the by-election, which had a low voter turnout, and took his seat in parliament.

Amid the rhetoric on the official ZANU-PF website, no mention was made of the shooting or the many other acts of intimidation: 'The resounding victory of the ruling party at the just ended Insiza parliamentary by-election is a blow to the MDC and its imperialist British and European Union sponsors. Cde Andrew Langa polled 12 115, while the MDC's Mr Siyabonga Ncube garnered just 5 102 in a crucial by-election seen as a litmus test to measure the two parties' popularity in Matabeleland. A total of 17 521 people voted during the two-day poll. Police and the Electoral Supervisory Commission described the poll as incident free.'[4]

Intimidation was also a factor in two Harare by-elections in March 2003, but the MDC candidates won easily. The state found it difficult to control urban areas, where people came and went to work every day and were more likely to share accounts of their mistreatment with reporters from the *Daily News*. City voters were also more exposed to the realities of life under ZANU-PF, because they had to join the food and petrol queues, whereas rural folk only heard about the difficulties of life in town.

In 2001 and 2002, the monthly human rights reports published by Amnesty International and other NGOs ran to several pages on average, but by 2003 they had become entire dossiers, often listing hundreds of victims.

Some cases from the first half of the year show how difficult it had become to avoid being caught up in the violence:

- In Kuwadzana, Itayi Tinarwo was trailed by unnamed youths wearing ZANU-PF T-shirts, cornered and beaten up. He lost five teeth.
- Soldiers entered a nightclub in the Harare suburb of Dzivarasekwa and beat up patrons on suspicion that they had taken part in a national strike called by the MDC. Clients were ordered to lie on the floor, where they were beaten with batons and pieces of wire.
- Isobel Gardiner and her husband Norman were assaulted on a farm at Ruwa, twenty kilometres east of Harare, and accused of supporting the national strike on 18 and 19 March.
- At another Harare nightclub, this time in Chikwana, soldiers sealed all the doors, then beat up the customers. After the assaults, the patrons were forced to undress on the dance floor and engage in unprotected sex with each other. One man was assaulted when he failed to achieve an erection. Despite several reports of injuries, the police later denied that the incident took place.
- On 18 April, Zimbabwe independence day, MDC supporter Tonderai Machiridza was assaulted by police for allegedly resisting arrest, and died of his injuries. When his friends tried to hold a memorial service for him on 5 May, they were dispersed by the militia.
- Four ZANU-PF youths raided the home of David Matinyarare, MDC Secretary for Information and Publicity, in the Mufakose district of Harare. They beat him with iron bars and stabbed him in the stomach. He was admitted to hospital and died three days later. The case was reported to the police, but no action was taken.
- MDC MP, Job Sikhala, was picked up by CIO near Harare and tortured for four days. He was subjected to beatings and electric shocks, and on release had to fly to South Africa for treatment. No action was taken against the intelligence agents.

During the week-long strike called by the MDC at the beginning of June, the situation got even worse, and the following report from Amnesty International sums up the terror:

On Monday, 2 June, the police and army conducted arbitrary attacks on opposition supporters. Across the country, more than 400 were arrested, at least five of whom were MDC members of parliament.

In the Harare suburb of Highfield, protesters were intercepted by the police and army, who fired live ammunition into a crowd. One person was shot in the leg, while many others were injured. At the University of Zimbabwe, riot police, army officers and war veterans cordoned off a march, firing tear-gas and using water cannons on student protesters. At least 49 students were taken to Parirenyatwa hospital for treatment.

On Tuesday, 3 June, MDC member Tichaona Kaguru and MDC councillor for Mbare, Sydney Mazaranhanga, were beaten by police and army officers who used whips, rubber batons and sticks. As a result of his injuries, Tichaona Kaguru died the same day.

On 4 June, 10 policemen arrived at the privately-run Avenues Clinic in Harare, where more than 150 injured people had been taken for treatment. After searching the hospital, the police abducted seven patients and took them away for questioning.

A quick search on the Internet would turn up hundreds of documented reports of people being tortured, assaulted and murdered by agents of the state, yet hardly any arrests were made. In most cases the police refused to respond, citing the violence as political and therefore outside their jurisdiction.

Yet, when MDC youths attacked ZANU-PF members, the situation was very different:

- In January, four police officers raided a house near Harare where twenty-one MDC youths were holding a meeting. The youths threw stones at the police, injuring one officer and damaging two vehicles. Reinforcements were called and all twenty-one were arrested.
- In February, Holland played a World Cup cricket match against Zimbabwe in Bulawayo, and when two spectators, Thamsanga Ncube and Similo Mpofo, waved their MDC membership cards in the grandstand, they were arrested and beaten by police outside the stadium.
- During the two-day stayaway in March, Constable Tarisa Matipira and the driver of a bus sustained burns when the vehicle was set alight by MDC youths at a shopping centre in the south of Harare. Within hours of the incident, seventeen suspects had been arrested and were denied bail. Several were tortured by a team of soldiers, police and CIO. One victim, Tonderai Murimba, had his toes broken, and an MDC Women's League secretary, Margret Kulinji, had a gun barrel forced into her vagina. A party youth leader, Steven Tonera, was so badly beaten that he died of his injuries. No action was taken against the torturers.
- During the same stayaway, residents at Budiriro near Harare assaulted a headmaster who refused to take part in the strike. Police arrested 108 people and remanded them each on bail of Z$10 000.[5]

The NGO Human Rights Forum issued a grim warning: 'The fabric of Zimbabwean society is at risk if the level of state-organised violence and torture is maintained or increased. Equally damaging would be the use of organised violence by ZANU-PF to suppress dissenting opinions and, in the same vein, MDC resorting to violent action as a means of expressing dissent.'[6]

ZANU-PF, of course, had a different view on who was responsible for the violence, and used their official website to level serious allegations against the MDC. Given the ruling party's track record on abuse of the truth, it would be hard not to take the claims with a cupful of salt, but the list is reproduced below in full:[7]

**ZANU PF members murdered by MDC during elections (2000–2002)**
Since its inception, the opposition has employed intimidation and violence to woe [sic] supporters. As a result a lot of ZANU PF supporters and officials have been killed by the opposition's hit squads. Below is a list of ZANU PF members killed by the MDC.

The party pays tribute to these sons and daughters of the soil who died on duty defending their country against the British sponsored MDC. While we remember and mourn them, we say they are not dead but merely fallen. They live in the collective memory of Zimbabwe.

1. **Cde Leo Jeke:** On 10 June 2000 at about 19h30, Cde Leo Jeke (29), a ZANU-PF supporter, was in the company of Emmion Makhulani, an MDC supporter, at Lundi Business Centre, Ngundu, Chivi. The deceased was wearing a ZANU-PF T-shirt while Makhulani was putting on an MDC T-shirt and the two were drinking beer together. Makhulani demanded that Cde Jeke remove his ZANU-PF T-shirt. When he refused Makhulani pulled a knife and stabbed him once on the neck. The accused collapsed and died on the spot. Makhulani was arrested and convicted for murder. He was sentenced to 12 years in prison.

2. **Cde Bernard Gara:** Bernard Gara (42) was beaten to death by MDC supporters at Baradzanwa Business Centre, Bikita. The alleged murderers who have since been arrested are Elias Machingura (25), Edson Mukwasi (27), Sarah Katandika (30), George Mhandu (25), Gratiano Tauya (30) and Tobias Mudede (25).

3. **Cde Cephas Majasi:** Cde Majasi, a settler on a farm previously owned by a white MDC sympathiser, was assaulted by security guards on 29 January, 2001 and sustained serious injuries which led to his death four days later.

4. **Cde Eswat Chihumburi:** Cde Chihumburi was, on 23 March 2001, among a group of ZANU-PF supporters who approached one Paurosi Taperwa Chimukuze Chigade of the MDC to discuss their differences. This did not amuse Chigade who armed himself with a shotgun and shot Cde Chihumburi, who died on the spot. Chigade is on remand pending his trial.

5. **Cde Dumukani Zondani:** Cde Zondani was on 10 June 2002 at TT1

243

farm in Waterfalls with other landless people waiting to be resettled at Blackfordby Farm, also in Waterfalls. At the instigation of the white farm owners, farm workers assaulted the group with knobkerries [traditional clubs]. In the process, Cde Zondani was assaulted until he became unconscious. He was taken to hospital where he died on arrival. Two of the farm workers were arrested and they are on remand pending trial.[8]

6. **Cde Febian Mapenzauswa:** On 14 July 2001, Cde Mapenzauswa and four others went to Tara Farm in Odzi where they were going to be resettled. The five were being led by Cde Godfrey Gola, the chairman of the ZANU-PF Mutasa District Coordinating Committee. The then owner of the farm, Phillip Bezuidenhout, was incensed by the move. Driving at high speed he struck Cde Mapenzauswa who had disembarked from his vehicle. Cde Mapenzauswa who sustained multiple and body [sic] injuries was driven to Mutare hospital where he was pronounced dead on arrival. Bezuidenhout has since been convicted and sentenced for murder.

7. **Cde Alexio Nyamadzawo:** Cde Nyamadzawo was, on 15 September 2002, stoned to death by farm workers at Bita Farm in Wedza where he was to be resettled. The deceased was among settlers who were waiting to be resettled at Bita Farm. Twenty-nine people were arrested in connection with Cde Nyamadzawo's death and are currently awaiting trial.

8. **Cde Fanuel Madzvimbo:** Cde Madzvimbo was stoned to death together with Cde Nyamadzawo by farm workers at Bita Farm on September 15, 2002. The assailants were arrested and are on remand awaiting trial.

9. **Cde Sikumbuzo Nyati:** An ex-combatant and ZANU-PF district coordinator for Nkayi, Cde Sikumbuzo Nyati (45) had a hand grenade thrown at him from an unidentified direction. The grenade exploded, killing Cde Nyati. No arrest has been made but investigations are continuing.

10. **Cde Limukani Lupahla:** Cde Limukani Lupahla was abducted at Lupane on 29 October 2001 by three people driving a white pick-up truck. His burnt body was discovered by a passer-by along the Old Victoria Falls/Bulawayo Road. Police discovered some shoeprints, pools of blood and vehicle tyre impressions at the scene. Four suspects who are members of the MDC were arrested and are on remand pending the setting down of the trial date. Cde Lupahla was a ZANU-PF youth leader in Lupane.

11. **Cde Cain Nkala:** Cde Nkala was kidnapped by about six men in front

of his family from his home on 5 November 2001. On 13 November two accused MDC members, Khethani Augustine Sibanda and Sazini Moyo, volunteered to lead the police to the place where they had murdered and buried Cde Nkala. His body was found buried in a shallow grave in the Norwood Resettlement area, Solusi. The accused persons are currently on remand pending their trial. Cde Nkala was a senior ZANU-PF official and Chairman of the Bulawayo War Veterans' Association.

12. **Cde Rambisai Nyikayaramba:** Cde Nyikayaramba (26) who was a ZANU-PF supporter was forcibly taken from her homestead at Makore Village in Gokwe to Manoti Business Centre on 24 December 2001. At the centre she was assaulted by suspected MDC members. Ten people have since been arrested and are on remand awaiting their trial.

13. **Cde Gibson Masarira:** Cde Masarira who was the ZANU-PF District Coordinating Committee [*sic*] for Zaka was on 9 January 2002 assaulted by MDC supporters at his homestead in Chiromo Village, Zaka. He was dragged into a nearby bush where they murdered him and left his body where it was discovered the following day. Four MDC members were arrested in connection with the murder.

14. **Cde Stanley Chitehwe:** Cde Chitehwe had an altercation with an MDC supporter, Raised Marufu, and the two fought, resulting in Cde Chitehwe's death. The incident occurred on 15 January 2002. Cde Chitehwe was a war veteran.

15. **Cde Tariro Nyanzira:** Cde Nyanzira was murdered by suspected MDC supporters on 8 February 2002. Her body was found floating in Mutorahuku River, Murambinda by a passer-by, Alex Choga. No one has been arrested but investigations are continuing.

16. **Cde Steven Maphosa:** Cde Maphosa was on 10 February 2002 on a bus with other ZANU-PF supporters wearing their party regalia. When they arrived at Budiriro Shopping Centre, they were confronted by MDC youths who hurled stones towards the bus. Cde Maphosa was struck on the head, fell off the bus and died on the spot. No one was arrested in connection with the murder and investigations are in progress.

17. **Cde Langton Siziba:** Cde Siziba was on 14 February 2002 drinking beer at Muwandi Beerhall, Kwe Kwe, when he was taken by five suspected MDC members who led him to a place near Plot Number 6, Eastclare. They assaulted him using bicycle chains and empty beer bottles. They were seen assaulting him by two passers-by, Simbarashe Ndhlovu and Tsanangurayi Inyathi. The deceased's body was found

lying in the road about 30 metres away. Cde Siziba was a ZANU-PF member. Investigations are still in progress.

18. **Cde Shelton Lloyd:** Cde Lloyd was asleep in a hut at Masvingo on 26 February 2002 when he was attacked by 20 MDC supporters. They entered the kitchen and assaulted him with logs, machetes and stones and set the hut on fire. He sustained serious injuries and died on the spot. Police investigations into the incident are continuing.

19. **Amos Misheck Maseva:** Cde Maseva was legally allocated plot number 20 at Lothiam Farm in Masvingo. On 8 March 2002 he was assaulted by five men. He died two months later from the wounds he suffered from the assault. The five have since been arrested and are being charged for the murder of Cde Maseva.

20. **Cde Ali Khan Manjengwa:** Cde Ali Khan Manjengwa was shot on 22 August 2002 at the Nyerere Flats, Magaba in Mbare, Harare and died on the spot. Four suspected MDC members have since been arrested and are on remand awaiting their trial. Cde Manjengwa was a member of the Harare ZANU-PF Provincial Executive Committee.

No matter how great the provocation or how justified an oppressed people may be in taking action to liberate their country, it is a writer's obligation to log all transgressions without fear or favour. To this end, I spent many months investigating claims that the MDC had also killed people, and most of my inquiries led to nothing. When I investigated claims that ZANU-PF members had been attacked, I invariably discovered that they had started the trouble, and some of them had been injured in the ensuing violence.

The high level of propaganda made it difficult to reach a clear verdict, but after extensive interviews with people in ZANU-PF, the MDC, the CIO and the exile communities in Britain, Botswana and South Africa, I was able to gather a fair amount of information about the deaths of three people: Limukani Lupahla, Ali Khan Manjengwa and Cain Nkala, and I have dealt with them in that order.

At the time of writing, all three murders are the subject of lengthy trials in Zimbabwe. I have thus avoided the use of any names other than those already in the public domain.

**Limukani Lupahla** was, it seems, an MDC supporter in the Lupane area of Matabeleland who had defected to ZANU-PF. The three people who abducted him on 29 October 2001 parked a white pick-up truck outside his house, then knocked on the door and told him they were from the CIO, and wanted to drive him to their office, where his help was needed in identifying some MDC youths they had arrested.

Lupahla went with them and did not realise he was in trouble until the truck headed out of town, at which point he was overpowered and handcuffed. The vehicle stopped in an area of bush along the old road from Bulawayo to Victoria Falls and Luphala was told to get out.

He was questioned about the local activities of ZANU-PF and tried to put up a fight, at which point one of the abductors sprayed his face with some kind of irritant that caused him to scream and fall to the ground. He was then beaten with a hammer and forced to divulge what information he had, after which he was strangled and his body burned.

Police later claimed that MDC youth and security guards Sazini Mpofu and Khethani Sibanda, who were arrested the following month on suspicion of abducting war veteran leader Cain Nkala, had been part of the team that murdered Luphala.

Grisly pictures of the dead man's charred body were shown on ZBC television news as evidence that the MDC was a violent organisation. But when police attempted to put together a case against the accused, there was little evidence to go on.

Despite this, the notion that the opposition had killed Luphala seemed to be an open secret among lower-level MDC party officials I spoke to, but I could find no evidence that any of the senior people in the movement had been consulted. It seemed more likely that local party chiefs, especially in rural areas, were taking matters into their own hands. Given the state of terror under which these people had to live compared with the relative safety of Bulawayo and Harare, where the national executive spent most of its time, it would not be surprising if rural communities had their own views on what constituted appropriate action against ZANU-PF.

**Ali Khan Manjengwa** was, by most accounts, a particularly nasty ZANU-PF provincial executive committee member, who led the torture and sexual assault teams in the Mbare suburb of Harare in the run-up to the presidential election.

He was responsible for a ZANU-PF youth group called Chipangano,[9] which orchestrated much of the peri-urban violence in 2002. Manjengwa had allegedly also been part of the team that murdered David Stevens, one of the first farmers to die after the land invasions began.

At the time of Manjengwa's murder, the MDC allegedly had evidence that he and his thugs were planning to murder Mbare East member of parliament Tichaona Munyani, and it seems almost certain that the MDC took a decision to eliminate him. Manjengwa was shot dead in Mbare on the night of 22 August 2002.

The police acted quickly, rounding up dozens of MDC supporters and interrogating them about the murder, and slowly they came up with a list of suspects.

On 28 August, a squad led by a Detective Inspector Henry Dowa arrived at the MDC office in Harare with a warrant to search the building for firearms and suspects, including Itayi Mudzingwa and Mambo Rusere.[10] Nothing was found, but the police tracked down Rusere's wife, who was taken into custody and allegedly tortured. In order to save her, Rusere came out of hiding and handed himself over to the police.

On 22 September, Rusere was taken to the Harare magistrate's court in leg irons, but was not asked to plead. On 16 October he was granted bail of Z$15 000, and although he was only a party youth leader, the MDC put up the cash.[11] Interestingly, the courts had not factored in the inflation rate, and while Z$15 000 had been a handsome sum of money five years before, by late 2002 it was the cost of a tank of petrol.

Rusere jumped bail and left the country, while Itayi Mudzingwa was never caught. The police arrested several other MDC members, including the party's intelligence officer, Solomon Chikowero, and a city councillor, Linos Mushonga, but were unable to prove a case against them.

By the middle of 2003, several of the party members who claimed to have been privy to discussions about Ali Khan's fate were living in Britain and South Africa, and spoke quite freely about the case, though no one admitted to pulling the trigger. They told me that Ali Khan had been placed under observation for a period of several months, until the fateful night when he was walking alone and the gunman was able to strike.

At the time of writing, the state has been unable to prove its case against any of the accused in Zimbabwe, and the *Daily News* has suggested that perhaps Ali Khan was killed by one of the many people who had been robbed, beaten and raped by his ZANU-PF thugs, the Chipangano.

While my investigations into the deaths of Limukani Lupahla and Ali Khan Manjengwa were quite straightforward, the third murder on my list was so complex a story that it might have been penned by Agatha Christie or Raymond Chandler.

The facts of the case were a matter of record.

**Cain Nkala** was born near Bulawayo on 9 November 1958, and after leaving school, he studied agriculture and metal work.

In 1977, aged nineteen, he went to Zambia and trained with the ZIPRA guerrillas before being sent to a Cuban-run camp in Angola for further instruction. Later that year he returned to Zambia and crossed into Rhodesia, where he carried out his first mission near Kariba. The ZAPU leaders were impressed with his natural sense of authority and promoted him to a junior command position, and from 1978 he led attacks in Matabeleland.

When the ceasefire was announced, he reported to the Gwayi assembly point south of Hwange National Park and was demobilised. In 1987 he joined the

Zimbabwe National War Veterans Association, and in 1998 was elected chairman of the Bulawayo branch.

Cain was married, with children, and lived in Magwegwe, a suburb of Bulawayo. He was articulate, deeply committed to the welfare of his members and a friend of former home affairs minister (and ZIPRA commander) Dumiso Dabengwa.

On Monday 19 June 2000, Cain and six other war vets were allegedly dispatched by persons unknown to murder a former ZANU-PF member, Patrick Nabanyama, who had joined the opposition and was working as an electoral assistant for David Coltart, an MDC candidate in the general election that was less than a week away.

Anyone who understood the mood in Bulawayo could see that Coltart, one of the town's leading lawyers, was set to beat the ZANU-PF candidate, Dr Callistus Ndhlovu, and the ruling party, apparently incensed that black voters were set to elect a white MDC member over their own man, had used the state media to attack him at every turn. Even Mugabe had branded Coltart a 'traitor' and a 'British agent', perhaps because he had played no small role in bringing to light the Fifth Brigade's atrocities.

But they were wasting their time. Coltart spoke fluent Ndebele and was hugely popular. Despite his busy practice, he always returned phone calls, made time to see his constituents and helped them with their problems.[12] In their desperate efforts to rig the vote, it is possible that some ZANU-PF members believed that Nabanyama might have information about his party's strategy for the last few days of campaigning. Or they might simply have wanted to hurt Coltart, who had become good friends with his assistant.

At approximately 4 pm on 19 June, three men knocked on the front door of Patrick's home in the suburb of Nketa. The door was opened by his children, who called their father. As he reached the door, he was grabbed by the three men in full view of his family and dragged screaming out of the house and about fifty metres down the road, where he was bundled into a white Mazda 323 in which four people were waiting. The car sped off towards town, and Patrick was never seen again.

The three men who had grabbed him walked back to their own homes. One of them, Simon Rwodzi, was known to Patrick's family, who gave his name to the police. But it was not until Coltart went to the police station on 23 June, the day before the election, that any action was taken.

Three weeks later, Rwodzi and the two other men who had taken Patrick from his home and forced him into the waiting vehicle were arrested, and claimed the abduction had been led by Cain Nkala.

The final line-up of suspects included Nkala, Rwodzi, Aleck Moyo, Howard

Dube, Stanley Ncube and Julius Sibanda, and despite allegations by the Attorney-General that Nabanyama might still be alive, it looked as though Nkala was set to take the rap for the crime.

Sources inside ZANU-PF told me that while Nkala was out on bail, he was traumatised by the accusations levelled at him. Simultaneously, a leadership battle was brewing within the WVA, with the more radical members seeking to oust Nkala and replace him with one of their own.

At the beginning of November, Nkala told his colleagues he was going to hold a press conference and reveal the truth about what was going on within both the WVA and ZANU-PF. But on the night of 5 November he was abducted from his home during an incident in which his wife was hit on the head. On 13 November his decomposing body was found in a shallow grave next to the road a short distance outside Bulawayo. A post-mortem revealed that he had been strangled.

When police removed the body, a senior reporter and camera team from ZBC in Harare were on hand to film the event. That night on ZBC news, several MDC security staff claimed to have committed the murder. But at their first court appearance, Sazini Mpofu, Khethani Sibanda and Remember Moyo all withdrew their confessions, saying they had made them only because they were being tortured.

Moyo told the court: 'I was handcuffed and police started assaulting and kicking me. They forced apart my legs and Detective Inspector Martin Matira kicked me in the private parts and I lost consciousness. They then took me to the Mbembesi Police Station where I was detained.'[13]

Two days before Nkala's body was found, Vice-President Joseph Msika publicly accused the MDC of murdering him and threatened: 'If they are looking for a bloodbath, they will certainly get it.'[14]

A surprised nation – largely unfamiliar with Nkala's name until his arrest – learned that he had been declared a national hero and that Mugabe would deliver the speech at his funeral.

Two days before the burial, dramatic scenes in Bulawayo were recorded on the Human Rights Watch website as follows:

On 16 November, war veterans and ZANU-PF leaders assembled in Bulawayo and marched to City Hall, under police escort and armed with axes, sticks, and whips. Along the way bystanders were targeted for violent attack, especially whites. One old woman had her windscreen smashed and was beaten. She later had to have glass surgically removed from her eye. Schoolchildren were also attacked.

The police took no action to stop the violence. At City Hall, marchers assembled to hear brief speeches against 'terrorism' from the march leaders: former home affairs minister Dumiso Dabengwa and local war veterans' leader Jabulani Sibanda. They then attacked City Hall, heading for the mayor's office. The mayor – a member of the MDC elected in September – had already fled but they ransacked his office, taking his briefcase and destroying papers. It was noted that ZANU-PF members of the City Council had not parked their cars at City Hall that morning, suggesting that the attack was premeditated. Still the police did not intervene.

The demonstration then went to the Bulawayo MDC office where police did nothing as the demonstrators knocked down a wall and smashed windows.

A twenty-litre plastic container of petrol was carried inside, and within minutes the building was on fire. The police formed a barricade to prevent anyone from dousing the flames. The report continues:

At this stage, none of those arrested in connection with the murder of Cain Nkala had been charged or had even been visited by a lawyer – in breach of the constitutional requirement that they be brought before a judicial authority within 48 hours.

The government press announced, completely incorrectly, that one Bulawayo MP, Fletcher Dulini-Ncube, had fled. In fact the reason he was not at home was that he was in Parliament in Harare. On his return to Bulawayo he handed himself in to police. Dulini-Ncube, an elderly diabetic, was held in police custody in very poor conditions. The authorities delayed several days before releasing him, even after a Supreme Court order granting him bail.

On Sunday 18 November, Nkala was buried at Heroes' Acre outside Harare, and Mugabe paraphrased President George W Bush's reaction to the attacks only two months earlier on the World Trade Center in New York and the Pentagon in Washington, declaring that, like America, Zimbabwe would not tolerate acts of terrorism on its soil.

He referred to the MDC and white farmers no less than twenty times as 'terrorists' who were, he said, on a mission to 'reverse our sovereignty, to reverse the right of the people to determine who should lead them, and trying to direct events in a way that suits foreign powers'.

'The MDC are perpetrators of political violence and crimes against humanity,' he said, and warned that 'their international sponsors should know that their days are numbered.'

In life, Mugabe had never even met the man he was burying, but the chance to denounce the opposition had been too good to miss.

Tsvangirai also made capital out of the case, claiming that the government was out of control and denying MDC involvement in Nkala's murder.

'We are shocked at this suggestion, because we are not involved in any crime and would not condone any crime,' he told a press conference in Harare. 'Anyone who commits the crime of murder must face the wrath of the law, that is the only way we can return this country to civil order. Our conscience is clear and we will not lose sleep over that.

'There is rampant lawlessness in Zimbabwe, which is leading to anarchy. The government has chosen to ignore all the violence perpetrated so far and is now applying the law selectively.

'We have rogue war veterans and ZANU-PF supporters who have committed serious crimes, but are still roaming the streets freely, and this is part of a wider agenda by ZANU-PF to beat up urban supporters of the MDC.'[15]

From the start there were signs that the story of the abduction was not as simple as it seemed. The *Herald* claimed that, according to unnamed eyewitnesses, Nkala was abducted by men carrying sub-machine guns, but since the police had placed Mrs Nkala under 'protective custody' and refused to allow anyone to talk to her, such reports could not be verified.

And while the state media thundered on, the private press was proclaiming just as loudly that the murder was an inside job. The *Standard* went so far as to quote an unnamed member of the dead man's family, who reportedly said Nkala had been in fear of his life because he had spoken out against the continued use of violence, and was even talking about moving to London.[16]

But, beyond the rhetoric, the issue had major implications for Zimbabwe. If Cain was killed by his own party in an effort to silence him, similar action might well be taken in the future to stop ZANU-PF members from testifying at the MDC's proposed justice commission. On the other hand, if the opposition did it, questions would have to be asked about the conduct the world might expect from a future MDC government.

At the time of writing, no case has been proved against any of those arrested for the murder.

I spent more than 100 hours interviewing members of both ZANU-PF and the MDC in an effort to get to the bottom of the story, and met several people who each claimed to have personally murdered Nkala. But journalists are sceptical of those who make bold confessions because it is not in keeping with human nature, and none of the men concerned expressed any remorse over the incident, so I doubt that their testimony was a statement of conscience. I put most of these claims down to bravado.

Some accounts sounded more plausible than others, but whichever way I looked at it, there were holes in the story, so I distilled the clues down to three possibilities. I attach no particular weight to any of them, and leave it to the reader to decide which version – if any – is the most likely.

## Scenario Number One

Cain Nkala and a team of accomplices abducted Nabanyama on the afternoon of 19 June and took him to a safe house outside Bulawayo, where they questioned him about MDC strategy. The interrogation got rough. Having tortured their victim, the men realised that if they released him, he would identify them, and that, as a lawyer, David Coltart would see to it that they were arrested and charged.

Nabanyama was therefore taken into the bush and murdered, his body burned and the ashes buried.

Nkala was a compassionate man who paid attention to the problems of his veterans, and, although Nabanyama was a political foe, the murder began to worry him. He suffered sleepless nights, and according to friends was haunted by his actions. In black Zimbabwean culture, there is a belief that if you kill someone who has not harmed you personally, the victim's spirit will drive you insane, unless you confess your guilt.

The abduction had been ordered at a senior level within ZANU-PF, and the men involved believed that the state would protect them. After being arrested, Cain found the stress too much to bear.

The leadership contest within the war veterans' movement had grown ugly, and with Nkala increasingly distracted by his own worries, he began to neglect his duties. It became clear that he was unlikely to maintain his position.

At the start of November 2001, he told his most trusted confidants that he could no longer take the strain and planned to go public with the facts of the Nabanyama case.

News of this reached the ZANU-PF leaders who had ordered the abduction, and they dispatched a team to kidnap and murder Nkala, after which they laid the blame on the MDC and made sure that the police and CIO extracted confessions under torture to back up the claim.

This scenario is supported by the fact that the government made such a fuss about Nkala's murder in a country where hundreds of people had died in political violence. To borrow a phrase from Shakespeare, perhaps they 'doth protest too much'.

The problem with this hypothesis is the risk it would have posed to ZANU-PF. If word ever got out (and Zimbabwe leaks like the proverbial sieve) that they had murdered Nkala, there would have been war between the party and the many veterans in Bulawayo who revered their leader.

And, if ZANU-PF was going to blame the MDC, why manufacture the story that Cain's abductors were carrying assault rifles, when it is widely known that the party has no access to such weapons? Finally, the MDC had an excellent intelligence staff that had infiltrated the war veterans' movement, but by the middle of 2003 they had not come up with the name of a single ZANU-PF member or war veteran who might have been involved in the murder.

*Scenario Number Two*

On the afternoon of 5 November, between four and eight young MDC body-guards and security officials were briefed at the party office in Bulawayo that their services would be required that night.

It was known that Nkala had been involved in Nabanyama's disappearance, and there were fears that ZANU-PF death squads were set to murder other members of the MDC, including, perhaps, one or more of the Matabeleland MPs.

At nightfall the team left Bulawayo in a pick-up truck belonging to the party and proceeded to a bar at Magwegwe, where they bought supper and had a few drinks for courage before proceeding to the Nkala home.

Cain was not there, and two of the men were dropped off and made their way into the garden, where they hid among the shrubbery. The truck parked nearby at a spot from which the driver could observe the house. Surprisingly, given the senior rank of the occupant, there were no guards on the property.

Shortly afterwards Cain arrived, and went inside to greet his family. The truck returned and parked in front of the house. The driver hooted and called out, 'Hey, my friend, come and see me.'

It was nothing unusual for WVA members to call on their boss at home, and Cain emerged and went over to the vehicle. The men in the garden came from behind, bundled him into the back of the pick-up and cuffed his hands.

As the vehicle pulled away, Mrs Nkala heard her husband's cry for help, and ran out of the house. In an act of great courage, she grabbed the rear panel of the pick-up tray and tried to climb aboard, but one of the gang hit her on the head with a stick and she fell to the ground. Mrs Nkala was later treated for a gash on her forehead.

Neighbours heard the commotion and came outside, but the action was over and there was nothing to see.

A little way out of town the truck pulled off the road into the bush, and the prisoner was told to get out and sit on the ground.

'I know who you are,' he told his abductors. 'You want to talk to me about the death of Patrick Nabanyama.'

He was questioned and gave information freely, saying that while he had not been present when Nabanyama was snatched from his house, he had conducted the interrogation, after which Nabanyama was shot by one of the veterans. The body was taken away for disposal, but Nkala did not know what had become of it.

Cain then revealed the name of the ZANU-PF official who had ordered Nabanyama's murder.

Nkala must have realised that he was about to die, but he neither cried out nor made any plea for his life. A few minutes later, he was strangled.

The police had no leads until several days later, when one of the killers got drunk in a pub and, in a quarrel with another man, boasted that he was not someone to be messed with, because he had been in the team that murdered Nkala. From there, it didn't take the police and CIO long to track down key members of the team, torturing each person they arrested in order to obtain information about the others.

By the end of November, six people had been charged: Sazini Mpofu, Khethani Sibanda, Remember Moyo, Army Zulu, MDC MP Fletcher Dulini-Ncube and the party's national director of security, Sonny Nicholas Masera.

As with the first scenario, this one has its strengths and weaknesses. The complicity of people associated with the MDC (acting under orders or on their own, depending on who one speaks to) appeared to be common knowledge in the party. And several of those arrested in connection with the murder had previously been tortured by the state or lost members of their family in acts sponsored by ZANU-PF, so they might well have had some enthusiasm for the mission.

But, in the *Herald* and on ZBC, it was claimed that the abductors had been armed, and despite countless raids on MDC offices and the inspection of thousands of vehicles at roadblocks, there have been no corroborated accounts of the opposition having access to automatic weapons.

Furthermore, if they were armed, why did the men go to the trouble of strangling Nkala? The area where he was killed was well away from any habitation, so the killers had no reason to fear that a gunshot would give them away.

And, with Nkala being the leader of the local veterans and with so much political violence going on, why were no guards protecting his home?

Before Khethani Sibanda was even arrested, Vice-President Msika had accused the MDC of murdering Nkala – but he had no way of knowing that the man was already dead. And the problem of prior knowledge doesn't end there.

According to statements in court by the police, they arrested Sibanda on Sunday 11 November, and he confessed to the murder at 7.30 pm the next day. The official police report stated that it was only *after* this that Sibanda gave them the first clues about the location of the body.

Yet Sibanda's lawyers produced a letter written by the Bulawayo police, which was delivered to a pathologist at 4.30 pm on Monday 12 November, asking for help with the Nkala post-mortem. That afternoon as well, police were dispatched to guard the grave site, from which Nkala's body was only removed the next morning, once the television camera crew arrived. The state was unable to explain these anomalies.

Given how much capital the state made out of the murder – and Mugabe's stout words on terrorism – the subsequent investigation was sloppy, and evidence was either ignored or lost. It seemed almost as though the prosecution did not want to get to the bottom of the matter.

Dockets on the murders were lodged with the Attorney-General's office in January 2002, only to be returned to the police to 'attend to certain aspects of evidence', a process that took nearly four months.

A law officer in the Attorney-General's office was quoted as saying that by April 'the docket has not improved much from what it was when it was initially submitted'.[17]

Senior officers had been assigned to the case and given unlimited resources, yet by the middle of 2003, more than eighteen months after the murder, their efforts to mount an effective prosecution were still floundering.

*Scenario Number Three*
In the run-up to the 2000 general election, senior members of ZANU-PF asked Nkala if he could arrange the abduction, interrogation and murder of Patrick Nabanyama. He agreed, assembled a team of trusted men, and together they carried out the mission.

When the team was eventually arrested, the party leaders told them that the Attorney-General would ensure that the charge was limited to abduction, since no body had been found, and efforts would be made to secure an acquittal. Even if the judge proved difficult, Mugabe would decree that all those accused of political violence over the election would receive a state pardon. This would not include acts of murder, but would cover alleged kidnapping.

But, when Nkala felt pangs of conscience and talked about wanting to spill the beans, it became clear that he would have to be eliminated before the accused were cross-examined in court. The problem was how to kill him without sparking a war between the veterans and the party. The answer was simple: get the MDC to do it.

It was well known within the MDC that the party had been infiltrated by ZANU-PF agents, any one of whom could have set in motion the idea of killing Nkala.

This would explain why there was no security at his home, and the authorities would have found out the location of the body from their source in the MDC.

In order not to give the game away, it was important to get a confession about the murder before retrieving the corpse, but even under torture Khethani Sibanda took more than twenty-four hours to admit to the killing.

Meanwhile, someone in the police had jumped the gun, sending off the letter to the pathologist and dispatching guards to the grave.

If Nkala did tell one or more of his abductors the name of the person who ordered him to kill Nabanyama, it would explain why there was such a half-hearted effort to get the case to trial or even to track down the real culprits, some of whom remained at large.

I have the greatest contempt for conspiracy theories, which rarely stand up to the randomness of daily life, but this one does hold some water.

Whatever the truth, the most important issue is that, by the time of Nkala's murder, Zimbabwe had slipped into a state of undeclared civil war, not only between ZANU-PF and the MDC, but even within the ruling party and the war veterans' movement.

The inter-party violence grew worse with the establishment of Green Bomber camps across the country. The youth militia would abduct MDC members and torture them, and the MDC youth would then raid the Bomber camps to rescue their people, and sometimes take prisoners of their own. From the interviews I conducted with both the Bombers and the MDC, it appears to have been rare for anyone to be killed in these games of tit for tat.

Measured by volume, there is no comparison between the terror perpetrated by the government and acts carried out by the MDC, but the outside world should not imagine that peace can be attained in Zimbabwe simply by pushing ZANU-PF out of power.

It will be important for a new government to set up the proposed justice commission without delay, so that both the victims and perpetrators of violence can bring their stories before a national inquiry. And if, in the process, illegal acts committed by the MDC are uncovered, then so be it.

Judging by the interviews I have conducted with victims of torture and violence, failure to deliver swift and transparent justice – and to put the most serious offenders on trial – will result in vigilante action. It takes only a cursory glance at the personal accounts in the appendix to this book to realise the degree of horror Zimbabwe has suffered, and to understand why some people would feel the need to settle scores, with or without the sanction of the state.

When democracy finally arrives, it will take a great deal of work to erase the culture of violence that has become a way of life for those on both sides of the political front line.

# 14

# When freedom comes

From the second half of 2003, Mugabe became increasingly irrelevant in the context of finding a solution to the crisis.

In the *Herald* and on ZBC, Jonathan Moyo continued to insist that, ultimately, the president would triumph over the international conspiracy trying to oust him from power, but the foreign press and the privately owned newspapers in Harare ignored his speeches.

Mugabe was no longer *running* the country in the normal sense, because the resources of government were being gobbled up by the daily crises of famine, foreign exchange shortages, AIDS, unemployment, emigration and popular dissent. And it was clear that his death or retirement would no longer be enough to satisfy the people.

In South Africa, the ANC continued to pursue its policy of 'quiet diplomacy', but also talked about how best to rebuild a future Zimbabwe. And in Europe and America, policy makers started calculating the cost of aid and assistance that would undoubtedly be needed by a post-Mugabe government.

The polite language of international relations had been replaced by an unequivocal demand for change.

US secretary of state General Colin Powell referred publicly to Mugabe as a 'tyrant' and accused him of 'violent misrule'.

The US, he said, was no longer talking about reform, but wanted to see Mugabe step down, after which 'a transitional government should take over and fix a date for fresh elections'. Once that happened, Powell believed, 'the US would be quick to pledge generous assistance to help restore Zimbabwe's political and economic institutions', and he suggested that other donors would follow suit.[1]

Powell's attack drew outrage in Harare, where Moyo called him an 'Uncle Tom', a pejorative term used for black people who submit to white authority.

But three days later, President George W Bush supported his foreign secretary when he told an African business conference in Washington that Mugabe ran a country where 'the freedom and dignity of the nation is under assault'.

Africa was a hot topic because Bush was preparing to make his first official trip to the continent in July, visiting Senegal, South Africa, Botswana, Uganda and Nigeria, and it was clear that, along the way, he would be seeking support for regime change in the strife-torn countries of Liberia, the Democratic Republic of Congo, and Zimbabwe.

The DRC was the easiest of the three, because Joseph Kabila had brought the rebel groups into a government of national unity, the war was winding down, most of the troops sent to the country by Uganda, Angola and Zimbabwe had withdrawn and a timetable for elections was being drawn up.

Liberia was a tougher case, with President Charles Taylor given to extremes of behaviour exacerbated by his alleged cocaine addiction, but armed rebel groups were making inroads and a limited number of American military forces had already been committed by the US government.

But Zimbabwe was a different matter.

Given his age, it was clear that Mugabe would have to step down sooner or later, but African leaders were hesitant to endorse the American view that the 2002 presidential election was illegitimate due to alleged rigging by ZANU-PF.

Since 2000, Zambia, Malawi, Uganda and Nigeria had all been accused of electoral fraud, and if the fairness of a poll became the sole test of legitimacy, then many of Africa's leaders would be in trouble.

But Bush would not be swayed. Little more than a week before his trip, he restated the conditions under which the US would help African countries.

'The world needs a new approach to foreign aid,' he said, 'and America is leading the way with the Millennium Challenge Account. Under my proposal, money will go to developing nations whose governments are committed to three broad strategies. First, they must rule justly. Second, they must invest in the health and education of their people. And third, they must have policies that encourage economic freedom.'

He singled out Zimbabwe as an example of an undemocratic nation where none of these criteria was being met.

In Pretoria, the ANC began to worry that the pending visit would see Bush, Powell and the US undersecretary of state for Africa, Walter Kansteiner, forcing Mbeki's hand to get rid of Mugabe.

An unnamed ANC policy maker told the *Washington Times*: 'This is going to be a tough couple of weeks for Mbeki. He will have to smile and will no doubt be delighted to be seen hosting the world's most powerful leader, but behind the scenes he will need to work hard to hold his party, and even his close supporters, together.'

The South Africans, he said, saw the continent as their domain, and comments by Bush and Powell, calling so directly for change in Liberia, Congo and Zimbabwe, had shocked the ANC.

'They are starting to fear that their refusal to take tough action on thorny issues, especially Zimbabwe, has created a vacuum which other countries, like the US, are moving to fill,' he said.[2]

But both sides went out of their way to make sure that a deal had been done before Bush set foot on South African soil.

The Americans had offered a multi-billion-dollar aid package for the rebuilding of Zimbabwe once Mugabe was gone and internationally supervised elections were set to be held.[3]

If Mbeki cooperated – and there was every indication that he would – a sizeable volume of the US-funded contracts would be awarded to South African companies.

On the night of Tuesday 8 July, Air Force One touched down at Air Force Base Waterkloof outside Pretoria, and Bush, his wife and his daughter were whisked away to the Sheraton Hotel.

The next morning, it was all smiles for the media when Bush met with Mbeki, and they went into a closed meeting for less than thirty minutes. Bush would be in South Africa for two days, but the African Union was having its annual conference in Maputo, and Mbeki had to fly out that afternoon. The rest of the time the US delegation would meet with business leaders and travel to neighbouring Botswana for talks with President Festus Mogae, before going on to Uganda.

Just before noon, Bush and Mbeki emerged and held a joint media conference. After statements on AIDS and the need to combat world terrorism, they allowed just four questions from the more than 200 journalists. Only two American reporters and two South African journalists were allowed to ask questions, which had almost certainly been submitted in advance.

One dealt with Zimbabwe, and although it had been addressed to Bush and touched on the apparent difference of opinion between Washington and Pretoria on the issue of how to handle Mugabe, Mbeki jumped in and spoke first.

'President Bush and myself are absolutely of one mind about the urgent need to address the political and economic challenges of Zimbabwe,' he said. 'It's necessary to resolve this matter as quickly as is possible.

'We have said, as you would know, that responsibility for the resolution of these problems rests with the people of Zimbabwe; and we have urged them – both the government and the opposition – to get together and seriously tackle all of these issues.

'I did tell the president that ZANU-PF and the MDC are, indeed, discussing. They are engaged in discussions on all of the matters that would be relevant to the resolution of these political and economic problems. So that process is going on.'

Bush concurred, adding that Mbeki was the 'point man' on the issue, and that America would back his efforts.

'He represents a mighty country in the neighbourhood who, because of his position and his responsibility, is working the issue. We share the same outcome. And I think it's important for the United States, whether it be me or my secretary of state, to speak out when we see a situation where somebody's freedoms have been taken away from them and they're suffering. And that's what we're going to continue to do.'

When one of the reporters reminded Bush that Tsvangirai had accused Mbeki of not being an honest broker, the US president chose his words carefully,

'Well, I think Mr Mbeki *can be* an honest broker.'

He stopped short of saying that his host *was* one.

Within minutes, Morgan Tsvangirai and Didymus Mutasa, ZANU-PF secretary for administration, had both issued statements denying Mbeki's claim that they were talking to each other about anything.

Zimbabwean journalist Michael Hartnack did not believe that Mbeki lied. Rather, he said, the president 'was misled by over-optimistic reports fed to his advisers by those given to minimising problems'.[4]

Kansteiner was in touch with Tsvangirai by telephone throughout the visit, would have known that the talks were not on, and would have been sure to brief Bush and Powell, but when Powell was asked to comment later, he glossed over the topic.

'With respect to what negotiations may be going on between parties, I can't speak to that,' he said. 'And what President Mbeki's role may be in it and what he may be doing, I can't speak to that either.'

Clearly, the Americans knew that there *were* no talks, and they didn't care. The Pretoria visit was the Bush administration doing what it does best: smile, agree to everything and then carry on with the original plan. In the speeches made by Bush during the rest of his time in Africa, he made it clear that Mugabe's days were numbered.

But when Air Force One left Waterkloof, Mbeki's status in the region was reaffirmed and his pride intact; the hard left of the ANC did not feel compromised, and relations between Pretoria and Washington were better than ever.

The only discernible difference was that Bush had made it clear he wanted to see a total change of government in Harare, whereas Mbeki favoured a new leader of a reformed ZANU-PF.

Either way, Mugabe had been rendered redundant, with no role to play in a future Zimbabwe, and clearly someone else would have the task of cleaning up the mess.

Of course, not everyone saw it that way, and Mugabe did have his defenders.

On their website, the AfroAmerica Network described him as brilliant, selfless, proud and 'a man of vision'.[5] However, the site gave no space to any of the criticisms levelled at Mugabe, and avoided matters of torture, murder and hunger.

Dr Daniel Tetteh Osabu-Kle, a Ghanaian-born professor of political science at Carlton University in Ottawa, Canada, had strongly defended the right of white Zimbabweans to be categorised as Africans, with the same rights as their black countrymen. But, he warned, they could not remain an elite group in possession of vast land holdings, when millions of blacks had nothing.

'African culture abhors greed, and holds fundamentally that all citizens have equal access to what Mother Nature has to offer.

'White Africans of Zimbabwe robbed the ancestors of black Africans of their land and gave it to their children. What the white Africans of today should know is that they are no longer Europeans, but Africans. Being Africans, they have to comply with African culture. Black and white Africans must have equal access to what Mother Nature has to offer.

'Mugabe is only enforcing African culture.'

In the view of Osabu-Kle, Mugabe was 'one of the greatest leaders Africa has ever produced'.

'Mugabe is walking in the shoes of the great Nkrumah to liberate all Zimbabweans from the shackles of neocolonialism and institutionalised racism and to give them peace … What Mugabe is doing in Zimbabwe today is part and parcel of the total liberation of the whole African continent. Those who have ears to hear, let them hear!'[6]

Closer to home, the ANC Youth League published several condemnations of South African opposition leader Tony Leon's stand on Zimbabwe. Leon, leader of the Democratic Alliance (DA), had repeatedly called on Mbeki to get tough with Mugabe, but in a press statement the Youth League alleged that 'the Tony Leon-driven Democratic Alliance and the Western power-mongers such as the brutal and ruthless Tony Blair's Labour Party regime and John Howard's Australia, are not concerned about the lives of ordinary Zimbabweans, but are bent on defending white minority property interests.

'What is common between British and Australian cowboy regimes together with their "racist surrogate" [DA] is their hatred for the indigenous people of Zimbabwe and passion to crook Africans their land [sic].'

As for the MDC, it was 'being used by racists who want to defend the ill begotten land of dispossessed Africans'.[7]

But the critics far outnumbered the praise singers.

Following a split in the War Veterans' Association, a rival organisation had been set up. The Zimbabwe Liberators' Platform (ZLP) grew rapidly, and one of its leading members, Wilf Mhanda, a former senior ZANLA commander, spoke out against the madness that had spread throughout Zimbabwe. He claimed that Mugabe had been 'arrogant, paranoid, secretive' and interested only in power from the start.

'We are the real war vets,' he told a media conference in Harare. 'The people who are now describing themselves as war vets and invading white farms are not really war vets at all. Often they are just thugs. We fought for freedom and democracy in this country, and what they are doing is quite the opposite.

'We would like to see a united front with the farmers against what is happening now. After all, today's white farmers are Zimbabweans and are contributing to the country.

'We can't afford to be neutral. What we say is: "Don't sit on the fence, because the fence is electrified."

'We made great sacrifices and now we want respect as the real war veterans. We do not want to see our name dragged through the mud by the criminals who are occupying farms.'

But he closed the meeting with a warning against the MDC.

'The answer does not lie in another almighty party,' he said. 'While we would like to see the MDC defeat ZANU-PF, we do not want it to become too powerful, either. It will need a strong opposition, but we do not want that opposition to be ZANU-PF. Most of all, we need restoration of the rule of law and a multiparty system with a proper democratic constitution.'

Thomas Mapfumo lives in the American town of Eugene, Oregon, but in the 1970s he was in exile with Mugabe, writing songs that stirred the ZANLA fighters to action.

His *chimurenga* or 'war-time' music was so popular that he sang at Mugabe's inauguration in April 1980, sharing the stage with reggae king Bob Marley.

For the first few years after independence, he was on the A-list for state functions, and wrote songs about the people's victory over minority rule. Barely a day went by without Mapfumo's music being played by the ZBC, and he was dubbed 'The Lion of Zimbabwe'.

A decade later, many of his songs had been banned, and Mapfumo used his music to criticise what he described as 'policies of injustice, brutality and oppression'.

A translation from one of his Shona songs reads:

You have caused hunger,
You have chased away capable farmers
Do the farming yourself
or do you just have a big mouth!

'I supported Mugabe in the beginning,' he said, 'but I was always keeping an eye on him. When they started talking about a one-party state, I started to realise they were selfish. We went from the frying pan into the fire with this man.'[8]

In 2003, his hit track *Vechidiki* [The Young Generation] sent a warning to the Green Bombers about the campaign of revenge that could follow Mugabe's demise:

They send you to do dirty work
And you just comply.
Be warned that you will die
For other people's evil deeds.

One branch of society that could have taken a stronger stand is the Church, which was outspoken during Smith's time in office, but remained almost completely silent in the 1980s and 1990s.

In July 2003, the Zimbabwe Council of Churches (ZCC) issued an apology to the nation.

'We have, with our own eyes, watched as violence, rape, intimidation, harassment and various forms of torture have ravaged the nation,' the council said in a statement.

'We have buried our people who have starved to death because of food shortages. While we have continued to pray, we have not been moved to action.

'We, as a council, apologise to the people of Zimbabwe for not having done enough at a time when the nation looked to us for guidance.'

But one churchman, Pius Ncube, Archbishop of Bulawayo, had long been vocal, condemning the government in the press and from the pulpit.

'We face an absolutely desperate situation in Zimbabwe and the government is lying to the world about it,' he told a conference of bishops in Durban.

'Our government continues to engage in lies, propaganda, the twisting of facts, half-truths, downright untruth and gross misinformation, because they are fascists.'[9]

Jonathan Moyo took to calling Ncube 'that mad priest', and the state began clamping down on what was said by churchmen. In June 2003, Sonykis Chimbuya, a pastor with the Church of Christ in Masvingo and regional human rights chairman of the ZCC, was detained by police after criticising ZANU-PF in one of his sermons.

'I was ordered not to say prayers which are political,' he later told the *Daily News*. 'They even told me that I should write down my prayers for them to scrutinise.'[10]

All this, according to Morgan Tsvangirai, was just further evidence that the government had become desperate and paranoid – but none of it, he warned, would save the president.

'The reality is that the opposition in this country enjoys the support of a majority of Zimbabweans, and we will prove that in free and fair elections.'

A second treason charge and a spell in jail after leading a week-long national strike in June had made him 'more determined than ever to campaign peacefully but forcefully to defeat Mr Mugabe's party', and he urged those being criticised by the president and his cohorts to 'take no notice of this personal vitriol. I have had my share of tantrums from the old man. It is something we have to live with until he goes.'[11]

It was the last line that reporters picked up on: the notion that Mugabe was doing little more than keeping the seat warm in the presidential office.

But, after twenty-three years of virtual one-party rule and the recent violence and lawlessness that had so corrupted the national values, could the MDC deliver the utopia they had talked about since 1999?

To some degree, that would depend on the mechanics of change. If ZANU-PF was to bow out gracefully (or under pressure from South Africa) and allow internationally supervised elections, which the MDC would undoubtedly win, the new government could take over the organs of state in an orderly manner, as happened in Zambia, Malawi and Kenya when the ruling parties in those countries lost power.

The danger would be if government under ZANU-PF collapsed altogether, and by the winter of 2003, at the rate that food and money were running out, that scenario was gaining currency.

The breakdown would first be felt in the outlying areas, leaving war veterans and the militia in charge. As was seen in Afghanistan and Iraq, the collapse of government often leads to chaos, plunder and poverty, and makes it hard for a new authority to gain control.

But even assuming a peaceful transition of power, a future government would face a daunting list of challenges and would have to:

- restore law and order;
- disband and neutralise the Green Bombers;
- feed the nation;
- rebuild the health system in a country where an estimated 3 000 people die every week from AIDS;[12]
- get back into school thousands of children whose parents have long been unable to afford tuition fees;
- root out corruption;
- bring home the skilled exiles;
- investigate crimes against humanity and prosecute offenders;
- stabilise the currency;
- track and recover the billions that have been embezzled;

- rebuild the commercial agriculture sector;
- restore investor confidence; and
- embark on a priority programme to rebuild the economy and create jobs for the 70 per cent of people who are unemployed.

A glance at the list makes it clear that a ZANU-PF government – even one determined to break with the past – would be unable to tackle thorny issues such as war crimes, corruption, embezzlement and land, which would require the investigation and possible arrest of almost all the party's MPs.

But a caretaker government, running the country while preparing for internationally supervised elections, could handle the most urgent issues.

The first priority would be to feed the nation, and this would require emergency imports of maize, wheat, cooking oil and even protein like milk, chicken and beef. Fuel would also have to be high on the list because, without transport, there would be no way of distributing the food.

While imports were being procured, law and order would have to be re-established to ensure that, when essential commodities arrived, they were not raided, pilfered or siphoned off to ZANU-PF – or MDC – cronies. The first step in this process would be to take control of the militia bases, but simply disbanding the youth brigades could prove dangerous. They have been so desensitised to violence and brutality that they would need to undergo some form of counselling and reorientation before they could be assimilated back into the community.

Many former Green Bombers have escaped into exile, but they are hard to find because they cannot talk openly about their past activities for fear of retaliation. In Johannesburg, for example, I interviewed more than a dozen male recruits (I also found two women who had joined the militia, but they refused to talk), and their stories brought home to me that they, too, are victims of the system.

One young man, whom I shall call Charlie, was living in Hillbrow and attending MDC meetings, although his new friends had no idea about his past life. This is what he told me:

I was working at a factory near my home in rural Matabeleland and things seemed to be going okay with my family. I was not yet married but I was ready to pay lobola to my girlfriend's parents, and I was also looking after my mother and my two young sisters, because our father had passed away some years before.

One Sunday, I was walking home from church when a group of Green Bombers met me on the path and asked why I was not at a ZANU-PF meeting, which was being held in our village. Before I could answer, they knocked me to the ground and started kicking me and shouting that I was an MDC sell-out. From there, I was taken to the local militia camp where some other boys and girls who had been picked up were also waiting. I knew some of them from the local area, but others had been brought from far away. One of the men had a broken arm because he had struggled when they grabbed him and he was very much in pain, but no one was doing anything for him.

We sat in the shade of a tree at the camp all day with no food or drink. That night, we were given some porridge and water, but we slept under the tree without blankets.

When I woke the next morning, the man with the broken arm was gone and I never saw him again. I was led to an interview with a senior Bomber and two war vets, and they told me that from now on the camp would be my life, and that my job and my family were not important any more.

They escorted me to my house and allowed me to pick up some clothes and blankets. I wanted to say something to my mother, but we were both too afraid to talk.

That night, I was led to an area of open ground next to the camp, and all the young Bombers were sitting there in rows. Those of us who were new had to sit in front.

Some of the militia had broken rules of some kind, and one had tried to escape, and we were going to watch them being punished.

The first one was dragged to the front of the crowd and questioned about why he had not been following orders. As he tried to speak, the militia leaders and the two war vets who had interviewed me started punching and kicking him.

He was crying and blood was coming from his mouth, and I felt sick. But the Bombers who had been in the camp for a while started cheering and laughing. Then I felt a pain in my back and someone had kicked me in the spine. I looked up and a senior Bomber was standing behind me.

'Are you not enjoying this,' he shouted at me. 'Would you like to be next?'

I still can't believe it, but I started cheering and shouting for the man to be punished further. I am so ashamed now when I think of how I behaved, but I was just thinking about my own survival.

Over the next few weeks, I was also beaten, and twice I was raped as punishment. And then, when I had lost all my human qualities, I was sent out with other militia to patrol the district and to chase out any MDC who might be in the area.

In the Bombers, there is never enough food and you are always hungry, and learn quickly not to trust anyone. If you find a vendor who is selling goods at more than the official price, or if you suspect someone of supporting the MDC, you have to punish them to your full extent. If you are soft in your judgment, one of the other militia on patrol with you may report the matter to the commanders, and that night you will find yourself being punished in front of your friends, who will cheer while you bleed and scream.

After listening to Charlie, I realised the magnitude of the task awaiting any new government. There are tens of thousands of youths who have been through the same experience, and international aid agencies will need to commit themselves to a long-term programme aimed at detraumatising the militia and their victims.

I have sent several young people to an NGO-funded counselling centre in Johannesburg where they received treatment for mental trauma, and one of the psychiatrists at the unit told me that the damage currently being done to society in Zimbabwe could give rise to a culture of crime, rape, domestic violence and social dysfunction.

Once food and fuel supplies had been secured and law and order re-established, the longer process of rebuilding the country and rehumanising its population could take place.

Many of the commercial farmers who were forced off their land have emigrated, but those willing to return to their farms – lying fallow and abandoned – would have to be encouraged to do so, in order to get food production back on track. Despite being evicted, the landowners still have legal title to their properties.

ZANU-PF MPs and their cronies who have been given farms would have to be moved, and a full land audit would be required to determine who owns what.

By the time of the Commercial Farmers' Union's sixtieth annual meeting in August 2003, less than 10 per cent of the 4 000 farmers who had been on the land in 1999 were still in production. Many, living in town with no income, depended on charity to survive. CFU vice-president Doug Taylor-Freeme told the meeting that the 2003 wheat crop was down to 10 per cent compared to the usual harvest, and even cash crops such as tobacco had fallen by more than 60 per cent. But he believed that, under the right conditions, many farmers would return to their properties.[13]

Clare Short is the former British minister for international development, whose portfolio included foreign aid. Short resigned in early 2003 over the Iraq war, alleging that Tony Blair had exaggerated the threat posed by Saddam Hussein, but she maintains a special interest in Zimbabwe.

'I think it would be relatively simple to rebuild the country once the political problems have been sorted out,' she told me at her office in London. 'The whole world will have to come to the rescue, and I believe they would.

'It won't take five minutes, but the country has plenty of good people and strong institutions. It is not like the Congo – that will take years to rebuild. I think Zimbabwe could progress fairly quickly.'

In Short's opinion, the high level of education among Zimbabwean exiles could aggravate the problem of reversing the brain drain, because so many of them have found jobs in their new countries. Still, she said, there would be some who would go home because of family ties, and it might be possible to set up an incentive scheme to encourage people to return.

On the vexed problem of land, however, there would need to be a fresh start.

'Having so much of the best land in the hands of a white minority was never healthy for the country, but the recent moves to reform the system have not been transparent and have created even more problems,' she said.

'There are several hundred thousand farm workers walking around without jobs, lots of cronies have been given land and are not farming it, and I think we'd have to get an impartial group to look at where the country is now and map out a way forward.'

But, she said, an even greater challenge would be to create jobs for the millions of unemployed who would rather work in an urban environment than eke out a living as subsistence farmers.

'The answer in any country is to create the right enabling environment so that the private sector can grow the economy,' she said. 'That ranges from small-scale business which needs micro financing, all the way through to foreign investment.

'The international community knows how to do those things, and although the Zimbabwe people have suffered terribly and the economy has shrunk so badly, I think recovery would move forward quite well, though it will take some years to even get the country back to where it was before the current crisis.

'But although Zimbabwe has been battered and broken – and a lot of people have suffered the same fate – there are strong institutions, and a lot of educated people, and they form the country's single greatest asset.

'Of course we need to also make sure that young people who have fallen out of the school system are pushed back into education, so that the tradition of learning is not broken and there is a new generation to take over in the future.'

In Washington, I spoke with Walter Kansteiner, who echoed what Short had said and agreed that most countries, including the United States, would be willing to help rebuild Zimbabwe, but believed they would first require definite change.

'There would need to be true freedom in the country first or we would risk Zimbabwe slipping back into trouble very quickly,' he said.

'Investors and institutions giving aid or soft loans are there for the long haul and the only solution that is going to provide sound, long-term guarantees is one that has the full consent of the Zimbabwe people.

'So before we can talk about rebuilding, we have to make sure that sustainable and irreversible change has taken place and that can only happen through truly free and fair elections. I think we are well past the point where cosmetic change would impress anyone, least of all the people of Zimbabwe.

'The kind of election we're talking about would include: repeal of undemocratic laws that disenfranchise exiles; unfettered monitoring by international observers; equal and unrestricted access to the media by all parties, a lack of intimidation; and transparency at every stage of the poll.

'Once that happened and there was no doubt about the validity of the poll, it would not be long before the international community, including the United States, got behind the new government.

'The first priority would be to re-establish commercial agriculture, because a hungry nation cannot be productive. Industry and manufacturing would also need a lot of attention and, of course, there would have to be some plan to entice millions of highly qualified Zimbabweans back from exile.

'But my own feeling is that, if the electoral process was totally clean, the resolve would be there to sort out the rest of the problems.

'However, we're only talking here about the physical well-being of the nation. Healing the emotional wounds of the past few years will be just as challenging because so many people have lost loves ones or been tortured or abused and some kind of justice will be needed before the country can be at peace with itself.'

Another challenge to face is helping the 2.3 million Zimbabweans who are HIV-positive. Hunger and a shortage of medication, including vitamin pills, have compounded the problem, speeding up the onset of full-blown AIDS.

The state hospital system has all but collapsed and would need large-scale refurbishment.

Non-governmental organisations, many of which have been closed down, would need to rebuild civil society and assist in the development of grass-roots democracy, while also keeping an eye on the new government.

In 2002, justice minister Patrick Chinamasa claimed that NGOs were bent on the overthrow of ZANU-PF, 'disguising their activities in semantics such as human rights, democracy and promoting civil society'.[14]

But in South Africa, local and foreign organisations have played a major role in developing a culture of tolerance, good governance and respect for human rights, and the same task would lie ahead for Zimbabwe.

But what about those responsible for the breakdown in human values – the torturers, legislators, war vets, militia leaders, army commanders and members of the CIO?

In London, Kevin Laue is an official with the international anti-torture group Redress, which by July 2003 was already investigating acts of abuse in Zimbabwe, with a view to prosecuting those who may have committed crimes against humanity.

Henry Dowa, a Zimbabwean police officer, was serving with his country's contingent as part of the UN Interim Administration Mission in Kosovo (UMNIC), when Redress received affidavits from MDC members in Harare, alleging that Dowa had tortured them during interrogation.

Laue appealed to UMNIC for Dowa's arrest and prosecution, but the UN Secretary General's special representative in Kosovo, Michael Steiner, said that while the charges levelled at Dowa were serious, his mission did not have the resources to mount a prosecution.

Among those who claimed to have been tortured was the MDC MP for Mbare East, Tichaona Munyanyi, who said he had suffered beatings and electric shocks while being questioned by Dowa.

MDC spokesman Paul Themba Nyathi said his party supported efforts to put the policeman on trial. 'Most of the people tortured by this man were MDC supporters, and when Redress approached us, we gave them the information they needed so that they could pursue the matter. The move is to stop impunity,' he said.

Two other victims who had been interrogated by the CIO (though not by Dowa) called publicly for his arrest. MDC MP Job Sikhala and human rights lawyer Gabriel Shumba were so badly tortured that they had to seek medical treatment in South Africa. Sikhala returned to Zimbabwe, where he called publicly for Dowa and others guilty of similar crimes to be put on trial, while Shumba, who had remained in Pretoria, added his legal expertise to the case.

'Under international law, torture is a crime that is prosecutable in any country, in any legal jurisdiction and at any time,' Nyathi said. 'The other alternative with a modicum of success is to urgently apply for a warrant of arrest in countries that have universal jurisdiction on their statutes, for example Belgium, Britain or France.

'It would be embarrassing for any state to refuse to fulfil such a grave obligation in respect of international commitments. Kosovo would then be obliged to extradite the suspect to the prosecuting state.'

When UMNIC refused to act against Dowa, Laue took up the issue with UN Secretary General Kofi Annan, and Dowa was taken off active duty in Kosovo pending investigation.

But Laue said this was only the first step in a concerted move to start war crimes trials against alleged suspects in Zimbabwe. 'Once we get evidence linking any officials to torture, we will do our best to make sure that they are prosecuted if they travel outside Zimbabwe,' he said.

In Harare, the director of Zimbabwe Lawyers for Human Rights, Arnold Tsunga, agreed.

'This should serve as an adequate reminder to law enforcement agents who are being implicated in torture that the day of reckoning will come, and it can be anywhere in the world,' he said.[15]

The idea of prosecuting those who commit gross violations in the name of government goes back to the Nuremberg trials of Nazi leaders after World War II, but a new precedent was set in the late 1990s when former Chilean strongman Augusto Pinochet was arrested in Britain on a warrant issued by former victims now living in Spain.

Pinochet was eventually sent home on the assertion that he was too frail – mentally and physically – to stand trial, but an important legal principle had been set: those alleged to have committed crimes against humanity, even former heads of state, could be arrested on foreign soil and on the strength of a warrant issued in a third country.

Following the Pinochet case, former Yugoslav dictator Slobodan Milosevic went on trial in The Hague; in the former Portuguese colony of East Timor, some 250 militiamen were charged – many in absentia – in connection with the death of almost one-third of the tiny country's population during twenty-five years of Indonesian occupation; in June 2003, a special court was set up in Cambodia to try members of the Khmer Rouge almost twenty-five years after their reign of terror resulted in an estimated 1.7 million deaths;[16] the trials of alleged perpetrators of genocide in both Rwanda and Sierra Leone are under way; and in Iraq the interim American administration is committed to bringing criminal charges against former members of Saddam Hussein's Baath Party.

In July 2003, the International Criminal Court, established a year earlier and based in The Hague, began investigating human rights abuses in the Democratic Republic of Congo, a process that at some point will almost certainly implicate some of the ZANU-PF elite. However, the court can only deal with crimes committed after 1 July 2002.

The United States has undermined the process by insisting that its own citizens should not be subject to the new court's jurisdiction, but this would in no way influence the arrest and trial of Robert Mugabe and his ministers, or members of Zimbabwe's armed forces, war veterans or youth militia. Indeed, given the international judiciary's pursuit of human rights abusers since Pinochet's arrest in London, it is hard to imagine how Mugabe and his colleagues might avoid arrest.

Human rights activist and gay campaigner Peter Tatchell believes that swift and transparent justice under a new government will be essential to the future peace of Zimbabwe.

'Putting the culprits on trial and drawing up a new democratic constitution to make sure the state can never again abuse its people, are, to my mind, two of the most important issues for Zimbabwe, post-Mugabe,' he told me when we spoke in London.

'Although there has been some exposure of the torture, rape and murder that have made this regime one of the worst dictatorships in recent history, a full commission of inquiry and a series of trials will almost certainly reveal a lot more horror. This is the only way justice can be secured and reconciliation can begin.

'It must be made clear to leaders everywhere that, if you abuse your power or allow others to do it in your name, you will be brought to justice and made to pay for your crimes.

'If Mugabe escapes justice, the message will be that governments can do as they please and that international human rights agreements are worthless bits of paper.'

Tatchell made world headlines on Saturday 30 October 1999, when he tried to arrest Robert Mugabe, who was on a private shopping trip in London.

As Mugabe's car left the St James's Court Hotel in Buckingham Gate, London SW1, where he had been staying, Tatchell, along with John Hunt, Alistair Williams and Chris Morris from the gay-rights organisation OutRage!, ran in front of the president's limousine and forced it to stop.

Tatchell opened the car's rear door, grabbed his quarry by the arm and shouted: 'President Mugabe, you are under arrest on charges of torture. Torture is a crime under international law.'

The president's bodyguards were caught unawares and didn't know what to do. When the British police arrived, they arrested Tatchell and his colleagues under the Public Order Act, and escorted Mugabe to Harrods department store, where he went on a shopping spree.

Mugabe refused to press charges, saying that he was unwilling to return to Britain to testify in the case. He has avoided London ever since, but in March 2001 Tatchell attempted another arrest in the lobby of the Hilton Hotel in Brussels. This time the bodyguards beat him unconscious while the Belgian police looked on.

The Australian-born Tatchell moves around London on a bicycle and lives in a council flat in Bermondsey. 'Peter lives like a church mouse,' says Marcelle d'Argy-Smith, former editor of *Cosmopolitan* and a personal friend. 'What's so wonderful about him is that he's ferocious. Some straight men look at him with contempt, but he's got more balls than all of them. He's practically a Hemingway hero.'[17]

In the 1970s, the black liberation struggle in Rhodesia was one of Tatchell's causes, along with a sackful of others ranging from independence for East Timor to gay rights in the communist-ruled Soviet bloc. He raised funds in London for ZANU's campaign against the government of Ian Smith, and later supported the ANC's struggle against apartheid. He was also one of the people behind the inclusion of gay rights in the new South African constitution.

But it was not just Mugabe's statements against gay people that changed his views on ZANU-PF.

'The evidence was there early on,' he said, 'only a few years after Mugabe took office and began slaughtering people in Matabeleland. The world ignored those massacres. That sent a signal to Mugabe that he could get away with anything and no one would protest. The world has, at last, woken up to Mugabe's tyranny. I hope he and his henchmen will be brought to trial when they leave office, in the same way that the former Yugoslav leader Slobodan Milosevic is now on trial in The Hague.

'There are some tragic parallels between the situation in Zimbabwe today and in the former Yugoslavia during the 1990s. In Bosnia, there were many reports of Serbian soldiers raping both men and women. It was the UN human rights commissioner, Mary Robinson, who raised the issue and demanded action to halt these sexual war crimes.

'The Serbian forces would sometimes line up fathers and sons and force the boys to perform oral sex on the fathers, after which both men and boys were raped by the Serbian soldiers.

'We are now seeing a similar pattern of sexual abuse emerging in Zimbabwe. Male and female rape is being used by ZANU-PF as a weapon of repression. Many torture victims and political detainees complain of sexual harassment and assault. Given the well-established precedent of putting Serbian war criminals on trial, the international community must ensure that Mugabe and his cronies are also brought to justice.

'If we fail in this, the message will be that governments can do as they please and then just apologise when they are removed from power, and everything will be okay.'

At the London-based Accountability Commission, which gathers and stores information for possible use in the trials of people accused of torture, David Banks is assembling dossiers on illegal means of interrogation.

'The Zimbabwe situation gives very great cause for concern because the abuse is being carried out on such a wide scale, and seemingly with the full knowledge of the regime,' he said.

'Given the reports I have seen coming out of the country, we would have to ask what international pressure is being brought to bear on Mugabe to stop this kind of abuse by those who claim they are acting with the authority of the state.

'And I have no doubt that the evidence we have already will be powerful enough to secure the arrest and conviction of people in government and members of the armed forces, police and CIO.

'It is a tragedy how rapidly the use of state-sponsored torture has escalated since 1999. The arrest of those responsible will be of great importance in a free Zimbabwe, both for reasons of natural justice and also to stop acts of personal retribution. Given the scale of the abuse, there are thousands of people who may feel the need to take revenge on those who have tortured them, and this will only lead to a fresh cycle of violence.

'I would therefore urge the international community to allocate money and resources to this project, and even to make sure that long-term assistance to a free Zimbabwe is linked to a new government's cooperation in securing the arrest, trial and, where guilty, the conviction and punishment of those who have committed crimes against humanity.'

Both Morgan Tsvangirai and his shadow minister for legal affairs, David Coltart, have consistently reaffirmed their commitment to a justice commission once their party is in power.

Along with these trials, there would be the need to recover money looted from the national coffers. In both Nigeria and Indonesia, new governments have had considerable success in finding and reclaiming stolen assets, and there is every reason to believe that Zimbabwe would be able to do the same.

As for the sale of state assets to Libya in exchange for oil, the MDC has made it clear that any agreements of this nature would be reviewed, and possibly cancelled.

'Deals with this illegitimate regime that have no sanction from parliament are illegal,' Morgan Tsvangirai told me. 'If they have been done behind the scenes, then that is a personal debt accrued by a dictator in that government,' he said.

Reforming the CIO would be a more difficult task, and there could well be a case for disbanding the organisation altogether and starting a new intelligence service, assuming the country needs one at all. Tough clauses in the constitution would need to limit the manner in which the state can spy on its own citizens.

The CIO has infiltrated the MDC and every aspect of Zimbabwean society, and, even in South Africa, its agents make an effort to keep tabs on the exile community.

When I was interviewing torture victims, a Zimbabwean living in Hillbrow approached me under a false name and claimed that he had been raped and beaten in the militia camps. I took him to Dr Len Weinstein in Sandton, who was treating other torture victims, but a medical examination did not support the claims this man had made.

'Andrew', as he became known to me, claimed to have only just arrived in South Africa, but I soon found out that he had been living in Johannesburg for four years and had been suspended from the MDC on suspicion that he was working for the CIO. I met with him several times and never let on that I knew he was lying, but eventually he sensed that the game was up, and did not contact me again.

Rebuilding Zimbabwe presupposes that there will be a single country to rebuild. Since 1998, various groups have advocated the secession of Matabeleland as an independent republic, while others have called for a federal system in which Zimbabwe is split into a number of autonomous regions.

The London-based Mthwakazi Action Group on Genocide and Ethnic Cleansing in Matabeleland and Midlands, an organisation dedicated to seeking justice for Gukurahundi, has vowed to campaign for self-determination, 'specifically in order to ensure that the Ndebele people never again endanger their security by entrusting it to evil plundering strangers bent on their destruction'.[18]

Although the Matabele make up only 20 per cent of Zimbabwe's population, 37 per cent of the opposition MDC's members of parliament come from the province, and should Tsvangirai become president, he would almost certainly face calls to reward their contribution, if only by upgrading the status of the Matabele history and language as part of the national culture.

A separate radio service (which existed in Rhodesian times) and some control over education in the province would go a long way to satisfying the valid notion that, since 1980, the southern tribes have largely been ignored by Harare.

But punishing the people who were responsible for the massacres of the mid-1980s would be the first priority for Matabeleland.

Sadly, there's not much that can be done for the Bushmen or San, who were the sole occupants of the country for 99 per cent of its human history, and are now extinct. In South Africa, the new coat of arms issued in 1995 has, at its centre, a picture of two San people, and it would be appropriate if Zimbabwe followed suit.

The last word in my story goes to one of the most talented people I have ever met.

Henry Khaaba Olonga was born on 3 July 1976 in Lusaka, Zambia, of a Kenyan father and a Shona mother. After the war, his family moved to Zimbabwe, where Henry was educated at the prestigious Plumtree Boys' School near Bulawayo.

His father, Dr John Olonga, had polio as a child, and encouraged his five children to maintain their physical health by playing sport. Henry chose cricket, and in 1994 was selected for the national team. He quickly rose to become one of the world's most respected players, excellent in the crease and a formidable bowler.

In 2000, he wrote and recorded a song called 'Our Zimbabwe', which told of a nation bound together by a painful past and a promising future, and it went to number one on the local hit parade.

But Henry was troubled by the abuse surrounding the 2000 general election and the presidential poll two years later.

'I had been talking to a prominent human rights activist who gave me a dossier prepared by the Catholic Commission for Justice in Zimbabwe on the massacres that took place during Gukurahundi,' he told me. 'It was terrible to read about the gross abuse, and I was disturbed by the recent wave of state-sponsored violence around the country. I began to think that people ought to speak out.'

During the 2003 Cricket World Cup hosted by South Africa, he did just that. Olonga and fellow batsman Andy Flower walked onto the pitch sporting black armbands, and TV cameras beamed the picture to millions of viewers around the world.

'We didn't discuss the protest with anyone beforehand, because we knew it would not be allowed,' said Olonga. 'Our contracts prohibited us from making any statements without prior management approval, so we had to wait until it would be too late for them to stop us.'

The rage in the government press in Harare made clear that both men would never play for their country again, and Olonga moved to England, where he joined the Lashings Cricket Club and launched a career in music.

'If I were to continue to play for Zimbabwe in the midst of the prevailing crisis,' he said, 'I would do so only by neglecting the voice of my conscience. If I lost everything, just for doing the right thing, I'd have no regrets.'[19]

'Everyone must realise they have to make a stand for what is right. Many issues are thrown around in this nation, but the real issues get clouded. In my opinion it's not about white or black, it's not about race. Sometimes it's not even about money. It's about what is right and what is wrong.'[20]

As for the future, Henry believes that things will come right, but that it could take a while.

'Zimbabwe is wounded and the wounds need to heal. What the country needs is accountability and transparency. Dictators thrive because they are not held accountable. There needs to be some kind of truth and reconciliation commission for the benefit of victims, and the perpetrators must be prosecuted.

'They can't get away with their wickedness, and they won't. They have been arrogant and drunk with their power. They are morally corrupt and have abused human rights. They have allowed their greed to destroy the economy and have shown no remorse. They have made truth unattainable with their propaganda and placed themselves above the law. If the law doesn't get them, then the angry people will – and of course, ultimately, God will.'

> Though I may go to distant borders
> My soul will yearn for this my home
> For time and space may separate us
> And yet she holds my heart alone
>
> We've been through it all
> We've had our days
> We've had our falls
> Now the time has come for us to stand
> To stand as one
>
> The night has gone and with the morning
> Come rays of hope that lead us on
> So we will strive to give our children
> A brighter day where they belong
>
> Now flies the flag our nation's glory
> We'll live with pride, inside our hearts
> As we all stand to build our nation
> This our land, our Zimbabwe[21]

# Epilogue

## Will South Africa go the way of Zimbabwe?

While I was writing this book, many people asked my opinion on whether the Zimbabwe scenario was likely to happen in South Africa.

Would the ANC or a successive government abandon democracy, embezzle funds, declare war on minorities and chase farmers off their land?

My answer was that, just because Uganda suffered under Idi Amin, it didn't follow that Kenya and Tanzania would go through the same experience. Likewise, there is no reason to believe that Mugabe's behaviour will spread to neighbouring states.

But I am no expert on South Africa, so I put the question to Moletsi Mbeki, a former journalist, deputy chair of the South African Institute of International Affairs and brother to President Thabo Mbeki.

Moletsi is a modest, approachable man who has been successful in business. In South Africa, he is known for speaking his mind on issues affecting the region.

'First of all, you need to establish why things went the way they did in Zimbabwe,' he told me at his office in northern Johannesburg. 'It was not about land, but all to do with the need of ZANU-PF to keep themselves in power against the will of the electorate.

'Land reform was necessary, but the way things have been handled in Zimbabwe was the problem and related to other pressures on the ruling party.'

So, I asked, could the same thing happen in South Africa?

'Zimbabwe and South Africa are very different cases,' he said. 'Here, we have a strong constitution with the kind of protection for human rights that was never written into the Zimbabwe constitution. We have a robust democracy, a free press, a limit on the presidential term, and, to answer your question, no, I don't believe South Africa will go down the same path as Zimbabwe.'

Next, I spoke to former South African president FW de Klerk, who was responsible for releasing Nelson Mandela from prison and negotiating a successful transfer to democracy in South Africa.

De Klerk agreed with Mbeki, but sounded a note of caution. 'It is up to the electorate of South Africa – voters of all races – to make sure that the freedoms they enjoy under the constitution are not tampered with or compromised,' he said.

'And the international community has a role too,' he added. 'In the rest of Africa, and even in parts of Asia, when human rights collapsed so badly in the latter part of the twentieth century, the world said nothing. That's one of the reasons why governments like the one we now see in Zimbabwe were able to entrench themselves in power against the wishes of their own people.

'Things have changed now and there is a lot more focus on freedom, but if any country, including South Africa, starts abusing its people or taking away their rights, then the world must be quick to act and not leave things until it is too late to rescue the situation.

'But the current South African government has made it very clear that they will not embrace the kind of behaviour we have seen in Zimbabwe, and, for now at least, there is evidence that they plan to honour that commitment.'

The views of Mbeki and De Klerk make sense, and in the first ten years since the introduction of democracy in 1994, the country has not gone through any of the trauma experienced in Zimbabwe's first decade under Mugabe:

- The press has not been nationalised, though there have been increasing efforts by the ANC to control the South African Broadcasting Corporation. Even so, there are plenty of independent and community radio stations, and even one TV network, in private hands.
- Corruption, where it was alleged to have occurred, has been reported in the media and investigated by the state, albeit with some resistance.
- Land claims have been tackled early and a transparent system of redistribution is in place.
- No effort has been made to disband opposition political parties.

But there is one area in which the problems facing the South African government mirror those of Zimbabwe: *Unemployment is running at a record high.*

In my view, it is this, and not the land debate, that should scare South Africans and other people who have a stake in the country.

Like ZANU-PF, the ANC has not scored well in its march on poverty and job creation, especially in rural areas.

A programme of decentralisation with strong incentives is required to encourage new investors to build factories and other projects in rural areas, where land hunger is likely to be worst.

In 2003, farmers in the midlands region of KwaZulu-Natal have been in running battles with unemployed youths who have started a campaign of violence in the region, aimed, they say, at driving commercial farmers off the land.

Nyanga Ngubane, KwaZulu-Natal MEC for Safety and Security, has taken a firm stand on the issue. 'Land invasions are illegal, and what is happening in Zimbabwe will not be tolerated [here],' he told a local black pressure group. But when asked about their aspirations, the young activists who had allegedly been stealing cattle, poaching game and assaulting farm workers were quick to agree that their first choice would be some form of employment.

And even if the government could find enough land to settle all the rural families who want to till the soil, how many of their children, now in school, would stay on the farm once they got their education?

In developing countries around the world, the trend of the past fifty years has been for the rural youth – notably those who have some education – to seek their fortunes in the city, and if you watch the bus terminals near Johannesburg's Park Station any day of the week, you will see people arriving from all parts of the country, each with a bag of clothes and a head full of dreams.

South Africa's worst land invasion took place in 2000 on Braam Duvenage's 4 000-hectare *Modderklip* farm near the Johannesburg suburb of Benoni, where some 40 000 people now live as squatters.

'The invaders have ruined my farm and it can't be rehabilitated,' says Duvenage. But when he won an eviction order in the Witwatersrand High Court, the state refused to move the squatters, and the local sheriff told him he would need to pay R1.8 million to have a private security firm drive the settlers off his property.

At the time of writing, the case continues, with Duvenage demanding that President Thabo Mbeki should appear in court and explain why his government has not acted in accordance with the earlier ruling.

The *Modderklip* invasion has some notable features. The settlers are not so much farmers as people who have drifted to the city and have nowhere else to live. Ironically, many are not even South African, but are political or economic refugees from Zimbabwe, Zambia and Mozambique.

But what about those who have participated in legal land reform programmes in rural areas?

According to a survey commissioned by the Department of Land Affairs to gauge the quality of life among those who have benefited from such schemes:

* 80 per cent earn less than R1 000 per month (less than US$4 per day);
* 28 per cent of households have no income at all;
* despite access to land, most families still spend more than half their money on food; and
* most crops harvested are used in the kitchen and do not generate income.[1]

These criteria all point to a class of people who are worse off than those in the cities, and if the continental trend is mirrored in South Africa, it is likely that – with or without land reform – rural folk will ultimately make their way to the cities and towns in search of a better life.

The emotional attachment is a different and more complex matter, and for most Africans, black and white, land is part of their folklore and psyche. But making a go of farming is just as hard in Africa as it is in Europe, Australia or America. Agriculture has become sophisticated, economy of scale is everything, and selling crops means being able to compete with those who can grow the same product cheaper, better and more quickly.

Ask a city dweller in London, Sydney, Dallas or Durban, and they may well tell you about their dream of one day owning a cottage in the country with veggies growing in the field, cows for milk, and chickens to provide meat and eggs for the table. But most will never get there, and even if they did, the produce they raised would cost them more than buying the same goods at the supermarket. And in black South Africa, with the new, expanded school system rapidly producing a generation who are better educated and more confident than their parents, aspirations will be increasingly material and urban.

As in Zimbabwe, land will be an emotional factor, but it will never be the real issue.

When authority is challenged, the threat usually comes from the urban poor. They were at the storming of the Bastille in 1789, and they led the Russian Revolution of 1917. In Africa, the call for an end to colonial rule found its voice in post-war urbanisation, and the townships were the main battleground in the fight against oppression and in the push for democracy in Kenya, Zambia, Malawi, Nigeria and, more recently, Zimbabwe. And the drift of rural people into the towns is more rapid in South Africa than it ever was in those countries.

Intellectuals lead the way with ideas, but it is only in the city that the ideas grow loud enough to make a difference. If the ANC's right to rule South Africa is ever called into question, the challenge is likely to come from that quarter, and, as in Zimbabwe, the main gripe will not be land, but the cost of living and unemployment.

It is the ruling party's response that will determine South Africa's future. 'The first decade of truly democratic rule in South Africa has been a success and is nothing like what happened in Zimbabwe,' FW de Klerk told me.

'But in politics,' he said, 'the future is never guaranteed unless the people themselves remain vigilant.'

# Appendix

## Testimony of torture victims

**WARNING:** *This Appendix contains explicit descriptions of torture and brutality that may distress or offend anyone of a sensitive disposition. These personal accounts form part of this book because to exclude them would invalidate not only the ordeal of the victims, but also the courage they showed in reliving their suffering at my behest.*

The issue of rape as a weapon of war is as old as human conflict itself. In recent times, it has featured prominently in war crimes trials at the international tribunal in The Hague, endorsing the world's determination that sexual abuse by members of armed or paramilitary forces cannot be brushed off as 'just one of those things'.

In times of conflict, rape can be classified in one of two categories. There is the rape of lust, when soldiers force themselves on defenceless victims who are in no position to resist. This is a serious crime and should not go unpunished. Then there is premeditated sexual abuse, sometimes conducted on a widespread scale, which involves the violation of men and women alike as punishment, or as a form or torture, and this has long been regarded as an even more abhorrent crime.

In Zimbabwe, the latter has been employed as a tool of oppression, and human rights groups agree that there is a case for some of the perpetrators to be put on trial.

My own ordeal at the hands of the war veterans and militia – and even the terror inflicted on white farmers (with the obvious exception of those who were murdered) – was as nothing compared to what the MDC's black supporters were forced to endure.

In January 2003, I began interviewing exiles in South Africa who had been detained by the CIO, army, police, war vets or the Green Bombers. I met people who had been branded with hot irons, buried alive in trunks, drowned and left for dead, axed, slashed and raped. In one case, a group of police, war vets and militia used police truncheons to anally rape a group of more than thirty MDC youths near Harare. I have not included this report here because it is too gross for publication.

As the 2002 presidential election drew nearer, agents of the state carried out ever worse acts with impunity. But the most serious violence involved the Green Bombers, a modern-day African equivalent of the Hitler Youth, their value system apparently warped by a daily diet of depravity.

Of the twenty-one women I interviewed, all but two had been raped at some point while in detention, and many had been forced to undergo oral, vaginal and anal sex repeatedly and over several days. Out of fifty-two men who shared their experiences with me, thirty-eight had been raped, and it soon emerged that a systematic programme of male rape, deliberately designed to break the morale of the opposition, had been implemented throughout Zimbabwe.

I selected ten men and four women whose cases were particularly gruesome, and found a doctor in Sandton who was willing to examine and treat them at no cost. In every case (except one which is dealt with in Chapter 14) their accounts of torture, rape and abuse were corroborated by the injuries he found.

Dr Len Weinstein is well known in Sandton and has spent nearly forty years specialising in cases of physical and mental trauma.

I have great admiration for the courage of the victims who had to relive their terror in order to work through it with me, but without Dr Weinstein's hours of unpaid professional assistance, I would not have been able to piece together the full horror of what had happened to them. In addition to the primary care and counsel he provided, Len also arranged for a mental trauma clinic in Johannesburg, funded by a non-governmental organisation, to treat some of the worst cases for depression and anxiety arising from their time in custody.

The transcripts that follow do not make pleasant reading, and I recommend that sensitive readers should skip the next few pages. I have neither embellished nor censored the accounts, allowing the victims to tell these stories in their own words. I have, however, presented the details in chronological order, whereas the victims provided them in random sequence, due to the distress caused by recollecting such horrific events. Most of the stories came out very slowly, over a period of between four and twelve hours, spread across anything of up to eight meetings, and some of them were told in a mixture of English and the subject's home language. The translations are mine.

The victims are not named here, because all of them have families in Zimbabwe, and I agreed at the outset not to use any information that could endanger their loved ones. However, full copies have been lodged with my publisher, and more than a dozen transcripts are in the hands of the Accountability Commission, a London-based organisation that assembles data for possible use in war crimes trials.

In every instance, the victims gave me permission to reproduce this material.

### CASE #1: Female (26) from Manicaland province

In the months before the presidential election, my husband had been very active with the MDC and had taken part in a raid on a camp where the war vets and militia used to stay. He and his men had gone there to rescue some MDC youths who were being tortured, and they managed to free everyone.

The problem was that the war vets were now hunting for him and the police were assisting, so he had nowhere to hide, and he told me that he thought it best if he went to South Africa for some time, and that I should follow later with our four-year-old son. I agreed that this was the best thing to do and he left, and we had no way of communicating.

It was some days before the election and two weeks since he had left when three of the war vets, dressed in police clothes, came to my house and wanted to know where my husband had gone. I knew they were not police because they had a mix of uniforms, one with just a police jacket over his own shirt and another with just police trousers, and none of them were wearing police shoes.

I told them the truth and said he had gone to South Africa, but they said I was lying and they beat me in front of my son who was screaming, but they did not hurt him. I lived in the rural area and our huts were close together, but no one in the village came to help me because we had all learned to be very afraid of the war vets. One man sat on me and another beat my feet with a stick, and it was so painful that I passed a motion inside my pants and it smelled very bad.

One of the war vets started shouting that I was a pig, and that all MDC women should be fed shit because that is what we enjoy. Then he made me put my hand into my pants and get some of my own shit on my fingers and wipe it on my face, but they did not make me eat it. Even so, it was terrible for my son to witness all this.

They now beat me with whips all over my body, but after maybe an hour they stopped, and said they believed my story and even apologised for hurting me and said they would now leave me alone.

That night I took my son and stayed with my sister and her family in the next village, and I was there for three days. The people at my village said that no one had come looking for me so I thought it was safe to go back. It is bad to be beaten anywhere, but when it has happened inside your own home, the room always feels bad, but I had nowhere else to go.

The first day, nothing happened, but the next night at around 1 am, I heard someone knocking on my door and I asked who it was. One of the war vets answered and said that unless I opened the door he would set fire to my hut. I asked him to wait a few seconds and, lucky for me, I put on my dress, because when I opened the door, he grabbed me by the arm and pulled me from the hut and another man put his hand over my mouth.

They dragged me away from our small collection of huts into the bush, and one of the men put a knife to my throat and said that if I screamed, he would kill me. I wanted to tell them I needed to do something about my son who was sleeping, but I was too scared that they would hurt him. So I kept quiet and we walked back to the dust road near the village and they took me back to their camp. I was still very sore from the beating and the journey was difficult for me, but they did not show any sympathy.

It was an hour by the time we reached their place and several men were still awake at that time, which was strange. I was dragged into a hut and the war vet who had first pulled me from my own house pulled off my dress and pushed me onto the floor. Then I was raped by the three men and others from the camp. It was dark and I couldn't see anything, but I could smell that some of them had been drinking. I don't know how many men did this but I was in very bad pain and still they kept coming.

Then one of the men asked me: 'Do you want to tell us now where your husband is?' but I could not even talk. He hit me on my face and then another two men raped me and the first man asked me again, but I think around that time I passed out.

They let me go the next morning, but I could not walk. I managed to crawl into the bush near their huts and lay there for some hours and finally, later that day, I got back to my house.

I had no passport and it was too dangerous to try to escape to South Africa with a child, so I sent my son to my mother and I found someone to help me get to the border and cross into South Africa, where I am now with my husband. I hope my son can join us soon.

*The family has since been reunited in South Africa.*

## CASE #2: Male (32) from Matabeleland – worked as a builder and helped with security at MDC rallies over weekends

In November 2001, I had been to a party near the town of Plumtree, on the border of Zimbabwe and Botswana. It was late afternoon, and I was on the way back to the bus station to catch my transport home to Bulawayo, when I saw a team of six Green Bombers talking with the people in the bus queue.

The Bombers were new in our area, and we did not know yet how much we should fear them. I had done nothing wrong and, in any case, there were some policemen in the bus queue, so I felt sure nothing would happen. I had not seen another gang of ten or more youths coming up the road behind me, and I was still fifty metres from the queue when they circled around me and one shouted: 'Oh, yes, it's you. We have seen you at the MDC rallies. You think you are a strong guy.'

Before I could say anything, one had kicked me in the testicles and another ripped off my hat and threw it over the heads of his comrades. I clutched my groin and, as I fell to the ground, they all began kicking me and spitting on my body.

I was groaning and the youths were screaming at me and the police in the bus queue must have seen what was going on, but no one came to help me. I heard a vehicle engine and a pick-up truck drew next to us, and the youths picked me up and threw me into the back, and jumped in and sat on me.

I could hardly breathe, and as I gasped, one of the boys took a rag that must have been used to clean the engine and stuffed it into my mouth. I could taste the dirty grease on it. Then they took another rag and tied it around my head so that I could not see where we were going.

It must have been forty minutes before we arrived at a deserted farmhouse somewhere between Plumtree and Bulawayo. The blindfold was removed, I climbed down from the truck, and they took off my shoes and shirt and I was led into the house. I think the electric power had been cut off, because there were paraffin lamps burning in some of the rooms.

I was taken into what looked like the living room, because it was big, but there were only some plastic garden chairs and boxes for furniture and there were militia and some war vets sitting on these.

What I saw was a picture from hell. About a dozen other MDC men and boys had been brought to this place and most were naked. Some had cuts and even bleeding wounds on their arms and legs. Others had fresh lines on their backs where they had been beaten. There were men on the floor, crying and groaning, some were curled up like they had been hit in the stomach, and one was chained to the window frame, where he was being whipped with a piece of hosepipe.

There was the smell of shit, blood and urine everywhere. I think maybe eight of the guys had been tortured and the other four were grouped together in a corner waiting their turn. Among these, I recognised two of the young men who worked under my command when we did security for MDC rallies. Some wore handcuffs and others had pieces of rope around their legs.

I was taken into the next room where a war vet called [name supplied] asked me about the MDC and their structures in Bulawayo. I told him I did not know anything, and some of the Green Bombers held my arms behind me while the war vet hit me in the stomach with his fist and across my face with his hand.

I was questioned for maybe an hour, and when I came back into the room, most of the MDC men had been taken away, but there were still three there, including the two who had worked with me. Now the war vet who had questioned me said I would need to show who was the boss of these boys.

'It is your choice,' he said. 'Either you can rape them or they are going to rape you.'

I told him that I would not take part in such acts, but there were many Green Bombers now, and they grabbed us and ripped off our clothes. I tried to fight, but was soon overpowered, and while we stood naked, the militia began stroking our private parts to make them erect.

I failed to respond because I was disgusted by what was being done to me and also because I was still in pain from the beating, but one of my subordinates became erect and I was then forced to bend over and he raped me. The sex went on between the boys and some of the Green Bombers also took part, and it was after midnight when we were all released and told that if we continued to support the MDC, we would be picked up again.

I could not go to the police, because I knew that they would probably just hand me back to the Green Bombers, so I took my things from home, and got a lift to the border and crossed into South Africa.

I have not forgotten the people who tortured me and I am waiting for the day when justice can be done to them.

*\* The victim underwent extensive psychiatric counselling in Johannesburg, after which he obtained employment as a security guard near Pretoria.*

## CASE #3: Male (23) from Bulawayo – worked as electoral assistant to an MDC member of parliament

It was early afternoon on Thursday 7 March, 2002, two days before the presidential election. I was on a bus going to visit a friend, and I passed through a rural area not far from Bulawayo where I had previously done some work for the local MDC MP.

A roadblock had been set up by the police and the youth militia and some war vets dressed in police clothes. They stopped the bus and made everybody get off. Then they told us to produce ZANU-PF party cards, and those of us who could not were sent to sit on the other side of the road.

When the search was complete, the party members were allowed to reboard the bus, which drove away. The rest of us had to sit and receive a lesson on why ZANU-PF is the only party that will be tolerated in Zimbabwe. This was a punishment, because people's belongings were on the bus and they had paid their fares. Now they would have to wait for the next bus and pay again, and try later to collect their goods at the bus stop.

Then one of the militia walked up to me and said he recognised me as an MDC worker. I was very afraid. He grabbed me by the shirt and dragged me to a police Defender vehicle, while other police and militia were kicking me. I was handcuffed with my hands behind me and pushed onto the back of the police truck.

First I was transported to the local ZANU-PF office, where I was taken to a small, dark room and blindfolded. They asked me to recite the names of all MDC members in my area, and when I said I could not remember such a long list, they beat me with sticks and kicked me in the back, buttocks and testicles.

The blindfold was removed, but the handcuffs stayed. I was now transported to a garage (filling station) owned by the ZANU-PF chairman for the district. I was taken into a back room and they put chains on my legs and left for a while. About six youth militia returned without the police, and they were carrying buckets of water. They made me kneel by one of the buckets and pushed my head under the water.

They held me while I struggled and then I passed out, and when I woke up, they were pushing my chest and making the water come from my lungs. My head was burning very much. Once I was able to breathe again, they put my head back into the bucket and kept doing this, pulling me out when I collapsed.

I don't know how many times this happened, but I thought my brain was burning because my head was so sore. They kept asking me to recite the membership list, which is some thousands, and when I would say some names, they would drown me again.

Finally, they threw me into a corner and said they were going to eat, but that if I was hungry I should drink more water. They also said that I would be held until after the presidential election, and that if Tsvangirai won, I would be killed. If Mugabe won, I might be released.

They opened the door and I could see that it was now dark outside. After that they left me alone. I was not given any food and the handcuffs and leg chains stayed on. Then, at about 10 pm, three new men whom I had not seen before came back into the room, and I was told that one was from the CIO and the other two were militia. The CIO man was about thirty-five years old and I can think that the youths were perhaps twenty-two.

They undid the chains and the leg irons and removed all my clothing. Then the two militia took off their clothes, but the CIO man did not. He sat on a chair and watched.

The militia lay me on my back and started playing with my penis, masturbating it until it came hard. They said that if I produced some sperms, I would be released.

I could see that the one militia had an erect penis. I tried to think of someone I loved to make my sperms come, and they produced.

The three cheered, then the CIO man said: 'Now it's our turn.' And he told the two boys, 'Satisfy your needs with this one.'

They turned me onto my stomach and the militia with the erect penis applied some kind of oil to my anus and put on a condom, and then he raped me. It was very painful and I screamed, and this seemed to excite him more. He reached from behind for my testicles and pulled them while he was raping me, and it was as though he wanted to remove them.

I was crying and there was a lot of blood. Now the second militia put on a condom and did the same thing, and I saw to my side that the CIO man had removed his trousers to his ankles and was masturbating, but he never raped me.

Both youths had very big penises and I don't know if they were selected for that by the CIO man, but they hurt me very much. While the second youth was raping me, he told the CIO man that he could feel a lot of blood inside my anus. The man replied: 'Just enjoy now, this night. If you rip his anus, the MDC will send him for treatment in England.'

When the rape was over, they put back my handcuffs and chains and left me without my clothes. I stayed in the room for four days and I could not go to the toilet because my anus was so painful. Finally some other militia came and undid my chains and told me to put on my clothes and leave.

When I was going home, I discovered that the presidential election was over and Mugabe had won. I was sad that I had not been able to cast my vote for Tsvangirai.

A few weeks later, I went to Botswana and worked there. In December 2002, the Tswana police caught me without an ID and I was taken to a holding camp for illegal immigrants. There we were all asked if we had ZANU-PF party cards, and those who did were taken away. I don't know what happened to them. The rest of us, who said that we supported the opposition, were given a lecture by one of the police to say that it was our duty for Zimbabwe and for Africa to overthrow Mugabe, because what he was doing was even hurting Botswana. Then they drove us to an unmarked area on the border and we walked back into Zimbabwe. I was so afraid that I might again be caught by the militia that I kept walking until I crossed into South Africa.

My problem is that my anus is still torn and it is still painful for me to go to the toilet. I cannot sleep at night with the pressure in my brain over this rape, and I think many times that it would be best just to end my life.

*Medical examination revealed serious rectal damage, which was treated. The victim has also taken part in a counselling programme.*

### CASE #4: Male (30) from rural Matabeleland

At the end of August 2002, I was picked up by war vets and militia in Bulawayo, because I was working in the MDC security department. They took me first to an empty farmhouse outside Bulawayo and beat me, asking for details of the next MDC meeting, our campaigns and whether we had any guns. I told them some things, which they already knew, but said I had never seen any guns and they beat me more with a sjambok (leather whip). I still was wearing my clothes, but was handcuffed with my hands behind me. This was around four in the afternoon.

At about 7 o'clock that night, I was led to a truck and they pushed me into the back of the pick-up. We drove to Nkayi outside Bulawayo, to another empty farm at a place I did not know. When I got out of the truck, they removed my shoes and my long trousers but left me with my shorts and T-shirt. I was taken to an area of trees and made to sit on the ground. They told me they were waiting for their leader, a war vet called [name supplied] to arrive.

About an hour passed, then I was told that the man had arrived, and someone put a blindfold over my eyes and led me into a farm building. They undid the handcuffs, removed all my clothes and lay me on the floor on my stomach. Then one of the war vets started to beat me on my buttocks with a sjambok, asking again about guns.

When he had finished, I was told to sit up and open my mouth, because they were going to urinate into it. I did as I was told and felt someone's penis on my lips and the hot urine squirted into my mouth. I spat it out and was pushed to the ground and beaten again with the sjambok. They sat me up again and told me they would repeat the exercise, and again a man put his penis into my mouth and urinated and I swallowed it. They told me to keep my mouth open and now an erect penis was placed on my lips and I could feel the pulse of a man masturbating himself. I heard him grunting and his semen flowed into my mouth.

I choked as it went down my throat and I vomited, and they shouted and swore at me and pulled me to the ground again and beat my buttocks with the sjambok. Then the process was repeated with several men, some with urine, some with semen, and I swallowed it all.

When they finally released me they removed the blindfold and I saw the people who tortured me. If I see them again, inside or outside Zimbabwe, I will kill them, even if it means going to jail. I can never forgive them for what they did.

My problem is that, a few days later, my gums started bleeding and this still happens. My brain is still heavy and crying with the experience, and although my wife is here now, we have not had sex since that time when I was abducted.

I left Zimbabwe, but the CIO visited my parents at their rural home and beat both my mother and father, asking for my whereabouts. Then they took my father outside and beat him separately while they kicked and beat my mother inside the hut. She later died of her injuries and I was not able to go home for her funeral.

I need to see a doctor to talk about my problems and also to check my mouth. But there are horrible things in my brain, when I think about what has happened to me. Really, I just want to die sometimes. It is so terrible.

*I interviewed both the victim's brother and father, who corroborated the story of his mother's death. At the time of writing, both the victim and his brother attend weekly sessions with a psychologist.*

# Notes

**Chapter 1**

1. Statistics Office and the Insurance Association of South Africa.
2. 'Expectations, perceptions and reality', by Peter Scott-Wilson. From *South Africa, The Good News*, published by Brett Bowes and Steuart Pennington, Johannesburg, October 2002.

**Chapter 3**

1. The Rhodes children and the years of their birth were: Elizabeth (1835), Herbert (1845), Edith (1847), Louisa (1848), Frank (1851), Ernest (1852), Cecil (1853), Frederick (1854, died at five weeks), Elmhirst (1858), Arthur (1859) and Bernard (1861).
2. Economic History Services.
3. *The Correspondence of Cecil John Rhodes*, Bodleian Library of Commonwealth and African Studies.

**Chapter 4**

1. Sphere Books, 1981.
2. Hamish Hamilton, 1981.
3. Congressional Record, US Senate, Vol. 133 No. 105, 25 June 1987; National Policy Analysis No. 23, Washington, October 1987.

**Chapter 5**

1. 'Zimbabwe News Chief Takes Hard Line', *Sydney Morning Herald*, 8 October 1980.

**Chapter 7**

1. *Mail & Guardian*, 2 March 2000.
2. *The Namibian*, 11 May 2000.
3. *Time* magazine, 5 January 2000.
4. Amnesty International report 46/014/2000, 8 June 2000.

**Chapter 8**

1. *Dancing Out of Tune*, Edwina Spicer Productions.
2. Media Monitoring Project Zimbabwe, update 2000/17.
3. ZBC TV news, 8 pm, 26 April 2000.
4. 'Military Terror Silences The Nation', *Horizon*, February 1999.
5. ZBC TV news, 8 pm, 15 February 1999.
6. In 2002, Ncube expanded his media empire by buying the *Mail & Guardian*, a weekly newspaper published in Johannesburg, which had earned a reputation for exposing corruption in both the former National Party and ANC governments, but which had consistently shown a financial loss. Following Ncube's acquisition, a number of white South Africans wrote letters to the editors of major

daily newspapers lamenting the *M&G*'s transfer to black ownership and predicting that, because of it, the newspaper would in future take a soft line on Thabo Mbeki and the ANC. In fact, the opposite proved true, and furthermore, Ncube moved the *M&G* into profit. I had always maintained that white South Africans understood little about the struggle for freedom in either their own country or the region at large, and this incident proved the point.

7. Media Institute of Southern Africa, 11 September 2001.
8. United Nations report, 19 September 2002.
9. *Daily News* (Zimbabwe), 5 November 2001.
10. Media Institute of Southern Africa, 3 December 2001.
11. Blair subsequently recounted his experiences in an excellent book, *Degrees in Violence* (Continuum, 2002).
12. Worryingly, in 2003 the South African government was drafting similar legislation, albeit with built-in constitutional safeguards.
13. The head of one of the leading private banks in Zimbabwe also put in some funds.

## Chapter 9

1. *Victims of Torture* by Eric Beauchemin, broadcast 16 May 2002.
2. Annual report, Amnesty International, 2001.
3. Reuters, 7 September 2001.
4. Published by Jonathan Ball, 2002.
5. By that time this trade had stopped and products previously bought

from neighbouring states were either rationed or unobtainable in Zimbabwe.
6. Four of the suspects were later arrested, and at the time of writing, were awaiting trial.

## Chapter 10

1. *The Age*, 22 March 2002.
2. *Hansard*, 22 January 2002.
3. *Daily News* (Zimbabwe), 14 January 2002.
4. *Daily News* (Zimbabwe), 14 January 2002.
5. *Daily News* (Zimbabwe), 23 January 2002.
6. *Guardian* (UK), 22 January 2002.
7. *Sydney Morning Herald*, 9 March 2002.
8. BBC *World Service*, 22 April 2002.
9. BBC *World Service*, 23 January 2002.
10. *Guardian* (UK), 23 January 2002.
11. *News24* (South Africa), 23 January 2002.
12. BBC *World Service*, 1 February 2002.
13. *Daily Telegraph* (UK), 4 February 2002.
14. *Independent* (Zimbabwe), 15 February 2002.
15. *Daily Telegraph* (UK), 23 February 2002.
16. *The Times* (UK) and *Daily Telegraph* (UK), 25 February 2002.
17. ABC radio is world class and rates well alongside the commercial stations.
18. OzTAM Five City Progressive Share Report for January–December 2002.
19. The impending election prevented Mugabe from attending, and he would thus not have been able to defend his actions.

20. *Daily Telegraph* (UK), 26 February 2002.
21. BBC *Online*, 6 March 2002.
22. 'Zimbabwe's False Friends', *New York Times*, 16 March 2002.
23. BBC *Online*, 24 March 2002.

**Chapter 11**
1. *Beeld*, 20 November 2002.
2. At the time of writing the price was around US$100, converted to Zimbabwe dollars at the black-market rate.
3. Sadly, on my next trip north a month later, it was raining. I had to swerve on the highway near Polokwane to avoid a collision and *Ernie* went off the tarred surface and hit a tree. The car was a write-off and was sold for scrap, but not before I removed the registration plate as a souvenir of our many adventures together in Australia and across southern Africa.
4. *Financial Times* (UK), 12 December 2002.
5. It's a little-known fact that, in 1963, Buthelezi played the Zulu king Cetshwayo in the feature film, *Zulu*, which depicted the British defeat at the battle of Rorke's Drift. The film also starred Michael Caine in his first major role.
6. *Buthelezi, A Biography* (Cass Publishers, 2003).
7. This issue was exposed by a report in *The Star* on 16 September 2002, but the practice continued.
8. 'Zimbabwe's Missing Millions', *Mail & Guardian*, 4 December 2002.
9. *Independent* (UK), 12 May 2002.

10. 'Labour's Asylum Policy Is To Fool the Public That All Is Well', *Daily Telegraph*, 16 December 2002 and 'How the Home Office Makes Life Easy for Terrorists', *Daily Telegraph*, 27 January 2003, both by Harriet Sergeant.
11. 'Suspect Lived in Brixton Before Joining US Flying School', *Guardian* (UK), 18 September 2000.
12. Set to the melody of a traditional Zulu wedding song, 'Homeless' (© 1986 Paul Simon/BMI) was written jointly by Paul Simon (of Simon & Garfunkel fame) and Joseph Tshabalala, composer and lead singer of the popular South African vocal group, Ladysmith Black Mambazo. English translation of the Zulu is approximate and has been paraphrased, and the sequence is incomplete.

**Chapter 12**
1. *Financial Times*, 22 February 2002.
2. *The Biography of Laurent Kabila*, ABC television (US), 2001.
3. *Zimbabwe's Military Connections in the DRC*, published by Zimbabwe Today, 2000.
4. *The Adventure Capitalist*, Center for Public Integrity, Washington, 2002.
5. Mahachi had never cut a strong figure within ZANU-PF, and, as a Manica, was not part of the Zezuru-Karanga mafia that dominated the party. In May 2001, he was killed in a car crash, and Sydney Sekeramayi, perhaps Mnangagwa's closest ally in ZANU-PF Inc., became Minister of Defence.

6. UN inquiry into the abuse of resources in the DRC, 2001–2002.
7. *The Adventure Capitalist*, Center for Public Integrity, Washington, 2002.
8. *The Adventure Capitalist*, Center for Public Integrity, Washington, 2002.
9. '85% of DRC Diamonds Smuggled out in 2000', *The Star*, 19 June 2001.
10. Sections of the UN report dealt with in this book relate to UN reference No. S/2002/1146. The original report was written in French and translated into English by the UN and documented in an official report to the Security Council, 16 October 2002.
11. *Mail & Guardian*, 4 April 2001.
12. *The Star*, 20 November 2002.
13. 'SA Probes Zim Role in Smuggling Racket', *Independent* (Zimbabwe), 22 November 2002, and SABC, 13 November 2002.
14. *ZW News*, 2 November 2002.
15. '$96 Million Looted from AIDS Levy', *Daily News* (Zimbabwe),10 April 2002.
16. 'Mugabe Buys Luxury Limo', *Standard* (Zimbabwe), 18 November 2001.
17. *The Opposition and Civil Society*, Institute for Security Studies, June 2003.
18. Robertson Economic Services.
19. *The Star*, 1 July 2003.
20. 'Few Have But Most Have Not in Harare', *Sunday Times* (SA), 22 June 2003.

**Chapter 13**
1. 'Freeing a Nation From a Tyrant's Grip', *New York Times*, 24 June 2003.
2. Clemency Order No. 1 of 1988.

3. Zimbabwe Human Rights NGO Forum, political violence report, October 2002.
4. *Insiza loss a blow to MDC and the British*, http://www.zanupfpub.co.zw.
5. Zimbabwe Human Rights NGO Forum, political violence reports, January–June 2003.
6. Zimbabwe Human Rights NGO Forum, political violence reports, January–June 2003.
7. ZANU-PF website: http://www.zanupfpub.co.zw.
8. This is a well-known case in which ZANU-PF and war veterans attacked the farmer and his workers, and one of their number was killed in the fracas.
9. *Chipangano* means 'agreement', but in the context used here, it does not translate readily into English. Essentially, it means that those who were part of the gang shared a bond of honour, which linked them together in their war against the MDC.
10. 'Police Ransack MDC Offices in Search of Murder Weapons', *Daily News* (Zimbabwe), 28 August 2002.
11. Bail deposit notice No. 512 428, case number 11578/02, 16 October 1902 (*sic*).
12. The government even moved the electoral boundary to include a large black township in the hope that voters would back ZANU-PF, but Coltart won the seat, defeating Ndhlovu by 20 781 votes to 3 193, a margin of 81 per cent.
13. *Herald* (Zimbabwe), 28 November 2001.
14. *Herald* (Zimbabwe), 28 November 2001.

15. 'MDC Did Not Murder Nkala, Says Tsvangirai', *Daily News* (Zimbabwe), 16 November 2001.
16. 'Come Clean Comrades', and 'Nkala Family Breaks Silence', *Standard* (Zimbabwe), 18 November, 2001.
17. *Independent* (Zimbabwe), 19 April 2002.

**Chapter 14**

1. 'Freeing A Nation From A Tyrant's Grip', *New York Times*, 24 June 2003.
2. *Washington Times*, 3 July 2003.
3. *Independent* (UK), 15 July 2003.
4. Comment from *ZW News*, 19 July 2003.
5. 'Black Man of the Year 2001', http://www.afroamerica.net/Robert Mugabe122001.html.
6. 'The wisest African leader of today', *Expo News*, Vol.7, No.12.
7. 'ANC Youth League Vindicated. Indeed DA is Using MDC to Bash the ANC', ANC Youth League, 10 April 2003.
8. 'Meet the New Boss, Same As the Old Boss', *Daily Telegraph*, 24 June 2003.
9. The Archbishop Denis Hurley Lecture, delivered by Archbishop Pius Ncube in Durban, November 2002.
10. 'Human Rights Activist Quizzed Over Prayers', *Daily News* (Zimbabwe), 25 June 2003.

11. 'Mugabe Is Paranoid About UK Coup Plot', David Harrison, *Daily Telegraph*, 22 June 2003.
12. The Archbishop Denis Hurley Lecture, delivered by Archbishop Pius Ncube in Durban, November 2002.
13. *Daily Telegraph* (UK), 7 August 2003.
14. *Standard* (Zimbabwe), 17 November 2002.
15. *Daily News* (Zimbabwe), 18 July 2003.
16. *Washington Times*, 7 June 2003.
17. 'Just a Zealous Guy', Ben Summerskill, *Observer*, 23 February 2003.
18. Details of the MAGGEM 2000 campaign can be found at http://members.aol.com/maggemm/ Historical.htm.
19. BBC, March 2003.
20. 'Why I Wore A Black Band For Zimbabwe', Andrew Meldrum, *Observer*, 16 February 2003.
21. © *Our Zimbabwe* by Henry Olonga.

**Epilogue**

1. *Quality of Life Report 2000/2001*, prepared by Citizen Services for the Directorate Monitoring and Evaluation division in the Department of Land Affairs.

# Select bibliography

Becker, Peter. *Path of Blood.* London: Longmans, 1962.

Beit, Sir Alfred, and JG Lockhard. *The Will and the Way.* London: Longmans and Green Co., 1957.

Blair, David. *Degrees in Violence.* London: Continuum Books, 2002.

Bulpin, TV. *Discovering Southern Africa.* Cape Town: Books of Africa, 1970.

———. *To the Banks of the Zambezi.* Johannesburg: Thomas Nelson & Sons, 1965.

Carey, Robert, and Diana Mitchell. *African Nationalist Leaders in Rhodesia.* Bulawayo: Books of Rhodesia, 1977.

Chan, Stephen. *Robert Mugabe, A Life of Power and Violence.* London: Tauris, 2003.

Chinodya, Shimmer. *Harvest of Thorns.* Harare: Baobab Books, 1989.

Cowen, Michael, and Laakso Liisa. *Multi-Party Elections in Africa.* New York: Belgrave, 2002.

Davidson, Apollo. *Cecil Rhodes and His Time.* Moscow: Progress Publishers, 1984.

Ellert, Henry. *The Rhodesian Front War.* Harare: Mambo Press, 1993.

Fothergill, Roland. *Mirror Over Rhodesia.* Johannesburg: Argus Printing and Publishing Company, 1984.

Hudson, Miles. *Triumph or Tragedy.* London: Hamish Hamilton, 1981.

Judd, Denis. *Empire.* London: HarperCollins Publishers, 1996.

Meredith, Martin. *The First Dance of Freedom.* London: Hamish Hamilton, 1984.

———. *Robert Mugabe, Power, Plunder and Tyranny in Zimbabwe.* Johannesburg: Jonathan Ball, 2002.

Museveni, Yoweri. *Sowing the Mustard Seed.* London: Macmillan, 1997.

Raeburn, Michael. *Black Fire.* Harare: Zimbabwe Publishing House, 1978.

Rosenthal, Eric. *Southern African Dictionary of National Biography.* London: Frederick Warne & Co., 1966.

Rothberg, Robert. *The Founder, Cecil John Rhodes.* New York: Oxford University Press, 1988.

Sculley, Pat. *Exit Rhodesia.* Ladysmith, KZN: Cotswold Press, 1984.

Smith, David, and Colin Simpson. *Mugabe.* London: Sphere Books, 1981.

Smith, Ian. *The Great Betrayal.* London: Blake Publishing, 1997.

*Spectrum Guide to Zimbabwe*. Nairobi: Camerapix Publishers International, 1991.

Storry, JG. *The Shattered Nation*. Cape Town: Howard Timmins, 1974.

Temkin, Ben. *Buthelezi, A Biography*. London: Frank Cass Publishers, 2003.

Thatcher, Margaret. *Statecraft*. London: HarperCollins, 2003.

*Today's News Today*. Johannesburg: Argus Printing and Publishing Company, 1956.

*Who Is Who in Zimbabwe*. Harare: Argosy Press, 1992.

# Glossary

**chimurenga:** armed struggle, as in pre-1980 guerrilla war in Zimbabwe – also used to describe protest music as popularised by Thomas Mapfumo

**Chinja maitiro!:** rallying cry of the Movement for Democratic Change, meaning 'Let's change the way we do things'

**girigamba:** slang term for the African dung beetle, used to describe Zimbabweans who cross the border into South Africa on foot, carrying their possessions on their backs

**Green Bombers:** ZANU-PF youth militia (also known as GBs)

**Gukurahundi:** the storm that washes away the chaff before the spring rain – name given to massacres by the Fifth Brigade in Matabeleland, 1982–87

**indaba:** meeting of African tribal chiefs

**kraal:** rural village or cattle pen

**kumusha:** rural and spiritual home

**kwerekwere:** 'gobbledygook' – Johannesburg street slang for African emigrants

**lobola:** bride price, traditionally paid in cattle

**n'anga:** spirit medium

**ncwala:** annual traditional 'first fruits' ceremony celebrated by the Matabele

**nyaradzo:** ritual that marks the end of one-year mourning period following the death of a family member

**mujhiba:** ZANU-PF collaborator

**murungu:** white person

**sjambok:** whip, traditionally made of rhinoceros hide

**Talibob:** nickname given to Green Bombers after the US invasion of Afghanistan

**veld:** stretch of open land or bush

**Voortrekkers:** nineteenth-century Afrikaner pioneers in South Africa

# Index

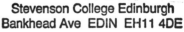